T0301662

NOT EXACTLY LYING

NOT EXACTLY LYING

FAKE NEWS
AND FAKE JOURNALISM
IN AMERICAN HISTORY

ANDIE TUCHER

Columbia University Press

New York

publication supported by a grant from
The Community Foundation *for* Greater New Haven
as part of the Urban Haven Project

Columbia University Press
Publishers Since 1893
New York   Chichester, West Sussex
cup.columbia.edu

Library of Congress Cataloging-in-Publication Data
Names: Tucher, Andie, author.
Title: Not exactly lying : fake news and fake journalism in American history /
Andie Tucher.
Description: New York : Columbia University Press, 2022. | Includes bibliographical
references and index.
Identifiers: LCCN 2021036120 (print) | LCCN 2021036121 (ebook) |
ISBN 9780231186346 (hardback) | ISBN 9780231186353 (trade paperback) |
ISBN 9780231546591 (ebook)
Subjects: LCSH: Fake news—United States—History. | Journalism—Objectivity—
United States—History. | Disinformation—United States—History. | Journalism—
Corrupt practices—United States—History. | Press and politics—
United States—History.
Classification: LCC PN4888.F35 T83 2022 (print) | LCC PN4888.F35 (ebook) |
DDC 071—dc23
LC record available at https://lccn.loc.gov/2021036120
LC ebook record available at https://lccn.loc.gov/2021036121

Columbia University Press books are printed on permanent
and durable acid-free paper.
Printed and bound by CPI Group (UK) Ltd, Croydon, CR0 4YY

Cover image: *Group of Newsboys on Frankfort Street near World Building. Witness,*
Fred McMurrry. Location: New York, New York (State) / Photo by Lewis W. Hine.
National Child Labor Committee collection, Library of Congress, Prints and
Photographs Division.
Cover design: Lisa Hamm

To the real journalists

CONTENTS

ACKNOWLEDGMENTS

What a pleasure that after years' worth of immersion in fakes I am finally able to extend genuine thanks to all those who have helped and cheered me on the way.

I am grateful most of all to the Columbia Journalism School and my friends and colleagues there. Special thanks go to my fellow faculty members in the Communications PhD program, Todd Gitlin, Michael Schudson, and Richard John, who took a deep interest in my project; to the program's great friend Anya Schiffrin, who generously shared her own work on disinformation and propaganda and did me the great favor of reading a portion of the manuscript; and to our exceptional community of current and former students. I couldn't have asked for a more supportive or nourishing intellectual home.

I had invaluable help from two assiduous, thoughtful, and resourceful research assistants, Joanna Arcieri and Cherie Henderson, and Cherie's finely trained AP editor's eye also helped improve several chapters in the manuscript. (Though I confess I didn't take *all* the adverbs out.) Dan Bischoff, who read the entire draft, is the perfect editor, possessing the rare skill of knowing both when to push me harder and when to save me from myself.

I had the good fortune to attend a number of workshops and intimate conferences where work in progress was shared, conversation was lively, ideas flowed, and friendships were born, and this book bears the imprint of each one. I am grateful to Mike Miller of the Social Science Research Council and to the other generous participants in the workshop "Media, Technology, and Democracy in Historical Context," especially Nicole Hemmer, Martin L. Johnson, and Jennifer Petersen. Hansjakob Ziemer presided over the rich and enlightening working group "Observing the Everyday: Journalistic Knowledge Production in the Modern Era," a project of the Max Planck Institute for the History of Science in Berlin in cooperation with the German Historical Institute in Washington, and I am especially grateful to Norman Domeier, Petra McGillen, Annie Rudd, and Heidi Tworek.

I had a wonderful time at the brilliant International Communication Association preconference "Objects of Journalism" in London organized by Chris W. Anderson and Juliette De Maeyer. Adeline Wrona, Juliette Charbonneaux, and the participants in the research project "National Cultures of Interviewing," Gripic CELSA Paris-Sorbonne, offered a stimulating day of talk about journalistic talk. At Columbia, Mark Hansen, Bruce Kogut, and the Study Group on Fake News hosted me for several spirited breakfast-time conversations. And warm thanks go to Martin Conboy and the participants in the conference "Popular News Discourse" held on a wintry Zurich day by the AHRC Research Network on journalism history.

Many people offered advice along the way, many others moral support, and some a bit of both. I'm happy to thank Emily Bell, Lynn Berger, Emma Briant, Mark Canada, Leslie Clark, Dan Czitrom, Ruth Ford, Marguerite Holloway, Bud Kliment, Jennifer B. Lee, Efrat Nechushtai, and the whole Tucher clan.

This book wouldn't exist without Philip Leventhal of the Columbia University Press; it was his idea in the first place, and his wise guidance is evident on nearly every page. The editorial staff at the press made the entire process smooth and effective, and I stand in awe of Annie Barva's sensitive, meticulous copyediting. I also wish to thank the two anonymous reviewers for their insightful comments and their encouragement.

I am grateful to you all—truly.

Portions of chapter 4 were derived in part from an article published in *Photography and Culture*, June 2017, copyright Taylor and Francis, available online: https://doi.org/10.1080/17514517.2017.1322397.

NOT EXACTLY LYING

INTRODUCTION

The media is—really, the word, I think one of the greatest of all terms I've come up with—is "fake." I guess other people have used it, perhaps, over the years, but I've never noticed it.

—President Donald Trump, interviewed by Mike Huckabee,
Trinity Broadcasting Network, October 7, 2017

Ralph Pulitzer hated fake news. In December 1912, just three months after the journalism school founded by his late father, Joseph, opened its doors on the campus of Columbia University, Ralph delivered a guest lecture to the eighty-odd aspiring reporters who made up its first undergraduate classes. "The public pays the newspapers their price in order to buy the truth about events," the new publisher of the *World* (New York) told them.

The newspaper which sells the public deliberate fakes instead of facts is selling adulterated goods just as surely as does the rascal who puts salicylic acid in canned meats or arsenical coloring in preserves. . . . For those who rightly regard journalism not as a business but as a profession, it is needless to point out the shame of distorting a minister of truth into a

messenger of lies. For the faker is a liar. If he perpetrates a so-called harmless fake, he is a harmless liar. If he is guilty of a fake that injures people,
he is not only a vicious liar but often a moral assassin as well.[1]

Not everyone agreed. In the 1880s and 1890s, many journalists had been
openly embracing the term, cheerfully applying it to the reader-friendly
art of enlivening ordinary stories with skillful tweaks and fanciful embellishments. There was, those journalists insisted, nothing harmful about
it; after all, as one Boston editor explained breezily in 1887, faking was "not
exactly lying."[2] And even though by 1912 few journalists would openly
admit to the practice, many still quietly indulged in it. The thirty-year-
long debate, however, concerned much more than the location of the line
between harmless liar and moral assassin. The debate over faking in fact
lay at the center of a vital struggle over the very nature of journalistic work
and who could be trusted with the truth.

Though this was the first journalistic debate to turn on the word
fake, it was nowhere near the first debate about journalistic truth, and it
certainly wouldn't be the last. Concerns about the authenticity and
authority of American journalism are exactly as old as American journalism. The social institution that is defined by its claim of a special
ability to get things right has always offered an irresistible cover for
groups, enterprises, and people (sometimes including journalists) who
willfully get things very wrong. News organizations have frequently
found themselves competing with other actors who are distorting,
manipulating, misunderstanding, or faking the prevailing journalistic
conventions in order to present "truths" of their own for motives or
reasons of their own that range from ignorance to entertainment to
commercial advantage to political or social control. Americans have
been bamboozled by false reports about incestuous monarchs, challenged by humbugs about murdered prostitutes and depraved nuns, and
propagandized by sensational tidings about splendid little wars and ugly
big ones. They have been entertained by faked films of battlefield heroics and faked photographs of jilted brides, horrified by fabricated
atrocities and pacified by cover-ups of real ones, and disinformed for
their own good by powerful and secretive spy agencies. They have been
misled by institutions of government into disastrous foreign interven-
tions, disillusioned by whoppers unnoticed by inattentive editors, and

beguiled by political partisans disguised as professionals. Sometimes they have actively participated in the fake.

Historians of journalism have traditionally emphasized its steady evolution toward a greater professionalism rooted in an ethic of public service and a commitment to seeking the truth. And that story does indeed fit many kinds and aspects and eras of journalism, which at its best has challenged malefactors, exposed corruption, borne witness to conflict, comforted the afflicted, and numbered the dead, along with simply offering people timely intelligence they could trust about everything from the price of gold to the chance of rain. But stories about truth are never only about truth; they're also about power, about control, about desire, about values. The history of American journalism is about much more than how people called journalists developed forms and conventions to gather, verify, interpret, and distribute accurate information. Those forms and conventions were designed to vouch for the accuracy of their contents: journalism was supposed to *look like* truth, and truth like journalism. But what if falsehood does too?

The current national preoccupation with "fake news" and "fake media" continues the urgent debate over what truth looks like and who gets to define it. This time, though, the conversation has been seriously complicated by the blurriness of the terms in question, terms that are closely identified with Donald Trump as their alleged creator. But those terms have also been applied to everything from the mischievous and the mistaken through the opportunistic and the satirical all the way to the predatory and the subversive. Although much of what has been denounced as "fake news" comes to the public through journalism, even more often it arrives through social media or popular culture. The perpetrator can be a government or corporate propagandist, a rogue reporter or an incompetent one, a partisan activist, an advertiser, a spy, a homegrown hacker, a foreign hacker, a bot, an entrepreneur, a troll, a conspiracy theorist, or a polarizing president with a Twitter account. It can also be your grandmother. False information has been blamed for influencing election results, worsening a global pandemic, tribalizing the public discourse, and reinforcing the wackiest of conspiracy theories, but no one seems to know how to rein it in.

So before we can even begin a meaningful analysis of the history of "fake news," we need to impose some order on that most protean term and define what each of the two words in it has meant—and hasn't meant.

By *fake*, I mean something that was *purposefully* untrue, created by people who understood, at some level and for whatever benign or devious purpose, that what they were saying was false or deceptive. Some of their readers or viewers may have caught on to the trick, but that was often incidental. The point was generally to mislead or manipulate the consumer. Unintentional errors are not fakes, though willfully blinkered reporting may be. Opinions or advocacy clearly expressed as such are not fakes, though partisan argument cast as impartial observation may be. And although failures by journalists to account for facts or attitudes that challenge prevailing mainstream social and cultural values represent another essential critique of how journalism works, that phenomenon lies generally beyond the scope of a book on the history of journalistic faking.

It's important to note that what news consumers or journalists or both have considered fake has varied widely over the years as expectations about what journalism should do and how journalists should work have evolved. Political invective in which zeal replaced fact, for instance, was seen as normal, even desirable in the newspapers of the early republic. In 1912, as Ralph Pulitzer well knew, the very word *fake* had not much earlier described a journalistic tactic admired in many circles for its rakish charm. And the adoption of new technologies for journalistic use has often begun with a period when "anything goes" before practitioners and the public can come to an agreement on what the rules for rendering reality with the new device should be.

Every era produces the fakes its circumstances demand and its opportunities afford, which discourages any effort to provide a historically situated taxonomy of fakery of the sort that scholars working mainly on contemporary journalism have been able to produce.[3] It also cautions researchers who use journalism-like works from other eras as historical source material to make sure they understand what they're dealing with. Fake news can warp the public debate in the urgency of the moment, but it can warp our understanding of the past, too.[4] The examples and case studies I have chosen to analyze here are ones I found to be representative of the problems, innovations, and contingencies of their particular times.

Of course, drawing conclusions about the intentions and understandings of people long gone can be challenging; what looked like a button-busting joke in one era might well scream "fraud!" to a historian far removed from that social and cultural milieu. But a textual-analysis approach that is based on wide reading, that considers the stories in the context of other contemporary events, and that is alert to stylistic cues, cultural resonances, and underlying allusions can lead to the careful drawing of plausible conclusions about the perpetrators, victims, beneficiaries, and debunkers of these efforts and about their relationships with power and authority.[5]

The more ambiguous word in the phrase "fake news" is *news*, which can apply to varieties of information and intelligence ranging from commercial advertising to political campaigning to social media posts about last night's frat party. My interest here, however, focuses on how fakers have persistently operated within the information system known as journalism and how they have manipulated the outward forms of that system to lay claim to truthfulness.

Journalism has always been something of an outlier among the kinds of work generally considered "professions." Unlike law or medicine, it has no requirements for education or credentialing; it resists most kinds of regulation; its area of expertise is ill defined; it seems "doable" by almost anyone; and it has no formal mechanism to disbar or defrock or yank the licenses of rogue operators. But journalists do engage in the practice of boundary work, asserting their legitimacy and professional authority by defining norms, behaviors, and ethics that they find acceptable in their discipline—chief among them accuracy, fairness, independence, and accountability—and by branding others as unacceptable.[6] That's what Ralph Pulitzer and other journalists were doing in the late nineteenth and early twentieth centuries with their explicit repudiation of faking. They were drawing a boundary line to separate themselves from their more disreputable colleagues, especially those in the yellow press, who could not be trusted to tell the truth.

For journalists, however, professional boundaries have turned out to have few effective sentries and insufficient strength to stop undesirables from ignoring them, dismantling them, or tunneling under them to pop up safely on the other side, and as the social institution that claims jurisdiction over the presentation of what's true, journalism has surprisingly little jurisdiction over its own practice. The disreputableness of "fake" news has helped shape the idea of what "real" journalism is, but, as I will argue, the creation of the norms and standards of real journalism have paradoxically helped produce something even more harmful to the body politic and the idea of truth than fake news. I am calling it *fake journalism*: the appropriation of the outward forms of journalism in an explicit effort to lend credibility to falsehood.

Fake news is deceptive *information*, which can operate entirely outside the world of conventional journalism. Fake journalism, in contrast, is a deceptive *practice*, an imposture that launches from some kind of authentic or authentic-seeming perch or platform to present false information or heavily partisan opinion or propaganda in a form specifically crafted to look or sound like "real" independent journalism rooted in impartial investigation and rigorous verification. (By "real" or "mainstream" journalism in recent times, I generally mean the likes of CBS, NBC, ABC, CNN, the *New York Times*, the *Washington Post*, and the *Wall Street Journal*, which occupied seven of the top nine tightly clustered slots in a survey released by the *Columbia Journalism Review* in December 2018 that asked people which news organizations they considered "mainstream."[7] Local and regional news organizations, too, often fulfill that role for their particular audiences.) For the past century and more, as the mass media have woven themselves deeper and deeper into the political system, fake journalism—CIA front organizations, spurious campaign tabloids designed to smear political enemies, billionaire-funded "investigative teams" avid to dig up dirt—has implicitly or explicitly attacked and undermined the credibility of professional or mainstream journalism as failing to uphold standards even as it pretends to uphold those standards itself. An important part of journalism history is thus the story of the clash *within* journalism between practitioners of the real seeking to defend their profession and perpetrators of the fake working to exploit it. At the heart of that struggle lies an urgent question: What happens to democracy when fake journalism looks more and more like truth and fake truth like journalism?

The first three chapters introduce the early American newspaper as a hodgepodge of truth, fiction, fakery, partisanship, and humbug, where news and commercial intelligence could mix with political argumentation, tall tales, hoaxes, serialized novels, social notes, and poetry. In large part a consumer good focused on giving the public what it wanted, the nineteenth-century newspaper offered a bargain to its readers: they accepted the responsibility of monitoring and evaluating the authenticity of everything they read, and in return they were empowered to choose for themselves what to believe. Not until the late nineteenth and early twentieth centuries did the expectation take hold among readers of the professionalizing press that everything they read was supposed to be true—an expectation immediately challenged by fake journalism that adopted the outward forms of truthfulness without making the commitment to it.

Chapter 4 analyzes how public attitudes about news media were prone to complication by the rise of new technologies—photography, moving pictures, radio—that often seemed to do the same kind of work as journalism without following any of the rules of journalism. Chapter 5 explores World War I as the first great clash between professionalized and fake journalism as government, military, and corporate propagandists elbowed the journalists aside in order to "inform" readers about the "bestial" enemy. Chapter 6 takes up the postwar backlash of disillusionment and mistrust that played out in the flowering of new kinds of newspapers that openly promised to entertain their readers without resorting to boring old factual information.

Another world war, as chapter 7 argues, brought new dilemmas for journalists torn between the professional imperative to report honestly and the human desire (backed up by government and military oversight) to make sure "our side" won. Chapter 8 describes how the demands and delusions of the Cold War led not just to creative new forms of fake journalism but even to the turning of fake journalism against journalists in the service of what was justified as the "greater good." Chapter 9 charts the public's growing mistrust in journalistic institutions and conventions— notably the traditional value of objectivity—as well as the disruptions and opportunities afforded to both fake and real journalism by the new formats of cable news and the internet. And chapter 10 carries into the twenty-first century and through the Obama years an analysis of the increasingly fraught relationship of journalistic "truth" with the very different "truths" of political partisanship.

After unsettling his audience of fresh-faced undergraduates with dire warnings about salicylic acid and moral assassination, Ralph Pulitzer shifted to a more upbeat tone. How, he asked them, could inaccuracies be reduced and faking eradicated? Pointing to the "gentlemen" (and the handful of ladies) arrayed in front of him, "You," he said, "are among the best remedies that I know of." The students had enrolled in the nation's second-ever journalism school to undergo training "not only in the technique but in the highest traditions of their life's work," he told them, thus demonstrating that they "regard[ed] newspaper work not as a trade but as a solemn trust." And they would, he assured them in his concluding flourish, "realize that truth telling is the sole reason for the existence of a press at all. That every time a journal prints a mistake it is performing an essentially abnormal function. That every time it prints a deliberate fake it becomes a degenerate and perverted monstrosity."[8]

A century later, Pulitzer's faith in both journalism and the possibility of truth have all but vanished from public life. It is no coincidence that perverted monstrosities are alive and flourishing.

1

"FALSE REPORTS, MALICIOUSLY MADE"

For two hundred years, news in the American newspaper was often untrue but less often fake. Its columns brimmed with items meant to tease or challenge or entertain readers, to offer them a sense of community or superiority, to persuade them of a partisan argument, to tweak a rival, to fill column inches in a time of news drought. Many of those items were not factually accurate, but since much of the time they were not intended to fool or deceive anyone, they weren't fake, either. News can be fake only if the public has a general expectation that all news should be true.

To be sure, declaring war against falsehood and claiming a special mission on behalf of truth have always been newspaper conventions. The first two people ever to publish newspapers in the English North American colonies announced that they were inspired to start their journals by a public-spirited desire to establish the truth—to correct the rumors, gossip, propaganda, and "false reports" that swirled through the public square. Both, however, printed reports that were demonstrably inaccurate. One was openly challenging the powers that be; the other was proudly claiming their imprimatur. One was purposefully spreading news that was fake; the other was duped by a compelling faker. Their radically different responses, aims, and outcomes neatly represent two poles of opinion at the dawn of journalism in America about what a newspaper ought to be and what a responsible newspaper editor ought to do.

The first known genuine American newspaper—that is, the first publication containing information about current affairs and intended to appear on a regular schedule—was issued in Boston on September 25, 1690. *Publick Occurrences Both Forreign and Domestick* was not the first product of the colonial press to offer timely accounts of recent events; Massachusetts printers were accustomed to producing the occasional broadside, pamphlet, special-occasion sermon, or one-time "publick newsletter" in response to political developments or important happenings. But this new sheet flaunted its intention to follow a growing European practice and become a recurrent visitor. It carried the optimistic designation "Numb. 1" and promised to come out once a month or even more often in case of a "Glut of Occurrences."

Its founder, the printer and bookseller Benjamin Harris, had begun his newspaper career amid the political and religious maelstrom of Restoration London, where yet another chapter was unfolding in the endless battle over the complicated bonds linking truth, falsehood, and power. As early as 1275, nearly two centuries before the advent of the printing press, English law recognized that untruths could endanger power: because spreading "false news or tales" could cause "discord . . . between the king and his people or the great men of the realm," anyone who did so was subject to prosecution. In 1606, however, in the reign of James I, English law recognized that truth, too, could endanger power. A new statute essentially criminalized any statement that disparaged the king or the government, defining as seditious libel even—or especially—criticism that had the hazardous quality of being accurate.[1] "False" news was anything that threatened the institutions of power.

By the time Harris began printing in London in the 1670s, the legal requirement that printers receive official permission for anything they set in type had lapsed, been reinstated, and then been tightened all the more. Like their predecessors both royal and parliamentary, King Charles II and his chief censor, Sir Roger L'Estrange, saw the job of the press as simple: to print the truth, which meant whatever was royally approved and officially licensed, and not to print anything that "disturbed or amused the minds of [the king's] subjects by Lyes or vain Reports," which was just about everything else. The "great business of Government," the king believed, was to "procure Obedience, and keep off Disobedience," and that would be impossible if ordinary citizens could send their ideas out into the wild at will. Like rebels and dissenters before them, Restoration-era anti-Catholics, antiroyalists, and other activists maintained their right to express in public whatever their consciences told them was true. The underlying theory, as John Milton had put it in 1644, was that if ideas were fairly debated in an open encounter, the ones that were true would inevitably triumph over those that were not. According to this view, the survival of fake news would thus be impossible: it would inevitably go down to defeat.[2] But theory was one thing, and the reality of human argumentation another, especially in an era of bitter religious and partisan divisions. Not even Milton believed in freedom of the press for Roman Catholics, who would, he was certain, inevitably despoil any fair and open encounter with polemic, provocation, and propaganda rather than reason. In the paper wars of Harris's London, "false reports" became potent weapons, as each side accused its opponents of maliciously, ignorantly, or greedily spreading them, and each claimed that its own goal was to correct the false reports of others—an implicit suggestion that "the truth" would need a strong helping hand if it were to end up on top. In fact, sometimes the suggestion was perfectly explicit. The *Monthly Recorder* of January 1682, for instance, complained bitterly that newspapers eager to "make their News sell" published reports without verifying them, while many others "abuse one another with Sham Letters of News, on purpose to do one another injury, by causing one another to publish things that are false."[3] False reports were not doomed to certain death after all—and not for the last time, *accusations* that others were peddling fake news for profit or mischief could be enormously effective weapons in those "open" encounters.

Harris, a fervent Anabaptist, soon compiled such a long record of legal troubles over his feisty anti-Catholic and anti-Stuart newspapers and pamphlets that he felt it wise to flee England, arriving in the Netherlands in 1685 and Boston the following year. In Boston, he was confronted with a new round of political pandemonium, this time a Puritan-led rebellion that ended up with the Anglican royal governor in jail. Taxpayers were revolting, hostilities with American Indians and the French were boiling, provincial soldiers were striking, and political factions were clashing over how to constitute a new government.[4]

Harris introduced his new project with a sturdy prospectus telling Bostonians exactly what to expect from him. He would provide a record of

"Memorable Occurrences of Divine Providence." He would offer intelligence that would help "people everywhere" both to understand public affairs and to prosper in their businesses. He would tell the truth and publish nothing "but what we have reason to believe is true, repairing to the best fountains for our Information." If he made any kind of "material mistake," he would correct it in the next issue. And he would expose fake news. Drawing on the familiar language of the paper wars back home in London, he began by declaring that "there are many False Reports, maliciously made, and spread among us." But then he went a step further: he encouraged his readers to turn in anyone doing the spreading and promised to publish in his paper the name of anyone exposed as "a malicious Raiser of a false Report." The first practitioner of American journalism was seeking to earn credibility in terms that sound strikingly modern: he would use only reliable sources, he would correct his mistakes, and he would sniff out and punish anyone who told lies. And it was surely no accident that he chose to preemptively label his own errors with a word suggesting only innocent lapses while damning others with accusations of malice and purposeful deception.[5]

For a recent arrival with so contentious a background to set himself up as a sort of public truth-police bureau would have been bold under any circumstances. But given the prevailing atmosphere of chaos and choler and the urgency with which competing factions were working to sway the political debate, Harris's stated goal was both high-minded and wildly audacious. Considering that he was printing what he pleased without securing the permission or formal license that was required in the English colonies just as it was in England, he seemed to be asking for trouble.

He got it. The paper, three pages of text with a blank fourth page and barely big enough to wrap a small mackerel, carried mainly local intelligence about daily life that had been gathered in person and secondhand (or perhaps third or fourth). Inquiring Bostonians read of outbreaks of fevers and smallpox, a destructive fire, the capture of two children by American Indians, the suicide of a melancholy widower, the progress of the colony's military expedition against Canada. There was a little overseas news, too, including reports about King William's military expedition into Ireland that had arrived in a letter delivered by ship out of the English colony of Barbados.

The governing council responded by almost immediately proscribing the paper and went about destroying the edition with such zeal that only a single copy of that sole issue is known to survive. That Harris was working "*Without the least Privity or Countenance of Authority*," as the council put it, was bad enough. But the paper also raised the council members' "high Resentment" because it contained what they called "Reflections of a very high nature" and "sundry doubtful and uncertain Reports."[6] According to the councilman Samuel Sewall, the group was especially irked by two particular items in the paper.[7] Harris's account of the military expedition in Canada included a sharp critique of the colonial authorities for their alliance with Mohawk warriors, who had abused French prisoners of war "in a manner too barbarous for any English to approve." And, Harris noted in a passing comment, the dauphin of France was gathering an army of Huguenots and disaffected papists to depose his own father, Louis XIV, because the Sun King was accustomed to "*lie with the Sons Wife.*"

Harris was not without important friends; his paper had the support of the prominent Puritan minister Cotton Mather and members of Mather's faction. But the editor was also a known malcontent who was flouting the law in a way that was particularly galling to the hierarchical society of seventeenth-century New England. In the midst of a passionate political debate in which rumor and falsehood were inevitable participants, he, a nobody, was claiming for himself the power to decide what Bostonians should and should not know and the authority to determine what was and was not true. Even the professionally nuanced disclaimer that tempered his report of the Mohawk abuses—he may not have gotten it precisely right, he conceded, "but this Account, is as near exactness, as any that could be had, in the midst of many various reports about it"—served only to remind his readers that the intelligence had been brought to them not by someone in an official position but by some guy named Harris who claimed he could tell the difference between lies and truth. (By 1692, Harris and the local authorities had reconciled with each other on purely practical grounds: Harris needed to earn money, and with the always meager ranks of Boston print shops further depleted by fires and deaths, officials had no choice but to hire as government printer the troublesome dissenter with the only press in town.)[8]

Old-school journalism historians with a romantic turn of mind have tended to see Harris as a hero whose voice was cruelly suppressed simply because he tried to strike a blow for conscience and liberty. In his history published in 1920, George Henry Payne, for instance, called him an "exceptional figure in the fight for a free press in both England and America," a "fine old Whig" who was "on the side of humanity and progress, to the very great displeasure of the authorities." (Payne didn't mention the less-than-humane incest story.)[9] But even historians with a more analytical point of view seem to have missed the twist embedded in the whole affair. Benjamin Harris—the proto-professional who had declared war on "false reports" and threatened to expose the perpetrators—was himself peddling opportunistic falsehoods. The report about Louis XIV's indiscretion with his daughter-in-law and the vengeful plotting by his cuckolded son was a calculated item of fake news.

How do we know? In the first place, Louis had no daughter-in-law at the time: the wife of his only son had died in April, five months before the paper appeared. (*Publick Occurrences* contained accurate European intelligence less than three months old, so news of the dauphine's death could certainly have reached a well-networked Boston printer by late September.) More important: any affair between the king and his son's wife seems extremely unlikely. The dauphine—who was known for being devout, multilingual, homely, and ill—had been bedridden for years before her death at the age of twenty-nine, and Louis himself, under the influence of his powerful and pious second wife, Madame de Maintenon, had long since given up his famously libertine ways. Nor does any historical evidence support the existence of a treasonous plot involving the incurious and affable dauphin, who all his life was, two historians have commented, "relatively untroublesome for the king by the standards of heirs-to-the-throne in France and elsewhere."[10]

Most important: whether Harris knew or not that his report was untrue, he must have realized that it was inflammatory. Yet the man who had promised always to seek out "the best fountains for our Information" and had declared war against "False Reports, maliciously made" nonetheless had consciously chosen that particular juicy story out of a multitude of other possible items he could have plucked from letters, foreign newspapers, and travelers' tales. He had nestled it casually in a stream of local intelligence about epidemics and fires whose verifiable accuracy would likely have lulled his readers into believing that even those stories they had *not* seen or confirmed for themselves were also true. And he could not have been unaware that the canard sounded just truthful enough to be plausible, especially to anyone who already disliked Catholics or kings or both. Louis had, after all, enjoyed many mistresses in his younger years, and the incest and the son's patricidal conspiracy added just the right outrageous frisson, exactly what anyone might expect of an absolute monarch who was also a papist.

Harris, moreover, was already experienced in the art of fake news; back in London he had been involved in the particularly egregious episode known as the "Popish Plot," the alleged Jesuit conspiracy to assassinate Charles II and launch a reign of terror in London. The whole thing was a fabrication, concocted by the ne'er-do-well religious chameleon Titus Oates, but Oates's accusations threw London into a panic and set off an orgy of investigations and executions. Harris's busy print shop had played a crucial role in bruiting the supposed plot, and in 1680 he was put on trial for sedition, where the lord chief justice blasted him as a writer of "false News."[11] Harris was pilloried, jailed, and fined. When he eventually turned up in Boston, though, he seemed poised to continue exactly as he had before. His new newspaper claimed the same noble-sounding purpose of "prevent[ing] false reports" as his trouble-making London newspaper had.

Publick Occurrences is ambiguous about Harris's source for the scandalous report about the king; it could have come from the letter that had just arrived via Barbados, but in any case he did not offer any identifying details about the letter writer. The news may well in fact have originated from the network of like-minded anti-Catholic activists Harris had known in London and the Netherlands. Especially creative and energetic in the distribution of scurrilous royal rumors was the community of French Huguenots who had begun flooding into the Netherlands in 1685, when Louis revoked the century-old edict that had protected Protestants from persecution.[12] For all his bold claims of authority over the truth and his declaration of war against falsehood, Harris was exploiting his status as truth teller to spread his own false reports in the service of a cause dear to his heart. He was, in other words, producing what has become a familiar kind of fake news: disinformation intended to undermine an opponent by exploiting a well-known soft spot. But his effort to disseminate fake news about a king, even an enemy king, even a Popish enemy king, drew a response that has also become familiar: he was shouted down by people who had more power than he did. Some guy named Harris should not have been surprised to earn sanctions rather than celebrations for attempting to usurp for himself the authority to declare what was and was not true.

BY AUTHORITY

The fourteen-year period that followed the suppression of *Publick Occurrences* was the very last era when it can be said for certain that not a single newspaper in America published a single item of fake news. That's because in those fourteen years not a single newspaper was published in America. Only in 1704 did the next journal appear, a two-page weekly published by the Scottish immigrant John Campbell, who had recently been appointed to succeed his father as postmaster of Boston.[13]

From the beginning it was clear the *Boston News-Letter* would be very different kind of paper in style and tone from the willfully provocative *Publick Occurrences*. Campbell's initial issue, dated April 17–24, 1704, included no promises, no manifesto on behalf of truth, no discussion of his methods, not even an explanation of his intentions; his only welcoming note was an invitation to readers to place advertisements, at "Reasonable" rates, about houses for sale or runaway servants. (Surviving for a year made him more garrulous; it was in his near-first-anniversary issue of April 2–9, 1705, that he called his paper a "Publick Good" designed "to prevent a great many false reports.") Just below the title banner was printed, in large letters, "Published by Authority," a strong signal that Campbell, unlike Harris, would not be treading on any official toes. The claim seems to have been more entrepreneurial than submissive, however, perhaps a bid for official business or a subsidy from the legislature; colonial officials never treated Campbell's paper as an official publication along the lines of the royally sponsored *London Gazette*. In any case, licensing in the colonies was already trickling away.[14]

Also unlike Harris, Campbell focused on matters that were safely international, not close to home; his interests were practical and commercial, not disputatious. Like his father, Postmaster Campbell had for some time been using his position at the communications center of the most important seaport in the English American colonies to gather information about world affairs. He compiled these findings into handwritten newsletters and sent them to a small list of colonial officials, merchants, and others who required access to current political and financial intelligence. Transforming the handwritten newsletter into the printed *News-Letter* offered the same goods on a potentially more profitable scale and began to establish news as a commodity with commercial value.

The content, appearance, and style of the *News-Letter* followed those of England's officially sanctioned *London Gazette*. Much of its fare had wandered in secondhand via ship captains, mail riders, travelers' letters, or London papers and usually concerned distant events of interest to the Boston merchants, political men, and other leading citizens who were Campbell's main audience: wars, dynastic marriages and deaths, international politics, shipping news, foreign commerce. Campbell worked his readers hard, assuming they were worldly enough to understand the context of the brusque and random snippets he lifted verbatim from sources he rarely even named. But those Bostonians who made it through, for example, the notice from the October 29–November 5, 1705, number that "yesterday" (which the attentive reader would have deduced to mean April 29) Prince Eugene (who was not otherwise identified) arrived at the imperial camp at Gavardo (not otherwise located) and dined with the Count de Leiningen (not otherwise described) could have prided themselves on their connection to the great affairs of the European world. Overt political commentary and visible partisanship of any kind were both rare and mild. Local laws and proclamations claimed some space, as did the occasional tragedy near home, such as the report in the November 5–12, 1705, issue that a five-year-old boy had been crushed to death in a cider mill at Muddy River outside Boston. That news was dispatched in thirty-eight words.

The issue of October 29–November 5, 1705, carried another story that stood out against all that conventional *News-Letter* fare like a cardinal in the snow. It concerned a young Quaker named Henry Burch, who had recently arrived in Boston from New York with a harrowing tale. Apprenticed as a teenager to a wicked uncle who tried to have him murdered, Burch had been badly injured in a pirate attack, sold as a servant to a Virginia planter, nearly drowned in a shipwreck, and cheated out of his inheritance. The *News-Letter* devoted nearly one-quarter of its entire weekly news hole to the tale, proudly noting that "This whole Information was taken from *Mr. Henry Burch's* own mouth." Campbell clearly believed the story to be true.[15]

It was not. Within days of the appearance of the story, previous hosts of Burch had revealed the young man to be a liar, an imposter, and a thief whose facial scar had apparently come not from a pirate's dagger but from a branding iron upon the order of some outraged magistrate. Mortified, Campbell strove to play down the blunder, pretending in the next week's issue that he had known all along about the young man's deception. He explained that he hadn't had room in the previous issue to recount the entire affair, so he had, "According to good Manners[,] . . . let [Burch] tell his Story first." But he also offered a reward for the capture of the youth, who had fled, and suggested punishing the "ungrateful Varlet" as a justification for having lavished so much attention on the tale.

> And now, I hope, this is become such an useful Story, That the Gentlemen my Subscribers will not complain either of the *Introduction* to it in our former, or of the *procedure* of it, in our present, *News-Letter.* Our *News-Letter* also, will, I hope sufficiently preserve its Reputation, if any Paragraph of it, not setting a thing in all its *true light*, shall in one weeks [*sic*] time supply all that is defective, and perhaps there are few Readers, but what have themselves now & then told a Story that needed a further *Elucidation.*

Although Campbell tacitly acknowledged here that his newspaper had been wrong to accept Burch's story as truthful and promised to correct any future mistakes, he also noted pointedly that anyone, even his own readers, could have made the same error. He insisted that the real problem was the "*Remarkable*" phenomenon that "a Blade should be so desirous to have such a formal Story Printed about himself, and yet that in less than 2 days time, he should be detected for an horrid CHEAT." The fault lay with Burch for lying, not with Campbell for believing.

It's hardly surprising that Campbell jumped at the Burch story, a timely, dramatic, and narratively satisfying tale that came directly from an interview with the protagonist. But whereas his attention to both the young man's yarn and its distressing aftermath does suggest a glimmering of something now recognizable as a reporter's nose for news, Campbell, unlike Harris, had neither an editor's eye for error nor an activist's yen for disputation. By resisting the idea that a newspaper publisher had any particular obligation to confirm his content or to expose a faker, he was also rejecting the special status that Harris had claimed for himself. No one, the editor of the *News-Letter* was saying, should have expected him to know anything or express any opinion about what he was printing; no one should have looked to him for certainty or confirmation. Authority? Not him. He was just some guy named Campbell.

REVOLUTIONS

The main story of the revolutionary and early national press is the evolution of the newspaper producer from "printer" to something more like "journalist." But that new being had a voice that sang of liberty and the public interest while delivering big dollops of propaganda, agitation, and falsehood.

By 1765, the American colonies were producing about two dozen newspapers with circulations ranging from an average of 600 to as many as 1,500 copies a week.[16] A few of them indulged in Harris-style provocations, at least for a while. The *New England Courant*—founded in 1721 by James Franklin and produced with the sometimes impertinent help of his apprentice and younger brother, Ben—launched crusades, picked fights, delighted in doggerel and satire, made fun of the local bigwigs, and endured official sanctions, but it finally subsided, exhausted, after less than six years. John Peter Zenger, the New York printer tried in 1735 for seditious libel because he manned the press for the wrong side in a newspaper war involving the governor, was sprung from jail after his lawyer dazzled the jury with his argument that it was legal for a newspaper to speak *truth* to power. But after his victory, Zenger, either chastened or just worn out, tempered the asperity of his paper anyway.

Most newspapers in these early decades resembled Campbell's dutiful record of occurrences more than Harris's trouble-making sheet. Generally impartial in politics, civil toward power, and more attentive to distant international news than to local affairs, newspapers were essentially tools of business, offering their mostly elite readers the sort of information they could use to profit in commercial affairs. They were tools for the printer as well. In most print shops, the bread-and-butter work consisted of handbills, blank forms, schoolbooks, religious works, almanacs, and, for the lucky, a lucrative stream of government documents. The newspaper was almost an afterthought, a way to advertise the shop's other wares, and printers had little incentive to risk offending any member of their very limited pool of customers by involving themselves in reporting local imbroglios or political debates.

Ben Franklin's editorial "Apology for Printers"—often cited as the most direct expression of the typical colonial printer's interpretation of a "free and open press"—forged a tidy connection between the financial and the philosophical imperatives of the print shop. Criticized in 1731 for printing a handbill advertisement that seemed to malign clergymen, Franklin, no longer his brother's bratty apprentice but the new proprietor of the *Pennsylvania Gazette* with profits to protect, argued it was wrong to assume that printers agreed with everything they set in type. In fact, he went on, they naturally acquired "a vast Unconcernedness" about the accuracy of what they were printing and looked at it simply as the product of their daily labor, a commercial good no different from a fireplace poker or a pair of shoes. Printers, he said, echoing Milton's imagery, "are educated in the Belief, that when Men differ in Opinion, both Sides ought equally to have the Advantage of being heard by the Publick; and that when Truth and Error have fair Play, the former is always an overmatch for the latter: Hence they chearfully serve all contending Writers that pay them well, without regarding on which side they are of the Question in Dispute."[17] Franklin was extending James Campbell's argument that newspaper publishers had no special authority over truth; in fact, he was praising that deficiency as a key tenet of a printer's vocational identity.

As the political crisis with Britain accelerated, however, and citizens—including printers—contemplated the daring and hazardous prospect of rebellion, the safe virtues of print-shop impartiality began to seem much less compelling. In the atmosphere of crisis, newspapers were, of course, essential for anyone who wanted to follow the latest political and military news, but they also took on new roles as participants in public life rather than disinterested observers of it. Newspapers rallied, they inspired, they inflamed, and, especially, they created a sense of community and common purpose for readers eager to discuss the issues of the day with each other or to contemplate the contours of the new political landscape. One sign of the papers' influence lay in the magnitude of their presence: between 1763 and 1775, the number of newspapers in the colonies nearly doubled, and circulations soared. Another sign lay in their orientation: more than twice as many papers supported the Patriots' side as the Tories', and many Tory printers endured boycotts, mob violence, and business collapse.[18] Printers who formerly worried that being too opinionated would lose them customers now had good reason to fear that *not* being sufficiently—and correctly—opinionated would do the same thing.

Some printers turned Patriot in self-defense; others embraced the revolutionary cause out of conviction; but most began to see themselves differently. In his "Apology" in 1731, Franklin had explained (though quite possibly with a dollop of Franklinian cunning) that he hadn't even had enough "Curiosity" to ask what the offending handbill had actually meant: all he did, he said, was set it in type. With the coming of the revolution, few printers would have betrayed that kind of indifference even in jest. Many of them were coming to think of themselves more as thinkers and activists than as mere craftsmen churning out yet another gewgaw. And their traditional view of their task as encouraging truth to emerge on its own from open public debate was increasingly tinged with the imperative of rebellion: to support their righteous cause by ensuring the emergence of the *right* truth.[19]

Sometimes, as with the writings of Tom Paine or John Dickinson, that could take the shape of inspiring rhetoric and courageous idealism, but it could also mean distortions, propaganda, and false reports in myriad guises, some of them creative indeed. The *Constitutional Courant*, for instance, was an obviously fake newspaper issued in 1765 in a single number that gave the name of the printer as "Andrew Marvel"—a pseudonym just one letter away from the name of the English poet and antimonarchical satirist who was a close friend of Milton—and his place of business as "the Sign of the Bribe refused, on Constitution-Hill, North America." Containing two screeds against the Stamp Act so fierce that not a single printer dared to publish them openly, this fake paper was designed solely to disseminate a message without incriminating the impassioned messenger.[20]

Benjamin Franklin's fake "Supplement" to the *Independent Chronicle* (Boston), in contrast, clearly intended to fool readers on the enemy's side into believing it was the real thing. Produced at his press in Passy, France, in 1782, just as the British government was about to open peace negotiations with the American rebels, the supplement looked authentic, carrying a serial number in an appropriate range and several genuine-seeming advertisements for land in Massachusetts. Its main content was two letters. One, allegedly written by John Paul Jones, the American naval commander often denounced as a pirate, insisted that it was not he but the English who were waging the "war of *rapine*." The other letter, addressed to the governor of Canada and supposedly intercepted by an American militia officer, described at grisly length a collection of hundreds of scalps of American adults, children, and infants that had been taken by the Redcoats' Seneca allies and packaged to be sent to George III as gifts. All of the scalps carried "Indian triumphal Marks" indicating how their unfortunate owners had been killed: "surprised in the Night," "burnt alive," "knocked down dead," "ript out of their Mothers' Bellies," and more. Franklin's hope, as he wrote to John Adams, was that if he could get the supplement reprinted in London, it would remind the British of the wartime atrocities that they and their allies had committed against American citizens. That memory, he continued, might make the British "a little asham'd of themselves" at the start of the peace talks. But the sheer luridness of Franklin's invention apparently aroused readers' suspicions, and the Whig politician Horace Walpole, for one, guessed the real author. Fakes that are too outré can fail to fool.[21]

Throughout the war, genuine newspapers, too, often crafted their accounts specifically to incite and inspire, and readers readily obliged. When in 1768 Britain sent troops to garrison the rowdy city of Boston, resistance leaders there began to compile a sort of running samizdat narrative of the outrages of life under Redcoat occupation. Installments of the "Journal of Occurrences" were regularly sent to the local press and then widely copied from paper to paper in other colonies. The tone was set by the first insertion, initially published in the *New York Journal* of October 13, 1768, which concluded by quoting the anonymous authors' instructions to the printer: "*The above Journal you are desired to publish for the general Satisfaction, it being strictly Fact.*"

The complaints about the quartering of soldiers and the confiscation of property do seem believable and generally factual. Much harder to assess are reports about, for instance, the married woman walking alone who was subjected to "great Indecencies" or the unoffending gentleman clubbed with a musket by an inebriated guard or the smallpox-ridden Irish immigrants who had been released from their ships to spread the disease in the streets. All of the items are from the *Journal* of November 24, and all of them could be perfectly accurate about life in a time of rebellion. But like the incest rumors that Harris chose to reprint about the Sun King, melodramatic accusations that an enemy was abusing respectable ladies, drunkenly assaulting innocent bystanders, and unleashing germ warfare in the public square were also classic propaganda weapons whose accuracy was much less important than their effectiveness at keeping the rabble—and everyone else—roused.

Similar cautions surround the accounts of the brawl sparked in Boston in 1770 by crowds of rowdy Patriots throwing stones and swinging clubs at the British military occupiers. Five Americans were shot and killed in the melee, a toll that under the circumstances could have been much worse. But news of what the *Boston Gazette* on March 12 called the "horrid massacre" ricocheted throughout the colonies, and Paul Revere's hand-colored engraving of the "Bloody Massacre" seared into its viewers' memories the horrifying—and completely bogus—image of Redcoats lined up in smart military order resolutely mowing down their defenseless victims at the captain's command.

The turn to emotional, engaged reporting on matters of intense public interest marks a radical change in the American newspaper. It is scarcely surprising that the pressures and exigencies of the war so often led to coverage that was bent or sensationalized; other wars would do and have done the same in the United States and elsewhere. More consequential a shift was the emergence of newspapers as active, essential, and opinionated participants in the democratic process. If a government was to be based on the consent of the governed, the governed had to understand what they were—and were not—consenting to, and newspaper editors were uniquely authorized to offer the information their fellow Americans required to decide.

CONGRESS MADE A LAW

Conducting a government rooted in the informed consent of the governed, however, turned out to embody enormous practical and moral challenges in which the new nation's newspapers were deeply implicated. What would happen if citizens, duly informed by their newspapers, disagreed on what they wanted their government to do? What would happen if different newspapers offered their readers different versions of what was "true"? What would happen if readers did not trust what newspapers told them in the first place? Faced with the task of actually building the representative democracy they had dared everything to establish, many Americans were surprised to find the country split by deep ideological disagreements over everything from the power of the government to the revolution in France.

From these divisions grew two parties whose adherents regarded each other's philosophical and political attitudes as wrong-headed, risky, even treasonous and each other's characters as dangerously lacking the civic virtue essential to a democracy. To plead their cases in the public square, Federalists and Republicans alike founded or funded feisty, opinionated newspapers, staffed them with committed political operatives, and devoted them to vigorous political argumentation and attack, at times in language of pyrotechnic nastiness. Benjamin Franklin Bache's (Republican) *Philadelphia Aurora* howled that the Federalist George Washington had "debauched" the American nation. William Cobbett's (Federalist) *Porcupine's Gazette* bellowed that Bache himself was an "atrocious wretch," an "ill-looking devil" with the "*toute ensemble*" of someone who had been left hanging for days on a gibbet. The (Republican) *Independent Chronicle* of Boston screamed that Alexander Hamilton, a Federalist, was "haunted by whores" and was a "lewd slave to lust."[22]

Much of this journalistic language was purposefully exaggerated and satirical, and readers understood it that way; not even Bache's bitterest enemies would have believed that he literally resembled a week-old cadaver with a stretched neck. But in the same piece Cobbett used equally extravagant language to ridicule Bache's support of the French Revolution and his subservience to the "cut-throats of Paris," thus linking personal invective to political argumentation and tacitly inviting readers to judge the credibility of both by the same standards. That could lead to complex calculations for readers about which news was fake and which was not—and which they chose to accept as true.

As the chief architect of the new nation's most controversial economic policies, the Federalist Hamilton had long been a target of Republican fury, including persistent (and unproven) accusations of personal financial mis-conduct. In 1797, the journalist and pamphleteer James T. Callender—who has generally been described ever since with such terms as *hack*, *sleazy*, and *scandalmonger*—broke the story that some six years earlier, while Hamilton was Treasury secretary, he had had an extramarital affair with Maria Reynolds and had made payments amounting to more than one thousand dollars to her shady husband. Whereas reports of the affair were not fake news—and given James Reynolds's apparent role as his wife's pimp, "haunted by whores" was not exactly an inaccurate description for Hamilton, either—the suggestion that the former secretary had been implicated in the schemes against the government was untrue but also eminently credible in the eyes of the many who already suspected him of financial malfeasance. In this case, Hamilton eventually chose to confess to the adultery in order to make the case that his payments to Reynolds were blackmail, not evidence of profiteering—which merely gave his ene-mies new grounds for attack. It also did nothing to elevate the tone of the public debate.[23]

So venomous grew the political and journalistic climate that in 1798, less than a decade after the Constitution mandated that Congress make no law abridging the freedom of the press, Congress made a law abridg-ing the freedom of the press: the Sedition Act, which among other provi-sions allowed for the punishment of anyone who "shall write, print, utter or publish . . . any false, scandalous and malicious writing or writings against the government of the United States, or either house of the Con-gress of the United States, or the President of the United States, with intent to defame the said government . . . or to bring them . . . into contempt or disrepute." The Federalist-dominated Congress denied that the act abridged the press at all, defending it as a permissible—even necessary—effort to protect the government's authority and to guard against Jaco-binism, whose effects in France were terrifying President John Adams's party. Opponents, however, denounced the act as yet another heavy-handed attempt to suppress dissent by defining it as sedition. Prosecu-tions under the act were begun or completed against nineteen editors, three politicians, and more than one hundred ordinary people who had in some way criticized or protested against the government. (Several more actions were begun under common law.) All but two of the defendants were Republicans.[24]

The act didn't last long; it lapsed after the Republican Thomas Jefferson was elected to the presidency in 1800, his victory driven in part by popular disapproval of Federalist overreach. The journalistic vitriol, however, lived on. Callender's success in exposing the scandal involving the former Treasury secretary had led Hamilton's bitter rival Jefferson to secretly support the journalist with money while Callender was assaulting another of Jefferson's political enemies, John Adams, for his "amazing depravity," his "more than common vileness," and other evils.[25]

After Jefferson became president, however, and failed to appoint Callender to the postmastership he wanted, the journalist turned against his former patron, too, publishing the most notorious and durable accusation of the era: that Jefferson had made a "concubine" of Sally Hemings, an enslaved woman in his household, and had fathered her children.[26] Only after nearly two centuries of outraged denial by historians and many of the president's legitimate descendants did a DNA study of Hemings and Jefferson family members finally compel a consensus that the accusation had *not* been fake news after all. The case was a prime example of the tenacity with which true believers can cling to the "news" they prefer, but even more it exemplified how readily a prevailing atmosphere of luridly partisan attack journalism can offer an excuse for true believers to dismiss as fake any facts they don't like.

THE PRESS TURNS COMMERCIAL

During the new nation's first half century, newspapers continued to focus mainly on opinion, argument, and invective, but in the 1830s the press began a revolutionary shift from purveying opinion to purveying information. That did not always mean, however, that it was purveying the truth.

The change began in the big eastern cities, where entrepreneurial printers more interested in profits than in politics imagined a new kind of newspaper that would appeal to a mass audience of ordinary readers who were less interested in politics than in their own daily lives. The new papers proclaimed their independence from party alliances, a stance that liberated their editors from the trammels of partisanship but also cut them off from the parties' financial and logistical support. The editors sought a wide readership in the booming population of city dwellers, many of them working-class immigrants or wanderers from the small towns and backwoods of the United States who were fascinated by their bustling, confusing, nerve-wracking, exciting new home. The newspaper proprietors took advantage of new technologies such as the steam press and invented new marketing tactics, such as hiring boys to hawk individual copies on the streets. With literacy rates strong, most New Yorkers could enjoy reading a bright human-interest paper, and with the asking price of just a penny most could afford to buy their own copy, too.[27]

The suddenly competitive mass-newspaper market put editors under intense pressure to fill their columns with material that would draw ever more readers and advertisers. The avenue to success, it turned out, lay in the timely presentation of snappy, sassy, or sensational stories about the events of the day, whether that meant a grisly murder or the new camelopard in P. T. Barnum's menagerie or the uproarious antics of yet another Irish person who had had too much to drink. Political independence did not mean political apathy; although the penny editors often did show clear preferences on the great issues of the day, they did so by choice (or from a shrewd understanding of their readers' convictions) and argued proudly that their reliance on the marketplace rather than on political interests for support rendered them inherently more trustworthy. The meat of the penny press was not opinion but *news*—and people wanted it. Very soon the circulation of the cheap papers was booming to five or ten times the reach of the city's traditional political and mercantile papers, which complained bitterly about their new rivals' tactics. As the more successful of these penny papers added weekly editions that circulated well beyond the cities, the distinctive editorial voices of journalists such as the caustic, canny James Gordon Bennett of the *New York Herald* and the virtuous, amiably eccentric Horace Greeley of the *New York Tribune* made them household names—maligned in some households, to be sure, but adored in others.

The penny press has been rightly credited with a range of innovations. It was the first U.S. journalistic institution to understand news as a commercial product that could be produced, owned, packaged, and marketed; the first to need (or even envision) the kind of observer/investigator known as the "reporter" to gather all that timely news; the first to actively seek a

FIGURE 1.1 A "News-b'hoy" looks as disreputable as the penny paper he is hawking.

Source: Lithograph, Sarony & Major. New York, 1847. Library of Congress Prints and Photographs Division.

mass audience among workers and middle-class citizens rather than the political and merchant elite; the first to recognize the immense appeal of human-interest and local news stories. It also was also the first to conceive of newspaper reading as interactive entertainment, the first to permit that mass of readers to see themselves as equal partners in their engagement with the paper, the first to use the language of democracy and egalitarianism to argue that all citizens, not just the powerful, had both the right and the ability to follow the news and to form their own opinions about it.

And the penny editors made the radical discovery that emphasizing facts and information rather than political opinion and argumentation did not have to mean sticking only to the truth. News that wasn't true, in fact, could be commercially successful for editors and wildly entertaining for the public; news, true or not, that challenged something reported by a rival paper could whip up readers and reap huge sales. In the earliest years of the New York penny press, the editors established their reputations as news organizations and inveigled their readers into the news-reading habit through the artful use of the peculiarly Jacksonian-era incarnation of fabricated news known as the "humbug." Mixed indiscriminately among the factual reports from the police court or the theater or City Hall were straight-faced stories about the huge telescope that offered glimpses of strange creatures on the moon, the traveler who had crossed the ocean by balloon, the withered crone whom the showman P. T. Barnum was billing as George Washington's 161-year-old nurse, or the recently discovered journal that revealed the fate of the lost African explorer Mungo Park, last seen more than thirty years earlier rounding the great bend of the Niger River past Timbuktu.

The editors of the New York papers the *Sun*, the *Herald*, the *Transcript*, and the *New Era* weren't telling their readers one way or another what to think about these odd reports; they were *asking* them, warmly inviting them, to enter into a spirited public debate over whether the stories were true or false and assuring them they had as much right as even the rich and powerful to make up their own minds. It was in the debate, not the eventual answer, that the appeal lay.

Barnum rode that insight to fame and fortune with the American Museum he founded in New York in 1843 and filled with marvels and "freaks": the fat boy, the Fejee Mermaid, the machine that could play chess.

A humbug, he insisted, was *not* the same as a lie. Humbugs, in his view, were intended to challenge, enlighten, and entertain—to spark a general conversation in which any visitors who paid the admission fee at the door were welcome to weigh the evidence and come to their own conclusions without deferring to anyone else. In fact, the way the Barnumesque humbug worked, at least as Barnum advertised it, bore some clear similarities to the way the press was supposed to function under the classically Habermasian ideal of the public sphere: by providing the grist for an open, rational-critical debate in which the best ideas, not the most powerful participants, would win, it formed citizens into a public (though the existence of mermaids was not exactly the kind of question of general interest the German philosopher had in mind). Lies, in contrast, were meant only to deceive. Lies formed citizens into suckers.

Being suckered was the great fear, a valid one in the striving, citified, and aggressively individualistic new society where many Americans were regularly encountering those previously legendary beings called "strangers" and where the old social conventions governing business and personal relationships were fading away. Questions of how to recognize authenticity and to protect oneself against the inauthentic loomed large. Being asked to make their own decisions about an entertaining humbug, whether that meant viewing Barnum's crone for themselves or reading about a wondrous balloon voyage, gave anxious New Yorkers confidence in their own powers of discernment as well as a pleasant and low-stakes workout in the arts of authentication. As another ringmaster would later assure followers, "We report; you decide."[28]

But the *laissez-penser* tone of empirical egalitarianism in the penny press wasn't confined to inconsequential humbugs about balloons and telescopes; it burrowed deep into genuine news stories as well. One of the first big competitive stories in the New York penny press came in 1836, when the teenage clerk Richard Robinson went on trial for the ax murder of Ellen Jewett in an elegant house of prostitution. Opinion about his guilt split largely along class lines. Middle-class readers insisted that Robinson, a prepossessing young man from a good family, had been framed by Jewett's madam in collusion with crooked police officials. Working-class readers, in contrast, were sure Robinson's wealthy and influential friends were buying exoneration for a murderer, and many elites tried (or pretended) to ignore the whole dreadful affair. The penny editors split, too, vociferously criticizing each other as corrupt or deceitful even as each was also printing fake letters, fake interviews, and fake scoops to underpin his own preferred version of the case.[29]

It sounded very much like another humbug as editors encouraged their readers to make up their own minds about the clerk's guilt with as much freedom and confidence as they did about the telescope's reach. The *Sun*, for instance, a paper with roots in the essentially defunct Working Men's movement and a clear sympathy for working-class readers, proclaimed on June 9, 1836, "that the public have now as good an opportunity of forming as correct an opinion of his guilt or innocence as the jury who tried him . . . and that the public have a right to express that opinion, whatever it may be, is undeniable."

Despite this familiar-sounding paean to intellectual independence, however, no one who had followed the paper's fervent two-month campaign to discredit the rival *New York Herald*, whose preferred suspect was the madam, and to brand the clerk guilty could have doubted which opinion the *Sun* considered "correct." (The *Sun* was right: Robinson *was* guilty. Even the *Herald* acknowledged it eventually, after the young man's protectors had stopped paying off the *Herald* editor.)[30] Many of the readers who chose to buy the anti-Robinson *Sun* rather than the pro-Robinson *Herald* were doing so to ratify their own opinion, not to shape it; they already *were* a public, and they were searching for its voice. The difference between this humbug and the one about the telescope was simple but real: when readers chose between possible truths, they were also expressing their thoughts about justice, fairness, life, and death.

Another journalistic clash over the true and the false had been sparked earlier that year by a young nun calling herself "Maria Monk." *Awful Disclosures, by Maria Monk, of the Hotel Dieu Nunnery of Montreal* was first published as a book—which was a massive hit, selling an unprecedented 300,000 copies in its first twenty-five years—but excerpts swiftly appeared in several newspapers, and it was in the papers that the battle over its authenticity played out.[31] In the book, which the young nun had supposedly dictated to a sympathetic Protestant clergyman, she described the monstrous debauchery she had witnessed upon entering the convent, where lustful priests and depraved sisters engaged in fornication, rape, torture, murder, and infanticide. The story went that when Maria herself became pregnant, she finally fled to save her baby.

In the prevailing atmosphere of intense nativist agitation, when many Americans feared that Jesuits were conspiring to undermine their institutions and establish the pope in the United States, the accusations were inflammatory. But even as furious American Catholics sought to refute the awful disclosures, powerful Protestant clergymen welcomed the "escaped" nun to New York, vociferously defended her story, and happily claimed most of the profits from the book. On January 18, 1836, the *Sun* justified its publication of lengthy excerpts with a disclaimer straight out of the penny-press playbook: it was giving the tale space out of

> our imperative sense of public duty, as conductors of a public journal, to expose crime to public abhorrence where it is detected, and to meet the just claims of our readers upon whatever subjects of interest that may be found in the columns of our cotemporaries [*sic*]. . . . [But] we do not, and indeed cannot, vouch for the truth of the appalling disclosures which this remarkable work contains. They may be true or they may be false, they may be partially true, or partially false, and we have no better means than are possessed by every reader to decide upon their truth or falsehood.

In stark contrast was the response of the New York grandee Colonel William L. Stone. The son of a Congregationalist minister and the brother-in-law of the president of Brown University, he was a historian and fiction writer in his own right and battled fiercely over literature with Cooper, Bryant, and Poe. He also engaged in a remarkable array of civic and benevolent causes, from abolitionism to the building of the Erie Canal. It was in his role as editor of a reputable and well-established mercantile paper, the *Commercial Advertiser*, that he visited the Montreal convent on what sounds very much like an investigative-reporting trip. Determined to test Maria Monk's claims, he scoured the place for secret passages and basement burial pits, sniffed the apothecary's jugs in search of the carbolic acid supposedly used to destroy the victims' bodies, and interviewed priests, nuns, outside seminarians, Maria's friends, even the local bishop.

His analysis took up one entire densely printed seven-column page of the *Commercial Advertiser* issue of October 8, 1836, and it was unequivocal: "MARIA MONK IS AN ARRANT IMPOSTOR, AND HER BOOK IN ALL ITS ESSENTIAL FEATURES, A TISSUE OF CALUMNIES." He was right, of course: the story was fake, born of a serendipitous collusion between a colorful character with a sensational story, on the one hand, and a powerful group eager to profit financially and politically from a tale they preferred not to scrutinize too deeply, on the other. Whether Maria believed her own account is harder to judge. Her mother had stated in an affidavit that the daughter had been "frequently deranged" since the age of seven, when she "broke a slate pencil in her head."[32]

Like the *Sun*'s handling of the Robinson murder trial, its coverage of Maria Monk's story represented the furthest possibilities of the humbug. Nobody's opinion counted more than anyone else's, not even its editor's; Benjamin Day was simply honoring his duty to submit the story, perfervid as it was, to public opinion. The approach had the advantage of sounding open and democratic to readers impatient with the traditional infrastructure of deference, while at the same time giving them permission to indulge in a ripping yarn that tickled fears they already had. It also absolved Day of any responsibility for spreading news that even many of his readers would have recognized clearly as false. But like the Jewett story would a few months later, it did even more. The mass press was already treating news as something that could be bought and sold and possessed and competed for, but this sort of humbuglike reporting pushed the commercial analogy even further: news was also something that could be tailored to suit the customer's preference, that had value only if it was chosen by a consumer. Beef stew or mutton? Red ribbons or yellow? Abused nun or faker? Pay your penny and take your choice.

Stone took a different path. As the editor of a serious newspaper dedicated to serious people, he, like many elite New Yorkers, abhorred the sensationalism and coarseness of the penny press. During the Robinson trial, his *Commercial Advertiser* often berated the cheap papers, noting for instance on April 28, 1836, that although they "are capable of exerting a beneficial influence upon the minds and morals of the people," they care only about increasing their circulation and thus "corrupt and mislead their readers, by ministering to the morbid appetite for horrors and excitement." Stone was no man to countenance intellectual egalitarianism. He was an editor of the old school, harking back to the more partisan era when the job of an editor was to tell readers what they should be thinking. In all his public roles, literary pugilist and civic leader as well as editor, he demonstrated that he saw himself as exactly sort of person who did have "better means than are possessed by every reader" to speak correctly about literature, morals, finance, politics, and public affairs.

To Stone, the Maria Monk affair was just one more episode that called for an authoritative voice to come in and set the record straight for readers who didn't know any better. His exhaustive investigation with its unconditional conclusion served a number of purposes: he exposed the nun's fake story; he implicitly chastised the penny papers for their refusal to do the same; and he staked out his own claim as an authority who had both the knowledge and the right to set the record straight. Stone's effort was high-handed, certainly, relying on a view of social deference that was growing ever more unfashionable. But it was also both a public-spirited assault against disinformation and a pioneering example of the willingness of the journalistic establishment to patrol its own boundaries and proclaim its own standards.

The effort was doomed. Stone's report brought on a flurry of vicious responses from Maria Monk's most ardent supporters, but her éclat soon dimmed, terminally tarnished by a string of sordid lawsuits over the book's profits as well as by her second pregnancy, this one impossible to blame on a lustful priest. Splashy and obvious humbugs such as the moon hoax largely faded out of the penny press, too, as readers' tastes changed, reporters got better at gathering authentic news, and editors who survived the first scrum of competition saw advantages in presenting themselves as more serious, more credible, more adult.[33] What didn't fade, however, was the sense, born in the humbug era and only sharpened by the ever-expanding market culture, of news as a commodity that could be—that *should* be—shaped to fit to the buyer's preference.

2

"IMPORTANT IF TRUE"

I t's difficult to speak sensibly about "*the* nineteenth-century news-paper"; after the turn toward the independent commercial press began in the 1830s, nineteenth-century newspapers, both individually and collectively, could be summed up with that resonant phrase "dog's break-fast." Readers and journalists alike did acknowledge and value the Enlightenment ideal that a well-conducted press was vital to the demo-cratic process. They took pride in the unique American tradition of press freedom and praised the newspaper's role in bringing to readers useful knowledge that would improve their lives.[1] But newspapers were also fulfilling a wide range of other roles, only some of which had any-thing to do with democracy, self-improvement, or even reality. For much of the nineteenth century, American newspaper readers were frequently, consciously, and happily consuming humbugs, hoaxes, shams, scams, jokes, japes, fakes, *and* timely, factual information about current events and deciding for themselves which was which.

As the concept of a newspaper as a commercially valuable and consumer-friendly commodity gradually outgrew the penny press and spread beyond the biggest eastern cities, more and more editors interested in earning both profits and influence were sorting out what their relation-ship ought to be with readers, advertisers, and news subjects. Some news-papers continued to focus on serving their elite readerships, sacrificing a broad influence to gain a prestigious one. Some owners became wealthy, well known, and powerful; some carefully nursed their battered type to the edge of illegibility and traded subscriptions for firewood, potatoes, or eggs. Some editors used every possible technology to push their circulations as large and as far as possible; some knew every one of their subscribers by name and their tastes in reading, too. Some maintained the earlier tradition of close financial and ideological relationships with political parties; some lived only to advance a cause, from temperance to abolition to free love, or trained their sights only on readers who were African Americans or Germans or women or Cherokees or Methodists. Some conscientious editors supervised extensive news-gathering organizations, while others tilted their chairs back in their ramshackle offices and copied their material wholesale from whatever other papers happened to wander in. Many readers regularly saw two or four or even more papers a day or a week, but others stuck to, or were stuck with, just one.

In this wilderness of newsprint, journalistic standards did not look particularly standard. Journalistic *criticism* did flourish, especially in the columns of rival papers hissing at each other; if anything kept reporters on the straight and narrow, it was the fear that their errors or short-cuts would be ridiculed in a competitor's columns. But other than the ideas that the stuff in the newspaper that was called "news" ought to bear a visible relationship to reality, that the editor ought to be independent of the wrong influences (whatever those were deemed to be), and that the reporter ought to be generally enterprising, nothing like widely accepted "journalistic norms" about how journalism should be done was much in evidence before the very end of the century. Nor were reporters driven by any strong or cohesive sense of professionalism or constrained by any of the now-familiar mandates for objective or impartial reporting.[2] In fact, norms did not even seem particularly relevant to all the stuff in the newspaper that wasn't called "news" and that took up so much of the column space of local, community, and advocacy papers.

The more serious papers—the evolving penny journals, the big-city papers with their growing budgets and growing staffs—did make modest marks with their efforts to set standards. The Civil War was a journalistic watershed as well as a political one as reporters competed to deliver the timely and accurate life-and-death news their readers craved. At the end of the war, a handful of reporters from important papers published memoirs seeking to craft their public image and explain what was vital and unique about their work.[3]

One of the earliest known book-length handbooks for aspiring journalists, compiled in 1889 from columns that had appeared in the new trade journal the *Journalist*, suggested that a common understanding about rules and protocols would be helpful to the profession. T. Campbell-Copeland's *Ladder of Journalism*, however, devoted many more of its pages to practical matters than to anything ethical or philosophical. Campbell-Copeland supplied detailed job descriptions for typical positions in the newsroom—managing editor, telegraph editor, drama critic, proofreader. He offered a chapter on "technical terms" and another on correct punctuation; he cautioned reporters against drinking to excess, accepting gifts, or having a "big head"; and he suggested that for an editor of a small-town paper to attend church "would be good for him in a worldly as well as a spiritual sense." The words *accurate* and *accuracy* appeared six times in the 115 pages of the handbook. That's exactly as many times as *neat* and *neatness* did.[4]

But even as some nineteenth-century journalists, along with their readers and the people they wrote about, were working to establish the terms that would govern the earning, bestowing, withholding, or losing of trust, believability was a secondary issue for many newspaper readers. Especially in the four-page weekly "country papers" that were the standard fare in smaller or remoter towns, where enough fresh, original news to fill the columns was hard to come by week after week, readers were accustomed to finding nuggets of intelligence nestled in columns full of sermons, poems, humorous sketches in regional dialect, old wives' remedies, serialized novels, travelers' letters, jokes, tall tales, and a riot of advertisements—for everything from get-rich-quick schemes to miraculous cure-all tonics to the ubiquitous Batchelor's Hair Dye, guaranteed to produce "no ridiculous tints"—nuggets that could sound as fantastic as the tall tales.[5]

Readers understood full well that some items that were *presented* as true might have been intended to tease rather than to inform and that others were never intended to look true at all; they were thoroughly accustomed to encountering within a single page a range of grave, playful, important, provocative, offensive, arch, and commercial items and to making their best judgments about which to believe. People understood, accepted, and took pleasure in knowing that the newspaper offered far more than the news and sometimes far less than the truth. They understood that any encounter with a newspaper required them to continually monitor their expectations and adjust their assumptions about the authenticity of what they read. The choice to believe was theirs.

Even content that was officially presented as news often came with an asterisk. Editors of country papers were perfectly open about how they went about gathering whatever bits of news did find their way into the columns: they stole them. Or, rather, they aggregated them, following the widespread and thoroughly acceptable tradition of "rendering unto Scissors the things that are scissors," as the hoary joke went.[6] They would snap up any out-of-town papers they could find, whether through formal exchanges with other editors or informal donations from travelers and neighbors, and copy into their own columns anything that struck their eye as momentous, interesting, funny, or peculiar. Whether that bit of news was also accurate wasn't necessarily part of the calculation.

Some editors disavowed any responsibility to say one way or the other, explicitly shrugging off the mantle of authority and placing the burden of proof on their readers. The task of "gatekeeping," defined as the "special responsibility—and ability—to decide what is news," is now seen as "central to claims about the unique place of the institution of journalism in the public sphere."[7] (We decide; you read.) But even though editors in the nineteenth century, too, accepted the task of deciding what was news, for them the work did not necessarily also encompass deciding what was true. One editor in upstate New York, burned by "mischievous" ship captains who spread false news among the "coffee-house loungers," warned his readers in 1809 that "as we always insert foreign accounts, *as they are*, we are not responsible for their correctness."[8] Such disclaimers were nothing like the nudge-and-wink gambits that in the 1830s would mark the commercially ambitious penny-press humbug; they represented the editor's frank admission that he didn't know any more than his readers did.

Others deployed the well-worn headline "Important If True" to express any number of subtle variations on the message "Well, we're not really sure." Even serious papers might use the headline to mark an item as a placeholder, staking a claim to a possible scoop but preemptively disavowing any responsibility if it later proved wrong. Such was the case when on December 22, 1863, the *New York Herald* attached it to a front-page item about three disabled Union ironclad ships abandoned in Charleston harbor. Like all of the metropolitan dailies covering the Civil War, the *Herald* was fiercely competitive, constantly navigating between the glory of being first with the news and the embarrassment of being mistaken, especially about intelligence that might be coming from long distances or even from behind enemy lines. In this case, it hedged, warning readers they should make some "allowance" for the possibility that the report, which had been taken from the Richmond papers, wasn't true. (Two days later the paper indignantly branded its former scoop a "complete hoax.") But when an editor in Pennsylvania reported that a Virginia paper had cited a letter from a man in Illinois who claimed to have heard from a military messenger that General Gaines's troops had been soundly defeated by American Indians on Rock River, his headline "Important If True" suggested he was not about to bet the farm that he had gotten the whole thing right.[9]

How readers evaluated the accuracy of distant and secondhand news is hard to assess. Local news was easy for them to judge. A pair of scholars who pored over thousands of letters and diaries in their exploration of how New Englanders in the antebellum era used the printed word in daily life found plenty of complaints about things the local paper had gotten wrong. But such things usually involved events the complainants were familiar with—a young woman annoyed that her ballroom finery was described incorrectly, a father who knew perfectly well that his son had *not* died of cholera.[10] It was easy to assess truthfulness when you had seen the truth for yourself.

Some of the routine features of the local press of the latter half of the nineteenth century, however, complicated the task of evaluating truth in the newspaper. Emotional stories of sudden death, thwarted love, or mistaken identity, for example—call them sob stories, pretabloid versions of the tabloid press, or simply hoary chestnuts—were often copied from paper to paper for months on end. They frequently displayed the accessories of factuality, but in an attenuated form, with abbreviated names and locations that grew less comprehensible the farther they traveled from the original source or with dates that remained "the 16th of last month" no matter how long a journey the item had taken. Typical was the story of the widowed Mrs. Blankenship of Allen County, Kentucky—no first name given—who set out on an unspecified autumn day in 1867 to do the washing and within minutes had lost all three of her children,

two to snakebite and one to drowning.[11] Although the story was peppered
with lavish details of the children's last moments, which no one could actually have witnessed, the invented embellishments may not have mattered
to readers willing to accept the item as either an emotionally honest
expression of a mother's anguish or a richly melodramatic tale understood to be more metaphorical (or fake) than accurate.

Another challenge to readers could be found in the weekly round-ups
of brisk, pithy bits of intelligence under headings such as "Miscellaneous
Items" or "Latest by Telegraph." They brought tidings of the world beyond
that were usually unattributed, often impossible for ordinary people to
verify for themselves, and frequently offering only a stingy peek at what
was obviously a larger story. Readers of the *Vincennes (IN) Western Sun*
of March 21, 1868, for instance, would have had no reason to doubt that
"Victoria has twelve grand children," and if they were regular newspaper
readers, they probably even knew that Victoria was the queen of England.
But no reasons were given to buttress the brusque report that headed the
column: "Mrs. Lincoln is not crazy, as reported." And farther down in the
same column came this item: "Rats cannot live in Alaska, because their
holes freeze up, nor in St. Thomas, because their holes are turned wrong
side out by earthquakes." Would readers have accepted all items as equally
valid because they all came in a newspaper? Or would they have mentally
sorted the rats and the queen into categories of the dubious and the true?

For some regional newspapers, distant readers were fair game for fake
news—or "tall tales," as their creators labeled them. A distinctively American genre with deep roots in oral culture, the tall tale was closely associated with the backwoods and the West, where it served as a symbol (and
a symptom) of the legendarily rambunctious spirit of the frontier and
emphasized its cultural distance from the stodgy and censorious East. Tall
tales were intended and expected to emphasize the chasm between the
insider and the outsider, between those who *knew* and those who didn't;
they lured victims into the embarrassment of gullibility while rewarding
the nongulled with the sweet solidarity of superiority.[12]

The archetype of the western tale spinner was Mark Twain, who in his
roistering youth as a local reporter in Nevada and California in the 1860s
perpetrated a number of "stretchers" and hoaxes, including the "Bloody
Massacre near Carson," the Miscegenation Ball, and the Petrified Man, a
body frozen into a pose that only the most careful reader would realize

was cocking a snook.[13] But while Twain's claims of fooling his readers tended to be inflated, his Ohio-born colleague William Wright, a.k.a. "Dan De Quille," balanced masterfully on the fine line between the bogus and the plausible, planting fabricated reports about surprising natural phenomena in dozens of local and national newspapers and magazines from New York to San Francisco. Among his surviving papers are carefully preserved letters from eminent eastern scientists pleading for a glimpse of the seven-foot mountain alligators and the eyeless hot-water fish they had read about under his byline, and each letter bore an annotation, probably by De Quille himself, chortling about the "professor" who was "sold."[14] In the West, the story of the eyeless fish was a tall tale, intended to tease rather than deceive; only in the East was it fake news.

Whereas hoaxes, japes, and outright fakes were most common in the miscellaneous columns of the country press, they still turned up on occasion even in the more serious metropolitan dailies. A closer look, however, suggests that some of them had ulterior motives; like the lunar telescopes and balloon voyages of the earliest penny-press era, they were actually games that challenged their readers to spot the joke. The notorious "wild animal hoax" of James Gordon Bennett Jr., for instance, is known to this day, but present-day readers often miss the point of the tale.

WILD ANIMALS BROKEN LOOSE

On November 9, 1874, Bennett Jr. devoted an entire page of the *New York Herald* to a lurid account of an "AWFUL CALAMITY," as the decked headlines screamed. "The Wild Animals Broken Loose from Central Park. TERRIBLE SCENES OF MUTILATION. A Shocking Sabbath Carnival of Death. SAVAGE BRUTES AT LARGE." At least forty-nine New Yorkers, the article went on to report, had been killed by the "wild, carnivorous beasts" that had escaped from the menagerie in Central Park when Pete, the huge rhinoceros, went on a ferocious rampage that destroyed their cages. The reporter, who had happened to be in the park at the time, described scene after scene of blood and mayhem as the animals took to the streets: a panther was "knawing [sic] horribly" at a dead keeper's head;

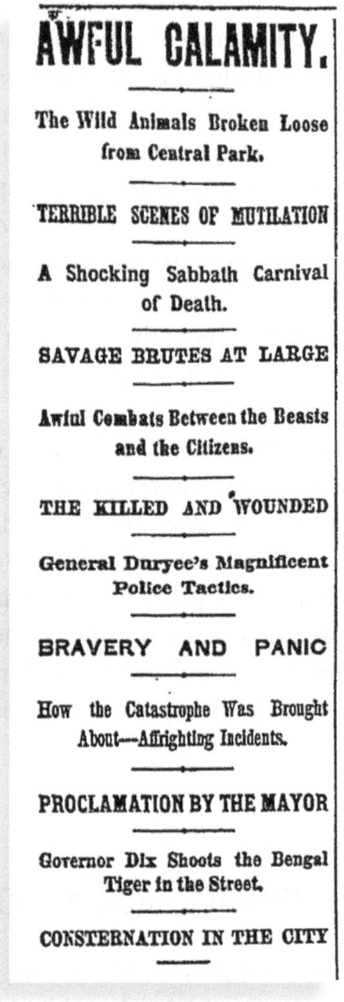

AWFUL CALAMITY.

The Wild Animals Broken Loose
from Central Park.

TERRIBLE SCENES OF MUTILATION

A Shocking Sabbath Carnival
of Death.

SAVAGE BRUTES AT LARGE

Awful Combats Between the Beasts
and the Citizens.

THE KILLED AND WOUNDED

General Duryee's Magnificent
Police Tactics.

BRAVERY AND PANIC

How the Catastrophe Was Brought
About—Affrighting Incidents.

PROCLAMATION BY THE MAYOR

Governor Dix Shoots the Bengal
Tiger in the Street.

CONSTERNATION IN THE CITY

FIGURE 2.1 The "carnival of death" that wasn't.

Source: *New York Herald*, November 9, 1874.

another keeper was trampled and gored by the rhino; a cougar buried his fangs in the neck of an aged lady in church; a tiger got aboard the ferry just as it left the dock and "mangled" the captive passengers. The reporter included a detailed inventory of animals yet at large and quoted the mayor's proclamation ordering everyone but the National Guard to stay home.

Not until the very last paragraph of the lengthy article—long after the point when many readers would have flung down their papers and rushed off to rescue their loved ones—did the reporter confess, cheerfully, that the whole thing was "a huge hoax, a wild romance . . . simply a fancy picture" that had occurred to him as he strolled by the animals' rickety cages and wondered: "How is New York prepared to meet such a catastrophe? . . . A little oversight, a trifling imprudence might lead to the actual happening of all." Many New Yorkers, however, who had believed the story and had spent moments or hours in a panicked search for children or spouses saw the "wild romance" differently. The *New York Times*, blasting the *Herald* the next day for its "intensely stupid and unfeeling hoax," ran seven letters from furious readers denouncing the "disgraceful outrage," the "canard," the "vilest fabrication." "If this article was meant to be funny," steamed one, "I, as well as hundreds of others, fail to see where the laugh comes in."[15] All seemed more offended at the heartlessness of the joke than the untruthfulness of the story, more upset that the newspaper had made them anxious than that it had lied.

For anyone at all familiar with the opportunistic, sensational, and crass *Herald*, neither the heartlessness nor the untruths could have come as a surprise. This time around, however, the paper that normally loved to flaunt its own excesses and bask in attention even when it was negative seemed abashed, uncertain how to spin what it had done. The next day the paper mentioned its hoax only briefly in a column that lengthily recalled two incidents elsewhere in which elephants had escaped their cages, then ended with the hope that its "narrative" would increase the vigilance over Central Park.

What the *Herald* seemed too embarrassed to admit is that it had misjudged what the reaction would be to a story that was never either *just* a mean-spirited (or simple-minded) joke or a ploy to get the cages fixed. One of the unstated goals of the *Herald*'s story was to snap back at a critic; just days earlier, the pioneering political cartoonist Thomas Nast of *Harper's Weekly* had mocked the *Herald* with an image based on an Aesop fable involving a chaotic cluster of wild animals.[16] But there was even more to the *Herald*'s piece. Like many hoaxes, this one was a satirical roman à clef in which were embedded a number of sly digs at well-known New York political leaders and other public figures, and, like a western tall tale, it was intended to bestow on its community of readers the pleasure of *getting* the in-jokes.

The digs were bipartisan, even multipartisan; the *Herald* always preferred art to consistency. A group of newspaper editors and local politicians, for instance, including Governor-elect Samuel Tilden, whom the *Herald* had supported, was said to have allowed a tiger and a lion to escape because they were "a trifle nervous from running." The piece appeared six days after election day, when they had run for office. The defeated incumbent governor, John A. Dix, who had bounced several times from party to party before settling as an anti-Tammany Republican, took just one shot to kill the Bengal tiger—a beast well known as Tammany's symbol.[17] A Malayan tapir burst into the portico of the Fifth Avenue Hotel where "General Gilmore" and General Benjamin F. Butler were conversing and bit Butler in the calf. General Q. A. Gillmore was in fact more likely to have bitten Butler himself than to have conversed with him, given that during the Civil War Butler had bungled an action in the Bermuda Hundred campaign and then fired Gillmore for it.[18]

And when the Honorable Richard Schell sought shelter from a bear, "I got into the house," he supposedly told the reporter, "but was almost summarily ejected, although I made an urgent appeal to be allowed to remain." Schell, as the *Herald* had reported on October 16, had just been nominated to fill a seat in Congress left open by the incumbent's death. It was a short-term vacancy that would send him to Washington for only three months, after which he would be summarily ejected from the House.[19]

Other false reports in the nineteenth-century press were specifically intended to deceive. In a politically polarized era when many newspapers maintained the tradition of open, enthusiastic, and financially implicated partisanship, journalists routinely inserted themselves into the political process. One such effort was so notorious its name still survives a century and a half later. The "roorback," wrote the word maven William Safire in his *Political Dictionary*, which went through several editions between 1968 and 2008, was "a fictitious slander, an outrageous lie intended to smear a political figure during the final stages of a campaign."[20]

The first roorback was spawned during the election of 1844 between the Democrat James K. Polk—the original dark-horse candidate—and the Whig Henry Clay, then on his third try for the presidency. The use of the mass press for political purposes was still in the experimental stage. Large-circulation campaign papers such as the *Log Cabin* of New York and Albany had played a surprisingly important role in the 1840 election, avoiding questions of policy whenever possible as they boomed William Henry Harrison—a wealthy and well-educated Virginia-born blueblood whose father had signed the Declaration of Independence—as a man of simple republican virtue who lived quietly in his log cabin and who enjoyed the plebeian tipple of hard cider.

But those same large circulations could also bring trouble as wider and faster distribution networks sometimes pushed news items farther than their creators had imagined or even wanted. The *Whig Standard* of Washington, DC, was delighted on September 17, 1844, to expose what it called "the unparalleled duplicity" and *"disgraceful, infamous fraud"* committed by an important Democratic campaign paper, the *Washington Dollar Globe.* Quoting two nearly identical prospectuses that the *Globe* had issued the previous May, the *Standard* pointed out that one, which was intended for circulation in the South, savagely denounced the "DISHONEST, FRAUDULENT AND EXORBITANT" tariff as a ploy by "MR. CLAY'S CONGRESS" to benefit "OVERGROWN CAPITALISTS." The prospectus intended for the more capitalist and industry-friendly North made no mention at all of the tariff. It certainly wasn't the first time that politicians made different promises to different constituencies, but the reach of the mass press made it easier to catch them when they did.

Fake news, too, traveled farther now. In August 1844, less than three months before election day, a small Whig paper in upstate New York published what it said was an excerpt from a book called *Roorback's Tour Through the Western and Southern States in 1836.* In the excerpt, Roorback was traveling in Tennessee when he came upon the "revolting" sight of an encampment of three hundred slaves. Forty-three of them, he said, had been branded on the shoulder with the initials of Democratic candidate Polk. Thurlow Weed, one of the most influential Whig editors in the northern states, immediately reprinted the story in his paper, the *Albany Evening Journal*, and it swiftly went the rounds of other Whig papers, all of them expressing horror and dismay.[21]

It wasn't the ownership of the enslaved people that caused the outcry; many Democrats supported or at least accepted the institution, and in any case the Whigs' candidate owned about as many slaves as Polk did. It was the branding, seen even by other enslavers as an unacceptable practice (and unbusinesslike, too, because a branded enslaved person was harder to sell). The intent was clearly to portray Polk as a man of low and vicious moral character.

Within days, however, an Albany paper that supported the Democrats blew up the *Journal*'s story. Both Roorback the man and *Roorback's Tour* were "shameful frauds," reported the *Albany Argus* on September 24, and as proof it reprinted the supposed Roorback excerpt side by side with an almost identical text taken from a well-known recent book, George W. Featherstonhaugh's *Excursion Through the Slave States* (1844). The creator of the Roorback extract had simply substituted Polk's name and neighborhood for the originals in *Excursion* and had completely made up the encounter with the branded slaves.

The more newspapers reprinted and weighed in on the contretemps, the more complicated it became. Faced with the implacable evidence of the Featherstonhaugh book, Whig papers reluctantly conceded the item was fraudulent, but that hardly presaged their surrender; most then went on to insist that the excerpt had been planted by an opponent scheming to discredit the party and its candidate. The squabble continued almost until election day, with Democrats offering a variety of evidence supposedly proving that the Whigs *knew* the excerpt was fake and Whigs countering just as vehemently that they had been entrapped by designing Democrats. The flagship *Albany Journal* even went so far as to threaten to sue its critics for libel.

The fake excerpt evidently originated with the Whigs, but it's difficult to assess now who was the first dupe and who knew when that "Roorback" and his book were fabrications. Several editors close to Polk claimed, with good reason, that the Whig cause had been badly hurt by the exposure of a tactic both dodgy and inept, but Clay had committed enough gaffes without anyone else's help that this one was unlikely to have been the decisive factor in his loss. Nor were the Whigs the only party to play dirty. Throughout the campaign, both the Democrats and the Liberty Party lobbed a variety of missiles at their opponent, as when a Vermont congressman neatly twisted a rhetorical comment of Clay's into the suggestion that he supported enslaving white people, too.[22]

But some clarities emerge from this debate. The creative deployment of parallel texts and dueling affidavits suggests an understanding that even fake news had to carry the *appearance* of truth for the partisans who expected their papers to buttress *their* side. Truth needed a shove in the right direction—some kind of realistic-looking evidentiary proof; neither an old-fashioned reliance on the inevitable victory of truth over falsehood nor an elitist conviction that readers would simply believe what their party paper said was enough. And persistence was a virtue. Because neither side backed down publicly, both sides were able to claim victory, and both allowed their partisans to keep their beliefs intact.

The Roorback hoax had legs. It was bald-faced; it confirmed the low opinion many Polk voters already held of Clay's trustworthiness; it was blessed with a piquant name. Its revelation as a hoax was also one of the very first exposés of fake political news in the era of the mass press, and although its exposure did not inaugurate a new way of electioneering— the contest of 1800 had long ago confirmed the effectiveness of vituperation and hyperbole in a presidential race—it did make clear the power of the mass press in political campaigns. And the term *roorback* instantly became a versatile insult that packed layers of meaning. A "roorback" was not merely a lie but a desperate lie, a stupid lie, a lie doomed to fail because of the liar's political and philosophical bankruptcy. Headlines touting this or that scam, scandal, or plain old gaffe as "another roorback" continued for decades. "Roorback" was the nineteenth-century precursor of the present-day politician's all-purpose slam of "fake news."

LEARNING TO COVER WAR

Like political reporting, coverage of the Civil War was fraught with inventions, embellishments, errors, and fakes that could often be consequential. Some of the challenges came simply from the learning curve. The Civil War was the first large-scale conflict in the United States to be covered by an independent commercial press, so reporters had few rules or precedents to guide them and little social status or capital they could leverage. Few professional norms addressing such questions as interviewing or quoting or structuring a story were yet in place, and strongly opinionated writing, often in a distinctively personal voice, remained the convention throughout the news columns. There were no unified understandings about press credentialing, no standards of access to the fields of battle, no formal agreements about whether reporters should wear uniforms or rustle up their own provisions or be treated as prisoners of war if captured. Some officers enjoyed drinking and chatting with reporters, while others threatened to arrest them as spies. Censorship was erratic and inexpert. News often had to be gathered and sent from battlefields far distant from working telegraph offices or railway tracks. And, as always, reporters had several publics in view: they wanted to please their editors and readers, to beat the guys at the rival papers, and to confuse and demoralize the enemy.

In the midst of a brutal all-out war, to be sure, journalists did sometimes fake the news to cover up their mistakes, disguise losses on their side, or boost the public's morale. In 1863, the *Knoxville (TN) Register* defiantly ridiculed other Southern papers for the frequency with which they published rousing accounts of triumphant bayonet charges straight into the teeth of the enemy, when in fact no one could present evidence that a single such encounter had ever occurred. Demonization of the enemy was another classic tactic. The Southern diarist Mary Chesnut chastised the Yankee press for reporting that was mere propaganda: "The Northern papers say we [Confederates] hung and quartered a Zouave," she wrote in July 1861, "cut him in 4 pieces—and that we tie prisoners to a tree and bayonet them. In other words, we are savages." But in the privacy of her journal she also displayed a rare and remarkable open-mindedness about the possibility that her own side could be equally culpable. "It ought to teach us," she went on, "not to credit what our papers say of them. It is so absurd an imagination of evil."[23]

Those who spoke in public about the other side, however, tended to be much less tolerant. During the tense standoff at Fort Sumter, for instance, as North and South jockeyed to cast the other side as the aggressor, several influential Southern newspapers copied all or part of a comment from the *Daily Missouri Republican* hurling accusations of biased reporting against a news-gathering organization that enjoyed a reputation for tending to its far-flung and varied subscriber list with reporting that was carefully neutral.

> We respectfully suggest to the telegraph [*sic*] that it is making a fool of itself. We thought at first that it had only gone crazy, but that which we took to be lunacy turns out to be a bad case of idiocy. . . . We pay that mythical corporation called the "Associated Press," for news—for facts. Instead of facts, it keeps continually poking at us nonsensical batches of owlish speculations, furnished by the cheap-panic-correspondents of the New York papers. If there were the least probability of these speculations

proving true . . . perhaps we might feel disposed to submit without a mur-
mur. But there is not.[24]

In wartime, even a carefully neutral stance could seem to be nothing but
fake.

Civil War reporters had plenty of help, of course, in their efforts to present their side in the most positive light; for every clear-eyed Mary Chesnut there were many more military and political leaders, soldiers, official
censors, and ordinary citizens colluding in encouraging and feeding stories that eased fears, assuaged griefs, and roused anger. But the war also
produced a counterpressure in favor of truthfulness. It was a vital story
of unprecedented complexity and urgency for readers and journalists
alike—a story for which accuracy took on paramount importance—and
reporters felt intense pressure to *get the facts right*. Reporters were closely
scrutinized not just by their editors and their public but also by rival
reporters from competing papers eager to pounce on their errors. It was
simply embarrassing to do bad reporting, to fumble news that everyone
was following so intensely.

That became clear as early as the first major engagement of the war,
the First Battle of Bull Run, fought just outside Washington on July 21,
1861. Confident that the U.S. Army could easily whip the rebels and
inexperienced at reading the chaos of battle, many correspondents for
Northern papers were so quick to fire off jubilant dispatches about the
Union army's triumph that they missed a late turn in the fighting that
sent the panicky bluecoats into a frenzied stampede of retreat. By the
time the extent of the rout had become clear, the military censors had
seized control of the telegraph, blocking many correspondents from
getting their updates through—which led to the spectacle of newsboys
crying the Union's "glorious victory" in the streets even as shell-shocked
and demoralized blue-coated survivors were flooding into the nation's
capital with very different stories to tell.[25] On July 22, the *New York Times*,
for instance, had published under the headline "Victory at Bull's Run—
Sumter Avenged" a report that "the news from the seat of war must
thrill every loyal American heart with deep emotion." And on the same
day the *New York Tribune* had run a decked headline announcing "A
GREAT BATTLE FOUGHT . . . Splendid Union Victory. The Rebels
Routed. Terrible Slaughter . . . Their Last Hope Gone."

There was plenty of blame to go around for the debacle, and the *Times*, for one, laid it all on the government censors. "We desire it to be distinctly understood," the *Times* insisted in a statement published on July 24, "that we are not in the slightest degree responsible for what, if done deliberately by us, would be branded as a wanton and reckless trifling with the feelings of the public. . . . It was an agent of the Government,—and not the conductors of the TIMES,—who suppressed the facts of this most important case."[26]

But readers who saw that facts they themselves knew were misrepresented in the paper tended to blame the paper, and they were often right to do so. Expressions of contempt for the failures of the press were a constant in letters, diaries, and other contemporary writings. A lieutenant in the Seventy-Ninth New York who had fought at Bull Run, for instance, wrote to his mother a gleeful correction of a report in the *New York Tribune* of July 28. The paper's account under the furious headline "How the Enemy Treated Our Wounded: They Stab and Burn Our Injured Men" had included an outraged description by another lieutenant from the Seventy-Ninth of how the enemy had "with great precision" continued to fire their cannons at a group of soldiers trying to carry their mortally wounded colonel off the field, eventually killing five with a single shell.

> You say you read in the *Tribune* the statement of the bearing away the body of our good Colonel, made by Lieut. S. R. Elliott, a reliable witness. Yes, my dear Mother, I was one of the little band mentioned in the paragraph, but regarding that dreadful bomb-shell which, exploding, killed five of us, I can only say that I didn't see it. The story originated with ————— [*sic*], the correspondent of the Tribune, who called one night in a beastly state of intoxication, upon Colonel [*sic*] Elliott to inquire the particulars of the fight. We were all some-what astonished at the particulars as they appeared the next day in the papers. . . . You see, Mother, what reports are worth.[27]

Nor was it just snarky junior officers who savaged the press. That fall, Henry Adams, who was in London serving as private secretary to his father, the U.S. ambassador to the United Kingdom, and writing regular unsigned correspondence for *New York Times*, reported that "nothing has done us more harm here than the bare-faced exaggerations and misrepresentations of our Press. People have become so accustomed to the idea of disbelieving everything that is stated in the American papers that all confidence in us is destroyed."[28]

In the face of persistent public criticism, some journalists began tentative efforts to repair their image, though both the results and the motives could be mixed. Among the most active reformers was the group of Civil War reporters from some of the big New York papers who liked to call themselves "Bohemians" in tribute to their rakish and unconventional approach to their work. Within months of the end of the war, three of them had produced fat volumes of memoirs about their adventures covering the conflict; more than twenty years later, they were joined by a fourth, whose narrative sounded every bit as timely as those of his colleagues.[29]

All lavished attention on the drama of the war correspondent's life—the hair's-breadth escapes, the brilliant scoops, the insouciant endurance of hardship and fear—but all also took pains to explain what made reporters and their work special. Junius Browne of the *New York Tribune*, for instance, wrote lyrically of the special talents the job required. A reporter's duty, he said, was

> to illustrate the situation so far as is prudent; to describe the movements, actions, and combinations of the forces; in a word, to photograph the life and spirit of the combatants for the benefit of the great Public, united to them by blood and sympathy, and who thrill and suffer with the gallant warriors, and mourn over and honor the heroic dead. . . .
>
> The ill-starred Bohemian has a most delicate and difficult task to perform. He must do his duty, and yet offend no one. He must praise, but not censure. He must weave chaplets of roses without thorns for the brows of vanity, and applaud modest merit without wounding pompous conceit. Every thing is expected of him—impossibilities and virtues more than human.[30]

But they also pointed out the indignities and vicissitudes peculiar to their work: the difficulties of their anomalous status as neither civilian nor soldier, the sticky ethics of having to depend for their safety and provisioning on the very people they were supposed to be covering, the inequity that wounded or deceased soldiers or their families were given pensions but reporters who had faced the same dangers received nothing. Together they were beginning to make a novel case: that reporters should be regarded as dedicated workers with special skills that not everyone had, workers who provided an essential public service—in other words, as authoritative professionals worthy of recognition and respect.[31]

They were also figuring out how to handle a vexing issue for any nascent profession: how to police their colleagues. The complexities of the question are evident in the decision made by two of the Bohemians to publicly criticize Junius Browne as a faker. Browne's story on the three-day battle of Pea Ridge in a remote and mountainous corner of Arkansas consumed more than a full page of the *New York Tribune* for March 20, 1862. Full of knowing details about the landscape, the local population, and the soldiers' actions, it also presented anecdotes of bravery and pathos, enumerations of captured men and weaponry, and an outraged account of the "shocking barbarities" committed by Cherokee troops under the command of Colonel Albert Pike.

Even though it sounded authentic, Browne's report and a similar one in the *New York World* were nothing but "shams," trumpeted the *New York Herald* on April 17, 1862. The only reporters on the field at Pea Ridge, it insisted, were its own Thomas Knox and a man named Fayel from the *Missouri Democrat*; the reports appearing in the other papers had been concocted, the *Herald* harrumphed, by men "sitting at their ease a hundred miles away" who only "pretend[ed] to have seen, and participated in a struggle of which they were as innocent as babes unborn." Given the *Herald*'s own long record of mendacity, provocation, and no-holds-barred rivalry, readers might well have been forgiven if they had dismissed this accusation as more of the same, but the *Missouri Democrat* was making the same argument in its columns on behalf of its own reporter.[32]

After the war was over, Browne's fellow reporters Albert Richardson also of the *Tribune* and Franc Wilkie of the *New York Times* offered their own confirmation of Browne's treachery. Neither did so in the publication that had actually committed the error, however, and each had a different goal in mind. The first exposé, by Richardson in his memoir, was mild. It mentioned two fake reports, did not specify either perpetrator by name, and insisted, inaccurately, that the reports were just "a Bohemian freak," the only accounts "manufactured by any reputable journalist during the war."[33] The whole thing sounds as if Richardson was trying to address the accusations raised by the *Herald* three years earlier and that he was more interested in defending his other colleagues and reassuring his readers than in working to define or uphold journalistic values. His message seems to have been "don't worry, *most* of us tell the truth."

Wilkie's memoir, which did not appear until 1888, was far harsher in its judgment (the hoax was "eminently offensive") and more explicit in its identification of the faker, mentioning Browne and only Browne by name. Wilkie's message seems to have been "you can trust me to tell you the truth about the guys who don't," but he also misdescribed some of Browne's errors, leading to other questions.[34] Were Wilkie's own errors just innocent slips of memory caused by the passage of years, or could he have been telling a fake story for obscure purposes of his own? We can't say for sure. And that uncertainty over what we actually know is precisely the experience of many of the readers who attempted to navigate the complex journalistic landscape for most of the nineteenth century.

Sometimes that didn't seem to matter. Newspaper readers wanted and expected to read truthful accounts of authentic events, certainly, but they were also accustomed to encountering drama, mystery, intrigue, combat, and humor in the same pages. They knew that facts could be slippery things, which the editor of their paper might leave them entirely on their own to evaluate. They were not surprised that the item on page 2 about the glamorous prostitute's murder and the item on the back page about the drunkard's redemption tended to incorporate very similar language, imagery, and moral sensibilities and that it was their own responsibility to determine the difference between the two. They understood that a newspaper might make a political argument that was more passionate than empirical. They saw it as perfectly normal and acceptable for the writers of all those short stories, poems, sermons, travelers' letters, jokes, and opinion pieces to use their imaginations, charm their readers, and strive for literary grace. They expected, in short, their newspapers to serve a wide range of interests and purposes, which included not just describing the world but also exploring, enjoying, adjusting, and revising it.

The emergency of the Civil War, however, made clear the stakes when readers didn't, couldn't, or shouldn't believe their newspapers. As the dog's breakfast that was the nineteenth-century newspaper became much less palatable, readers and journalists alike pondered what might replace it and how. Some possible answers would arise toward the end of the century from a wide-ranging debate over a journalistic phenomenon that was openly, cheerfully, and explicitly referred to as the "fake."

3

"NOT EXACTLY LYING"

The debate over what would come to be called "faking" actually began five or six decades before the term describing the practice even entered the journalistic lexicon and focused at first on the particular and "contemptible" journalistic tactic of the interview. But the controversy that began in the 1830s fed directly into decades' worth of contentious discussions about the larger realm of journalistic fabrications, fancies, and frauds; about when, if ever, it was acceptable to fudge the truth; and about who had the authority to claim jurisdiction over the truth in the first place. By the 1880s, when the word *fake* itself had become a term of art central to discussions of journalism practice, it was batted about and battled over, its import manipulated and its meaning redefined, its application claimed as a boon and denounced as a bane, its effects embraced as a public good and decried as the symbol of all journalistic failure. The rise, heyday, and fall of the fake made up an essential element in the evolution of the *profession* of journalism in the later nineteenth and early twentieth centuries.

But it started with the interview. The practice was, as the influential British journalist W. T. Stead wrote in 1902, "a distinctively American invention," and whether one admired the American journalistic enterprise as entrepreneurial, deplored it as crass, or dismissed it as incapable of conveying the truth, nothing seemed to sum up that enterprise better than the emerging reportorial practice of walking up to people (or stalking or ambushing or tricking them) and *asking them questions.*[1] Yet the tactic that would eventually become accepted even beyond the United States as "the central act of the journalist" was an unnatural construct that posited but often manipulated a network of trust binding reporter and subject, reporter and reader, and subject and reader. Even now, as accustomed as we are to the rituals and conventions of the interview, watching or reading one can still be a "deeply disturbing" experience that leaves us with unanswered questions about the power balance between reporter and subject, about complicity and betrayal, about manipulation and aggression, about whose ideas are actually being represented.[2] In the infancy of the interview, the questions were even more fundamental: How was trust to be earned for a new and very messy endeavor that had few established rules, was practiced by nameless and often disreputable people, and, it quickly became clear, offered particularly rich opportunities for fakers and falsifiers to strut their stuff? Why should readers even believe the conversation ever happened, let alone that it was accurately rendered? And should they care if it wasn't?

The interview was invented at precisely the same time as the *reporter* was, part of the infrastructure created in the 1830s by the new independent mass press to gather and disseminate timely, fact-centered, commercially valuable information about daily events. For a while, no one even agreed on whether *interview* was a noun or a verb, let alone what the expectations and norms of an actual interview ought to be.[3] Although it didn't call itself one, the piece most often cited by journalism historians as the first interview published in a U.S. paper appeared within three years of the beginning of the penny press: James Gordon Bennett published a verbatim conversation he claimed to have had with Rosina Townsend, the madam of the murdered prostitute Ellen Jewett, in the *New York Herald* on April 16, 1836.[4] Bennett began his first-person report by explicitly establishing his credibility, noting that he had brought with him a witness who could swear to the authenticity of his account. He went on to describe himself grilling the madam while she "scowled, and averted her flashing eye," displaying, he said, "the eyes of the devil," a soul of "passion and malevolence," and a "perturbed spirit." Lending his readers his own eyes, Bennett was obviously intending them to see Townsend as a guilty woman.

Yet although Bennett may have been among the first newspapermen to *think up* the idea of the interview—no small achievement, to be sure—he probably wasn't the first to actually conduct one; the "first journalistic interview" was almost certainly a fake. The first decade or so of the penny press was, as we have seen, an era of casual humbug, when editors justified many stories of dubious accuracy with the democratic-sounding conceit that their readers would be happy—or at least able—to figure out the truth for themselves. Bennett and his paper openly sided with the accused clerk Robinson, insisting that Townsend was involved in the plot to kill Jewett. The madam, moreover, was reported by another paper to have denied that the interview ever happened. Although her denial could, of course, have been planted as another bit of fake news, many of the details noted or quoted by Bennett were flatly contradicted by other papers as well as by court testimony. He seems to have woven a glamorous vision of what a high-class house of prostitution should look like without ever actually having set foot inside the one at 41 Thomas Street.[5]

To those readers who chose to share his conviction of Robinson's innocence, however, Bennett's invention made him a champion, an enterprising activist on behalf of their right to know about matters of public interest that also happened to be highly titillating, an expert guide who went where they could not tag along and revealed the darkest secrets of an exotic world that most of them could barely imagine. Brought to them by a person who claimed knowledge superior to their own and gathered through tactics they could not themselves reproduce, the ostentatiously incriminating "interview" presented bona fides that were as persuasive as they were novel. Best of all: they *felt* true to life.

Bennett's fabrication embodied the paradox of the interview as it took root as a journalistic tactic. On the one hand, the interview could be a powerful reportorial tool, an efficient way for journalists to find things out quickly and directly. An early and by all appearances genuine interview by the widely trusted Horace Greeley of the *New York Tribune* illustrates the sturdy effectiveness of the form. In the 1850s, a time when Americans were intensely curious about the new Church of Latter-Day Saints and especially its sensational ideas about marriage, Greeley traveled to the church's headquarters in remote Salt Lake City and had a conversation with the Mormon leader. Among his questions for Brigham Young was this blunt one: "What is the largest number of wives belonging to any one man?" Well, Young replied, "I have fifteen." And on August 20, 1859, the *Tribune* published the conversation just like that, in Q&A format.[6] The interview seemed clear, authoritative, informative, and eminently sensible, too, a logical extension of the emerging understanding of *reporting* as the craft of finding things out: if you want an answer, just ask someone who is in a position to know.

Reporters also deployed the tactic of interviewing as evidence that they were performing a unique role as the eyes and ears of the public. We are, the message went, in a position to converse with the important and knowledgeable people whom our readers can't. We can talk to the people our readers wish they could approach. We can unveil—or we can *seem* to unveil—intimate secrets and can ask the most personal questions of anyone from a high-class madam to a Mormon polygamist. By publicly asserting they were bringing the words of powerful or protected people straight to the public, reporters were acting to democratize knowledge even as they were making clear that they themselves were the essential link in the information chain. Their claim to be both enterprising and authoritative marked a great leap from the deferential modesty of John Campbell and other forebears who declined to burden their readers with their own judgments about what was true.

The interview was also an infinitely versatile tactic, an essential component of the journalist's tool kit. Snagging a good interview certainly made a reporter look smart, but sometimes snagging any interview at all kept a reporter employed. In the out-of-the-way towns and settlements where not much happened and interesting polygamists were in short supply, reporters struggling to fill their columns came to see the interview as a great way to fill space—a way to build a story out of the merest wisp of raw material. Beginning journalists were often advised to make the rounds of the hotels in town, where they would always find someone new to talk to. The art of interviewing, commented one experienced journalist in 1904, was "a blessing to the correspondent located where things aren't 'tearing up jack' every day."[7]

But the way the interview worked was deeply disturbing to the many observers who saw it as the dodgiest aspect of the whole brazen and disruptive enterprise of reporting. Numerous contemporaries, including the social and political elites whom reporters most wanted to pursue, denounced the tactic as rude and intrusive, disrespectful to important traditions of deference, an assault on the privacy and dignity of the interviewee; the entire practice was, carped a highbrow cultural critic, "in every respect a thoroughly contemptible business, which honorable journalists should shun as they would shun contamination."[8]

But the problem with the interview wasn't just its coarseness; it was also seen as literally incredible, just another newspaper item to approach with practiced skepticism. Nobody could confirm that a given interview was authentic, critics charged, and, even more to the point, nobody had any reason to trust anything a *reporter* said in the first place. Because getting a job as a journalist required little in the way of wealth, education, apprenticeship, or social capital, it tended to attract footloose and unconventional types ill suited to more traditional work. Ingenuity, persistence, boldness, and a strong competitive streak were valued among the fraternity; politesse, book learning, and financial ambition were not. All of this meant that the American reporter quickly developed a not unmerited reputation for being nosy, unruly, and crude, for hating soap, loving beer, and doing anything and everything to please the editor and get the scoop.[9]

So there they were, those disreputable creatures with lager on their breath, badgering their betters; there they were, claiming that they had gotten a military general or an important official or a titan of business to personally tell them something. "Ludicrous," scoffed a Brahmin editor and columnist for *Harper's* magazine. Why would any readers believe, he wrote, that they might "quote a gentleman or lady as holding certain opinions because of a reported conversation printed in a newspaper"?[10] In another column, the same writer dismissed the notion that readers should accept on faith any quotation a reporter attributed to Senator A or Secretary B. "Who feels sure that the Senator or the Secretary has said it?," he challenged them. "Who will guarantee the security of the anonymous account which the editor himself must receive upon his general confidence in the character of his agent?"[11]

Surely it would not be the reporter.

THE INTERVIEW AS FAKE

Readers in fact had good reason to be suspicious that some reporters were just making up stuff. Bennett's faked conversation with Rosina Townsend was no early outlier but a preview of what was to come. Everything that made genuine interviews so valuable for reporters and readers alike—their authoritative air, their offer of intimate insider details, their nod to the public good and the democratization of knowledge, their potential for high-wire showmanship—was redoubled in the fake interview. As an added benefit—or hazard—the interview could offer readers an apparently authoritative confirmation of exactly what they wanted to hear or what the editor or publisher or confidential source wanted them to hear. As the commercial press spread across the nation and the competition for readers and scoops grew red hot, interviews were more and more routinely embellished, redacted, spiced up, clarified, rectified, and amplified.

Many reporters, not in the least abashed to let on what they were doing, took professional pride in explaining exactly how their embellishments benefited their subjects or the public or both. The interview process, they said, was more of a collaborative enterprise than a stenographic one. It was, they insisted, a public service, resting on their affirmative duty to improve comments from speakers who were inarticulate, wordy, or plain dull. "Nearly every man has a good story hidden away somewhere in his head," wrote an editor, "and it is the correspondent's business to get it out, and apply his art to the polishing process for the press. It is rare indeed that a man will object to having you improve on his language."[12] The author of a handbook for aspiring young reporters published in 1894 instructed them that "the best writers of interviews now put their matter in much the same shape as that used by a popular novelist. . . . If conscientiously done by a writer who knows his business, more than half the words credited to the speaker may never have been uttered by him at all, and yet the report as a whole may be fairer to him and please him better than would a verbatim interview written after the old style."[13] These reporters were flaunting their professional expertise, but the special skill they claimed lay in improving reality, not in rendering it. (We make it better; you enjoy it.)

Some journalists maintained that their subjects actually expected their aid. The young Theodore Dreiser, for instance, who began his brief journalism career in the early 1890s, recalled in his memoir that when he interviewed the boxer John L. Sullivan for his thoughts on exercise, the pugilist responded: "Exercise! What I think? Haw, haw! Write any damn thing yuh please, and say John L. Sullivan said so. I know it'll be all right." The future novelist obliged. "I adored him," Dreiser confessed. "I would have written anything he asked, and I got up the very best interview I could and published it, and I was told afterwards that it was fine."[14]

Dreiser also made good use of a variation on the standard advice to find good interview subjects by scouting the hotels. Assigned by the *St. Louis Globe-Democrat* to try his hand at its regular "Heard in the Corridors" column devoted to the hotel-guest beat, Dreiser quickly found that "one could write any sort of story one pleased,—romantic, realistic or wild—and credit it to some imaginary guest at one of the hotels, and if it wasn't too improbable it went through without comment. It was not specifically stated by the management that the interviews could be imaginary," Dreiser went on, but the assistant city editor tipped him that the previous columnist "never tried to get actual interviews except once in a while," and Dreiser's own inventions soon won him a permanent assignment to the column.[15]

While a good—or especially creative—interview could bring acclaim to the reporter, some subjects understood that they stood to benefit as well. A Philadelphia editor who expressed nothing but contempt for reporters enamored of the "little and undignified" tactic of interviewing went on to "expos[e] the secret" that their subjects, too, sometimes committed "fraud" by staging their own interviews. In those cases, the editor explained, an important man who "in the awfulness of his dignity, does not wish to appear in the light of seeking to 'put himself right' before the public" would quietly arrange with the paper to send a reporter to pose a set of prearranged questions for which he had already prepared answers.[16]

Yet most of the time the balance of power in the interview situation favored the journalist. Reporters could hound subjects, ambush them, twist their words; subjects could merely complain and then have their complaints dismissed as nothing more than expressions of morning-after regret for their frankness. One unnamed politician complained to his friend, a best-selling author, that he was "powerless to do anything to prevent the falsehoods" that constantly appeared in the press. The politician told his friend that "he had no paper of his own in which to reply. If he submitted to interviews, he was misquoted, and false emphasis was laid upon unimportant statements. If he refused to be interviewed, it made no difference. He was reported as saying things he never said, and the 'interviews' were written, anyway, by 'enterprising' reporters, who must have so much matter for their daily papers."[17]

Not surprisingly, therefore, reporters who did attempt actual conversations with public figures often found them more contentious than collaborative. In those cases, the journalists might argue—perhaps disingenuously—that their duty to their paper and their readers came before their responsibility to the subject. In an article in the recently established trade journal the *Writer* in 1889, a reporter named John Arthur began by staunchly defending the integrity of newsmen on "all reputable newspapers," who are "almost always gentlemen, and are possessed of more honor and brains than they are generally given credit for." But since a reporter has just one job—to "get news"—he "can go in a round-about way after his news without in any manner debasing his manhood." And if he is assigned to interview someone who absolutely refuses to respond to his queries, then "no scruples of conscience keep me from obtaining my information through a third party, and 'faking' my interview accordingly."[18]

There it is: *fake* news, so called. In one of the earliest applications of the term *fake* to U.S. journalistic practice, the reporter openly admitted that he had made up an interview without ever talking to the subject. In fact, it was more than an admission; it was a boast.

The boaster was, however, flaunting his creativity and his public-spiritedness, not his deviousness. The very choice of the word *fake*, whose use had previously been entirely confined to actors, confidence artists, sporting men, and other denizens of the demimonde, seems to have been intended as a tribute to the raffish and free-spirited tradition of the Bohemian reporter.[19] The *Writer* was fascinated by the word, treating the term as a bit of insiders' cant and the practice as a guild member's hallmark. In the third issue of the journal, for instance, in 1887, one of its editors, William H. Hills, lauded the sort of New York newspaper that required a reporter to "be able to 'fake' brilliantly to do the work well. He must be a skilful romancer, and it will not hurt him any to be a poet. . . . His style must have the quality of the French *feuilleton* writer and the snap of a Rocky Mountain stage-driver's long-lashed whip."[20]

In another issue, Hills defined faking as "not exactly lying," and if we are to believe John Arthur, the reporter with the undebased manhood, he in fact did *not exactly* invent his interview out of whole cloth. Though he did not speak directly with Person A, he did seek information about Person A from Person B, who knew Person A. As Hills put it, faking entailed "the supplying, by the exercise of common sense and a healthy imagination, of unimportant details, which may serve an excellent purpose in the embellishment of a despatch. It differs from lying in this delicate way: the main outline of the skillfully 'faked' story is strictly truthful; the unimportant details, which serve only the purpose of making the story picturesque, and more interesting to the reader, may not be borne out by the facts, although they are in accordance with what the correspondent believes is most likely to be true." Although Hills did offer the dutiful warning that "the less [faking] the correspondent does, the better" and cautioned reporters who faked "habitually or extensively" that they might find themselves unemployed, he didn't seem to mind that readers might find themselves misinformed.[21] Like John Arthur, he was more concerned with the danger to the journalist's job than to the public's understanding or the interviewee's pride.

Although the practice of the interview had a special affinity with faking, reporters were eagerly carrying the techniques of the fake into most of the other beats in the newsroom. Some journalists clearly considered faking to be a harmless in-house pastime that could lighten the tedium of their daily grind, and for others it offered the opportunity for some friendly one-upmanship over their rivals. Many reporters also cheerfully asserted that they were giving their readers what they liked. After dispatching the obligatory caution that faking could be an "edged tool" with the potential to wound even a skillful practitioner, the author of the reporters' handbook published in 1894 went on to assure his neophyte readers that "truth in essentials, imagination in non-essentials, is considered a legitimate rule of action in every office." No one, he said, wanted reporters to "fall into the dull and prosy error of being tiresomely exact about little things like the minutes and seconds or the state of the atmosphere or the precise words of the speaker. A newspaper is not a mathematical treatise."[22] In this view, the newspaper's primary job was to please its readers; its primary identity was as a consumer good.

Faking also allowed reporters to fill in gaps, to make stories more appealing, to portray life in ways that actually *felt* true, maybe even more true than boring old reality. If the downed telegraph wires kept distant reporters from getting firsthand news about the terrible tornado in St. Louis or the high-society wedding was scheduled to take place uncomfortably close to the paper's deadline, a little entrepreneurial pinning and tucking of the information they did have available would allow any decent reporters to turn in persuasive accounts of events they hadn't actually seen for themselves.[23] Some reporters even maintained that their readers would be more likely to appreciate a story characterized by vivid details than they would a piece that stuck to what one writer dismissively called a "bare recital of facts."[24] And the reporters had good evidence for their confidence. Accustomed as many newspaper readers already were to inventions, embellishments, and entertainments of all kinds in their news diets and comfortable with the task of navigating from the factual to the fictional and back again through the pages of their chosen journals, they were well primed to see faked details as benefits, not bamboozlements—as humbugs, not frauds. Both fakers and their readers could see faking as a consumer-friendly activity.

MANIPULATING THE FAKE

Yet the strenuous jolliness over faking didn't persuade everybody and didn't last long. Some of the backlash came from other journalists who cherished much loftier visions of the role of the newspaper. After John Arthur proudly parsed his scruples for readers of the *Writer,* for instance, Harriette Robinson Shattuck—a journalist, suffrage activist, and author of a manual on parliamentary law who wrote under the gender-obscuring name "H. R. Shattuck"—pounced in the very next issue on what she called Arthur's "astounding confession." The journalist "has no special ethical privileges or excuses," she wrote. "A reporter is a man (or woman) and has a soul, for which he is responsible." And since the "rights" and the "scope" of the press were "wellnigh unlimited," her piece argued, "is it not time, then, that its *duty* should be considered as correlative to its *right*?" Shattuck was not talking about giving consumers what they wanted; she was focusing on public service, conscience, morality, and duty, all qualities that could not possibly apply to a fake.[25]

Journalists were not the only Americans to cherish an aspirational view of what journalism could do and how it should serve the public, and reporters who embraced faking gradually found that they were losing control of their narrative. Many continued to defend the practice as harmless and reader-friendly, and many readers remained its friends. But these defenses of faking also served as clear acknowledgments to the world that journalists did *not exactly* tell the truth, and their critics noticed. Both inside and outside the profession, commentators were soon turning the term against its supporters, deliberately recasting it as a tactic less endearing than a simple aversion to mathematics and in the process manipulating its flexible meaning to serve purposes of their own.

Dr. S. A. Rogers, for instance, identified as the president of the Tennessee State Board of Health and quoted in the *Chicago Tribune* in 1893 under the headline "No Yellow Fever at Memphis," had good reason to sound touchy about the inaccurate reports sent out by cable that the deadly disease had returned to the Tennessee city. Still struggling to recover economically, politically, and demographically from the devastating epidemics of 1873 and 1878, Memphians would have dreaded another threat to their image. So Dr. Rogers, insisting that "there is no foundation whatever for the fake [report] telegraphed [to] the Eastern newspapers," threatened to seek out the correspondent responsible in order to punish him "to the fullest extent of the law."[26]

It was a cagey move. Calling the misstatement merely an "error" would clearly not have garnered as much public attention, conveyed as much outrage, hinted so well at his state's victimization by elites, or blamed a scapegoat of such proven efficacy, all of which were swiftly and smartly accomplished with his use of a single richly resonant word. In fact, some alter ego of Dr. Rogers could have been indulging in an even more baroque stratagem. Although dozens of newspapers printed some version or other of the denial, a search through the most common newspaper databases failed to turn up a single paper, eastern or otherwise, that had published the false report in the first place. The official bulletin of the Board of Health, moreover, which does confirm the contention that no one died of yellow fever in Memphis in August, does not actually confirm the existence of a Dr. S. A. Rogers: the name of the sitting president of the Tennessee Board of Health is given as Dr. J. D. Plunket. The suspicion lingers that some interested citizen, eager to make a splashy case for the salubrious charms of postfever Memphis, was purposefully manufacturing a canard in order to grab attention with an outraged repudiation. He was manipulating his readers' familiarity with the way fakes worked in order to fake a self-serving fake.[27]

Other cries of "fake!" were much more insidious. Throughout the Jim Crow era, much of the white press in the South essentially operated as a propaganda machine, aggressively supporting white supremacy with news that *should* have been labeled *fake*. Lurid fabrications about "unspeakable" crimes committed against white women by "bestial" Black men routinely included calls to lynch the alleged attacker. Drives for the disenfranchisement of Black voters were shot through with vague but dire-sounding threats of imminent "Negro domination" or "Negro rule."

In Wilmington, North Carolina, in November 1898, a volatile campaign season culminated in the Democrats' expulsion at gunpoint of the interracial elected government and the murder of dozens of Black citizens by a vigilante mob purposefully whipped up by Democratic and white-supremacist leaders. Among the buildings burned down by the mob was the office of the *Wilmington Daily Record*, a Black-owned daily whose

FIGURE 3.1 Ruins of the printing press of Alexander Manly's *Wilmington Daily Record* after his newspaper building was burned by a white mob in 1898.

Source: North Carolina Collection, University of North Carolina at Chapel Hill Library.

sharp editorials had been seen as casting aspersions on the virtue of white women. The incident was, some historians have observed, the first successful coup d'état in American history. The white editor of the *News and Observer* (Raleigh), which published a steady stream of inflammatory stories about alleged crimes and villainies by local Black people and their allies, later boasted that his paper had been "the printed voice" of the insurrection. "We were never very careful about winnowing out the stories or running them down," Josephus Daniels recalled breezily in the autobiography he published in 1941. "When these county chairmen and local leaders would come in with terrible stories, they were played up in big type."[28]

The white southern press, however, had its own view of what newspaper faking meant. When the crusading editor and activist Ida B. Wells published statistical evidence in her Memphis newspaper showing that the true purpose of most lynchings was not to punish the rapists of white women but to terrorize and control Black men, her furious opponents branded everything she said as a lie, often in terms linking her credibility to her race. The *Memphis Appeal-Avalanche* inveighed against the "negro adventuress" and her "career of triumphant mendacity"; the *New York Times*, at that time a minor enterprise that richly merited the label "failing," blasted her as a "slanderous and nasty-minded mulattress"; the *Baltimore Sun* excoriated the "absurd concoctions of this colored female missionary"; and even as the *Clarion Ledger* of Jackson, Mississippi, acknowledged there was a "large amount of truth in what she has told," it nonetheless savaged her "limber, double-hinged tongue" and the "thousand lies about the South" she told in aid of her "brutish brethren."[29] In 1892, in a direct attempt to silence her entirely a mob destroyed her newspaper office. Undaunted, she set out on a series of lecture tours in the United States and Britain, further infuriating her opponents by dragging "outsiders" into the debate.

On July 29, 1894, the *Atlanta Constitution*, which under its late editor Henry Grady had become perhaps the most outspoken journalistic champion of white supremacy, came up with a new way to brand Wells a liar. That day the paper unfurled the headline "Glad to Get Truth; English Papers Know That They Have Long Been Imposed On" over a piece claiming that Governor Northen of Georgia had "set them straight on one of the Ida Wells fakes." The *Constitution* was pleased to report that Governor Northen had persuaded the London weekly *Spectator* it had been wrong to believe stories drawn from Wells's reporting about particularly gruesome acts of torture and murder of African American women and children. According to the *Constitution*, the *Spectator* published a correction explaining that it had gotten the story from "American correspondents, who are supplying falsehoods to the English press for the sake of obtaining a few dollars. . . . We are glad to get reliable contradiction of such stories."[30]

Anyone could be called a liar. Branding Wells's reporting as "fake" took the assault a step further. It didn't just undermine her credibility; it didn't just exploit enduring stereotypes about African Americans as tricksters and fabulists. It also associated her with everything that was greedy, sensational, and untrustworthy about the mass press and reinforced the historic southern resistance to "outside interference" in local affairs, especially those involving race. The effect was to draw explicit connections among a cluster of free-floating ideas and beliefs that already inspired many white southerners' hatred and mistrust and to bind them together into a potent and persuasive package of pure emotion masquerading as information. All of this mounted enough of a distraction to foreclose any possibility of actually engaging with Wells's argument.

In a now-familiar pattern, however, the accusations of faking masked a more complicated story: the real faker in the case was the *Constitution*. The *Spectator*, a longtime and vigorous opponent of slavery that had become a harsh critic of the South's epidemic of lynching, did print the Georgia governor's denial verbatim. But when the *Constitution* then reprinted what it said was the British journal's comment, it subtly edited the quote to make it sound much less equivocal than it really was. What the *Spectator* actually said was, "We are very glad to have this contradiction, and sincerely hope it is absolutely true; but it is American correspondents who supply this false information to the English newspapers."[31]

The *Constitution* was doubtless confident that its overwhelmingly white readers would find it both easy and convenient to believe that the uppity Black female activist was a faker. Yet to make the case for what it saw as a larger truth, the paper resorted to a fake of its own. This tactic was both paradoxical and increasingly successful: a news organization offered false information to assure its readers that the (truthful) information they disagreed with was false, in the process undermining their readers' trust in all news organizations except the very one peddling the untruths.

In another now-familiar pattern, however, other newspapers escalated the battle over what was fake, offering corrective information to assure their readers that the untruthful information they disagreed with *was* false. After the destruction of her paper in Memphis, Wells continued her antilynching crusade in the leading Black journal *New York Age*, aggressively refuting any accusation that her reporting was fake. It's a safe bet that neither the *Atlanta Constitution* nor the *New York Age* very often succeeded in reaching readers of the other or persuading them to change their point of view, but that wasn't the intention; both papers focused on serving their own readers with the news and opinions that confirmed their own convictions, whether they were verifiably accurate or not. In the past, calling something in a newspaper a humbug or a tall tale was an invitation to a debate. Now, crying "fake" was increasingly seen as a smear—which was itself often rooted in a fake.

As the fake lost its luster, newspapers that were accused of the practice, however defined, worked to figure out the appropriate response. In 1892, the *Boston Globe* came up with one that proved remarkably durable. The paper, New England's biggest and at the time possibly its crassest, must have been feeling on top of the world on October 10 when it served up a sensational scoop in the hottest local story in decades. For more than two months, local and national newspapers had been squabbling over whether a stolid, church-going spinster of thirty-two could possibly be guilty of the grotesque crimes for which she had been arrested: the savage ax murders of her father, a prosperous but parsimonious businessman, and her stepmother in their home in Fall River, Massachusetts. But under the page 1 headline "LIZZIE BORDEN'S SECRET," that day's *Globe* flaunted a long and lurid saga that claimed to provide the answer.

Based on "Startling Testimony from Twenty-Five New Witnesses," the article reported that Andrew Borden's younger daughter had been quarreling with her father for weeks over his will. She had tried to bribe the maid not to speak of the dispute. She had been seen on the day of the murder leaning out of the window just after awful cries and moans had issued from the house. Later, when she was in custody, she had kicked her visiting sister Emma in the shin and cursed at her, and she had been overheard making incriminating statements in her sleep by officers who had cut a peep-hole in the wall of her cell. The capital-letter secret, which her father had discovered on the night before his death: Lizzie was pregnant out of wedlock, and at least one witness said that she (or someone who looked exactly like her) had been a guest several times at a New Bedford hotel in the company of her uncle.

It was a spectacular story. Unfortunately for the *Globe*, it was also spectacularly untrue. Immediately disputed by the police, defense counsel, and other newspapers, the tale was quickly revealed to have been fabricated by an unsavory private detective named McHenry and sold for $500 to the *Globe* reporter Henry Trickey, who had been so intent on beating the competition that he had swallowed the steamy mess whole, apparently without doing even the most basic shoe-leather work to confirm what McHenry was feeding him.

Cornered, the *Globe* gulped hard and acknowledged that its great scoop didn't stand up to scrutiny. "Detective McHenry Talks," ran the huge decked headline on October 11. "He Furnished the Globe with the Borden Story. It Has Been Proven Wrong in Some Particulars." Actually, a more accurate headline would have used the phrase "*most* particulars," but readers could figure that out for themselves once they began reading the long article that followed, placed in the same prominent front-page position as the discredited piece had occupied. It began with Trickey's exhaustive account of his negotiations with McHenry, who had wanted $1,000 for what he said was "great stuff" revealing the prosecution's case and who was clearly made out to be the instigator of the affair. (That the *Globe* paid for information in the first place, information the seller himself hinted had been stolen, seems to have been generally regarded as a routine matter barely worthy of comment.)

Then on page 6 the *Globe* bared its breast. In four long columns, it reprinted a succession of damning quotations from rival newspapers, alleged witnesses, and others, each of them sturdily denying aspects of its own previous day's story. The rival *Boston Journal* had called the whole story "A FAKE," and the *Globe* quoted that. The *Boston Herald* denounced the story as "a tissue of lies," and the *Globe* quoted that, too. Lizzie's sister said she had never heard of most of those twenty-five witnesses named in the original *Globe* article, and the *Globe* quoted her as well.

The next day, October 12, the paper continued its public mea culpa, running on the front page a triple-column, double-leaded boxed story headlined "The Lizzie Borden Case" that offered Borden a "heartfelt apology for the inhuman reflection upon her honor as a woman" and tendered its regrets to her uncle and "any other persons to whom the publication did an injustice." The *Globe* "comes out in this manner because it believes that honesty is the best policy, and because it believes in doing what is right." It continued:

> We prefer to build up rather than to tear down, to help rather than to injure, to carry sunshine and not sorrow into the homes of New England.
>
> When we make a mistake, whether through our fault or not, we believe that justice to our readers demands that we should fairly and honestly and boldly proclaim the fact in the same conspicuous place in The Globe where the error was committed.

The display of remorseful candor seems to have worked—and the *Globe* made sure its readers knew that, too. Also on the front page that day, it ran a follow-up under the preening decked headline "Honest Amend. Globe Apology Pleased Its Readers. . . . 'Manly Thing to Do,' Said Mr. Oliver S. Howes. Mr. E. A. Tuttle: 'An Open, Honest Stand. McHenry's Acts Condemned by Fair-Minded Citizens." The *Globe*, this article went on to say, "has made friends for itself here tonight with its dignified action" and "had taken a step that called forth the admiration of all who recognize honest desire for reparation." (We correct ourselves; you applaud.)

The *Globe*'s "dignified action" and its self-congratulatory coverage of that action were in large part a defensive ploy: the paper must have been terrified that its pyrotechnic lies would earn it a libel suit. (For the duration of the case, the *Globe* did indeed "build up rather than tear down" Lizzie Borden, offering a generally soft, even supportive assessment of her conduct. She was acquitted, no one else was ever charged with the murders, and to this day she is widely considered guilty.) Nor was there anything dignified in its immediate decision to throw all of the blame on the dodgy detective and his alleged accomplices in the Fall River Police Department without also acknowledging the recklessness and possible malfeasance of its own reporter—who was reportedly indicted by the grand jury on charges of witness tampering and just days later, while on a hasty and unexplained trip to Canada, was "by accident" run over by a train. The *Globe* published a series of flowery tributes that mourned Trickey's "tragic" death, praised his loyalty, energy, and cheeriness, and alluded only briefly and cryptically to "mistakes" caused by an excess of youthful enthusiasm and competitive spirit. Many other local news-papers chimed in to run tributes of their own, putting their rivalries on hold to help exonerate and protect a member of their professional frater-nity and to ensure that the blame remained with the outsider McHenry. (At the time, none of them treated the reporter's mysterious death as any-thing but an unfortunate mishap.) The *Globe* reprinted a number of those tributes, too.[32]

Yet even as the paper, with the help of its colleagues, worked to shift the burden of responsibility for the possibly libelous aspects of the report away from the profession itself, it did *not* deny that the report had been bogus in the first place, nor did it offer excuses for having been the agent of what the police reporter for a rival paper later called "the most gigantic 'fake' ever laid before the reading public."[33] To be sure, this fake was such a whopper that it's difficult to imagine any defense that would not have sounded ludicrous: the story concerned not a boxer's views on exercise but a heinous murder of enormous public interest; the errors that got into print were not charming embellishments but extravagant and possibly libelous fabrications that were easily disproved; and the competitive pressure from local papers was fierce. But having been forced into transparency, the *Globe* then seized command of that narrative, working to repair its credibility and reassert its authority by acknowledging and correcting the mistakes in the story. It was helping to establish what would gradually become the standard mainstream response to journalistic failures: public confession, public correction, and a public statement of and recommitment to the standards and boundaries that governed professional journalistic work.

By present-day standards, the *Globe*'s decision to protect the misbehav-ing Trickey rather than to drum him out of the profession disqualifies the incident as a full-blown example of what communications scholars refer to as "paradigm repair." Journalists' responses to the transgressions of Janet Cooke and Jayson Blair come readily to mind as more recent examples of the strategy to identify, uphold, and repair the norms of their profession by essentially blackballing colleagues who violate them.[34] But a more important element of the Trickey affair was the *Globe*'s insistence on treat-ing it as a *professional* matter, rightfully and effectively handled by the professionals themselves—professionals who could be trusted not to excuse it or cover it up, as Junius Browne's colleagues had apparently done for twenty years after his Pea Ridge fabrication. Professionals would tell the truth even if it hurt.

THE YELLOW PRESS VERSUS THE PROFESSIONALS

The battle over faking grew even sharper beginning in 1895 with the rise of the "yellow" press—William Randolph Hearst's brand-new *New York Journal*, Joseph Pulitzer's popular *World* (New York), and other metropolitan papers that deployed sensationalism, screaming headlines, vividly colored comics, fat Sunday editions, and gaudy illustrations to run up enormous circulations among mostly working-class and middle-class readers, especially recent immigrants. For the many fans of the yellow papers, harmless newspaper fakes seemed to sum up everything that was jolly, entertaining, and populist about the mass press. For critics of these papers, however, a fake could never be harmless, symbolizing as it did everything that was vulgar, dishonest, and wrong about that same press. In their eyes, the descriptors *fake* and *yellow* were virtually synonymous. As the *Courier Journal* (Louisville) put it under the heading "The Business of Faking," the "chief business, of what are called the 'yellow journals'" is "deceiving the public systematically and continually. . . . They are conducted on the theory that the public is a fool." Even more scathing about the "garblings, the misrepresentations, the unvarnished lies and the evil purpose . . . [and the] frenzied, hysterical, lying incendiarisms" of the yellow press was the generally humorous magazine *Puck*, which argued nonetheless that the "common-sense decency of the people" was a better remedy than censorship.[35]

The most notorious transgression by the yellow press was its coverage of the Spanish-American War. When in 1896 Spain sent General Valeriano Weyler to Cuba to crush the resurgent rebellion, the rival New York papers the *Journal* and the *World* ratcheted up their already ferocious rivalry, hurling themselves into a ruinously expensive competition for readers that was lofty on hype and abysmally low on fact. At first, as Spanish officials maintained tight censorship over U.S. correspondents in Cuba and routinely expelled those they disapproved of, the papers made up for the paucity of eyewitness news from their own reporters by accepting eagerly and uncritically a stream of atrocity stories obligingly provided by a "junta" of Cuban rebels and supporters based in New York. The journalists who did manage to file from the island, meanwhile, met the hometown competition by inventing melodramas of their own: nonexistent rebel armies on the march, phantom victories over Spanish troops (the same town was reported as invested and destroyed twice in three days), the treacherous murder—by poison!—of a rebel leader who had in reality died in a routine battle, phalanxes of beautiful Amazonian warriors wielding machetes.[36]

Soon, however, dozens of correspondents began streaming in, including Hearst himself, who chugged to Cuba in a steamer specially fitted out as a floating newsroom and crammed with friends, staffers, servants, and at least a couple of mistresses. The *World*, which could not match Hearst's paper in either cash or chutzpah, often found itself merely worrying at the ankles of the *Journal* as it ran manufactured or glitzed-up features on "suppressed" official cables that revealed the truth about the sinking of the *Maine*, on rough soldiers strip searching delicate Cuban ladies, on rebel maidens spirited out of the clutches of bestial Spanish officials, and on the beheading of "forty" Spanish guerrillas by "exasperated" Cubans. In the latter case, the *Journal* had exaggerated the number by tenfold, but Hearst typically managed to combine a grudging acknowledgment of his undeniable error with an attack on rival editors who had not traveled to Cuba.[37]

Of course, the coverage included fake interviews. On March 19, 1898, the morning *Journal* ran on its front page an interview with Assistant Secretary of the Navy Theodore Roosevelt. Under the huge headline "ASSISTANT SECRETARY ROOSEVELT, THROUGH THE JOURNAL, SAYS THERE WILL BE NO BACKDOWN," the paper reported the imminent dispatch of four double-turreted battleships to Key West. During the conversation with the paper, Roosevelt reportedly veered from discussing naval strategy into floridly complimenting his interviewer, remarking on how "cheering" it was "to find a newspaper of the great influence and circulation of the *Journal* tell the facts as they exist and ignore the suggestions of various kinds that emanate from sources that cannot be described as patriotic or loyal to the flag of this country."

Roosevelt immediately issued a statement through the Associated Press (AP) denying he had ever spoken with any *Journal* reporter on the matter. Then when the *Journal* cheekily asked him if he "contemplated" challenging the interview, the secretary went back to the AP with an even stronger repudiation. "I do not contemplate denying the story," Roosevelt said icily; "I have already denied it in the most unequivocal terms. . . . [Y]ou yourselves should have known that no such interview as that could possibly have come from me, if for no other reason than that I have never given a certificate of character to the Journal." He later added that he as well as everyone he knew "would as soon think of dealing with a mad dog as to give [the *Journal*] an interview."[38]

The *Journal* continued to follow its usual strategy, refusing to back down or admit the fake and repeatedly lambasting Roosevelt for lying. But the sheer unlikelihood that the assistant secretary of the navy would have stopped in the middle of a loose-lipped discussion of naval strategy to toss a bouquet to a notoriously crass paper argues that much if not all of the interview was indeed fabricated. To the *Nation*, which considered Roosevelt's letter a "model" response, the moral of the episode was clear: respectable people should stop "conniv[ing]" with the yellow papers by remaining silent when they printed bogus interviews. "Conversations with prominent persons have now become one of the principal journalistic modes of influencing public opinion," the *Nation* opined. When interviews were genuine and decently reported, they could be at best useful, at worst silly. "But the yellow journals have long ceased to report anything conscientiously, and this devilish industry is directly promoted by the habit of nearly all public men of letting fraudulent interviews with them, or invented stories about them, pass without notice."[39]

The continuing outrages by the press, in other words, were partly the fault of those public men and women who were too embarrassed or too discreet or too high-minded to complain when unscrupulous journalists co-opted their names and put words into their mouths in a setting that lent an air of authority and authenticity to messages that possessed neither. By genteelly refusing to dignify the abuses with their attention, victims of the nefarious power of the press were in fact enabling their abusers.

The persistent legend that it was the bellicose rhetoric of the yellow press that incited the American public into demanding intervention in Cuba—a legend encouraged at the time by the always self-aggrandizing Hearst and embraced later by some seeking a defensible explanation for a ridiculous war—has been widely debunked by scholars. It's true that in their frantic race for circulation the yellow New York journals drove each other to extremes of jingoistic fervor, but their coverage served more to confirm opinions their readers already had than to change anyone's minds, and their influence did not extend much beyond their own city.[40] The frenzied reporting did, however, have another consequential effect among those who did *not* routinely follow the yellow papers: it confirmed the widespread opinion that the mass press was circulation mad, untrustworthy, and riddled with fakes.

Nor was the nonyellow press exempt from justified criticism. In an era dominated by big businesses and corporations, big banks, big fortunes, big cities, and big-league corruption, big newspapers, too, were increasingly seen as no friend to the little guy. There were numbers to prove it; by 1900, advertisers were on average claiming as much as half of a paper's column inches and providing more than half of a newspaper's income, with many of those ads making wild promises and fake claims about products that turned out to be disappointing, ineffective, or even—as in the case of patent medicines and adulterated foods— deadly. Newspaper executives could occasionally be heard acknowledging among themselves that the journalistic imperatives of public service ran a pale second to the business imperatives of their own private enterprise. As the circulation manager for the *Boston Globe* told a convention of his fellows in 1901, "In printing a newspaper, the primary object is to make money."[41]

By the beginning of the twentieth century, the credibility of the U.S. press was at a crisis point. At the same time, the vast changes rippling through U.S. society were bringing fakery into increasingly noisy clashes with other intellectual, social, and economic developments. Many Americans were intrigued by the straightforward cultural outlook known as "realism" that was percolating through literature, art, photography, and other forms of expression and by emerging modes of scientific inquiry that were based on reason and systematic observation and carried out by neutral and uninvolved observers. Businesspeople, professionals, public servants, and others needed accurate and reliable sources of information to operate successfully in an increasingly complex industrialized economy. Progressive reformers who saw political partisanship as a corrupting influence on public life worked to undo the traditional ties between journalism and party politics, while among their other targets for reform were the sort of the ruthless merchants and corporations whose deceptive advertisements dazzled so many readers.

For all of these interests, a professionalized approach to journalism that valued impartiality and reason offered an antidote to the untrustworthy, lowbrow, and crude characteristics of the yellow press. Such an approach could benefit the newspaper, too, earning it a readership that was more respectable—and, not incidentally, better heeled. Decency, rationality, civic responsibility, and a public commitment to the primacy of the verifiable *fact* served as class markers that attracted readers and advertisers who liked to think they shared those qualities.[42]

Newspapers that wanted to be taken seriously, notably the *New York Times* after its purchase by the ultrarespectable Adolph Ochs in 1896, used the yellow press as their foil in carrying out what scholars refer to as professional "boundary work." They aimed to mark the acceptable and unacceptable ways of doing journalism and branded themselves as professionals holding the moral high ground over disreputable and unprofessional colleagues such as Hearst, who brazenly printed whatever would sell and rarely admitted his mistakes.[43] Throughout the first decades of the twentieth century, the serious papers gradually claimed jurisdiction over the social task of gathering, verifying, and distributing factual information about the world.

They established standards and codes of ethics that emphasized their independence and autonomy and promised accountability. They sequestered much of the miscellaneous flotsam that had been so common, the fiction and the jokes and the poetry, into clearly marked sections or even dumped it entirely. They increasingly supported the idea that reporting was a special skill that required special knowledge and training and that a college or university might be the right place to learn that skill. They valued reporters with discipline, self-effacement, and respectability more than those with imagination and Bohemian verve. They developed a new language for journalism, a set of communicative conventions—a neutral tone, a standardized format, a studied empiricism, an emphasis on corroboration and verification—that both embodied and reinforced their claim to be representing the world as it truly was. They spoke to and for a certain kind of readers, the kind Ochs characterized as "thoughtful, pure-minded people."[44]

The serious papers were also promoting a new kind of contract to those thoughtful readers, relieving them of the traditional responsibility—or, perhaps, the traditional opportunity—to decide for themselves what items in the paper they preferred to believe. The burden of determining truth was shifting from the reader to the newspaper and from the citizen to the expert authority, and papers functioned less like a partner in an intimate two-sided conversation than like a lecturer clinically dispensing wisdom to scribbling students.[45] It was a subtle reorientation of the conventional idea of the newspaper as a consumer good: buying a "serious" newspaper meant buying and accepting as a default the idea of a ready-made truth. (We report; you believe.)

A critical element in this new contract was the respectable papers' repudiation of all forms of the fake, but especially the fake interview, as the epitome of all that was indecent, embarrassing, untrustworthy, and inaccurate about the yellow papers. Faking was the opposite of everything that the respectable press claimed to do; no newspaper that faked could ever be considered serious or professional, and a professional newspaper was one that never faked. By the turn of the century, the very word *fake* had been transformed from a jolly compliment to a term of opprobrium, taking on a bleaker and shiftier hue and creeping into the general discourse to apply to a multitude of frauds and deceptions well beyond the journalistic. "Fake butter peddlers" were imposing yellow-tinted margarine on unknowing customers; horticulturists complained about the "fake pecans" that were really hickory nuts; and the disgruntled and defrauded slapped the label on everything and everyone from hypnotists to insurance claims to weather forecasts—and sometimes even on truths they wanted to discredit or smear. When an outbreak of bubonic plague in 1900 threatened to devastate San Francisco's economy, many of the city's newspaper editors joined state and local leaders in dismissing the warnings from public-health officials as "plague fakes."[46]

Serious journalists, meanwhile, brandished the term as an apt description of everything they and their reports were *not* and emphasized their own scrupulous accuracy, accountability, and uprightness by promiscuously dismissing as "fake" just about any of the sins a bad journalist might commit: padding telegraph dispatches, running tacky contests, making deals with sources. And in a tactic familiar to present-day news consumers, social critics gleefully worked to refute ideas, facts, or events they disagreed with by challenging the coverage not as partial or erroneous or misinterpreted but as outright faked. In 1914, for instance, Max Sherover published an eighty-page screed devoted to "fakes in American journalism." An active socialist who wrote and lectured in support of party ideals and served as editor of several socialist publications, he swept under the capacious category of "fake" everything from "harmless" hoaxes, stupid errors, and sensationalized crime reporting to what he characterized as brazen attempts to benefit advertisers, hush up political scandals, and manipulate public opinion against unions and peace activists. U.S. journalism, he argued, "holds the record for faking."[47]

Even as the respectable press worked to establish the boundaries of a new profession, many of their despised rivals clung all the harder to their traditional offerings of sensationalism, entertainment, and emotional gratification, finding the greatest profitability in retaining *their* distance from those boring and bourgeois papers concerned only with information. William Randolph Hearst, as always, showed more interest in circulation than in service and continued to glory in the coruscating garishness of his paper as its main selling point. The *Denver Post* remained faithful to its nickname, "Bucket of Blood," a reference to the crimson-painted walls in the editors' office as well as to the matching ink they broke out for their favorite headlines.

Chicago retained its reputation as an anything-goes newspaper town where reporting was performance art intended as much to dazzle and discomfit rival newsrooms as to appeal to readers. It was a congenial home for the likes of Ben Hecht, who as a sixteen-year-old runaway had bumbled his way onto the staff of the *Chicago Journal* and become adept at "picture chasing," the delicate art of burgling photographs of murder victims from the homes of their grieving families. He would later reminisce about the "exclusive news" he gathered in the city streets. "Tales of lawsuits no court had ever seen," he recalled, "involving names no city directory had ever known, poured from my typewriter. Tales of prodigals returned, hobos come into fortunes, families driven mad by ghosts, vendettas that ended in love feasts, and all of them full of exotic plot turns involving parrots, chickens, goldfish, serpents, epigrams and second-act curtains. I made them all up."[48] It's difficult to imagine that readers presented with a steady stream of ghosts, vendettas, and parrots in the streets of Chicago didn't catch on, at least sometimes, to the fakery.

Other papers struggled to determine where they fit in the changing journalistic landscape. For some, emerging professional standards were just as useful as weapons against competitors as they were as guideposts for themselves. Plenty of fake interviews about serious matters continued to appear, but now they often had two distinct audiences: the readers who enjoyed them and the rival newspapers that rushed to challenge them through the ostentatious invocation of journalistic ethics.

There was, for instance, the medical journal that debunked an interview the *New York Times* conducted with a doctor claiming a cure for alcoholism. The journal seemed nearly vibrating with glee as it pointed out the hypocrisy of the "lofty and pure" *Times*—the "censor of public morals" that "utterly abhors both fakes and fakers" and heaps "fervid rhetoric and scathing invective" on unworthy subjects—disseminating news that it failed to recognize as fake.[49]

There was the single week in February 1908, during a particularly volatile economic season, when dozens of newspapers reprinted or quoted from interviews reportedly conducted with two of America's best-known financial titans. The conversation with the eccentric multimillionaire Hetty Green, otherwise known as the "Witch of Wall Street," that first appeared in a Boston paper was quickly and almost universally dismissed. And J. Pierpont Morgan, who in another age would have been "a 'condottiere' of the Renaissance," as the morning *World* opined, "or even a Mongol conqueror," allegedly told the paper that he considered the financial crisis a good tool for keeping workingmen in line. That interview, too, was widely denounced as a fake, a particularly flimsy one; any decent newspaperman, noted the *New Outlook* with disdain, knew how hard it was to get an interview with the reclusive mogul. "The editor who accepted it as genuine," it groused, "was guilty of the most extraordinary ignorance or the most extraordinary credulity."[50] The *World* stood by its story, the authenticity of which remains unclear.

And then came the byzantine affair of the kaiser's indiscretions.

THE KAISER SPEAKS

In July 1908, with tensions in Europe simmering, the well-known journalist William Bayard Hale snagged a rare interview with Kaiser Wilhelm II of Germany when the unstable sovereign was in a dangerously voluble mood. The incendiary item was debated, rejected, revised, suppressed, revived, and allegedly reconstructed in dueling versions whose authenticity sparked a searing debate that was still bobbing up nearly a decade later. But the most important element of the story was never which if any report of the kaiser's words was genuine. More revealing are the many different editions of the stories that were told *about* the fake-or-not interview—the various ways that nearly all of the players manipulated for their own purposes the general and long-standing suspicions, expectations, and assumptions about credibility, fakery, and how yellow the press actually was. Whether a paper faked or not was in the end less consequential than who *accused* it of faking, who *believed* it was faking, and why.

At the heart of the affair lay the perennial combat between Pulitzer and his nemesis Hearst, who had rebranded the *New York Journal* as the more patriotic-sounding *New York American* after some critics blamed William McKinley's assassination on the paper's relentless assaults against the president. The rivalry, however, had become more complicated than it had been during the cutthroat days of the Spanish-American War. Although Pulitzer was widely seen as too popular to be entirely respectable, he was nonetheless more principled than Hearst and the other yellow compatriots with whom he was often lumped. (In fact, this dichotomy played out in the two editions he published: the somewhat soberer morning *World*, known in the office vernacular as "Senior," and the callower *Evening World*, "Junior," which he had founded in 1887 to compete with the city's traditionally coarser and more lurid afternoon papers. Pulitzer always preferred "Senior," but "Junior" held a clear edge in both circulation and visibility.)[51] Having arrived in the United States from Hungary as a penniless teenager with barely a word of English, Pulitzer built his success in New York in the 1880s on lively, vigorous, often sensational reporting specifically directed toward the city's huge immigrant population. He took particular pride in cutting a decidedly unstodgy figure. The story goes that at one point when Pulitzer felt the paper was losing its snap, he decided the problem was that no one on the staff got drunk, and he ordered his business manager to go out, find a man who did, and hire him at once.[52]

But he also genuinely considered journalism to be a public service dedicated to "the cause of the people," not the "purse-potentates," as he had put it in his inaugural editorial back on May 11, 1883. And he insisted that even the liveliest reporting could also be accurate, though the day-to-day realities of the hypercompetitive world of urban mass journalism not infrequently conflicted with the exhortations of "Accuracy, Accuracy, Accuracy!" displayed on printed cards plastered around the newsroom. His later-life efforts to improve the practice of journalism by establishing a professional school at Columbia University and a set of aspirational prizes were inspired in some measure by his remorse over the excesses he had countenanced in the heat of the war in Cuba and his circulation battle with Hearst.[53]

The kaiser's interview tested that old wartime rivalry afresh. The talkative emperor favored Hale, a onetime Episcopal clergyman who had become the *New York Times*'s literary editor, with a string of remarks about global affairs so incendiary that the editors of the *Times*, true to the traditions of gentlemanly statecraft, went straight to President Theodore Roosevelt to ask him whether they really ought to publish the kaiser's comments. Goodness no, replied Roosevelt; publication, he believed, would "jeopardize" not only "the peace of the world" but also the reputation of the *Times* because the kaiser was certain to repudiate the interview and "many readers would also believe that the *Times* had faked it."[54] With the German Foreign Office also expressing its strong displeasure, the *Times* spiked the article. Hale then sold to the highbrow *Century* magazine a new version from which the most inflammatory remarks had been blue-penciled out by a German ministry official. But even as the presses were rolling, Berlin, gripped by second thoughts, enlisted the American ambassador to help pressure the *Century* into canceling the piece altogether. The editors obligingly stopped the presses in the middle of their run and locked the sheets away.[55]

The reprieve was only momentary. By that point, rumors about the interview were rampant and copies of various excerpts, notes, letters, and drafts were floating freely around newsrooms and government offices on both sides of the Atlantic. On November 20, Hearst's *American* leapt splashily into print with what it said was a synopsis of the suppressed interview that it had obtained through channels of its own. The day after Hearst's bombshell, Pulitzer's *World*, dismissing its rival's version as "irresponsible" and "inaccurate," published what it called the "first authentic synopsis" of the interview. The two summaries, each just a few brief paragraphs long, differed in wording but were similarly sensational, touching on the decadence of Great Britain, the inevitability of war among the

European powers, the danger to white nations of Britain's alliance with Japan, the advantages of unity between Germany and the United States, and the personal bitterness between the kaiser and his uncle, Edward VII of England.[56] Both were widely republished throughout the American and European press.

The yellow papers' actions left German officials doubly infuriated, not just by the public humiliation of the kaiser but also by the meddling of the lowbrow foreign press in high matters of state. That lowbrow reputation did, however, offer to the German chancellor, Bernhard von Bülow, a credible basis for his program of damage control. The chancellor simply accused the American papers of purveying fakes, which given their reputation was not a hard case to make. As the kaiser authorized an official denial of the interview, the chancellor ordered the Foreign Office to brand the *World's* synopsis as a "clumsy swindle . . . crude mystification and an invention from A to Z."[57]

Many publications, especially American ones, accepted the synopses as both genuine and toothsome, but others, led by the *New York Times*, clung to the story line that the pieces were inauthentic, while Hearst's *American* belligerently and continually insisted that its own version was genuine and the *World's* only a "garbled hodge-podge" of stolen material. Hale publicly repudiated both synopses, reserving special scorn for the *World's* piece; it was, he proclaimed, choosing his words with obvious care, "the most arrant rubbish—pure invention—an absolute fake."[58] Through it all, the *World* appeared unperturbed, running an elaborate front-page explanation of how the paper had worked directly with Hale to confirm that every word in the piece was accurate.[59]

As always, the news rolled on, and by November 25 the story had essentially vanished from the pages of the *World*, elbowed out by timelier events, such as the escape of Nellie the elephant from the Hippodrome. Then suddenly, on November 30, the *World* abruptly reopened the affair with a stunning about-face. Deep inside the paper, on page 8, under the tiny headline "Correction," the paper confessed that its "painstaking inquiry" had uncovered "no convincing basis of fact" for its synopsis. "Not afraid to admit its errors," the paper acknowledged that "the Kaiser could not have uttered . . . some of the 'stupidly absurd words' attributed to him" and concluded that it "sincerely regrets the published synopsis of the Hale interview as mistaken, misleading and mischievous."

But even as the paper said it was sorry, it did not *exactly* say it was wrong, and it made clear that whatever had gone amiss was entirely the fault of Hale, who, it insisted, had examined and approved the proofs before publication. The frustrated journalist, said the paper, had doubtless been angling to get his suppressed scoop into print at last without taking responsibility for leaking it. The whole affair could "very well serve the Rev. Dr. Hale's self-interest," it concluded, "while gratifying his extreme vanity and his appetite for further international notoriety."

To this day, Hale's role and motives remain both enigmatic and suspect. His son, writing in the *Atlantic Monthly* in 1934, insisted that the elder Hale had acted honorably throughout.[60] But the erstwhile clergyman was a certifiably dubious character, or at least he had become one by the time of the Great War, when he began secretly collecting a princely annual salary of $15,000 (about $400,000 today) as a writer and adviser for the German propaganda operation in New York. By some accounts, he remained on the German payroll even after Hearst hired him in May 1916 to go to Berlin as a special correspondent. (Though Hearst was a famous Germanophile, he reportedly did not know of Hale's other job.) Late in the war, after his secret second career was exposed, Hale exiled himself to Munich, where he died in 1924.[61]

WHAT IN THE *WORLD*?

Repudiating the story must have been a harrowing decision for the *World*. A controversial interview fraught with global intrigue was the sort of story the paper lived for: it riveted the world's attention and showed the paper to be a player in international politics; it kept the competition on its toes; and its publication in the face of disapproval from foreigners and elites reconfirmed the paper's reputation for feistiness, fearlessness, and dedication to the little guy's right to know. The paper in fact had a very recent precedent for its refusal to bend to pressure: it had stood by the suspect J. Pierpont Morgan interview that had also dabbled in sensitive political matters. Now its very visible act of professional contrition and penance was presenting an irresistible target for ridicule and schadenfreude to its most merciless journalistic rival and to the world at large as well.

Nearly a decade later, in late 1917, with the kaiser's "inevitable" war finally raging, the *New York Tribune* reexamined the incident and came to a startling conclusion that was quickly supported by a number of other papers: the *World*'s synopsis had been genuine. The question, however, remained: Why had the *World* backed down? On that point, the *Tribune* was baffled. "The only man who knows why it did so is dead," it wrote. "That was Joseph Pulitzer himself."[62]

The affair remains murky. It's not impossible that pressure from Berlin or Washington rippled into the *World*'s newsroom as it had into the *Times*'s; a cryptic telegram to Berlin from the German chargé d'affaires in Washington *could* be interpreted as saying that Roosevelt was applying pressure on the *World* and the *American* to retract the story.[63] But even though Roosevelt had boasted to several correspondents of his success with the *Times*, his letters mention no personal intervention into the *World*'s decision. The bull-headed Roosevelt and the bumptious Pulitzer detested each other, moreover, and just as the interview kerfuffle was unfolding, Roosevelt was also embarking on what would become a Javertian effort to have the *World* convicted on charges of criminal libel over its aggressive reporting on possible corruption in his signature Panama Canal deal. Neither side ever backed down; Roosevelt kept losing in the courts, and even though the *World* fell short of proving its accusations, it never withdrew them, either, insisting in bold editorials that it could not be "muzzled."[64]

So although it's also not impossible that Pulitzer offered a humiliating surrender to Roosevelt at precisely the same time he was grandly insisting he would never surrender to Roosevelt, the scenario taxes the imagination. Nor did the Washington diplomatic world seem to feel much urgency over the whole affair. As the chargé noted in his cable, "the better press" in the United States was accepting Hale's repudiation of the synopses, while "local government circles" were dismissing the articles in the two "known scandal sheets" as having no broader significance.[65] The yellow papers' reputation for sensationalism and fakery may actually have been insulating them from outside pressure by elites and foreigners who underestimated their influence and disdained their mass appeal.

But if it's true that nobody pressured the *World* to recant, why then would it have felt compelled to correct a "fake" that was largely true all along? The issue seems to be that the *World* had derived its synopsis *not* from Hale's suppressed *Century* article but from a document it must have obtained either confidentially or illegitimately. The language of the *World*'s synopsis is very close to that of an unauthorized letter that an unnamed *New York Times* executive secretly sent to Lord Northcliffe, the British press baron, recounting what Hale had privately told the *Times* editors about the kaiser's shocking comments. Those were precisely the comments about Britain's degeneracy, Japan's dangerous ambitions, and other such matters that the German Foreign Office would later slash out of Hale's *Century* article. The *World* was thus correct in saying that its information had come through Hale, but Hale's public (and accurate) insistence that the synopsis had not come from his *Century* piece badly undercut the paper's position. The *American*'s "synopsis," meanwhile, was *also* genuine in its own way; it was an almost word-for-word transcription of parts of another private letter, one that Hale had dashed off to William Reick, the *Times*'s general manager, reporting on the incendiary conversation he had just had with the kaiser. Hearst simply continued to bluster that the *American* had gotten it right and the *World* had faked it.[66]

So the *World* seems to have been in the awkward position of feeling unable to defend itself against accusations of faking because it had to keep its genuine source secret. If that was indeed the case, the paper's decision to issue the embarrassing correction would have been an unforced—and impressive—demonstration of its professional integrity and not incidentally of its difference from Hearst. On November 25, the *World*'s brilliant and prickly chief editorial writer, Frank Cobb, told Pulitzer in a confidential memo that the publication of the synopsis had been handled in "an unfortunate manner." To the disinterested reader, Cobb wrote, the *World*'s publication of a mysteriously sourced interview a day after Hearst claimed to have done the same thing looked as if the *World* were simply countering the *American*'s fake with one of its own. Although he believed that the synopsis was "substantially true," he wrote, "it seems to me that the thing was handled like a fake, that it had all the ear-marks of a fake and conveyed the impression of a fake. . . . [I]t seems to me the best thing the World can do is to drop it completely." The next time the *World* made more than a passing reference to the story was to correct it.[67]

The *World*'s dilemma illustrates the tension faced by papers caught between their traditional orientation toward empirically casual entertainment and the increasing emphasis on the public performance of journalistic rigor. The problem for Cobb was that even if the synopsis was "uncontestably true," the circumstances of its publication made it "impossible to convince the average reader of that fact . . . [and] every word of it might as well be uncontestably untrue."[68] In other words, if it walks like a fake and quacks like a fake, it hardly matters that it is *not* a fake. The *World* had fallen into exactly the trap that Roosevelt had warned the *Times* against, foolishly sacrificing its credibility in a battle with an unbeatable foe.

The reader is left with the tickle of a suspicion that the *World*—like the *Boston Globe* with its "manly" confession that also managed to shift the blame to the shady detective in the Borden case—was hoping to repair its integrity by "confessing" it had been innocently entrapped in a falsehood by the devious Hale rather than by continuing to defend its active involvement in a tainted truth. Like the *Boston Globe*, the *World* may have determined that it was better to be seen as fooled than as fake; by casting its error not as fraudulence but as credulity, the paper could be seen as claiming a painful honesty as its hallmark and a professional commitment to accuracy as its goal. By taking responsibility for that credulity, furthermore, the paper appeared to be generously exempting its readers from having to acknowledge any of their own.

It seems fair to suggest that all the Sturm und Drang over what the press said about the indiscretions of the emperor of Germany did not, in the end, have much effect on public opinion or on the peace of the world, either. The kaiser was already in trouble, as was the peace. The people who already thought the yellow press was bold and antielitist would not have been disabused. The people who already dismissed anything the yellow press said would have continued to disbelieve it. And the *World*'s dicey reputation in many quarters outweighed and long outlived its self-sacrificial attempt at candor. On December 1, the day after the correction ran, headlines pummeling the paper for its "fake" appeared everywhere from the *Montreal Gazette* ("New York World Retracts: Admits the Alleged Kaiser Interview Was a Fake") to the *Rock Island (IL) Argus* ("New York World Admits That Its 'Kaiser' Interview Was a Fake").

Scholars have ever since routinely ignored or dismissed (or, quite possibly, never read in the first place) what the *World*'s synopsis actually said, readily accepting instead the word of the more powerful von Bülow, the more respectable *New York Times*, and the (temporarily) saintlier clergyman-journalist Hale. One exhaustive scholarly analysis of the political consequences of the affair even remarked upon the "curious" fact that the *World*'s synopsis "bore in its most important points an uncanny resemblance" to Northcliffe's notes, even as the analysis brusquely dismissed the paper's version as entirely "spurious," "concocted," and "sensational."[69] It was the yellow press; of *course* it would have faked.

The incident makes clear that although issues of journalistic authority and credibility were at its center, the debate was about much more than whether a given story was true; it also had to do with what readers, newsmakers, and journalists expected and wanted to be true. As each party to the episode battled to seize control of the narrative for its own purposes, the flexible and sometimes muddled meanings of the term *fake* were manipulated and exploited, in the end sowing even more doubt about what was genuine and what was not. Diplomats and politicians discredited a damaging but true story by branding it a fake. A journal that prided itself on its reputation as decent and trustworthy spiked the story for fear that its genuinely truthful account would be seen as a fake. A devious journalist eager to draw attention seems to have leaked his own hot story and then loudly repudiated it as a fake. A pair of hypercompetitive newspapers nourished their long rivalry by slamming each other for being caught in a fake. And finally, one of those rivals, eager to improve its standing and distance itself from its disreputable competitor, branded its own true story as a mistake to save it from being seen as a fake. News consumers were free to choose and find validation in whatever vision of journalism and version of world politics they preferred.

After Joseph Pulitzer died, in 1911, his son Ralph worked to haul the *World* at last out of the shady precincts of the yellow press. In his address the following year to the very first class of the new Columbia Journalism School, Ralph seized the opportunity to launch an explicit and full-throated repudiation of fakery. "The faker is a liar," he thundered to the students. "If he perpetrates a so-called harmless fake, he is a harmless liar. If he is guilty of a fake that injures people, he is not only a vicious liar but often a moral assassin as well."[70]

Ralph Pulitzer acknowledged that the breathtaking pace of the newsroom and the huge amount of material the editors handled each day made inaccuracies (and thus both embarrassments and lawsuits) almost inevitable. He nonetheless pledged allegiance to the creed of his father, for whom accuracy had been "a religion," and within a year had established a True Church of his own.[71] In a dramatic gesture designed to slay the fake once and for all, he set up an in-house *World* Bureau of Accuracy and Fair Play, whose mandate was to expose, acknowledge, and publicly correct mistakes and deliberate fakes that had managed to sneak into the paper. Bureau staffers, alert for errors, combed through each edition, invited readers to submit complaints directly to their office, and recommended the firing of reporters and correspondents who got too many things wrong. This was accountability on a grand and calculatedly visible scale— accountability that, again, served as libel proofing as well.[72] (We confess error; you excuse it.)

When the editor Isaac White sent his first circular letter to dozens of local editors, stringers, and other contributors explaining the plan for the Bureau of Accuracy and soliciting their comments, most responded with approval, though occasionally with a sardonic tinge. "I know of no newspaper where such a department is more needed," wrote the editor and publisher of the *Walton (NY) Chronicle*. "Congratulations on the fact that one of the greatest American newspapers is turning over such an important new leaf, and is ready to dispense with the inaccuracy and faking that has been one of its strongest characteristics during the many years that I have read it."[73]

But even as most editors made the expected noises about the importance of getting things right, some resisted, drawing on the traditional journalistic defense of "harmless" fakes: they were simply trying to please readers by "infusing 'life'" into otherwise drab copy.[74] It was the tension between accuracy and snap all over again: everyone knew that the emerging set of communicative conventions known as "journalistic" writing that was intended to embody a pledge of scrupulous empiricism often went hand-in-hand with deadly dullness. As Lincoln Steffens famously recalled of his training on the *New York Evening Post* in the 1890s, "Reporters were to report the news as it happened, like machines, without prejudice, color, and without style; all alike. Humor or any kind of personality in our reports was caught, rebuked, and, in time, suppressed."[75]

Even though the term *fake* had lost its luster, in the eyes of many readers its spirit had not. "To my mind," one of Isaac White's correspondents responded, the effort to alleviate the drabness "is so general throughout the country and so well received by the reading public, that a paper dropping it entirely because of the hazard it involves will be at something of a disadvantage."[76] Several correspondents picked out the creations of the "Winsted man" as particularly deserving of mercy. The reporter and editor L. T. Stone, also known as the "Winsted Liar," had put his small Connecticut town on the map with his decades' worth of yarns in the *Evening Citizen* about the naked wildman who haunted the local woods, the tree that grew baked apples, and any number of variations on the hilarious theme of chickens laying eggs, all of them considered more charmingly imaginative than deceptive.

In fact, not even the fake-slaying *World* was itself entirely immune to that sort of charm. On March 21, 1913, three months after Ralph Pulitzer soberly cautioned the budding journalists at Columbia against publishing "adulterated goods," the front page of the *Evening World* carried the arresting headline "4 O'CLOCK LIZARD BITES—THEN YOU DIE ON THE HOUR." The piece was reportedly based on an interview with a garrulous old salt about the natural wonders of the Bahamas, such as the samsonian bug, which eats the feathers off chickens. But it was the titular lizard that was truly amazing. No matter what time it bit you, the article informed readers, you would die the next time the clock struck four, morning or afternoon. The tale was picked up and copied by several other papers, all of which topped it with coy headlines or added arch ledes but chose not to distinguish it in any obvious physical way from any other news story in their columns.[77] A harmless fake.

The visibility of the Bureau of Accuracy was waning by the end of World War I, and it did not survive the paper's sale in 1931. But the bureau and the four o'clock lizard symbolize two competing visions of journalism at the beginning of the twentieth century. The lizard story had appeared in the *evening* edition of the *World*, "Junior," the more sensational edition that had been designed to compete with the cruder side of the mass press. No such reptile would have been allowed to slither into the pages of "Senior," the morning *World*, the paper that had worked so hard to salvage its reputation by presenting the kaiser's interview as a mistake rather than a fake.

The *Evening World* still made room to honor the old tradition that people might enjoy choosing for themselves what to believe and what was true—that a newspaper's role was to entertain as well as to inform and that there *were*, indeed, such things as harmless fakes. The morning *World* was taking a newer-fangled approach. Readers, it was saying, wanted to know that what they saw in the paper was accurate and that the work of authentication had been done for them by serious people who knew the difference between the truth and a fake and would stand up and correct their errors, no matter how embarrassing. The way to guarantee accuracy, accuracy, accuracy was to unequivocally condemn the fake by demanding professionalism, professionalism, professionalism.

4

"I BELIEVE IN FAKING"

Obscure tattoos of dots and dashes resolve into news of events not yet an hour old! Tragic images of bodies on a battlefield arise out of baths of stinky chemicals! Disembodied human voices exhort and inform from a box in the parlor! New communication technologies inevitably undergo tryouts as tools for making journalism. Innovators always seek ways to apply the new device or thing to the fundamental journalistic task of providing people with truthful information about the world—to make the gathering and presentation of news faster or more intimate or more efficient. But new technologies also have a tendency to confound the expectations that launched them; once loosed into the wild, they often end up filling purposes and responding to needs no one ever predicted. Innovators *also* always find novel ways to use those same devices or things to beguile, challenge, manipulate, and exploit people's expectations about receiving truthful information. New communication technologies also inevitably undergo tryouts as tools for faking journalism.

Between the 1890s and the 1920s, the efforts to improve journalism and the efforts to exploit technologies entangled themselves in particularly consequential ways. At the same time that many journalists were forging new understandings about their professional relationship with accuracy and truth, users of three important communication technologies—two new and one repurposed—were also figuring out how those processes worked and what advantages and limits they brought to the representation of real life. As with any new technology, each of the three "'enter[ed] into' the determination of its own utilities, suggesting new ideas for its own definition," write the authors of a classic study about unanticipated uses of the refrigerator, of all things. "What [technologies] are good for is a consequence, not a determinant, of their use . . . [and] they contribute to the definition of the problems for which they are the solutions."[1] Each of the three turn-of-the-century communication technologies helped solve the problem of representing truth in a different way.

Photography was half a century old, and the practice of retouching—or, as it was often called, "faking"—had become widely accepted by the time members of the new profession of "news-photographer" began to stake out a separate identity for themselves. In the new motion-picture industry, the emphasis was on commercial entertainment, but anything went as long as the audience did too, and nobody was keeping track of the boundaries between entertaining "actuality" films and actual entertainment. And the magical, other-worldly realm of the ether where radio dwelled offered so welcoming a haven for the faker that the federal government finally acknowledged that there ought to be a law—or several.

PHOTOGRAPHY FAKES THE REAL

When photography was introduced in 1839, it was seen as capable of expressing a "more absolute truth," as Edgar Allan Poe raved, that is "*infinitely* more accurate in its representation than any painting by human hands."[2] By the end of the century, however, photography had picked up the debate over the practice of journalistic faking right where the newspapers' debate left off.

It didn't take practitioners long after the introduction of photography to glimpse the potential to exploit people's changing ideas about the nature of truth and reality. The archetypal example is offered by the former engraver who in Boston and New York in the 1860s and 1870s collected hefty fees in advertising himself as "William H. Mumler, Spirit Photographic Medium." He took pictures of dead people, or so he said: having arranged his living sitter in a conventional pose for a standard studio portrait, he would then retreat to the darkroom and after a while emerge

FIGURE 4.1 Mrs. Tinkham and a spectral friend.

Source: Albumen print, William H. Mumler, Boston, 1862–1875. Digital image courtesy of the Getty Open Content Program.

flourishing an image that plainly showed the ghostly figure of a lost loved one hovering over the sitter's shoulder or behind the sitter's chair. It just *happened*, he said; somehow or other, a magical combination of lens and light was able to pierce the veil of death.

Derision and denunciation poured from all corners. Professional photographers protested his assault on the integrity of their craft, reporters and scientists defended logic and reason against a charlatan, and opportunistic politicians leapt into action to protect the public welfare against a cheat. Even P. T. Barnum weighed in, the man who had built his triumphant career on the shrewd exploitation of the distinction between the genially engaging humbug and the malicious fraud. He scoffed at credulous clients such as the woman who took comfort in having a spirit photograph made of her dead son and then, believing her brother to have been killed in battle, bought one of him, too. When soon afterward the "dead" brother returned home alive and well, Barnum snorted, she refused to be shaken in her belief in the process. Some "evil spirit," she said, had taken his form in order to deceive her.[3]

Yet this woman was not alone in her staunch refusal to be disabused. Especially in an era overrun with death, many of Mumler's customers preferred to accept supernatural solace as a gift not to be questioned, certainly not to be withered by the disdain of experts and elites: they made a conscious choice to bypass those heartless authorities and embrace the truths they could see in the fake. In 1869, when Mumler was hauled into a Manhattan courtroom for a preliminary hearing on charges of larceny and fraud, dozens of his supporters and believers rushed to the courthouse to present evidence on his behalf and to declare their faith in the kinder, gentler reality he offered them. After a three-week investigation, the judge declined to send the case to the grand jury. He was, he said, "morally convinced that there may have been trick and deception practiced by the prisoner," but he could not deny that the prosecution had failed to show how Mumler had pulled it off.[4]

It was a stinging defeat for rationalists and skeptics and an open acknowledgment that the role of photography was more complicated than Poe and others had imagined. Expecting it to present nothing more than a spitting image of real life was obviously much too simplistic, and failing to acknowledge its potential to defraud was clearly naive. The *New York World* (not yet owned by Joseph Pulitzer and still bearing its original, Gotham-rooted title) had been among the most aggressive challengers of Mumler's claims. On the day after the case was dismissed, the *World* ran a column that began with what sounded like a lamentation for a lost faith:

> Who, henceforth, can trust the accuracy of a photograph? Heretofore, we have been led to believe that nature, the whole of nature, and nothing but nature, could be "took"; but now whither shall we turn when it is possible for Henry Ward Beecher, say, to be presented in the embraces of a festive *fleurette*, or the ghost of the late lamented be delineated with a

rawhide in the hand hectoring a gang of negroes in a cotton field? What ravage will this possibility make of private reputation, and what confusion entail on the historian of future times. Photographs have been treasured in a belief that, like figures, they could not lie, but here is a revelation that they may be made to lie with a most deceiving exactness.[5]

But acknowledging the possibility of fraud also opened the possibility of liberation from literalness, and embedded in the piece is the sly recognition that even a photograph that lies can convey a kind of truth. The possibility that the wildly famous and widely worshiped Reverend Beecher might be portrayed cavorting with a "festive *fleurette*" doubtless sounded shocking to some, but the scenario wasn't entirely hypothetical; by that time, rumors of his philandering had been following Beecher for years.[6] (His spectacular trial on charges of adultery with his best friend's wife lay nearly six years in the future.) And the *World* piece went on to ask, with a ponderous heartiness, what would happen to "marriage by photograph" when pen pals could exchange images of themselves with aquiline noses subbed in for their snubs. Rather than a lament, the *World*'s comment was in fact a winking confirmation that nothing was what it seemed and no appearances—photographically captured or not—were to be trusted.

As encounters with photographic images became more and more common in everyday life, Americans grew increasingly comfortable with the myriad ways in which they could be ambiguous, complex, deceptive, or playful. Just as consumers did with the relationships between newspaper accounts and literal accuracy, they were also gaining experience in navigating and evaluating the slippery relationships between photographs and "absolute truth." The photographic tinkerers who figured out how to give a sitter three arms or to plop his disembodied head, eyes wide open, on a platter were sharing a bemused chuckle over the unexpectedly rich pleasures of a new parlor game. The artistes who staged elaborate studio tableaux of dying maidens, winged cherubs, fairy-tale characters, biblical personages, and other fantastical scenes were indulging their creativity and experimenting with the conventions of realistic representation. Not one of their customers either could have or would have believed that the photographer had been calmly dismembering and re-membering his sitters in the studio or had just happened by at the moment when Little Red

Riding Hood encountered the wolf. The images were *realistic*, but nobody took them as *real*.[7]

Meanwhile, the trailblazing Alfred Stieglitz and other pictorialists, determined to prove that photography was every bit as demanding a craft and as expressive an art as painting or drawing, used sponges, brushes, stumps, and darkroom panache to enhance their negatives and prints with shadow, mist, light, and feeling. And in commercial portrait studios, techniques variously known as "retouching" or "handwork" became routine. Over the objections of a few purists who saw mechanical manipulation as an admission of the photographer's failure, others insisted that their job was to give their sitters exactly the reality they had ordered and paid for.[8] "It would seem to me," one practitioner wrote in a trade journal in 1897 under the title "A Plea for Retouching," that "if a person of sixty years wants for any reason to be made to look as near thirty as possible, the nearer the photographer can come to hitting the mark the better it will be for him. The main thing, I take it, is that the photographer, being in the business not for the love of it so much as for a living, had best get his living in the easiest way possible for himself and with the most satisfaction to his patrons."[9] A "more absolute truth" was whatever the customer with the wallet said it was.

But it wasn't just portraits, artistic scenes, tableaux, and other malleable bits of reality that Americans expected to see tweaked, doctored, and beautified. It was also the sort of work that present-day news consumers would readily place in the category of "photojournalism"—a concept and a word that in the nineteenth century did not exist.[10] Some photographers did make images of news events, to be sure, but those images were neither a large nor an influential part of the national photographic output in part because the available technology tended to fail abysmally at the task of systematically capturing and distributing realistic, useful images of current events. News often breaks fast, but the cameras of the era were slow and cumbersome, and the developing processes finicky and difficult to manage on the fly. Until about 1880, it was not technologically possible to reproduce photographs cheaply and quickly enough for the daily press. When the halftone process did come along, it tended to produce images that were murky, unattractive, and, in the opinion of many, *less* informative than the engraved illustrations that an artist with a good eye, an enlightened imagination, and a deft hand could produce. For decades after photographs were possible in the mass press, they remained nearly invisible there.[11]

All of this meant that daguerreotypes or carte-de-visite images of even those news events that moved with a stolidity more congenial to the photographer's apparatus—the first-ever surgery performed under anesthesia, the packed-in crowd at a presidential inauguration, the iconic piles of bodies on Civil War battlefields, the locomotive after the crash, or the ruins after the fire—lacked the reach, the timeliness, the accountability, the contextualization, the commercial value, and the explicitness of a good newspaper report.

Those mechanical limits also helped shape the ways people thought about images of current events. Since the new medium of photography stood completely separate from and outside of the familiar information system known as "journalism," consumers who did happen to encounter an image of a news event had no reason to place it into a special category of its own or to bring different expectations about its truthfulness than they did to other kinds of photographs. Nor did photographers who documented current events feel any obligation to use particular techniques or follow different ethical imperatives for their work than the ones that were routine for their studio-bound colleagues. When the Boston daguerreotypists Southworth and Hawes, for instance, colluded with a team of physicians to restage for the camera their epoch-making surgery on an anesthetized patient, or when Alexander Gardner and Timothy O'Sullivan heaved the bodies of fallen soldiers into more dramatic scenes on the field at Gettysburg, they, too, were following convention and in their own way presenting images that were realistic, not real.[12]

TENSIONS OVER FAKING

In the first decades of the twentieth century, the persistent tension over how photography related to reality became entangled in the ongoing debate over journalistic faking. By that point, newspaper faking had generally been repudiated—by name if not always in practice—as the symbol of everything that was unprofessional about journalism. But at exactly the same time, commercial and artistic photographers were consciously beginning to use the otherwise discredited word *fake* to describe practices for which they already had perfectly good words, such as *retouching* and *handwork*, to describe. Just as some journalists had done with newspaper faking in its feckless and often endearing youth, some photographers were beginning to describe their version of faking as a harmless indulgence, a service to the public, a license to be creative, and, best of all, a way to give their public *better* truth, *realer* truth.

When faking was well done, argued one contributor to a trade journal, it did not necessarily "make the photograph more truthful to Nature, but . . . it should *seem more* truthful, which is by no means the same thing." As another practitioner declaimed in an address before the Photographers' Association of America, "I believe in faking, I admire legitimate faking, successful faking, faking that produces the results desired," and in his summation he urged his colleagues to overcome the "falseness of ultra-realism" to attain "not literal, but *spiritual* and *eternal* truth." The speech was hailed with "prolonged applause."[13]

At the same time, however, a different view of truth was taking hold among a new breed of photographer, a breed so novel it gave itself a formal introduction. "Every newspaper of importance employs a staff photographer," explained a contributor to the *American Annual of Photography and Photographic Times Almanac* in 1900. "To all parts of the city and country—indeed, all over the world—the newspapers are sending photographers to gather the news with camera as well as with pen. These bright, active, daring young men are now recognized as news-photographers, and their work is known as news-photography."[14]

The evolution of this new kind of photography was driven by a variety of developments. Technology helped: photomechanical processes were finally producing images acceptable for publication in the daily press, while lighter cameras, faster shutters, more versatile lenses and flash devices, and more efficient darkroom processes made possible the capture of more lifelike images. Shifting aesthetics also played a role as prominent practitioners such as Stieglitz began gravitating toward the more naturalistic style that would become known as "straight" photography. But the news photographers also had a professional model: the newspaper journalists who were establishing their identity as principled and credible by emphasizing their differences with the sensational and fake-filled mass press. Like the newspaper reporters, the news photographers insisted that their work offered a faithful and objective representation of reality that eschewed retouching, "handwork," or the intervention of a human sensibility. "This news-photography tells news-stories truthfully," the *American Annual* correspondent continued. "None of the inaccuracies of the pen, no fiction, no exaggerating of facts, no news that is not news. A camera does not lie. It shows people as they really look, reproduces scenes with realistic exactness. No chance here for the city editor to make the ugly young woman suicide a beauty, no need of 'faking' a picture of events that are happening on the other side of the world."[15]

There it was: news photographers *had no need of "faking."* Just as newspaper journalists had done before them, the emerging cadre of professional photojournalists distinguished themselves from others working in their own arena with their pledge to be authentic and publicly committing themselves never to manipulate the news or to tamper with reality. Repudiating the fake had become a critical measure of the professional, and the trade journals made sure people knew it, too, trotting out egregious examples of failures. There was, for instance, the paper that printed a two-year-old picture of the great fire in Baltimore when it couldn't procure one of the great fire in San Francisco or the paper that paid a young woman ten dollars to impersonate a suicide victim by slipping a noose around her neck and allowing herself to be strung up for a few seconds in front of the camera. But "the fake photo is generally discredited in your really high-class newspaper," one author assured readers in an explicit act of intraprofessional boundary setting; the "better class of papers" never uses them.[16]

In the decades since Poe had hailed the capacity of photography to express a "more absolute truth," its relationship with truth had revealed itself to be much less absolute than advertised. Photography, it turned out, not only offered inspiration for the artistic soul and delighted the experimenter and the amateur but could also lend itself to trickery, encourage fraud, and value commercial success over authenticity. In staking its identity on its rejection of faking, embellishment, and manipulation, the emerging field of news photography made clear that it was willing to police its own borders and to cast out the miscreants who might damage its reputation. The specialty that would become known as photojournalism was already casting its lot with the journalistic side of its heritage and rejecting the slipshod values of the photographic side.

In the 1920s, the coming of the tabloid press would challenge all that.

PICTURES BEGIN TO MOVE!

A celluloid locomotive rushes heedlessly toward the two hundred or so customers who have paid a franc apiece to huddle in front of a screen in the dark basement of the Grand Café in Paris. Terror-stricken audience members leap from their seats and run screaming for the exits.

Or not.

The story that spectators were faked out by the Lumière brothers' virtual train is to some extent a fake. No known contemporary eyewitness account, journalistic report, or police file confirms any frantic exodus from the Grand Café that spring evening in 1896. Most moviegoers of the time, although surprised or even disconcerted by what they were seeing, also knew perfectly well that the image on the screen wasn't about to run them down, and the enduring tale gently mocking their primitive panic in the face of a new technology is what one film historian calls "cinema's founding myth."[17] But the lasting appeal of that myth helps to illuminate the questions—some old and familiar, some new and unique to this technology—presented by the efforts of early audiences to make sense of realistic pictures that moved.

The founding myth survives in part because it conveys something important about the birth of any significant technology—those moments when people are figuring out what it might do, what it can do, who will control it, and what it all might mean for daily life. *This new thing will change everything,* goes the common refrain, long before anyone knows exactly what will change or how; *this is bound to have an enormous influence on people.* And obviously technologies often do.

A frequent cadenza in that common refrain, however, involves what might be called the Myth of the Clueless Other: the fervent conviction that it is only *other people* who are frightened or manipulated by whatever the new machine has brought forth. It is only the childish, the befuddled, or the backward, like the stock turn-of-the-century "Uncle Josh" character who was the bumpkin star of gramophone recordings and even a film of his own released in 1902, *Uncle Josh at the Moving Picture Show*. The frequency of that response serves as a sharp reminder of the caution required any time we try to evaluate what fakers, fakees, and observers say about any incident of mischief, falsification, or fraud. All of them, of course, bring interests of their own to bear in the shaping of their particular accounts, and any claim by any actor that "Ha ha, we fooled them all!" should be just as much a red flag for the historian as another's conviction that "Ha ha, no one can fool me!"

Assessing its impact is especially complicated for a medium that from the moment of its birth had so intimate an association with the world of commercial entertainment even as it promised to provide a new kind of authentic information about the world. The primary and secondary literature about the first years of the movies is full of conflicting stories about credibility and credulity: filmmakers faking scenes, filmmakers boasting about their ingenuity in faking scenes, filmmakers faking reports about how audiences viewed fake scenes, viewers understanding and enjoying fake scenes, viewers being fooled by fake scenes, historians insisting viewers were fooled by fake scenes, historians insisting viewers knew perfectly well the fake scenes were fake. The conversation about who was fooled, who was not, and why was as much a part of the process as the efforts to fool were. And that conversation took on special importance for the history of fake news when just a few years after the commercial introduction of film, moving pictures went to war for the very first time, and the technologies that had made possible the gleeful production of tricks, humbugs, and games took their uneasy place within the larger journalistic landscape where *fake* had begun to sound like a dirty word.

From its very beginning, the entire category of "film" had a complicated relationship to reality. The very first customers who wanted to watch a movie did not go "to the movies"; most of them went to the vaudeville house or the penny arcade or the tent show, where they could enjoy watching magicians, minstrels, acrobats, actors, comedians, female impersonators, and maybe even an elephant between those brief reels of flickering images dancing on a screen. Motion pictures were widely considered, at least by the highbrow, as just another lowbrow entertainment for the heavily immigrant and working-class urban masses, just another feature of the sometimes squalid world of commercialized mass leisure. As such, the moving picture was closer to a purchased novelty to enjoy in a public space than to an information system with obligations to the truth.[18]

That view would be given an authoritative corroboration in 1915 when the Supreme Court legalized censorship of the movies, ruling that because they were "a business, pure and simple" rather than journalism, they were not covered by constitutional protections of free speech. But the court was also effectively arguing that the new technology of moving pictures had such an unprecedented and powerful ability to sway the emotions and undermine the morals of susceptible people sitting with strangers in the dark that the guardians of public order and public decency *had* to be able to control its activities. Film would not be the last technology to raise the hackles of the moralist or to earn the semiofficial label *social problem* through its framing in the public arena as both dramatic and harmful.[19]

But it was the novelty of film more than the opportunity for immorality that piqued the attention of the earliest viewers. Like the dog's-breakfast newspapers of the nineteenth century, the seconds- or minutes-long films made by such pioneering U.S. and international companies as Edison Studios, Biograph, Vitagraph, Lumière Brothers, Pathé, and others made spaghetti of the lines between real life and fiction, between enlightenment and entertainment, between credible information and cheerful fabrication. For the earliest camera operators hauling around their bulky machines, the goal was to find "anything outdoors that moved rapidly," as one early cameraman recalled: that onrushing train, a swarm of factory workers, a streetcar trundling down a city street, a firefighting crew at work, cowboys branding calves, even the inauguration of a president or the coronation of a czar.[20] Not infrequently, moviegoers could catch glimpses on the screen of passersby casting bemused glances into the camera lens, testifying to the unseen but evident presence of the photographer and casually acknowledging the open secret behind the magic.

"Actualities" such as the milling factory workers and the oath-taking president could reasonably be categorized as realistic, even (accidentally or not) journalistic, capturing as they did genuinely spontaneous or newsworthy activities of daily life. But very soon came films of people in studios performing activities of daily life *as if* they were spontaneous: a man sneezing, a couple kissing, a strongman flexing, a señorita twirling, or, in one titillating instance from 1897, a woman in a ball gown being disrobed and bathed by a maid. (Georges Méliès's future wife wore a body stocking for that one, but she certainly *looked* nude.)[21]

Much of the thrill of these brief reels lay in their playful refraction of real life. "For the first time in the history of the world," gushed the *World* (New York) about the film showing the "Widow Jones" and her suitor nuzzling and pecking for eighteen seconds, "it is possible to see what a kiss looks like." That the smooch had been staged rather than snatched—the fond couple was reproducing a scene from a popular play at the *World*'s request—did not diminish its audiences' genuine pleasure; the kiss *looked* true, or true enough, a fleeting slice of real life magically captured, preserved, and shared with a theater full of shadowy onlookers.[22] For most of these features, the filmgoer's most common reaction was neither panic nor confusion but pleasure—"an undisguised awareness (and delight in) film's illusionistic capabilities," one scholar has argued. "The audience's reaction was the antipode to the primitive one: it was an encounter with modernity."[23] And a hallmark of modernity was complexity.

Commercial pressures and rivalries soon elbowed these simple plotless films aside in favor of more creative, even fantastic fare, often using actors, sets, costumes, and shooting scripts. "After all," recalled Albert E. Smith— who with his partner J. Stuart Blackton founded Vitagraph in 1897 and within a year was almost ready to pronounce movies *over*—"how long would the imaginative American mind be intrigued with a tree bending in the wind or a man milking a cow?" Smith used stop-motion photography to make a story out of the wooden figures from his daughter's toy circus and another out of Mr. and Mrs. Hayseed's acrobatic misadventures with the mesmerist.[24] Thomas Edison's studio churned out brisk comedies that featured such surefire gambits as people toppling off chairs and people falling into water, and its hit twenty-second film of a pair of cats sparring in tiny boxing gloves presaged a deathless genre of feline performance art.

Among the most extravagant innovators was Georges Méliès, a French wizard of trick photography and special effects, whose films were often shown either legally or as illegal copies in the United States. He made a lady vanish, shot a rocket into the eye of the Man in Moon, and in *Un Homme de têtes* (1898) had himself filmed theatrically lifting three copies of his own head one by one off his shoulders, laying the jolly noggins on a table, and then joining them in a vocal quartet to the tune of a banjo. Other Méliès films, however, fell into a more ambiguous category, deploying actors, stages, sets, and scripts to re-create real-life events. The most popular, *Le Sacre d'Édouard VII*, had its premiere in London in 1902 on the day that King Edward VII was crowned and included all the pomp and majesty that anyone would expect of a proper coronation: swords and regalia, thrones and canopies, kneeling and strutting, sweeping capes and towering wigs, a balcony full of richly dressed ladies peering down as if from an aerie. But because filming was forbidden in Westminster Abbey, Méliès studied up on protocol, built a set, and hired a wash-house attendant and a dancer to play the royal pair.[25]

Audiences loved the film despite its liberties with the truth, or quite possibly because of them. The fantasist Méliès never pretended to be doing otherwise, openly labeling this film and his other reconstructions—scenes from the Greco-Turkish war of 1897, the eruption of Mt. Pelée, an eleven-part series on the Dreyfus trial—as "Artificially Arranged Scenes."[26] Who cared that they were not strictly authentic if they offered a way for people who were not world travelers to witness grand disasters or for those who were not dukes or duchesses to get close to the new king? Who cared as long as they looked "true"?

Other popular filmed reconstructions involved realistic presentations of historic events centering on people long dead. In Edison's *Execution of Mary, Queen of Scots* (1895), for instance, a blindfolded and richly dressed lady kneels before the executioner, an unobtrusive stop-motion edit allows for the substitution of a richly dressed dummy, the ax falls, and the unfortunate royal's head bounces and rolls on the floor. (It's ghoulish but not gross: there's no blood.) The genre of historical reconstruction was already familiar to the many Americans who had thrilled to the live reenactments of the Battle of the Little Bighorn and other "actual and realistic scenes from life" that were perennial hits at Buffalo Bill's traveling "Wild West" shows or onstage at circuses, fairs, and vaudeville houses.[27] Like the living, breathing actors dressed up as Custer and Crazy Horse, like the openly acknowledged newspaper fakes, like the artfully posed photographs of Christ on the cross and Red Riding Hood in the wood, moving-picture reconstructions of actual or quasi-actual events were never intended to deceive. They instead presented audiences with scenes that looked every bit as heroic or romantic or poignant as their own imaginations could picture, allowing them the thrill of feeling part of the action unfolding in wild mythic spaces while fully appreciating the safety of the bleachers. Even more satisfying than reality, these entertainments improved on reality while keeping it securely under control.

MOVIES GO TO WAR, OR THEREABOUTS

The outbreak of the Spanish-American War in Cuba brought new tensions to the infant filmmaking industry and new urgency to questions of credibility and trust. Suddenly, a genre known for offering everything from fantastic amusements to unembellished slices of life was embracing a novel assignment: making moving images of actual combat. Film, in other words, was doing work that resembled journalism. Ultimately, the resemblance remained notional only because many of the filmmakers who boasted that their work was true to life were also using increasingly ingenious tactics to fake it. In that, however, the filmmakers were not much different from the politicians, the military and public figures, and the print journalists who did their best to turn a quarrel with Old World Spain over its treatment of New World Cuba into a "splendid little war" with noble intent and glorious outcome. The opportunistic saber rattling over what was in fact the accidental explosion of the battleship *Maine* was only the most visible example of the dominance of flag waving, fury, and fantasy over fact in the public conversation about the conflict.[28]

Like their colleagues in print, filmmakers rushed to claim a piece of the action in the war that many Americans saw as a ticket admitting their young nation to a place among the world's imperial powers. Also like their colleagues in print, filmmakers understood that news consumers would have different expectations about how films portraying actual news events would look compared to, say, films of tomcat palookas in boxing gloves. But, again, like their colleagues in print, or at least the yellower ones, many filmmakers were at the same time facing overwhelming pressures (or exploiting irresistible opportunities) to reel in bigger and bigger audiences with sensational and jingoistic reports of America's prowess in the field. The competition was ferocious not just between rival filmmakers but also between filmmakers and the enormous pack of correspondents who were covering the war in every other possible journalistic form and in some nonjournalistic ones, too. The flood of information was immense. So was the flood of fake information. And so were the difficulties of figuring out the difference.

For instance: Theodore Roosevelt and his pell-mell "charge" up San Juan Hill. Everyone, it seemed, had something to say about TR's exploits, and the something they said was occasionally even true. Already in 1898 a figure larger than life, Roosevelt—a preternaturally energetic dynamo and publicity hound who had gone cowboying in the Wild West, fought corruption in the New York State legislature, and worked to clean up New York City's venal police force—had been hankering all his life for a chance to experience firsthand the ultimate test of manhood. As soon as war was declared, Roosevelt resigned his position as assistant secretary of the navy to take a commission as lieutenant colonel in the volunteer cavalry unit that quickly became known as the Rough Riders. He swiftly found all the acclaim and all the thrills he could have desired during the sharp action on the first of July around San Juan Hill, where the Rough Riders and several other regiments, including an all-Black unit of Buffalo Soldiers, assaulted and took the heights while enduring heavy casualties.

The news, the legend, the realism, and the accuracy came in every variety. Visual representations of the engagement at San Juan casually claimed a verisimilitude they seldom merited. In rousing drawings such as *Colonel Roosevelt Leading His "Terrors" in the Famous Charge at San Juan*, newspaper sketch artists who had probably never left the United States portrayed the dauntless colonel brandishing a sword at the head of a troop of soldiers flourishing their rifles and just raring to climb that hill.[29] The popular artist and sculptor Frederic Remington, who traveled to Cuba to write and make illustrations for *Harper's* and Hearst's *New York Journal*, later produced the large oil paintings *The Charge of the Rough Riders* (1898) and *The Scream of Shrapnel at San Juan Hill* (1898), which elevated the ephemeral engravings into full-rigged narrative dramas. On July 8, the *Journal* unfurled a huge double-page headline over what it called "Actual Scenes on Cuban Battlefields, Photographed for the Evening Journal," with a caption that billed them as "the first actual photographs which have come from the scenes of the bloody fighting." But since the practical difficulties of photomechanical reproduction meant that "actual photographs" were still rare in the deadline-driven daily press, the caption eventually got around to conceding the obvious. The rough, muddy engravings of battle scenes the paper ran were merely "actual photographic transcriptions" intended to "reproduc[e]" the product of the camera. Paradoxically, the genuine photographs that had become commonplace in popular magazines such as *Leslie's Illustrated*, *Collier's*, and *Harper's* were perhaps the *least* persuasive visual form as camera operators grappled with recalcitrant equipment, dangerous battlefields, difficulties of access, and the constant fug of smoke that often made their images seem less realistic than the sketch artists'.[30]

Print accounts, too, ran the gamut of credibility. The war hawk Hearst, true to form, mixed huge headlines, provocative illustrations, eye-catching stunts, heavily embellished reports, and patriotic bombast about what he loved to call "the Journal's war"—including dispatches he delightedly wrote and filed from the field over the body of his wounded correspondent— and a stream of argumentative bulletins needling rival papers for alleged fakes and mistakes. Serious organizations such as the *New York Times*, the *New York Evening Post*, and the *Chicago Daily News* struggled to balance their coverage, disdainfully avoiding the excesses of the yellow press while still striving to grip their readers' attention. Some five hundred newspaper correspondents and photographers reportedly made their way to Cuba, many of them from local journals stretching their resources thin so they, too, could make heroes of their own hometown volunteers.[31] Stephen Crane covered the action for Pulitzer's *World* and almost immediately repurposed some of his best material for a collection of short stories, *Wounds in the Rain*, which were virtually indistinguishable in style from his journalism. His attention to Roosevelt was notably restrained compared to that of most other papers; in one of his dispatches, he even bluntly dismissed one of the Rough Riders' first engagements as a "gallant blunder" caused by their "remarkably wrong idea of how the Spaniards bushwhack."[32]

Perhaps the most influential reporter on the Rough Rider beat was Richard Harding Davis, a careful tender of his own image as the archetype of the dashing foreign correspondent. In a rare example of an internal protest against Hearst's brand of journalism, Davis had quit the *Journal* the previous year. He was angry that an illustration by Frederic Remington showing a young, comely, and stark-naked woman being pawed by three "brutal Spaniards" had been grafted onto Davis's report that Spanish officials had searched the clothing of Cuban ladies suspected of carrying messages to the rebels.[33] (The women had in fact been strip-searched, but in private, by matrons.) Davis's principles, however, did not stop him from continuing to report for *Scribner's* and other publications, with such color and brio that he would be widely credited with making Roosevelt's national political career. Davis did not whitewash the squalor and confusion of war, and an attentive reader of his account of the fighting around San Juan Hill would even have understood that the action, although certainly courageous, was no glorious charge with flags flying and bayonets glinting in the sun. Roosevelt had in truth led a deadly slog by a mass of unmounted troops through the tall grass and under the guns of Spanish sharpshooters to take Kettle Hill, then supported other units in their successful attack on the steeper (and more euphoniously named) San Juan Hill.

But for readers thirsty for romance and heroism, Davis's story—which appeared in *Scribner's* in October 1898, by which time most of the U.S. troops had returned home and the Cuba adventure was already fading into misty nostalgia—offered plenty of images that were much more memorable than the ones of sweat and blood. In one indelible passage, Davis wrote of how "Roosevelt, mounted high on horseback, and charging the rifle-pits at a gallop and quite alone, made you feel that you would like to cheer. He wore on his sombrero a blue polka-dot handkerchief, *à la* Havelock, which, as he advanced, floated out straight behind his head, like a guidon."[34] (Roosevelt, to be sure, contributed lavishly to his own legend: Mr. Dooley, perspicacious alter ego of the Chicago columnist Finley Peter Dunne, commented that TR's account of the campaign should have been entitled *Alone in Cuba*.[35]) Two years later William McKinley would choose Roosevelt as a running mate largely on the strength of his moment of military glory, and a year after that McKinley's assassination made the former lieutenant colonel into the president of the United States.

The many filmmakers who dashed off to Cuba soon realized that their balky, bulky motion-picture cameras were not actually very good at capturing pictures of motion, at least the brisk and unpredictable motion characteristic of warfare. The cameraman Billy Bitzer, for instance, who lugged along more than a ton of storage batteries to power Biograph's monster-size camera, didn't even try to get close enough to film the divers recovering bodies from the *Maine* and simply shot what he could see of the ship from the shore.[36] The footage brought back from the theater of battle by Edison's men ran heavily to such scenes as soldiers being tossed in a blanket or marching by in ranks or fording a river or embarking on boats or raising flags on boats or disembarking from boats. All of them were scenes that could be captured in daylight, in safety, with a camera sitting tranquilly on its tripod; none came close to the gloriously tumultuous vision of TR at full gallop trailing his polka-dotted pennant. And to theatergoers expecting their first real glimpse of the furious face of war, watching their brave soldier boys tumbling around in a blanket probably felt about as exciting as sitting through the actuality of the sneezing man.

So most of the filmmakers were soon presenting alternatives using the same kinds of stratagems and tricks they had deployed to part Queen Mary's head from her shoulders or to bring wooden circus toys to life. Méliès, who didn't bother actually traveling to the Caribbean, offered French viewers a series of his characteristic "Artificially Arranged Scenes," at least one of which included a whimsical workaround to the problems of access that plagued cameramen on the spot, such as Bitzer. In *Divers at Work on the Wreck of the* Maine (1898), figures dressed in deep-sea diving suits and huge helmets putter about the wreckage of a sunken ship and pull out a dead body—a flabby and obvious dummy—as live fish dart through the scene. The camera operator had shot the piece through both a layer of gauze, which created the hazy underwater atmosphere, and the glass walls of an aquarium, which provided the fish.[37]

For Edison, Biograph, Vitagraph, Amet, and the other U.S. film companies on (or somewhere near) the fields of battle, however, the war was too serious for whimsy. Primed by unequivocal titles such as *Shooting Captured Insurgents* or *Cuban Ambush* or *Skirmish of Rough Riders*, eager viewers of Edison films hissed and cheered at rebels being lined up against a wall and shot by Spanish soldiers, U.S. troops firing and horses dashing through the smoke, heroes waving their hats as they charged, warriors throwing up their arms and keeling over dead. Nowhere within the film or in the company's publicity materials was any acknowledgment that the rousing action scenes were reenactments, that they had been filmed not in Cuba but around the hilly terrain near the inventor's West Orange studio fourteen miles from Manhattan, or that the "soldiers" had been enthusiastically impersonated by rakishly costumed off-duty members of the New Jersey National Guard. The Edison company's catalog noted that in the film of the insurgents' execution, "The flash of rifles and drifting smoke make a very striking picture," while the ambush boasted "fine smoke effects" and the skirmish featured a troop of riders "leaving behind them a great cloud of dust and smoke" as they advanced up the road. All the statements were true, and all placed more emphasis on the drama, excitement, and realism of the *image* than of the event—more on its entertainment value than on its news value.[38]

The catalog was intended mainly for film distributors rather than for the moviegoers, but the theme of realistic representation was repeated in newspaper commentaries that were much more public, although not necessarily more spontaneous. A very few papers did express mild criticisms; the *Tyrone (PA) Daily Herald* groused that "the war-graph was like the war, a trifle short. The comic pictures were enjoyed, but the war scenes were hardly up to expectations." (Unfortunately, Tyrone's nitpicker didn't specify exactly what he or she had expected in the first place.) Much more common in the news columns were paeans to how "life-like" the films were, how "marvelously realistic," how well the device Edison had taken to calling the War-Graph "reproduces moving, breathing scenes, majestic battleships . . . shown in actual motion."[39] It's a fair guess, though, that many of the bubbly items were not journalistic reports but "puffs," those ubiquitous offerings that looked like news items but actually served up subtle (or not so subtle) product plugs free of charge as lagniappes for advertisers—yet another form of fake news.[40]

Long after the war, some filmmakers enjoyed revealing how they had pulled off their most ingeniously "realistic" effects. The Vitagraph cofounder Albert Smith described in his 1952 memoir how after the *Maine* explosion he and Blackton quickly produced a brief film they called *Tearing Down the Spanish Flag*, which showed Blackton's bare arm reaching into the frame to rip a miniature Spanish flag from the top of a miniature flagpole and then hauling on a cord to raise the equally miniature Stars and Stripes. But when the footage of the tiny props was projected on a thirty-foot screen it had a "sensational" effect, Smith recalled, "and sent us searching for similar subjects. With nationalistic feeling at fever pitch we set out to photograph what the people wanted to see."[41]

What the people wanted to see. Smith seems to be suggesting here that Vitagraph was simply good at divining and responding to popular sentiments that had bubbled up, spontaneous and pure, into the public square—which is as incomplete an explanation of the pressure for war as is the widely debunked myth that the yellow press was responsible for whipping up the whole thing. In the aftermath of the *Maine* disaster, people did flock to "patriotic" films such as Vitagraph's, but those patriotic films also helped push the public temperature high and maintain it there. To keep their public satisfied took art, craft, and guile, and so Smith and Blackton did not hesitate to employ any of those skills.

When audiences began clamoring for images of the great sea battle in Santiago harbor that the filmmakers had completely missed, the undaunted duo re-created the naval encounter on a tabletop in their studio using a hobbyist's arsenal of canvas, wood, cotton, thread, and gunpowder, with models crafted from large commercial photographs of the ships and with smoke supplied by Smith's wife's cigarette. The whole thing, he recalled with pride, had "an atmosphere of remarkable realism." He did acknowledge that "this was a serious compromise of the real battle, but it was hardly a time to weigh deceptions. . . . Jim and I felt less and less remorse of conscience when we saw how much excitement and enthusiasm were aroused by *The Battle of Santiago Bay* and the thirty-minute-long *Fighting with Our Boys in Cuba*."[42] As he had done with the Spanish flag film—and as newspaper fakers had done before him—Smith was essentially arguing that they couldn't help it; the public *wanted* them to fake.

When the partners did manage to travel to Cuba, Smith recalled, sailing on the same ship as Roosevelt and his men, they shot reels and reels of combat footage, including some of the famous charge. That footage, however, turned out to be a visual disappointment, nothing like the magnificent assault described in so many newspapers and magazines. It was "more picking their way through the heavy thicket than charging. This was the assault. Nothing glamorous or hip-hip-hooray or George M. Cohan; the mean vicious deadly business of tracking an enemy who at any moment might be leisurely drawing a bead on the small of your back. It was not until Blackton and I returned to New York that we learned we had taken part in the celebrated 'charge' up San Juan Hill."[43]

It's unclear whether this particular bit of undistinguished footage of the "charge" survives.[44] It's even unclear whether the pair actually made it to Cuba at all; historians have been squabbling for years over whether Smith's wry and vivid account of traveling to the war zone is just as fake as his film of the battle in the harbor.[45] Yet even if Smith had never set foot on the battlefield or seen the charge for himself, his retrospective account of the "mean vicious deadly business" was in fact much more true to life than the epics of glory and glamor that had been turned out by so many of the reporters and filmmakers on the scene. Smith's subversive candor came half a century too late to have any role in shaping the public image of the rough-riding Roosevelt. But in 1898 a true-to-life presentation of men on foot picking their way through a thicket would scarcely have been *what the public wanted to see*. (You imagine; we provide.)

TO BELIEVE OR NOT TO BELIEVE

Obviously, people liked the war films; contemporary accounts teem with references to theaters full of wildly applauding viewers. But the inevitable next question—whether people actually *believed* what to the present-day observer seem to be hopelessly obvious fakes—is both nearly irresistible and not particularly informative. Like any attempts to get inside the minds of people long dead, it's extremely difficult to answer empirically. This one is complicated even more, however, given that so much of the contemporary "evidence" for popular perceptions is rooted in that endless old conversation of mystification, mythologizing, and one-upmanship about who duped whom and who was duped by the new technology. Given how commonly the Clueless Other was invoked by producers, commentators, viewers, and others intent on confirming their own status as nondupes, it's refreshing to come across someone like the former assistant editor at Vitagraph who in 1938 recalled Smith's "notorious hoax" with the model ships. "They tell stories today about contemporaneous audiences being completely hoodwinked by this," he wrote, "but I do not believe they could have been—really. I saw the subject some years later, privately, as a curiosity. It was brazenly crude—even for then."[46]

Rather than rehashing the old debates, we might instead ponder *how* the public chose to see the war films and what they expected from them. Rather than posing the simplistic query "Did viewers believe what they saw on the screen?," we might consider how the films fit into audiences' overall diet of information—journalistic and otherwise—about the war and how their existing relationships with other intelligence and entertainment systems shaped their approach to this one.

Describing the scene as "marvelously realistic" may have meant that the on-screen image of the battleship at sea looked just like the real battleship at sea—*or* that the image constructed out of canvas, cotton, and cigarette smoke looked surprisingly like a real battleship at sea, just as Smith and Blackton's charming wooden circus, although unmistakably a toy, nonetheless looked surprisingly like a real one. Viewers may have accepted images of hat-waving, gun-toting skirmishers as faithful slices of real life that had actually played out right in front of the camera lens—*or*, like the spectators filling the bleachers at Buffalo Bill's Wild West show, they may have seen the dust-ups as satisfying embodiments of what they *imagined* a real-life skirmish with the enemy might look like.

Audiences may have regarded the films that "reproduc[ed] moving, breathing scenes" as perfectly satisfactory in their own right—*or* as admirably clever stratagems to surmount technological impossibilities, like the *Journal*'s imitations that supposedly "reproduced" the "actual" photographs that no one expected it could print in its pages. Audiences may have been bemused by seeing so many different versions of the San Juan charge by so many different filmmakers—*or* they might simply have agreed that the point of all of them, like the point of Richard Harding Davis's melodramatic written account of the same charge, was not their authenticity but that they "made you feel that you would like to cheer."

A distinctive element of film-going was that it required viewers to enter into a particular physical space, one that in its ostentatious devotion to spectacle was as different as could be from their own ordinary home surroundings. Newspaper advertisements from the era offer glimpses into what the film-going public encountered on an evening out at the vaudeville house or entertainment palace. Generally appearing in the columns headed "Amusements," the film ads joined a cheerful jumble of other listings that testified to the vast bazaar of commercialized leisure pursuits, available in cities large and small, that beckoned the bored to taste the delights of comic skits, dramatic readings, magicians, tumblers, minstrel acts, live theater, opera, and myriad other pleasures.

A few film presenters emphasized the information value of their war pictures. While the fighting was still raging, Keith's Union Square Theatre in New York didn't just offer "Still More New War Scenes" from Biograph but also promised to get "By Direct Communication the Very Latest War News" and announce it from the stage.[47] Most of the time, however, the goal was first and foremost exactly what the newspaper heading promised: amusement. The Roof Theater of Chicago's Masonic Temple, for instance, opened its summer season with a bill featuring everything from acrobats to xylophonists and including the War-Graph, which "Present[ed] New and Beautiful Series of War Pictures—the Latest Sensation. And Other Great Acts."[48] An ad in the *Detroit Free Press* for a "palace of amusement" called the Wonderland enticed viewers with Biograph's "Fine List of Novelty Pictures," which included "Bathing Girls' Hurdle Race" followed by "4th Inf. U.S.A., distinguished in the Battle of San Juan Hill."[49]

In Atlanta, the Hibernian Hall advertised a Christmas-season benefit on behalf of the Sisters of St. Joseph Loretto Convent that was anything but sacred, featuring "Edison's War-Graph: Life, Motion, Realism—the 'Rough Riders' will thrill any American heart. Don't miss the wonderful entertainment of the nineteenth century!"[50] In the *New York Times*, the Eden Musee, already famous for its wax figures of "All the War Heroes" and the huge collection of war films it would air one after the other for hours at a stretch, was touting its Hungarian Gypsy musicians along with cinematograph pictures of San Juan and Santiago.[51] And Hazard's Pavilion in Los Angeles advertised a Great Republican Rally for the gubernatorial candidate on Thursday night and Edison's reproduction of "40 Grand Views—Exciting Scenes. . . . War ships under full steam firing their great guns" on Friday.[52]

So for those who paid their quarter or half-dollar and sat down to watch the "new and beautiful" gunfights that came on after the acrobats had tumbled onstage and before the xylophonists took up their mallets, to cheer on the hurdling bathing beauties and then the veterans of San Juan Hill, to tap their toes to the czardas and then clap their hands for the Rough Riders, to support the nuns by thrilling to the "wonderful entertainment" of the age, to hear a rousing campaign speech and then witness a rousing naval victory, the war films were just one element in a barrage of genres and sensory impressions that were all the more intense for being shared with hundreds of rapt strangers.

In his famous essay on the picture palaces of Weimar Berlin and their "cult of distraction," Siegfried Kracauer described the characteristic mixture of live and on-screen entertainments offered in those palaces as *"the total artwork (Gesamtkunstwerk) of effects"* that "assaults every one of the senses using every possible means." He argued that the discontinuity between the flat, two-dimensional nature of film and the vivid three-dimensionality of live performance made clear that the moving pictures were merely illusions.[53] But two-dimensional or not, war films did share other, more important qualities with the other acts on the bill of entertainment. All of them were seen as more engaging than enlightening. All enticed viewers with sensation and emotional engagement. Racing bathing beauties were exciting; what viewers saw of the war was exciting. Prestidigitators were magical; what they saw of the war was magical. Acrobats were spectacular; what they saw of the war was spectacular. The question whether what they saw of the war was *true*—whether people knew that they were seeing the hills of New Jersey rather than Cuba, whether they saw through the fakery of the miniature boats in the canvas tub—seems rather beside the point.

Yet the war films differed from the comedians, the violinists, and the other entertainers in one consequential way. Besides the world of spectacle, the films were also deeply entangled in the widespread jingoistic support for the "splendid" conflict that would culminate in a brutal intervention in the Philippines and firmly establish the United States in the ranks of the imperial powers of the world. Whether the films were seen as presenting a truthful picture of the war or not, they *were* seen by many as presenting a positive and patriotic picture of the war, a picture that both encouraged and confirmed public support for the endeavor.

The vast edifice of public information about the fighting, which also included the respectable press, the yellow press, magazines, paintings, illustrations, spectacles, fiction, and tales told by both heroes and "heroes," was in large part riddled with illusion, sensation, enthusiasm, and fakery. As just one part of that edifice, the films obviously didn't bear sole responsibility for either causing or supporting the war, and they most likely just blended into and reinforced the hoopla. But given the high stakes of the war, anything that contributed to the flow of information about its conduct took on enormous importance.

The yellow press, which like the films sought to entertain and like the films also claimed to be true to life, has been strenuously criticized for its signal failures in reporting on the war. But it did have a counterforce within its own ranks: the small but increasingly influential part of the newspaper press that was staking out an identity as respectable, trustworthy, accurate, and vocally opposed to faking. Throughout the war, papers such as the *Chicago Daily News* and the *New York Times* frequently expressed their disgust for the "tremendous whoppers" disseminated by the yellow journals. Four days after the explosion of the *Maine*, E. L. Godkin's highbrow *New York Evening Post* let loose a blast of indignation at the sensational press's "gross misrepresentation of the facts [and] deliberate invention of tales calculated to excite the public."[54] The respectable papers were not just carrying out their professional duty in covering the war in a way they saw as responsible but also conducting professional boundary work by branding other papers as *not* responsible, not credible, and not living up to what the respectable papers were working to establish as acceptable journalistic standards. The mainstream papers were claiming the authority to police their own profession, to call out blunders, and to demand corrections. Even though that authority was often ignored or ineffective, it also represented a pioneering effort by journalists to hold other journalists accountable for failures, fumbles, and fakes.

The film industry was different. In its earliest years, it included no such authority, self-proclaimed or not, and no such division, acknowledged or not. Filmmakers pursued innovations and jostled for ever-greater audiences; they revealed their own fakes as a sign of their cleverness or undercut rivals by betraying the latter's fakes; they asserted their own savviness and ridiculed Clueless Others. But none measured their success by their contributions to the public good, and none staked their reputations on their fidelity to truthful information or their principled refusal to fake. Censors, official or otherwise, might object to too much flesh or too much crime or too much canoodling in darkened theaters, and the film industry would gradually set up policing mechanisms of its own, such as the National Board of Review of Motion Pictures and the Hays Office, to head off regulation from the outside. But the concern was decency, not accuracy: no internal professional boundaries marked off the credible from the fabulous; no producers of films carried out boundary work to exclude any of their fellows as fakers; and no studio would demand another studio correct its fabrications or mistakes.

In 1922, with *Nanook of the North*, Robert Flaherty invented the form that would come to be called the full-length "documentary." His film purported to follow an Inuk named Nanook, his family, and other Inuit as they went about their daily lives in the Canadian Arctic just as their ancestors had for generations before them. But although Flaherty did drag his cameras to Hudson Bay, much of the action he filmed there was as staged, manipulated, or invented as Edison's "Cuban" adventures in New Jersey had been. The Inuit had not actually hunted walrus with harpoons for years and were much more comfortable with guns; the seal they pulled out through a blow-hole in the ice after a comic tug-of-war had really been dead the whole time; the igloo was built without part of its wall so the cameras could fit in. But *Nanook* didn't really break any rules for documentary making because rules for documentary making didn't yet exist. Flaherty's intent had not really been to replicate reality but to preserve images (heavily romanticized, to be sure) of a traditional society about to be swallowed by a modern world, and if that meant faking the traditions, it was all in a good cause.[55]

The film industry was born at exactly the moment when both newspapers and news photographers were struggling to professionalize themselves. It began developing its identity at a time when citizens were making critical decisions about who they were as a nation. Yet even though the affordances of the new technology of film could have earned it an important place in both the journalistic professionalization project and the public debate, it instead devoted its ingenuity to entertaining viewers with costumed armies and bathtub navies. "What [technologies] are good for is a consequence, not a determinant, of their use," Bruce Hackett and Lauren Lutzenhiser remind us, and "they contribute to the definition of the problems for which they are solutions."[56] If entertainment was what film was good for, faking was *not* defined as a problem. And it needed no solution.

NOISES IN THE ETHER

Of the new communications technologies of the era, radio was both the uncanniest and the most chaotic. The realm known as "the ether" or "the airwaves" that began to reveal itself in the later nineteenth century was a frontier where the navy and commercial shippers and inventors and entrepreneurs and amateurs jostled to stake claims, a frontier controlled by no single authority and operating largely free of gatekeepers and rules. The ether itself was a commodity both finite and invisible, filled with chatter that was audible only to those who possessed a magic talisman made of tubes or crystals, comprehensible only to those who knew the code, and often difficult to scrutinize, preserve, or even trace. Although the consumer of photographs or films could make judgments about their authenticity and credibility by examining the work that went into their creation, the radio listener was confronted with the challenge of evaluating a technological product that had no evident authors and no visible "handwork."

For those listeners coming to be known as "hams," however, the perplexities of the ether offered irresistible opportunities. An anarchic breed of amateurs and tinkerers, they built their own crystal sets using hardware scraps and electrical leftovers and viewed the airwaves as their slightly more grown-up version of a backyard treehouse—on which the "No Gurls Aloud" sign was often still hanging. For many middle-class American boys and young men at the beginning of the twentieth century, who were torn between conflicting social pressures toward a traditional gentility on the one hand and a hearty, self-reliant, Rooseveltian manliness on the other, becoming adept with a mysterious and potent new technology offered a socially acceptable escape into a realm where parents couldn't follow and sweethearts and sisters wouldn't, a place where expertise and ingenuity were prized and the normal rules of decorum didn't apply.[57]

Ethereal chaos ensued. The hams interfered with messages destined for President Theodore Roosevelt on his visit to the fleet off Cape Cod; they clogged the airwaves just as the U.S. Navy's Great White Fleet was making its triumphal return home in February 1909 from its year-long goodwill tour around the world. As they reveled in the Wild West freedom of the airwaves and fought any attempts by private companies and the military to control them, some graduated from overenthusiasm to mischief. "Amateurs would send out fake orders to naval vessels, purporting to come from admirals; they broadcast false distress calls and had Coast Guard and other vessels running wildly about, trying to find the ship in distress. . . . There being no law to cover most of the amateurs' tricks, few or no police searches were made for them, and the names and locations of the worst offenders were unknown. When remonstrated with by air, these were apt to respond with curses and obscenity."[58] Picture the amateur operator darting into the ether, pulling a prank, and melting away again to snicker over his feat with his comrades: it was just as easy and just as rewarding for a ham with an outlaw streak to disrupt the ether in 1910 as it would be for a hacker with an outlaw streak to do so in 2020.

But in April 1912 the deaths of 1,500 men, women, and children in the frigid North Atlantic sparked some big changes for the hams and for wireless operators in general. After the first distress call came in from the Marconi man on the crippled *Titanic*, amateur operators up and down the U.S. coast took to their transmitters to plead for news, share rumors, and sow misinformation; to this day, no one knows for sure whether the message "All Titanic passengers safe; towing to Halifax" that was reprinted in dozens of newspapers was an unfortunate error or a brutal hoax. In the aftermath of the unthinkable catastrophe, fingers pointed everywhere, some of them directly at the hams—the "wireless triflers" or "wireless pirates," as some editorialists called them. Having gotten in everyone's way by swarming the airwaves during the attempts at rescue, they should, some thought, be held responsible for the "cruel and heartless . . . bogus messages" that had tantalized the world with a flare of false hope. Particularly incensed were British officials, who complained that the false information had caused reinsurance rates at Lloyd's of London to fall by half and who hinted darkly at plots to manipulate the financial system.[59]

The chaos, along with revelations about the numerous failures, missteps, and mysteries involving even official wireless communications, helped lead four months later to the passage of the Radio Act of 1912 to regulate the ether. Among its provisions was the requirement that anyone who operated a radio transmitter, including amateurs, be licensed and that transmissions by anyone "not engaged in the transaction of bona fide commercial business by radio communication"—that is, anyone who did it for fun—be confined to the least desirable part of the spectrum. And down near the end, in section 7, the act provided "that a person, company, or corporation within the jurisdiction of the United States shall not knowingly utter or transmit, or cause to be uttered or transmitted, any false or fraudulent distress signal or call or false or fraudulent signal, call, or other radiogram of any kind."[60]

The act represented Congress's first significant assertion of its power to regulate the airwaves as a public good. Although it focused on point-to-point communication and did not actually mention broadcasting, the act can arguably also be seen as a landmark moment when the federal government claimed the power and the will to ban fake news from the public airwaves. With both enforcement and compliance spotty, however, it was also the first of many instances of regulations that had no teeth. In any case, the Radio Act's restrictions on the hams became moot in 1917, when as a wartime measure the navy took control of the airwaves and ordered all amateur activity shut down. Nevertheless, the Radio Act of 1912 would not be the last time the government would make a stab at policing lies in the ether—and hams would not be the last fakers that government would try to rein in by law.

5

"WE DID NOT CALL IT PROPAGANDA"

Everything about the Great War surprised people. The smoldering tensions Europe had managed to contain for years—imperialist, nationalist, militarist, economic, even familial (given how many of the continent's crowned heads could call Queen Victoria "grandmamma")—suddenly flared into armed conflict because an open car made a wrong turn in an out-of-the-way Balkan capital and inadvertently delivered its august passengers straight to the startled assassin who thought he and his co-conspirators had already missed their chance. The sunny Progressive Era faith that reason, science, efficiency, and goodwill could solve the problems of modern society was crushed under four appalling years of industrialized carnage that no one could figure out how to stop. A "Great Push" on the Somme that Allied leaders were sure would finally break the stalemate in the trenches chewed through nearly twenty thousand Tommies in its first hours, killed or wounded more than one million soldiers on both sides before it was halted four months later by the approach of winter, and in the end bought the Allies a grand total of about six miles of territory. Governments, armies, corporations, and the increasingly massive media made intense efforts to keep enlistments up, morale strong, and public support unwavering throughout the accelerating catastrophe by stepping up an unprecedented blitz of disinformation. It was World War I that gave propaganda a bad name, shifting the generally innocuous term referring to the organization of mass information into a synonym for manipulation and deceit by institutions of power.[1]

And in a final shattering surprise, a clear message emerged from the wreckage of battle: that kind of propaganda gave journalism a bad name, too. Not so long before the war, serious U.S. journalists had confidently been presenting themselves to readers as authoritative professionals with special skills for telling the truth and exposing the fake. During the war, however, government and military propagandists usurped the journalists' jurisdiction over the presentation of factual information and their authority to police their own profession.

Even more, at times the propagandists usurped the very guise of journalism itself, marking the beginning of what we might call "fake *journalism*." Whereas the term *fake news* has referred to a wide range of hoaxes, jokes, deceptions, disguises, and mistakes in the information published by news organizations, *fake journalism* is a better term for the creation and spread of disinformation by institutions *pretending* to be or *acting like* news organizations, in forms crafted to *look* as if they were authentic productions of an independent press. Fake journalism had been impossible before the establishment of real journalism, professionalized journalism based on agreed-upon ethical and practical principles and carried out according to accepted standards. Fake journalism—a phenomenon that would only grow in power and influence—worked by appropriating and exploiting the credibility and authority that real journalists had been striving so hard to earn. Sometimes it attacked the credibility and authority of individual real journalists, too.

After the war was over at last, genuine journalists found themselves mistrusted, embarrassed, on the defensive—in part because of their own flawed war reporting but also because of the lingering taint of the government's fakes. They also found themselves outrun by a new kind of newspaper whose jaded readers didn't even seem to care whether it told the truth or not and by the maturing technology of radio that was making up its own rules as it went along. Serious journalists found themselves starting nearly from scratch in an effort to reclaim their jurisdiction over the provision of truthful descriptions of the world and prove their differences from the fakers.

SELLING THE GREAT WAR

Almost immediately after the German invasion of Belgium in August 1914, the British and French governments launched propaganda operations to create and distribute leaflets, books, posters, illustrated newspapers, news reports, and films both at home and abroad. All sought to compensate for the less-than-compelling military and diplomatic rationales for the war by offering a visceral one: saving civilization from barbarism. The Germans, the messages went, were subhuman savages lusting for conquest and led by a kaiser who, as many still remembered, had in 1900 urged the German troops departing for the Western intervention in the Boxer Rebellion to be as ruthless against their enemy as Attila the Hun had been against his. (Helping to refresh that recollection was a poem written in 1914 by the arch-Briton Rudyard Kipling that began, "For all we have and are / For all our children's fate / Stand up and take the war / The Hun is at the gate!") Although the Germans tried hard to match the Allies with propaganda efforts of their own—including a direct attempt at fake journalism, the secret purchase in 1915 of a fading New York newspaper called the *Evening Mail*, which did not regain any luster under its new masters—their efforts were never as good either at making their own case or at the essential propagandistic task of demonizing their enemy.[2]

The Germans did, of course, have much to answer for. The invasion, a gross violation of Belgium's neutrality, was carried out with immense brutality against soldiers, civilians, and property. By the spring of 1915, moreover, German destroyers were shelling British shore towns, German zeppelins were raiding Allied cities from the air, and German ground troops were lobbing chlorine gas at Allied soldiers in the field. (The Allies would soon begin compiling their own records of chemical warfare, aerial bombings that killed civilians, and other "uncivilized" actions.) And on May 7, a German U-boat sank the British passenger ship *Lusitania*, killing nearly 1,200 civilians, more than 10 percent of them U.S. citizens. Public outrage among the Allies and the Americans, who at this point were still officially neutral, was scarcely soothed either by Germany's (accurate) insistence that the passenger ship had been carrying munitions or by the German embassy's reminder that it had given fair warning by placing ads in a number of U.S. newspapers in the days before the liner's departure cautioning Americans that "travelers sailing in the war zone on ships of Great Britain or her allies do so at their own risk."[3]

As the war ground on in Europe, American newspapers served their readers a jumble of eyewitness accounts, intrepid scoops, censored reports, adventure yarns, fabrications, repackaged propaganda, fake films and photographs, and pontifications; it was left to readers to sort them all out. Like correspondents in other wars, the eager U.S. reporters who rushed to cover the Great One found themselves subjected to rigorous censorship and news management by the warring powers. Visual images in particular were seen as so potentially dangerous to morale and security that in the early days the belligerents strove to ban cameras from the front entirely, whether in the hands of professionals or amateurs, and they were always strictly controlled.

Even so, ingenuity and persistence could pay off. Journalists told stories of dodging military authorities or cajoling or fibbing or bluffing their way through; they pulled off larky professional coups such as wending their way to the front by bicycle or horse-drawn cab; they were arrested in war zones, thrown into prisons, threatened with execution as spies. The censorship wasn't always airtight, but the leaks that were flaunted in U.S. papers did not necessarily represent a triumph for the truth. The veteran muckraker Will Irwin later recalled that some newspapers, "conspicuously one in the metropolis" (the sort of locution that usually referred to Hearst's paper), "used to enrich the carefully censored dispatches of [their] correspondents in Paris or London with vivid, harrowing and imaginative details . . . and [to] head them with the correspondent's by-line."[4]

As always, the rivalries, confusions, and limitations of war reporting could transform even the most diligent reporters into fabulists, purposefully or not. Those still or movie cameras that did make their way into combat weren't actually much use, failing so miserably at capturing the tumultuous actions of battle that faked images were more common than real ones. The November 1915 issue of *Literary Digest* described for U.S. moviegoers exactly how the combat scenes they saw in the theaters had been staged by costumed actors in the "quiet country footpath[s]" back in England.[5]

Many American reporters, thrilled to be part of the manly adventure of battle, deliberately and delightedly cultivated the persona of the devil-may-care war correspondent who laughed at danger and did any-thing for a good story. Even more eager and even less credible were the amateurs, the business travelers and other ordinary citizens whom some American editors pressed into service as acting correspondents in an effort to outflank the belligerents' restrictions on their genuine reporters. As the longtime New York journalist Emmet Crozier wrote in 1959 in his book about U.S. reporters on the Western front, some of those laymen approached their task "with a holiday spirit." One of the "shameless fak-ers" allegedly turned in a masterpiece beginning: "I was riding on a train near Paris when we suddenly heard shooting. The train stopped and we got off and looking over a hill we saw a battle in full swing. As I looked, I saw one soldier jab another through the head with a bayonet."

That shameless faker, Crozier quickly assured his readers, was immediately stripped of his credentials. It was, he insisted, "irrespon-sible amateurs" like that one, not his own professional colleagues, who most vigorously exploited the understanding that "atrocity tales had a news value considerably higher than routine war stuff" and that even the most "improbable and absurd" stories could be printed with-out verification.[6]

But the nonamateur Crozier was hardly guiltless; his book, he con-fessed, was in part a four-decades-late penance for his own youthful complicity in faking war stories. As a rookie on the *New York Globe* in the fall of 1918, chafing at being tied to the rewrite desk while colleagues were sending sizzling dispatches from the Meuse-Argonne, he had accepted without question the dramatic stories regularly brought in by an old legman named Moore, who insisted he got them from schmoozing with veterans returned from the war zone. "At the time," Crozier conceded, "I must have known some of his tales were contrived but if I had misgiv-ings, conscience was stilled by the thought that Moore was supporting an invalid wife and needed my help to keep his job. Besides . . . it was my only chance, albeit vicarious, to be a war correspondent."[7] There again, the desire for drama overcame the boring old mandate for accuracy.

Whereas most U.S. news organizations, like most of their readers at that point, were either neutral or isolationist about the war in Europe, the cor-respondents on the ground ran the gamut. The ace *New York Tribune* correspondent Richard Harding Davis likened the German soldiers after the sacking and burning of Louvain to "men after an orgy" who were "incoherent with excesses"—which, he insisted, he could see even though the Germans had locked him inside a railway carriage during most of the rampage.[8] Then, a week after Davis's report appeared, five U.S. correspondents who had been covering the German advance sent the AP a telegram, widely reprinted, in which they pledged their "professional and personal word" that most of the reports of atrocities in Louvain were "groundless" and that "refugees with stories of atrocities were unable to supply direct evidence." (Two of the five signers wrote for the noticeably anti-British *Chicago Tribune*.)[9]

Unlike most Europeans, in other words, U.S. readers during the first years of the war could be exposed to news and perspectives from all sides. But the ready availability of that torrent of coverage brought news consumers a challenge of its own: the task of reconciling for themselves the wildly differing viewpoints and widely divergent facts about what was going on overseas and deciding which reporters and news organizations they could—or *preferred* to—trust as truthful. (We report; you pick what you like.)

Those decisions may have become somewhat easier in May 1915, less than a week after the sinking of the *Lusitania*, when the British government released the so-called Bryce report, the result of its official examination into the atrocities allegedly committed by German soldiers during their invasion of Poor Little Belgium the previous summer.[10] The accusations were incendiary, the alleged conduct violating not just the rules of war but also the most basic tenets of humanity: according to the report, surrendering soldiers had been bayoneted, prisoners abused, women raped, children mutilated, civilians massacred, hostages killed, houses plundered, towns burned, cultural treasures demolished.

The report certainly sounded authoritative, offering a wealth of intimate details allegedly taken directly from people who had witnessed the events. And it was published under the imprimatur of Lord Bryce, a widely respected scholar who had been a Liberal member of Parliament and an ambassador to the United States. But with its emphasis on luridly sexualized violence committed by brutish aggressors against pure and defenseless victims, this official publication was also a masterpiece of propaganda that exploited and reinforced the public's righteous fury over what was already being widely described in the Allied press as "the rape of Belgium."

As few readers at the time allowed themselves to notice, however, the depositions that were the basis of the report would never have stood up in court, having been gathered from soldiers and Belgian refugees who had not been placed under oath and who did not attach their names. Most of the commission members apparently felt pressured *not* to challenge the image of the blood-crazed Hun that was the British government's best selling point for the war. Assuming a stance of calculated passivity, the commissioners did not check facts, reinterview witnesses, or verify evidence presented in the depositions.[11] They did not, in other words, confirm the allegations—but they would not deny them either. The denials came later, after the war, when several investigations debunked most of the report's findings as heavily sensationalized. No one ever produced a single handless Belgian baby.

But in 1915, in the midst of an unexpectedly savage conflict that had not, in fact, ended by its first Christmas, the fake news worked. Translated into thirty languages and lengthily excerpted, often with scathing commentary, by newspapers around the world, the report helped imprint a lasting image of Germans as subhuman monsters on whose defeat depended the fate of civilization. As British officials had hoped, reaction was particularly intense in the United States. The language of the coverage was profoundly emotional, the tone urgent and usually unskeptical.

"BRYCE REPORT SHOWS MURDER LUST AND LOOT," screamed a typical front-page headline in the *Oregon Daily Journal* (Portland) of May 12, 1915; "British Government Commission Investigating Alleged Atrocities in Belgium Convinced Stories Are True. NO PARALLEL FOR THE LAST THREE CENTURIES."

"TERRIFIC ARRAIGNMENT OF GERMANS IN BELGIUM," bellowed the *Richmond (VA) Times Dispatch* on May 13; "Deliberate and Organized Massacres of Civilian Population, Accompanied by Horrible Outrages, Fully Established."

"TERRIBLE DESTRUCTION INFLICTED ON BELGIUM," howled the *Charlotte (NC) Daily Observer* on May 16; "All the Rules of Warfare Violated by German Hordes." In a weird hierarchy of victimhood, a *New York Tribune* editorialist ranked the (mostly fabricated) sexual abuse of Belgian women as more noteworthy, even more thrilling, than the (genuine) deaths of American women on the *Lusitania*. "While our own women were only slain," the piece declaimed, "those of Belgium were outraged."

Reading the Bryce report, "we Americans will feel the thrill of admiration, of wonder, that came with the first news that Belgium had chosen to fight, to die, rather than to submit. We who had Lexington, Concord and Bunker Hill behind us understood and glorified the resistance of Liège and Antwerp."[12] Poor Little Belgium!

THE UNITED STATES GOES TO WAR

Deeply conflicted about joining the fighting in Europe, in November 1916 Americans reelected President Woodrow Wilson, who ran on the slogan "He kept us out of war." Less than six months later, he took the country straight into it. The about-face, building for months, was finally sparked by the release of the Zimmermann telegram and the Germans' decision to resume all-out U-boat warfare in the North Atlantic. By then, Wilson already had support from many American legislators and citizens who agreed with the idealistic mission of asserting progressive U.S. values in the world or the more combative one of saving innocent victims from the savage invader, while others looked forward to the economic boom that waging large-scale war could bring. But the White House knew it would take some strenuous work to unify the divided country and gird everyone for the necessary sacrifices to come, from taxes raised to lives disrupted to sons and husbands lost. That was where the Committee on Public Information (CPI) came in.

The CPI was *not* sowing propaganda, or at least its leaders and advocates insisted that it wasn't. Established by executive order in April 1917, the CPI preferred to think of its task as a public-relations campaign using the most modern and efficient methods of persuasion to convince civilians of a necessary truth: that fighting to save democracy was both essential and just. The committee was headed by the fiercely progressive journalist George Creel and included three cabinet members, among them Secretary of the Navy Josephus Daniels, whose newspaper had been the proud "printed voice" behind the Wilmington coup of 1898. After the war, Creel would applaud the committee's efforts as "a vast enterprise in salesmanship, the world's greatest adventure in advertising," and boast that "there was no part of the great war machinery that

FIGURE 5.1 An unsubtle reminder of the "rape of Belgium" urges Americans to buy Liberty Bonds, ca. 1918.

Source: Library of Congress Prints and Photographs Division.

we did not touch, no medium of appeal that we did not employ. The printed word, the spoken word, the motion picture, the telegraph, the cable, the wireless, the poster, the sign-board—all these were used in our campaign to make our own people and all other peoples understand the causes that compelled America to take arms."[13]

He also insisted, in italics, that the CPI had been "*in no degree . . . an agency of censorship, a machinery of concealment or repression. Its emphasis throughout was on the open and the positive. . . .* We did not call it propaganda, for that word, in German hands, had come to be associated with deceit and corruption." (Many Germans, meanwhile, including

General Erich Ludendorff, were blaming their humiliating defeat on their own inferior propaganda, arguing that their side had lacked the "iron will" to emulate their enemy by using words as ruthlessly as weapons.)[14]

Indeed, the CPI, heavily staffed with progressive journalists, in many ways felt like a huge muckraking magazine, sharing with the muckrakers a genuine belief in the value of truth and a moral certainty that giving what they preferred to label "publicity" to accurate information and facts would spur readers to make the right choices and take the right actions.[15] Not calling the committee's work "propaganda," however, was itself a piece of propaganda. Here was an enormous government enterprise deploying the government's vast powers and resources to "fight for the *minds* of men," as Creel put it, and "for the 'conquest of their convictions,'" and he did not exaggerate in his claim that "the battle-line ran through every home in every country."[16] The CPI provided textbooks for schoolchildren and suggested subjects for cartoonists; it sent film stars on speaking tours and produced movies about liberty loans; it set up information bureaus to reach women and union workers and African Americans and the foreign born; it slapped up recruiting posters that promised the enlistee he would get the girl and told the girl she should reserve her heart for the enlistee.

The CPI reached deep into journalism, too, its Division of News distributing thousands of press releases that carried a range of tidings both morale boosting and belligerent as well as the daily *Official Bulletin*, America's first-ever government-produced daily paper. The *Bulletin* served up carefully vetted information about government regulations and presidential addresses, announced new laws, reported the latest statistics on draftees and liberty loans, and offered suggestions for how citizens could help the war effort, from planting vegetables in the backyard to driving Red Cross trucks in France. Although the CPI's own publications were not quite "fake journalism"—the government didn't hide its involvement—the newspapers around the country that happily filled their columns with the CPI's offerings didn't always make clear where these reports came from or how they were different from the work of the paper's own reporters. The Division of News also served as a "central information bureau," as Creel dubbed it, offering a convenient one-stop shop for overworked reporters struggling to nail down a story. Insisting that his role was not to exert control over what the newspapers printed, Creel argued that voluntary self-censorship by the press would keep undesirable items *out*.[17] But the CPI's diligent distribution of its own versions of the "news" and its standing offer to ease the workload of stressed-out correspondents everywhere gave it enormous influence over what went *in* the news, too.

The CPI's activity was focused on a clear message: supporting the war was patriotic, and questioning it subversive. But other official and quasi-official mechanisms worked to ensure that subversives, however defined, were rooted out and punished. The Censorship Board—on which Creel served, along with the notoriously reactionary postmaster general Albert Burleson and a clutch of military men—was empowered to keep "dangerous" publications from entering or leaving the country. New laws billed as wartime necessities to guard against sedition, sabotage, espionage, threats to the president, and trading with the enemy were interpreted so broadly that citizens could be jailed and publications could be banned from the mails for expressing even the mildest reservations about the war effort. The most famous victim, the socialist leader Eugene Debs, was sentenced to a decade in prison for a speech discouraging men from enlisting: "You need to know," he had told his audience, "that you are fit for something better than slavery and cannon fodder." The Justice Department welcomed the vigilant help provided by the quarter-million civilian volunteers of the American Protective League as they spied on neighbors, broke into private homes, stole mail, infiltrated socialist and pacifist groups, and bullied aliens and draft resisters, all in the name of sniffing out and punishing "disloyalty."[18]

Unlike reporters on the home front, correspondents on the front lines could cherish no illusions of independence. Objections by members of Congress and a sharp campaign of opposition by many newspapers had foiled President Wilson's efforts to claim broad powers of control over the press at home. But he heartily endorsed the strict regime of censorship imposed by military authorities on reports from the field of battle that could essentially transform the columns of war news into government-approved fake journalism. Any reporter who wanted credentials to accompany the American Expeditionary Force had to get his newspaper to post a $10,000 bond guaranteeing his behavior as "a gentleman of the Press." Correspondents had to agree to submit all copy to military censors. They could not name names or cite locations; they could not quote any officer without permission. And they had to swear, in writing, that they would "convey the truth to the people of the United States"—a delicate task, indeed, given that they were also specifically forbidden to report anything that would lower morale, "embarrass" their country, or help the enemy.[19]

Wrangles with the press officers were common. Some clever reporters who devised stratagems for evading censorship, such as sending their copy home in private letters or travelers' luggage, found that officialdom had plenty of ways to strike back. The former sports editor and drama critic Heywood Broun, a perennially rumpled pacifist with a sturdy disdain for the officer class, did a six-month tour in France for the *New York Tribune*, a Republican-leaning paper with little love for Wilson. In January 1918, after Broun's return home placed him beyond the reach of the military censors, the *Tribune* ran his savage articles exposing the army's colossal supply failures and slamming military censorship as oppressive, undemocratic, and untruthful.[20]

Creel responded with ferocity. Seizing on minor factual errors Broun had made—and admitted—in a later piece about lapses in security for generals traveling by sea, Creel blew them up into a bill of attainder against both the reporter and the paper, standing them before what he called the "moral firing squad of patriotic reprobation" in retribution for their "work in aid and comfort of the enemy."[21] Doubtless by design, Creel's focus on the potentially perilous (and generally imaginary) consequences of Broun's modest slips rather than on his critiques of the genuine supply snafus and the burden of censorship offered military authorities a publicly palatable excuse to relieve the *Tribune* of its $10,000 bond. The army and the government were indulging in the classic maneuver of transforming a journalist's small mistakes into acts of malicious fakery, specifically to undermine the credibility of a persistent critic.

In this feverish atmosphere, where critical commentary could be treated as treason and extremism in the right cause was lavishly rewarded, government officials had plenty of assistance distributing propaganda and fake news in the guise of truth: many Americans eagerly volunteered their help in spreading the word. Rumors, slanders, atrocity stories, and fabrications leapt like trench lice from newspapers to citizens, citizens to citizens, citizens to newspapers, often undergoing embellishment and "improvement" along the way. One particularly durable and devastating canard that began circulating internationally in the spring of 1917 offers a case study in the lasting power of a well-crafted propaganda lie and the enduring damage a fake could do to public understanding.

THE PHANTOM CORPSE FACTORY

From London to Paris to Hong Kong to Singapore to Sydney to Rio de Janeiro to Washington, DC, newspapers trumpeted the shocking story: the Germans were bundling up the bodies of their own dead soldiers and hauling them to *Kadaververwertungsanstalten*, "corpse-exploitation establishments," where their fat was boiled down to make grease for munitions and their bones were ground up for pig feed.[22]

Although the "corpse-factory" fake seemed a spontaneous sensation, it was in fact carefully crafted by powerful institutions of government in quiet collusion with two of Britain's most influential news organizations: the press empire of Lord Northcliffe, which included both the million-plus-circulation *Daily Mail* and the lordly *Times*, and the Reuters news agency, which had clients around the globe. What began as a cluster of accounts—chiefly in quasi-official Belgian refugee papers and the French press—about Germans desecrating cemeteries and abusing corpses was given new life after two Northcliffe journalists seized on an offhand report they found in a Berlin newspaper about a factory that processed *Kadaver* into fats and bone meal. Opportunistically mistranslating the word that Germans traditionally used to refer only to *animal* remains, the *Times* and the *Mail* then swiftly elaborated the deliberately misleading item into a lurid saga about "Hun Ghouls," which they first reported on April 16, 1917, and then expanded the next day—not incidentally, less than two weeks after the United States had entered the war against Germany—and which was immediately picked up by Reuters.

The publication of the story evidently had the covert approval, if not the outright encouragement, of the British government. In 1917, both Northcliffe himself and the general manager of Reuters held positions in the official propaganda operation. The government had also just brokered a secret deal giving itself majority ownership and control of the news agency, which was now regularly sending telegrams to its unknowing international clients that were, as the Foreign Office had requested, "composed in the interest of the Government"—in other words, fake journalism. Letters from indignant readers and arch nondenials from British politicians kept the corpse story bubbling for weeks. Northcliffe did his part to impress the message on the newest—and freshest—Allied power with a widely circulated opinion piece cautioning Americans that "the killing of the Prussian cobra is a slow task, but one essential to the future happiness of the world." The piece included a studiously matter-of-fact reference to Germany's material deprivations. "[H]er soap, largely mixed with clay, sells for $1.25 a pound," Northcliffe told America. "She has to boil up her corpses to obtain fats to make glycerin for the manufacture of explosives. She needs oil of all kinds."[23]

Steady readers of war news who might have been suffering from atrocity fatigue were surely reawakened by this story with its shivery frisson of the ultimate in ghoulishness and its extravagant confirmation of the general mandate to hate the Hun. With so many publications around the world vouching for the story, who could doubt it was true? Some pro-Allied newspapers and some readers did publicly question the truth of the story or point out the translation "error." A number of the most important U.S. papers chose not to mention the tale, and the *New York Times* suggested in a brief piece on April 20 that the whole thing could have been "somebody's notion of an April Fool joke," a ritual that was "customary for German papers to indulge in." But the story was both omnipresent enough to sound persuasive and disgusting enough to sound truthful to many readers already steeped in two and a half years' worth of increasingly creepy propaganda about atrocities committed by the bestial foe.

In fact, the "corpse factory" attained something close to immortality, continuing to inspire debate and fake news for years after the war ended and most governments pulled back from the active management of the news. More than a century earlier, in 1782, as the peace talks between Great Britain and the new United States were getting under way in Paris, Ben Franklin had tried to further humble the supplicant enemy with his fake newspaper full of exaggerated accounts of British atrocities. In 1919, as the latest war birthed the latest round of Paris peace talks, former Allied soldiers and prisoners of war—or men claiming to be former Allied soldiers and prisoners of war—were doing essentially the same thing with elaborate atrocity tales of their own, many of them involving corpse factories.

A particularly florid story in the *Los Angeles Times* of March 21, 1920, featured the sensational wartime experiences of a Canadian named Arthur Vanderbilt Post, a "wearer of the Victoria Cross, one-time Victory Loan lecturer, [and] witness in the Allies' case against the Hun leaders," who was working in Los Angeles at the time as a nurse. In 1913, the article reported, Post had been in Berlin looking after his mother's property, and when he refused to spy for the Germans, the "Death Head hussars" came for him and hustled him off to a labor camp. His sufferings were epic. Fed little more than coffee made from ground coconut shells and bread so hard it was cut with a hatchet, he had by the time of his release dwindled to ninety-seven pounds. From 4:30 in the morning to 9:00 or 10:00 at night, he was forced to toil as a "dissector" in a huge soap factory, where trainloads of soldiers' corpses were delivered every day; the "details of the operations . . . are not printable."

The bodies of thousands of babies killed by the milk famine of 1915, Post said, were cooked down into fats for kitchen use. After his father died of mistreatment, the body vanished and presumably went straight into the boilers. And as punishment for predicting a German defeat, Post and eight others were hung naked by their thumbs on a barbed-wire fence all night—when his thumb slipped out of the cord, an officer nailed it to the post—and then were forced to choose between having their eyes gouged out or "being mutilated in another manner" that the *Los Angeles Times*, as a family journal, discreetly did not name. Nor did the paper report which punishment Post had chosen, though he obviously wasn't blind.

An Arthur V. Post did exist. Most of the biographical details mentioned in the article match the ones recorded in the 1920 census for a twenty-nine-year-old man of that name, a nurse lodging at the Los Angeles YMCA who was a Canadian citizen born to a German mother. Notices in a handful of newspapers show that in April 1919 Arthur V. Post gave a few lectures at YMCAs, Rotary Clubs, and vaudeville houses in a cluster of towns mainly in Indiana, at least once as a volunteer for a Victory Loan event and once at a gathering advertised as restricted to men; several of the papers commented on his frail health, calling him "a physical wreck" or describing him as heavily bandaged.[24] But no documentary evidence supports his contention that he won the Victory Cross or that he testified before a parliamentary committee.

And, of course, nothing at all confirms the whole purple saga of the baneful hussars, the soap factory, the boiled babies, the father's lost corpse, and the literally unspeakable mutilation on the barbed wire. The tale seems to have been created by a damaged man with a vivid imagination who appropriated elements of several widely circulating atrocity stories, exaggerated them even more, and cooked them into a compelling narrative. In the "authentic" corpse-factory story, of course, the product was not soap but lubricants for munitions, while the spread-eagling of the Canadian-born Post on the fence carries echoes of another well-traveled atrocity story, about the "Crucified Canadian" who after the second battle of Ypres had been pinned alive to a door or a tree or a cross by German bayonets. That Canadian's story had never been definitively confirmed either.

None of those discrepancies and extravagances, however, stopped the *Los Angeles Times* from wholeheartedly embracing the dubious story, which it ran on the front page of its popular Sunday feature section on March 21, 1920, under the portentous headline "Truth About Hun 'Human Soap': Famous War Mystery Is Authoritatively Cleared Up Here by Prisoner Who Served for Years as 'Butcher' in German Factory Fed by Corpses of Men." It began no less authoritatively: "The truth concerning one of the war's most famous mysteries—the widely-circulated and oft-denied (by Germans) story of how Germany, desperate for lack of fats, turned great industrial establishments into saponification works for making soap out of human bodies shipped from the battlefield—was told here by Arthur Vanderbilt Post, wearer of the Victoria Cross, one-time Victory Loan lecturer, witness in the Allies' case against the Hun leaders and long an unwilling 'butcher' in a Hun human-soap factory."

This isn't the place to explore Post's motivations other than to suggest that he seems to fit into the large category of trauma fantasists epitomized by Binjamin Wilkomirski, *né* Bruno Dösseker, whose harrowing "memoir" of surviving the death camps of Nazi-occupied Poland as a tiny child alone in the world won brief worldwide acclaim in 1995 before it was exposed as a complete concoction, though whether fraudulent or delusional was never clear.[25] More relevant here are the motivations of the autocratic and powerful *Los Angeles Times*. Why, after barely mentioning the corpse factory even at the height of the war, did the paper choose years later to publish and aggressively defend a lurid and inflammatory story told by an obviously fragile soul, a story it must at least have *suspected* was fake?

The timing of the article suggests a familiar explanation: the news was faked in the service of politics. The pro-Republican *Times* had strongly supported the signing of the Treaty of Versailles with the reservations added by Henry Cabot Lodge and was bitterly disappointed when after months of contentious debate the Senate voted it down for the second time. That vote came on Friday, March 19. Just two days later, on Sunday, the *Times* ran the corpse-factory story. In that same Sunday issue, just three pages after the Post story, the paper published an opinion piece entitled "Policies of the Peace Pact," which castigated Wilson for "plung[ing] his party into the ditch." Americans, it said, had tolerated the waste and expense of the Democrats' war because they believed its ends would be achieved. But they "have now seen the peace of victory beaten, in the Senate by Democratic votes," it said, "and they will not forget. Those long lines of trenches filled with American dead in the Argonne forest and on the banks of the Marne now rise up in poignant memory. Two hundred thousand voices are asking, Was it for this we gave our sons?"

Any attentive reader of the first four pages of the feature section could have made the connection: Was it for this that the Arthur Posts of the world were unspeakably mutilated by the Huns? Although, of course, they hadn't been. But by embracing and publishing Post's fake atrocity story, the *Times* was offering an interpretation of events that may not have been accurate but that felt true, inviting any of its readers who had also been disappointed by the failure of the treaty to remind themselves of the stakes of the war and to share in a satisfying howl of rage over the betrayal by their leaders. It was also lobbing among its readers a bombshell that would have every potential to either fizzle into a deserved disillusionment toward the press or to blow up in their faces the next time the same enemy came around.[26]

For years after the end of the war, those abused corpses refused to stay buried, but as more and more citizens began to weigh the war's gigantic toll against its puny accomplishments, qualms about the power of government propaganda grew, chagrin took hold, longtime critics grew bolder, and, eventually, the cadavers began to smell. In October 1925, the former chief of British army intelligence aroused a "storm of criticism" when he claimed in a bibulously incautious after-dinner speech in New

York to have invented the corpse-factory story as a piece of disinformation. "Much indignation has been expressed in the press," the *New York Times* reported several days after the speech, "that the British Army should stoop to such propaganda methods."[27] The intelligence chief, insisting he had been misquoted, was summoned to the War Office; opposition members of Parliament demanded explanations; the prime minister and his cabinet waffled and hedged; defenses and accusations flew; newspapers around the globe weighed in, and critics weighed in on the newspapers.

The whole episode culminated on December 2, 1925, in an embarrassing scene in the House of Commons. With the German chancellor and his foreign minister looking on from the visitors' gallery, British foreign secretary Austen Chamberlain made it official: Berlin had denied the corpse story, and His Majesty's government accepted the denial. It was essentially a confession that the British government, in collusion with the British press, had done exactly what they claimed never to have done, exactly what they had accused the Hun of doing all along: inciting citizens to support a war based on propaganda and fake news. They had lied and then lied about lying.

Duped citizens noticed. Many of the U.S. papers that ran one or both of the AP's brief stories about Chamberlain's confession topped their articles with brutal headlines: " 'Corpse Factory' Propaganda Story Established as a Lie" in the *Public Opinion* (Chambersburg, Pennsylvania) (December 5, 1925); "Admits Lie" in the *San Bernardino County (CA) Sun* (December 6); "Boiling Dead Only a War Lie: British Propaganda Tale Is Officially Admitted Fib" in the *Billings (MT) Gazette* (December 4). That single blunt syllable *lie* fairly vibrated with the mortification and resentment of a nation coming to understand it had been bamboozled into supporting the war by leaders who did not tell it the truth, about the corpse factories and about everything else, too. Left unaddressed, however, was the fact that all three of those papers, along with many others, had also lied; the British government may have been producing fake journalism, but the Allied press had helped by disseminating its fake news. Each of the three papers just quoted had vouched for the accuracy of the corpse story by approvingly publishing some version of it in April or May 1917.[28] Familiar local papers, respectable big-city papers, popular mass papers— all had joined in, passing the deception along and cooperating in the gulling of America on matters literally of life and death.

Duped citizens noticed that, too, and in their anger over having fallen for a fake, many of them vowed never to believe another story of wartime atrocity again. That stance would have disastrous consequences when the same enemy returned even more savagely twenty years later. "'Atrocities' had come to be looked on as synonymous with 'lies,'" wrote George Orwell, who knew as much about propaganda as anyone. "But the stories about the German concentration camps were atrocity stories: therefore they were lies—so reasoned the average man." Public-opinion polls bore him out; in 1943, Gallup found that more than half of the Americans it surveyed either dismissed reports of the mass murder of Jews as mere rumor or had no opinion on the matter. But it wasn't just "the average man" whose reasoning was fallacious. Also in 1943, a high-level British intelligence official dismissed reports that the Nazis were gassing Poles to death because, said Victor Cavendish-Bentinck, the accounts "remind me of the story of employment of human corpses during the last war for manufacture of fat, which was a grotesque lie and led to true stories of German enormities being brushed aside as being mere propaganda." A generation later the most notorious hoax of World War I was continuing to taint the public debate, teaching precisely the wrong lessons about war, trust, and fake news.[29]

6

"NOTHING THAT IS NOT INTERESTING IS NEWS"

Few institutions of American life emerged unscathed from the shambles and disillusions left behind by the Great War—the pervasive sense that progress was a delusion and idealism naive, that "the masses" were biddable bundles of irrational emotions, that facts were unreliable, and that democracy might well be unworkable. But the embarrassing success of wartime propaganda, boiled bodies and all, was particularly tough on the reputation of journalism. Just a generation earlier, a portion of the U.S. press was proudly proclaiming its differences from the yellow papers, dividing the journalistic landscape into two categories: papers that could be trusted and those that couldn't. Newspapers in the first category, the argument went, were professional. They were credible. They were authoritative. They would get the facts straight. They would serve the public good. They understood their power and used it judiciously. *They would never fake.*

Now, however, the evidence seemed clear: they would, and they did. They were, in fact, no better than hucksters, devoting their enormous reach and power to manipulating the public's desires and fogging the public mind like any snake-oil salesman. All those boundaries the professionalizing journalists had worked to draw between decency, credibility, and authority on the one hand and the fake-filled yellow press on the other were coming under challenge by critics, by readers—and by other journalists. The muckraker Upton Sinclair, for instance, turned his scrutiny on his own profession in his screed *The Brass Check* (1919), which argued that newspapers essentially prostituted themselves on behalf of powerful corporate and political interests and worked to undermine anything that challenged their power. In the category of challengers would later fall Sinclair himself, whose run for governor of California in 1934 as a Democrat with a "socialist" plan to end poverty inspired furious opposition from, among others, Irving Thalberg. The Hollywood mogul produced a series of newsreels under the bland title "California Election News" that apparently used scripts, actors, and clips from feature films to create alarming but fake images of a state overrun with "hoboes" and "bums" looking for government handouts.[1]

The profession's internal boundaries were not the only ones under stress. Journalists were also struggling to strengthen the wavering borderlines between themselves and two quintessentially modern practices whose main product was also information—or so their practitioners claimed. Like journalists, advertising and public-relations (PR) agents insisted they were offering a public service, providing people with the intelligence they needed to make good decisions in their daily lives. Like journalism, advertising and PR were suffering image problems after their implication in the disastrous management of the Great War. All three professions were confronting similar and painful questions about the possibility of objective truth, the uses of deception, and the credibility of experts and authorities in an increasingly consumer-oriented society. And all were facing an increasingly cynical public who saw little difference between the persuaders and the reporters.

As mass-market advertising boomed into a big business in the early decades of the twentieth century and agencies took an increasingly powerful role, some advertising professionals found themselves grappling with a challenge similar to the one that the "respectable" journalists had been dealing with: embarrassing colleagues who blatantly lied about their rivals' products or touted the miraculous cures wrought by patent medicines that often included undisclosed toxins such as alcohol and opium. And some advertisers found a similar solution: professional boundary work. The practitioners who saw themselves as offering crucial information to consumers sought to draw a bright line between themselves and the fakers who were interested only in parting dupes from their money.

In 1911, the Associated Advertising Clubs of America launched a campaign for "truth in advertising" and endorsed a model statute—introduced
by the industry magazine *Printers' Ink* and eventually adopted in some
form by a number of states—that classified as a misdemeanor the prom-
ulgation of any advertisement that "contains any assertion, representation,
or statement of fact which is untrue, deceptive or misleading." Intended
in part to reassure the public and in part to fend off federal regulation,
the movement set up its own local and national "vigilance groups"—the
seeds of the Better Business Bureau—to keep an eye open for deceptive
ads, respond to complaints, and advocate for ethical standards.[2] It sounded
like the *World*'s Bureau of Accuracy and Fair Play all over again, a profession's effort to police its own borders by claiming jurisdiction over what
was true and what was not.

But like many efforts at self-regulation, the advertisers' vigilance actions
tended to be more conciliatory than forceful. And "truth" itself, it turned
out, had a more flexible meaning in the world of advertising, where outright lies were frowned upon but hyperbole, enthusiasm, and rhetorical
flourishes—exactly the kinds of things that if done by journalists would
have been scorned (or defended) as "faking"—were readily accepted as just
part of the job by even the staunchest upholders of professional virtue.
Even the original form of the Food and Drugs Act of 1906 inadvertently
reinforced that message. The Supreme Court ruled in 1911 that although
the act would have made it illegal for one Dr. O. A. Johnson of Kansas
City, Missouri, to present deceptive facts about the ingredients in the "can-
cerine tablets" he peddled, it could not stop him from stating his (false)
opinion that his tablets could cure cancer.[3] (A later amendment to the act
prohibited fake claims about therapeutic benefits but required proof that
the claims had been made with fraudulent intent.)

After the war, in any case, advertising was moving away from traditional appeals based on the qualities or performance of the merchandise
("Listerine: the safe antiseptic") and embracing newer methods of persuasion rooted in the murky world of subconscious emotions—methods
that often had little to do with "truth in advertising." The story of the
young woman doomed to be "often a bridesmaid but never the bride"
because she failed to use mouthwash was sad, unsettling, perhaps even
frightening—but was it "untrue, deceptive, or misleading"? Was it even a
"fact"? Could any "facts" be trusted anymore?

Even bolder in the use of the new methods of persuasion was the young discipline of public relations, a discipline that some practitioners, despite the unsavory odor of the term, preferred to call "propaganda." Chief among those was Edward Bernays, who in 1928 published a book with precisely that blunt title. (His eventual nickname, "father of public relations," tacitly acknowledged that the word *propaganda* had a PR problem.) Bernays's own most masterful propaganda campaign made the case that the right kind of propaganda was good for democracy. Drawing on both his experience working for the CPI and on the insights of his uncle, Sigmund Freud, he argued in *Propaganda* and other books that most people did not think rationally or individually; they were instead ruled by unconscious desires and were captives of the "group mind." It was only a small group of "natural" leaders, those who understood the mind of the ordinary person, who could expertly "organize" the chaotic scrum of public life; only those leaders could carry off "the conscious and intelligent manipulation of the organized habits of the masses" that was essential for allowing "vast numbers of human beings to live together as a smoothly functioning society." That's why propaganda, Bernays concluded, was "an important element in democratic society."[4]

But under whatever name, the goal of Bernays-style propaganda in peacetime was not to convince people they must fight to save the world for democracy; it was to exploit their emotions in ways designed to make them eat more bacon for breakfast or refrain from bobbing their hair.[5] And the real beneficiary of those behaviors was not the world order or even the world's consumers, well fed and well coifed though they might be; the beneficiary was the meatpacker or the hairnet company that had quietly hired the PR counsel in the first place to scientifically manipulate breakfast eaters or long-haired women into behaviors they might not otherwise embrace and to do so without their realizing they had been manipulated. The information, the motives, and the operators were all as fake as the connection to democracy. As the *Nation* put it in a review of *Propaganda*, PR was simply a way of "perfum[ing] the malodorous" and "mak[ing] the worse appear the better cause."[6]

For some Americans, these disturbingly dark arts of advertising and PR seemed indistinguishable from what journalism had become—and it was hard to argue with them. Silas Bent had a long career as a journalism professor, a publicity man for the Democratic presidential campaign of

1920, and a reporter or freelancer for some of the country's most important papers, including Hearst and Pulitzer journals as well as the *New York Times*. That wide-angle perspective informed *Ballyhoo* (1927), his critique of the "salesmanship and showmanship" of the press. Bent reserved particular scorn for the press's intimacy with advertisers and press agents, which made it impossible for citizens to tell which news was objectively, factually sound and which had been crafted to serve the interests of someone with a fat wallet. A single December issue of the *New York Times*, Bent reported, contained 147 stories that "almost certainly" came from publicity sources, 82 that had not, and 26 that were uncertain. That meant that a total of 60 percent of the content of the nation's flagship paper came from paid publicity men. (We report; you go shopping.) As barbed as Bent's accusations were, however, they were neither new nor shocking. As one reviewer of *Ballyhoo* put it, "He has used about five times as much evidence as is necessary. . . . [The book] proves the obvious."[7]

It seemed undeniable to anyone who cared about democracy and the public good that journalists were failing in their essential duty to keep citizens informed about matters involving the general welfare. Or as Walter Lippmann put it bluntly in 1919, "The present crisis of western democracy is a crisis in journalism."[8] The most famous postwar critic of journalism (in fact, one of the most famous critics of journalism ever), Lippmann, once an acolyte of Woodrow Wilson and the most progressive of Progressives, had become been deeply disillusioned by the successes of the wartime propaganda campaign and the lost opportunities of the peace conference. Part of the problem, he believed, lay in generally unrealistic expectations about the role of citizens in a democracy. Most people were incapable of forming an adequate vision of the world as it really was. It wasn't that they were stupid (which the advertisers and PR professionals often seemed to suggest). Distracted and busy with their daily lives, they simply had neither the time nor the specialized knowledge nor the incentive to comprehend an increasingly complex environment, and the pictures of the world they formed in their heads, satisfying though they might have been in explaining events, were also inevitably distorted and oversimplified. Most journalism simply fed those distortions.

The best remedy was not to change the way people thought; that was asking too much of them. The best remedy was to change the way

journalists thought. Journalists, Lippmann argued, should be better educated. They should establish themselves as the experts that most people
could not or would not be and put their expertise to work to inform people
rather than to manipulate them, as Bernays and his ilk would do. They
should learn to approach their work logically, critically, dispassionately,
with a scientific rigor. They should base their work on observed facts, not
on the shifty sands of opinion or values or emotions where the PR and
advertising people were to be found. And if they published falsehoods—
well, *something* ought to be done.

"We ought to know the names of the whole staff of every periodical,"
Lippmann wrote in *Liberty and the News*. "Each article should be documented, and false documentation should be illegal. . . . One wonders next
whether anything could be devised to meet that great evil of the press,
the lie which, once under way, can never be tracked down. . . . Would it
be possible then to establish courts of honor in which publishers should
be compelled to meet their accusers and, if found guilty of misrepresentation, ordered to publish the correction in the particular form and with
the prominence specified by the finding of the court? I do not know." He
did not know; the question of how to correct errors, Lippmann conceded,
was difficult and "full of traps." It was clear, though, that the public's
"growing sense of being baffled and misled" by the press could not be left
unaddressed.[9] Taken together, his suggestions about what to do bore
echoes of the solutions embraced by the turn-of-the-century newspapers
that had sought to distinguish themselves from their yellow colleagues:
claiming an independent voice, following specific methods of gathering
and verifying evidence, conforming to expressive conventions, subduing
the personality of the reporter, cracking down on errors and fakes. But
Lippmann pushed the idea further with his emphasis on professional
training, "in which the ideal of objective testimony is cardinal. . . . It does
not matter that the news is not susceptible of mathematical statement. In
fact, just because news is complex and slippery, good reporting requires
the exercise of the highest of the scientific virtues."[10]

It was here that the term *objectivity* became firmly associated with journalistic professionalism, though it was often used in a sense that was not
quite what Lippmann had in mind. His point was not that journalists
should free themselves of all bias and opinion; rather, he was arguing that
journalists should consciously sequester fact from opinion, conducting
and testing their work with a scientific rigor that would keep their

inescapable biases from compromising their accuracy. He was referring to the *practice* of journalism, not to the *attitude* of the journalist. But in a world brutally aware of the power of propaganda, the pull of PR, the inevitability of human subjectivity, and the cynicism of the "expert," it was the attitude that caused the most concern. Journalists embraced objectivity in part as an aspirational ideal, in part in an effort to distinguish themselves from PR and advertising, and in part as a defensive ploy against the inadmissible conviction that a truly unbiased stance was not in fact possible.[11]

In any case, objectivity was not the vision of journalism that came to characterize the postwar era in the popular mind, and experts were quite definitely not the people in whom most Americans chose to place their trust. The journalistic landscape of the 1920s and 1930s, to be sure, was sprawling, multifarious, and volatile, but if any one kind of journalism seemed to sum up the postwar period for the general public, it was the wildly popular new genre tagged by a contemporary with the lasting label *jazz journalism*. Both jazz music and tabloid newspapers, the writer Simon Michael Bessie argued in 1938, were "denounced as vulgar, depraved and vicious," doomed to early death. Both, however, he said, had respectable forebears, both served popular needs, and both represented "the true rhythm" of the times.[12]

For both, moreover, a defining element was improvisation. Tabloid journalists as well as jazz musicians valued creativity and expressiveness, challenged what were seen as "highbrow" traditions, and strove to build emotional connections with their audience. Both tabloids and jazz won legions of fans. But for those who saw journalism as a profession and a critical public service, that sort of "artistic" approach could be much too creative and emotional, and going "lowbrow" could undermine critical understandings that lay at the heart of how journalism was supposed to function in a democracy. Jazz journalism was precisely the opposite of what Lippmann and other serious critics had in mind. It was also much more popular.

THE TABLOIDS COME TO TOWN

As the penny press did in the 1830s, and as the yellow press did in the 1890s, the tabloid press in the 1920s shook up the mainstream journalistic landscape like a randy teenager crashing the country club. Also like their predecessors, the tabloids could be uniquely skilled in divining the needs and aspirations of their readers. In the 1920s, those needs included a passionate desire to leave behind the horrors of the previous decade and to reject the arrogant and stubborn elites who had caused them. Many Americans embraced the novel offerings of the *modern* world: widespread (though not universal) prosperity, new liberties (for some) to arrange their own lives, new forms of literature and art and dance, new playthings such as automobiles and silk stockings and cigarettes, new thrills such as speakeasies and urban life and sex without strings, new kinds of heroes such as movie stars and athletes and gangsters. Those offerings, however, also brought deep new anxieties about the withering of traditional values in a giddy world and new efforts, sometimes violent, to defend old ideas of power and authenticity. When the Ku Klux Klan reemerged in 1915, it aimed its fire not only at African Americans but also at immigrants, adulterers, divorcés, Jews, Catholics, bootleggers, city people, and others who were seen as transgressors against the moral order of the rural white Protestant male.

The *Daily News*, the first of the U.S. tabloids, was founded in New York in 1919 by a grandson of Chicago's biggest press mogul and modeled on Lord Northcliffe's spicy *Daily Mirror*. The *Daily News* "is going to be your newspaper," it announced on June 24, 1919, in its first issue. "Its interests will be your interests. Its policy will be your policy. . . . We shall give you every day the best and newest pictures of the interesting things that are happening in the world. Nothing that is not interesting is news." Within six years, the "interesting" little paper was reveling in the highest circulation of any daily in America and was closing in on the unprecedented figure of a million copies a day.[13]

In 1924, the Hearst organization, which seemed incapable of *not* competing ferociously with any new journalistic enterprise that came along, launched the *New York Daily Mirror*, and that same year Bernarr Macfadden, a devotee of "physical culture" who was often dismissed, not unfairly, as a nut, added the garish *New York Evening Graphic* to his stable of "true" romance, detective, and confession publications. Other cities from Miami and Chicago to New Orleans and Los Angeles soon had tabs of their own, but it was the tireless antics of the hypercompetitive tabloids of Gotham and their constant efforts to scoop each other that defined the genre.

Every bit as noisy, obstreperous, sensational, and cheap (in all senses of the word) as their penny and yellow forebears, the tabloids also brought new elements to the popular press. They were the first daily papers to focus on photographs, the bolder and bigger the better. They were also smaller in size than the broadsheets, which signaled their dedication to the kind of readers who unfurled their morning papers on the subway rather than in the limousine. "You can hang to a strap," the *Daily News*'s first issue promised its readers, "and read it without the skill of a juggler to keep its pages together." But the tabs' purported scorn for elite audiences in favor of a mass readership didn't mean elites never sneaked peeks at the mass press. Nor did papers on the staider end of the spectrum always resist the pressure to report on murders, bank heists, thrill killings, divorces, celebrity misbehaviors, bootleggers, sports heroes, and other hot stories just to keep up.

Besides size and illustration, a more consequential distinction separated the tabs and their popular forebears. As sensational and circulation hungry as the penny and yellow papers had been, most of them had also insisted that their prime concern was the public good. Even as the early penny editors fought over spicy details about murdered prostitutes, they also spoke of their "public duty" to enlighten and inform their mainly working- and middle-class readers. The latter readers had the same right as society's elites, the editors assured their audience, to educate themselves, to take part in public life, and to make decisions about questions of the general welfare.[14]

Joseph Pulitzer announced in the first issue that his paper, the *World*, would be devoted to the cause of "the people," not the wealthy, and it combined coverage of crime and war with genuine crusades to improve the lives of New Yorkers, especially those who—like Pulitzer decades earlier—had arrived as immigrants. Even Hearst's *New York Journal*, with its emphasis on "the journalism that ACTS," cast itself as a campaigner against injustice and wrong-doing that could accomplish what inept institutions—government, the police—could not. By the turn of the century, editors often spoke about their "news judgment," emphasizing their particular obligation to present news that served the public good.[15] The claims were sometimes merely strategic, even disingenuous, but they represented an obligatory obeisance to the traditional view of American journalism as a service to democracy and public life and the newspaper as a responsible servant.

In the 1920s, however, even as Lippmann and other critics were bemoaning the crisis in journalism, the tabloids were blithely ignoring not just the crisis but also the rhetoric of the public good that in the aftermath of the Great War tended only to bring back sour memories of journalistic failure, government propaganda, and those fakes and "lies" by misguided elites. The new papers offered a different vision of what journalism was all about and sealed a different kind of compact with their readers. Drawing a direct line between news and entertainment, the tabloids emphasized the public's pleasure instead of the public welfare. The avowed enemy was not injustice, inequality, or wrong-doing but tedium. The duty of the newspaper was not to promote informed participation in democratic life but to find amusement in striking events of daily life. Invisible in the tabloids' mission statements and other editorial comments was any claim to institutional authority or professional expertise, any declaration of fealty to even so basic a journalistic value as accuracy.

It was a striking variation on the classic strategy of paradigm repair: rather than joining with their colleagues to uphold professional norms by rejecting or casting out those who violated them, the tabloids purposefully cast *themselves* out by rejecting the professional norms. The self-banishment liberated them to build their own journalistic paradigm, one that unapologetically embraced the hucksterist spirit of the age: tabloid readers were not citizens but satisfied news consumers; the newspaper editor was a merchant whose job it was to provide the satisfaction.

The hottest rivalry was between the two more respectable (or at least less disreputable) publications, the first-comer *Daily News* and the *Daily Mirror*, which in its own self-introduction saw and raised the *News*'s promise of "interesting" news with a pledge to give its readers "90 percent entertainment, 10 percent information." Lest even that favorable ratio sound intimidating, it added that it would present that modest little 10 percent "without boring you" and concluded with an appeal to readers "to write and tell us what they DO NOT LIKE. DAILY MIRROR's motto will be 'short, quick, and make it snappy.'"[16] Explicitly disdaining the traditional journalistic roles of gatekeeper and authoritative interpreter, the *Mirror* was promising to tell its readers not what some out-of-touch

Bigfoot thought they *should* know but rather what they decided on their own they *wanted* to know. (You decide; we report.) The penny papers of the 1830s, too, had drawn a large working- and middle-class readership by expressing deference to their readers' own judgment, but they had done so in the language of egalitarianism and democracy. The tabloids spoke the language of pleasure.

Predictably, the competition pressed both papers but particularly the perennial second placer into an upward spiral of splash, exaggeration, and outright fakery. Their rivalry was in fact directly responsible for pumping up a sordid tale of middle-aged infidelity into perhaps the hottest murder story in a decade notorious for torrid tales of death. In September 1922, when the *Daily News* was still the only tabloid on the block, a young couple enjoying a stroll down a lovers' lane in rural New Jersey stumbled across the bodies of Edward Hall, the married rector of a local Episcopal church, and Eleanor Mills, the sexton's wife, who sang soprano in the church choir. Artfully posed under a crabapple tree, the bodies were strewn with steamy letters in Mills's handwriting. Hall's widow and her two brothers were questioned, but after the grand jury declined to take action, interest in the case faded.

Nearly four years later, however, in July 1926, Hearst's new *Mirror*, desperate for a story that could catapult the young paper past the *Daily News*, seized on some alleged "new evidence" brought forward by a dodgy character involved in an unrelated divorce suit and then campaigned relentlessly and successfully for the reopening of the case against the widow and her brothers. The tabloids' tenacious attention pressured even the more respectable papers to delve into the story to keep their readers from straying; the *New York Times* reportedly devoted more space to the case than any other paper did, though its publisher was said to have insisted that when the ultrarespectable paper covered such stories, it was purveying not sensationalism but "authentic sociological documents."[17] That November as many as three hundred reporters converged on the modest Somerset County courthouse to cover the sensational trial, the high point of which was the incriminating but dubious testimony of the "Pig Woman," an eccentric local hog farmer who was dying of cancer and had to be carried into court in a hospital bed.

Throughout the trial, the *Mirror* kept up its tireless and highly creative efforts to brand the defendants guilty. It reported, for instance, with no visible evidence, that the widow had spent the enormous sum of $2,000 a week to get "the dope" on the prosecution's witnesses, and it ran a cartoonish drawing depicting one of Mrs. Hall's brothers at the crime scene. Its editor, meanwhile, sent a telegram to the widow's lawyer defending the paper's accuracy and daring him to sue. Upon their acquittal, Mrs. Hall and her family did just that. (No one else was ever charged in the murders, which remain officially unsolved. In 1964, the well-known defense attorney William M. Kunstler argued that the culprits were Ku Klux Klansmen offended at the couple's immoral conduct.)[18] The family's eventual victory and the unspecified settlement Hearst was ordered to make to them, however, were barely covered in the press; most of the papers that mentioned them at all used only a cursory AP summary that was short on both detail and fuss.[19] Nobody seemed to care that the settlement essentially proclaimed to the world that the *Mirror*'s reporting had been egregiously, criminally fake. The *Mirror* had never claimed to be any kind of authority in the first place, so who could blame it now? The paper had fulfilled its promise: it had entertained. That was all anyone had expected from a tabloid bearing Hearst's name.

Even more freewheeling than the *Mirror* and the *Daily News* was the *Evening Graphic*, whose eye-popping luridness and frank promise to "throb with those life forces that fill life with joyous delight" soon earned it the nickname *Porno-Graphic*. "We intend to interest you mightily," the paper announced in its first issue, and, like the *Mirror*, it promised not to impose its own news judgment on its readers. "If you read it from first to last and find anything therein that does not interest you," it asserted chummily, "we want you to write and tell us about it." And most importantly, it stated, "we intend to dramatize and sensationalize the news and some stories that are not new." Although Macfadden was wont to claim that a paper like his "can be made to appeal to the masses in their own language; that it can be made so true and real that it will penetrate the hearts and souls of the readers," his mission statement also made the clear case that without drama and sensation, news was neither true nor real but a bore. Without ever actually using the word, the *Graphic* was acknowledging that it made the news interesting by *faking* it.[20]

It faked pictures, too. Indeed, all the tabloids played with the feature that was most central to their identity. The *Mirror* did it with the crime-scene drawing, and when an earthquake centered in eastern Canada

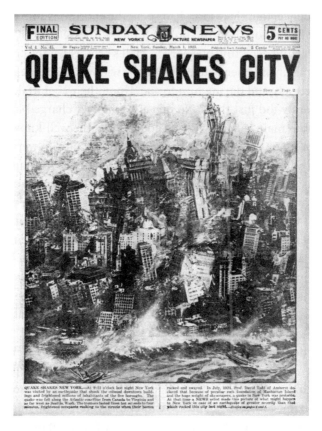

FIGURE 6.1 The *Daily News* (New York) shows readers what *might* happen the next time there's an earthquake.

Source: Final edition, March 1, 1925.

caused rattles and flutters in New York, the *Daily News* final edition for March 1, 1925, ran a hallucinatory full-page image under the headline "QUAKE SHAKES CITY" depicting skyscrapers buckling and swaying, smaller buildings tumbling into rubble, and tiny ships tossing helplessly in the coastal waves. But that, too, was a drawing, clearly so labeled; it showed "what might happen to New York in case of an earthquake of greater severity than that which rocked this city last night." The illustration was more whimsical than realistic, which would have been instantly clear to the millions of alert New Yorkers who had failed that day to be flattened by falling debris. (The *Daily News*'s most notorious illustration, however—the clandestinely shot photograph of the convicted murderer Ruth Snyder at the moment of her death in Sing Sing's electric chair in January 1928—was so outrageous that some readers seasoned in tabloid tactics may well have assumed it must have been a fake.[21])

The *Graphic*, however, under its demonically brilliant editor Emile Gauvreau, was inspired to create something meatier than a mere drawing, something new that would make people talk. Gauvreau called that something the "composograph" and reportedly trademarked the term; Stanley Walker, a legendary city editor of the *New York Herald Tribune*, called it "part photograph and part nightmare."[22] Nobody called it "photojournalism," and, like the tabloids' sensationalized reporting, it pointedly disdained the professionalizing values claimed by colleagues in the mainstream press.

The paper's first composograph was inspired by the *Rhinelander v. Rhinelander* trial of 1925, a steamy case that turned on explosive issues of racial identity, class privilege, and "exotic" sex. Soon after turning twenty-one, Kip Rhinelander defied his patrician family to marry Alice Jones, the twenty-five-year-old daughter of a Black coachman and a white cook. Within weeks, however, the continued pressure from his family and the frenzied coverage of "RHINELANDER'S COLORED BRIDE" in the tabloid press pushed Kip into seeking an annulment on the stated grounds that his wife had hidden her Black ancestry from him. At the trial, Alice's attorney countered with an electrifying ploy. Escorting her and her mother into a jury room from which spectators and press had been barred, he directed his weeping client, who was wearing only underwear beneath her long coat, to pull aside her clothing so that the jurors could see the skin of her breast, back, and lower legs. The point was to demonstrate her body looked so obviously "colored" that Kip, who acknowledged having slept with her before they were married, must have known all along she was not white. (The jury would agree; the annulment was denied.)[23]

Kept out of the jury room but desperate to cover the salacious episode, journalists faked the details. *Daily News* reporters compensated for the absence of photographs by dreaming up garish word pictures based on what they imagined happening behind the closed doors. One journalist vividly described how the young woman shrank "like a frightened animal before the cold appraising stare of twelve good men and true" and clung to her mother as "the half bewildered jury of business men and farmers circled around her."[24]

The *Graphic* compensated for the absence of photographs by dreaming up—a photograph. The paper hired a showgirl from Earl Carroll's "Vanities" to strip down and pose with drooping head before a group of anonymous onlookers arranged in something that looked like a courtroom. After the photograph was snapped, staffers in the art department pulled out the paste pots and affixed atop each body in the picture a stern-looking but genuine headshot of one of the principals in the trial. Over the caption "Alice Disrobes in Court to Keep Her Husband," the published composograph showed the female figure from behind, with her face obscured and her body naked except for a brief slip pulled down to her hips. Plainly visible to the *Graphic*'s readers were her entire back and the curve of one breast. Plainly visible to the ogling men in the composograph would have been much more. And plainly visible to the genuine jurors in the private room would have been quite a bit less.[25]

No one from either the *Daily News* or the *Graphic* had witnessed the display of Alice Rhinelander's body, but both the *News*'s report and the *Graphic*'s image played up the luridness of the scene with invented details presented, minus the slightest qualification, as accurate. Both portrayed Alice as a passively erotic object to be leered at by strange men who had been given official permission to do so. Both redoubled the public humiliation of her ordeal. The *Daily News*'s version, describing the all-male jury stalking and cornering her as if she were prey, presented clear and disturbing undertones of menace. But it was the *Graphic*'s image—sensationalized, novel, and, on top of that, apparently imperishable—that most compounded the complexities of the fake.

Not only did the titillating *Graphic* image pack a visual wallop that the *Daily News*'s prose report could not match, but it also continues to do so, frequently reprinted to this day in scholarly and popular literature and easily retrieved online by a Google search. The durability of the image recalls the persistent debate over whether displaying photographs of victims of cruelty and violence offers a salutary lesson against repeat violations or merely victimizes them afresh with each new spectator's gaze—but with the twist that Alice Rhinelander's enduring victimization comes from a fake image, one showing a mortified woman with her name but someone else's body.

Other composographs served up sizzle and zing that were more giddy than scandalous. On March 17, 1927, after squeezing out dozens of stories about Rudolph Valentino in the seven months since his hysterically mourned death from appendicitis, the *Graphic* introduced its first installment of the movie idol's ghost-written autobiography with a front-page picture showing him in a toga standing with the late and equally beloved tenor Enrico Caruso, also wearing a toga. The two were looking over a crowd of nearly naked runners sprinting up a grand staircase toward other scantily clad figures gathered on a platform. The huge headline screamed: "Rudy Meets Caruso! Tenor's Spirit Speaks!"[26]

In heaven, that is.

The story was a triumph of pawky mystification. Editor Gauvreau never pretended that his cameraman had humped his Speed Graphic right up to the Pearly Gates and captured the moment the dead Pagliacci ushered in the dead heartthrob. By clearly captioning the image as a composograph, he chose instead to flaunt both the paper's guilelessness and its ingenuity. But the caption also noted that the actor's wife, Natacha Rambova—whose real name was Winifred Hudnut and who was actually his ex—had "received his spirit messages," which had been "taken down by George Wehner, the psychic." It was the information gathered by Wehner, a fixture in high-society spiritualist circles, that had been used to prepare the illustration. (Those half-naked runners, the caption explained, were a "spirit audience from a lower plane about to greet a troup [*sic*] of spirit actors who play in spirit world theaters.") The *image* on the front page, accurately labeled as a composite, was thus available for interpretation as something other than an out-and-out fake. The *information* on the front page, in contrast, was presented with all apparent sincerity as a communication from a dead man to his pseudonymous not-quite-widow that had been plucked from the ether by a shaman to the stars. People loved it. The story sent the *Graphic*'s circulation numbers soaring to eight hundred thousand, one of its highest peaks ever.[27]

So what was it about the fake story that appealed to those eight hundred thousand readers? In his fullest comment on the topic, Gauvreau noted, with placid resignation, that despite the clear label *composograph* on the *Graphic*'s illustrations, most buyers of the paper were "under the impression" that all the images were unretouched photographs. That comment, to be sure, appears in the chapter on the "Rip Landecker" divorce trial in Gauvreau's very thinly veiled roman à clef about life at a fictional paper called the *Daily Comet*, but attentive readers will evaluate the editor's novel as neither more nor less truthful than his memoir. In a comment on the coverage of the divorce trial, the respected trade journal *Editor & Publisher* seemed confused by the whole affair, referring to the *Graphic*'s picture as a composograph but nonetheless lamenting that the image of the nearly nude bride in the jury room was "the most shocking news-picture ever produced by New York journalism."[28] But given that *E&P*, which had recently absorbed the pioneering industry publication the *Journalist*, took pride in presenting itself as an authority on the profession, it may well have been overzealously patrolling professional boundaries between "news-pictures" and entertainingly fake images that had not in fact been breached at all.

The same questions about credulity have long swirled around the supermarket tabloids that are the *Graphic*'s spiritual descendants. In her study of the motives driving buyers to the racks at the grocery checkout counter, S. Elizabeth Bird identifies several different kinds of readers. Some, she found, buy the papers ironically, as a self-conscious joke or as an adventure in slumming. Others read selectively, believing, for instance, in ESP but not in UFOs and seeing no inconsistency in branding some kinds of stories credible and others absurd. Some enjoy challenging authority by embracing a publication that debunks elitist scientific ideas about the occult and the afterlife.[29]

The *Graphic* doubtless had readers in all of those categories, but given the remarkable variety of straightforward truth claims, hedged truths, muddled truths, and open fakes embedded in the Valentino story alone, a large swath of the *Graphic*'s readers probably numbered among those who, as Bird puts it, seemed to "enjoy reading tabloids *as if* they are true, playing with definitions of reality, wondering if it could be so."[30] By refusing to present themselves as interpretive authorities, all three New York tabloids had entered into explicit or implicit bargains with their readers that decisions about what was news, what was true, and what was real would be left up to the readers, not to the elites. But the *Graphic* did the most to live up to the naughty, nutty, improvisational spirit that Simon

Michael Bessie called the "true rhythm" of the Jazz Age (and that others, not entirely without reason, called "vulgar, depraved and vicious"). Its goal wasn't for readers to believe the paper; its goal was for them to buy it.

LYING OVER THE AIR

It was still seen as uncanny, even bewitching. It still seemed to ensnare listeners' attention and loosen their critical faculties. But now radio was reaching larger audiences; it was literally taking a place in the family parlor and adding a voice to the household conversation. And some of what that intimate, insinuating voice was telling listeners was offensive, deceptive, or flat-out wrong. Audiences, broadcasters, and government were for the first time facing hard questions about what, if anything, should be done when, say, a preacher used the public airwaves to tell his huge audience that the Catholic Church had assassinated three former presidents and who should do it.

The end of the Great War had liberated the airwaves from the U.S. Navy's grasp and sparked the transformation of "wireless" into "radio"—from a technology used mainly for point-to-point communication into a commercially supported broadcasting system. Exactly what would be broadcast, to whom, at whose expense, and under whose control were matters of debate among moguls, cabinet officials, the navy, Congress, the courts, visionaries, and ordinary citizens. Some saw the airwaves as a public resource that ought to remain free, open, and dedicated to the "public interest," whatever that might be. Some glimpsed dazzling possibilities for profit and power and launched epic corporate battles to control the infrastructure of the industry. Some feared that allowing advertising into the sanctum of the home was a prospect beyond the pale, while others embraced the idea as both pragmatic and inevitable as a business model.[31]

The passage of the Radio Act of 1927 eventually established the basic framework of the broadcast system, a weird hybrid consisting of raw material—the airwaves—that was owned but not controlled by the public, that was subject to regulation by the government, and that was exploited mainly by the private sector. The act specified that the broadcasting spectrum would be overseen by the newly established Federal

Radio Commission (FRC). Private entities deemed to be operating for the public good could be licensed to operate over the public airwaves, with strong structural advantages built in for the larger and profit-driven or "general-purpose" organizations at the expense of so-called propaganda or nonprofit ones. Commercial sponsorship and on-air advertising were tacitly welcomed. Monopolies and censorship were prohibited. Although the FRC was mandated to consider whether potential licensees would be operating in the "public interest, convenience or necessity," no one knew exactly what that meant. "A precise definition of such a phrase," the commissioners noted primly, "which will foresee all eventualities is manifestly impossible."[32]

From the beginning, a few pioneers were envisioning a genre as groundbreaking as photojournalism: radio news. It had a rocky start. One of the first scheduled programs ever aired by a commercial radio station was a news special, the broadcast by Pittsburgh's KDKA of the returns from the presidential election of 1920 live as they came in. But the program was more a publicity stunt designed to sell radio receivers—Why buy a set if there's nothing to listen to?—than a civic-minded commitment to informing the citizens, only a tiny number of whom were even able to receive a radio broadcast at the time. In any case, the broadcast could barely be called *journalistic* work: the announcer simply waited for the *Pittsburgh Post* to phone the station with the latest update from the wire services.[33] Other stations began to feature regular segments in which announcers read news over the air, but those, too, simply credited (or pillaged) the columns of the local newspaper.

A few stations launched bold experiments in a wholly new genre, the broadcasting of live events. In those cases, the rules were often made up on the fly, understandings were forged on the sly, and a medium that relied on the ear plus the imagination left plenty of room for manipulation or outright faking if events went awry. In 1924, for instance, when the two major political parties announced they were inviting microphones into their nominating conventions, enthusiasts embraced the promise of an intimate, behind-the-scenes peek into the ultimate smoke-filled room. As a pundit rhapsodized in the July issue of *Popular Science Monthly*, "Who dares say that through radio, through the better understanding of politics and political issues that it will bring to the average man, some day may not be realized the long existing dream of patriots—a perfect government?" The same issue of the magazine included an ad for the RCA Radiola Super-Heterodyne model, which made that promise explicit. "No 'influence' needed this year for a gallery seat," it promised. "It used to be all for the delegates' wives and the 'big' folks of politics. Now it's for everybody."[34]

Eventually, everybody could hear the whole long, sweaty, agonizing fight on the floor of Madison Square Garden as the Democratic delegates tussled their way through a record 103 ballots before collapsing into a compromise and nominating the innocuous John W. Davis. At one point, Norman Brokenshire, then an eager young WJZ leg man, took over the microphone while his boss went out to lunch and, seizing on his moment in the spotlight, launched into a rapt description of a vigorous fistfight on the floor. His horrified chief rushed in to switch the feed to a musical interlude, hissing to his assistant "in words of one syllable" that the party had granted broadcast rights to WJZ "on the distinct understanding that no disorders of any kind would be reported."[35] For the first time, journalists were making decisions in real time about how to cover the events unfolding in front of their eyes, which could involve making deals with their subjects about when the broadcasters should avert *their* eyes. It could also sometimes include making dupes of listeners who believed that the thrilling new technology that could bypass the "'big' folks" would never be guilty of faking. "Everybody" could still be fooled.

Later that summer Brokenshire was sent to Mitchel Field on Long Island to cover the gala reception honoring the crews of two Army Air Force planes in the midst of a five-month aerial circumnavigation of the globe. At the last minute, however, the reception was rescheduled, which to Brokenshire's chagrin no one had thought to mention to the radio station. With a "deep hole" to fill live on the air, the desperate announcer rousted two of the pilots from their naps. In front of the microphone, the airmen obligingly shuffled their feet to mimic the sound of a bustling receiving line while weaving tales of their adventures. "When it was all over," Brokenshire recalled, "I nearly passed out on the mat." He eventually decided not to tell his superiors: "Who was going to be helped if I told what had really happened?"[36] The giddy subtext to this and to most live radio news: if he never told his superiors, would they even know he had faked a report that had floated off into the ether, leaving no physical traces behind?

Episodes like the unexpectedly rowdy convention and the rescheduled gala in 1924 underlined the new and very real possibilities of gaffe and embarrassment inherent in covering news events as they happened. Even so, executives at NBC and CBS followed a policy requiring that news—and everything else on the radio—should be broadcast live and only live; material recorded ahead of time, be it a president's speech, a journalist's commentary, or a correspondent's report from the field, was permitted on the air only in very rare instances.[37]

To some extent, the ban on using prerecorded material reflected concerns inherent in the nature of a technology that promised intimacy and immediacy but presented its ephemeral evidence only to the ear, not the eye. Listeners who thrilled to the belief that the Bakelite-clad device in the parlor connected them directly to the great events unfolding in the world would feel confused or even deceived, executives felt, if they discovered that the events in question had happened days earlier and somewhere else. E. P. H. James, a sales and promotion manager at NBC in the 1920s and 1930s, recalled later that the networks "utterly and completely refused" to use recorded material, which was "considered to be a sort of hoax to play on the listener." And the great CBS correspondent William Shirer, broadcasting from Europe on the growing Nazi menace, acknowledged that, for listeners, knowing they were hearing events "as they happened, the very second," was "the new dimension that radio gave, and it was exciting."[38] Listeners who couldn't have absolute faith that the voices on the radio were who, where, and what they said they were might as well be listening to fake news.

But the reasons for the ban on prerecorded material were actually more complicated and sometimes less admirable than a sensible concern about credibility, and the original target of the ban was not war correspondents but phonograph records. Early federal regulators saw it as a waste to use the magic of the airwaves to broadcast something as banal and ubiquitous as a prerecorded platter; early radio executives saw an existential threat in the possibility that popular singers would record their own programs and then bypass the radio to distribute them. New syndication arrangements eventually loosened some of the rules, but the powerful networks remained firm, refusing to make exceptions even for the news divisions. As war in Europe grew increasingly likely, CBS executive William S. Paley listened to passionate arguments from Shirer and Edward R.

Murrow that since war doesn't stick to a schedule and bombs couldn't be relied on to fall exactly where and when a microphone was at the ready, news broadcasts ought to be able to use recorded material. The argument, Shirer recalled, "seemed so simple, so logical. But Paley was adamant." Paley's biographer, citing her interview with the executive, noted that the blanket prohibition at CBS and NBC against airing any recordings whatsoever, designed as it was "to protect lucrative [live] entertainment programs" from competition, ended up "subordinat[ing]" the imperatives of journalistic news gathering "to the dictates of business."[39]

Throughout the 1920s, however, news on the radio remained only a modest presence generally overshadowed by music, drama, talks, comedy, the megahit *Amos 'n' Andy*—as well as faith healers, hellfire preachers, politicos, hucksters, and quacks. Long before news became a radio staple, entrepreneurs of all sorts were learning to exploit the intimate, emotional—and live—capacities of the radio voice to knit large audiences into loyalists. Some were motivated by beneficence, others by ambition or greed; some promised spiritual salvation, others potency in bed. When the FRC set up shop in 1927, it faced fundamental questions that had never been an issue with privately owned print media: if when allocating licenses the commission was supposed to consider how well a broadcaster using the public airwaves would serve the "public interest, convenience or necessity," what exactly did that mean, and what violated those tenets? In the aftermath of the abuses of the Great War, with the Supreme Court taking a new interest in cases involving First Amendment issues of free speech and free press, what should—what could—the government do to regulate the uses of the airwaves?

In a series of decisions, the FRC began tentatively allowing itself a wide range of powers. It could, it decided, pressure an announcer not to use "indecent" language. It could silence a quack doctor who used the airwaves not for the public good but for his private gain. It could even punish people who spread lies over the air. In one famous case, the commissioners refused to renew the license of a fire-and-brimstone radio preacher accused of, among other transgressions, filling his broadcasts with "misstatements of fact" and making "a reckless use of facts."[40] The Reverend Robert Shuler of Trinity Methodist Church, South, in Los Angeles, was broadcasting fake news, and the new radio commission decided it could—and should—intervene.

Known to his many fans as "Fighting Bob," the preacher, who had begun broadcasting over KGEF in 1926, was usually fighting mad, in a state of near-perpetual rage against what he saw as rampant unrighteousness, vice, and sin. "Unless you have been attacked by Rev. 'Bob' Shuler," the hometown *Los Angeles Times* reported in 1930, "you don't amount to much in Los Angeles," and the paper considered it only fitting that a city so full of superlatives should also be the home of "the champion 'ag'inner' of the universe." The *Times* listed an array of people and institutions that Shuler had denounced on KGEF, from the pulpit, or in his magazine. Some of the individual politicians he named may well have had their shady moments, but other targets of his wrath included such evils as the public library (for carrying "heathen" and "anarchistic" books), the YWCA (for holding dances that lasted into the night), the Jews (for undermining American idealism), the government (for its "vicious, putrid officials"), the *Times* (for disagreeing with him), and the Catholic Church (for everything from controlling the press to killing Lincoln, Garfield, and McKinley).[41] Although Shuler was sued several times for libel over comments in his magazine, the juries had either deadlocked or acquitted him, apparently reluctant to ascribe his motives to malice.[42]

In January 1931, after a local businessman challenged Shuler's license renewal, the FRC held a hearing into his fitness as a broadcaster. Shuler testified willingly, embracing the labels *extremist* and *agitator* and justifying his mission as "mak[ing] it hard for the bad man to do wrong in the community" and "as easy as possible for good men to do right." He had indeed, he acknowledged, done "some foolish things," and not infrequently throughout the hearing he conceded that he had used information he had gotten secondhand or anonymously and hadn't checked. But, he insisted, his comments were always intended for the public good, and in any case they were protected by his right to free speech.[43] Dozens of witnesses testified in his support.

The prosecuting team, however, presented stacks of transcriptions of Shuler's broadcasts along with refutations from those he had targeted to make the case that his assaults weren't merely intemperate and personal; they also bristled with mistakes and fabrications. "Witness after witness," as the *Los Angeles Times* summed up one day's proceedings, "accused the broadcasting pastor of Trinity Methodist Church of radioing misinformation, false statements, destructive opinions and ignorant comments on various public matters."[44] Some of the alleged lies bordered on the silly,

such as Shuler's claim that the University of Southern California was training young women for vaudeville, "commercial dancing," and life as "a
'Follies' queen." (It was just innocent "folk dancing," said the university
president.)[45] Numerous other charges, however, were much more consequential: that Shuler had undermined a murder trial with false accusations of jury tampering, for instance, and had fabricated an inflammatory story that the California Board of Health required aspiring waitresses
to strip naked for medical examinations.[46]

When the FRC delivered its verdict in November, it carefully explained
that it wasn't censoring Shuler; it didn't have that power. It was instead
simply exercising its "duty of determining whether the standard fixed by
law has been or will be met by the use of a broadcasting license." Lies did
not meet that standard. Shuler's offensives against churches, public officials, and the courts, the commission opined, sowed antagonism between
religious denominations, were sensational rather than educational, and
were "oftentimes based upon ignorance of fact for which little effort had
been made to ascertain the truth thereof." When he didn't have facts, he
resorted to innuendo, said the commission, and his broadcasts were filled
with "reckless use of facts" and "misstatements of fact and insinuations
based thereon." All of which led the commissioners to the unanimous conclusion that the "public interest, convenience and/or necessity would not
be served by the granting of this application for renewal of station license."[47]
A year later the U.S. Court of Appeals of the District of Columbia upheld
the commission's decision.

Cracking down on false and misleading information over the public
airwaves, insisted the FRC, wasn't a violation of the First Amendment. The
commission hadn't exercised prior restraint, which would have been
impermissible; it hadn't interfered in Shuler's broadcast or stopped him
in advance from saying anything he liked; the case was a policy issue, not
a constitutional one. All the commission had done was use the evidence
of what Shuler had actually said in the past to judge his fitness to continue broadcasting, and much of what he said had been untrue.

Not everyone agreed. After the Supreme Court refused in January 1933
to hear Shuler's appeal, his attorney, Louis G. Caldwell, who had been the
FRC's first general counsel, pointed to the Court's recent ruling in *Near
v. Minnesota* (283 U.S. 697 [1931]) that prepublication censorship of even a
"malicious, scandalous and defamatory" item was unconstitutional. Criticizing the commission for giving the realm of radio much less freedom

of expression than the press had, Caldwell argued that broadcasters could be put out of business for speaking words over the air that if printed in a newspaper would be protected by the First Amendment.[48] But for many that was the point: words spoken over the air simply had more power and posed more danger than words set down in cold print.

The voluminous transcripts of the hearing, the decision, and the appeals make a convincing case that Shuler used the radio to reach huge audiences by means of persistent, egregious, and often consequential lies. He was obviously a pain in the neck for many prominent Angelenos: an embarrassingly puritanical figure in a city eager to consider itself modern, a powerful man worshiped by a listenership both large and biddable, a crank who exploited the special powers of radio to spread stories that could be as damaging as they were outlandish. But the commission's argument that it was banning Shuler for his "reckless use of facts" didn't quite tell the whole story, and political considerations seem to have come into play, too. In their appellant's brief, the preacher's attorneys submitted evidence that seemed to show that some of their client's charges of corrupt dealings by public officials were in fact accurate.

The FRC's case would have been much purer if so much of the opposition to the renewal of Shuler's license had not come from people he had blistered—among whom numbered, perhaps not incidentally, one of the attorneys representing the businessman who had brought the complaint.[49] Also telling is that even though California had passed a "slander bill" in June 1929 extending the laws of press libel to cover speech on the radio, it wasn't the courts of law that finally brought him down.[50] His opponents apparently felt that an investigation by a broadly empowered government agency into whether Shuler broadcast fake news would be more effective than yet another legal case struggling to produce evidence of his malicious intent. Fakes were easier to prove than malice.

The bottom line is that the FRC's decision to pull Shuler's license allowed it to shut up an inconvenient agitator with an authoritative one-two punch: dismissing what he said as untrue (even if it wasn't, exactly) and denouncing on-air untruths as bad for the public. In any case, in its series of groundbreaking decisions the government was claiming that when it came to policing the public airwaves, it had the right to make value judgments about the indecency of cuss words, the greed of quacks, and the truthfulness of gadflies. The ether truly was a different kind of place, a place too dangerous to be left unpoliced. If the indecent, the greedy, and the false had gone about their business in print rather than on the air, none would have drawn such intense scrutiny.

THE SERIOUS PAPERS STRUGGLE

As the tabloids raked in the readers by freeing them from the tedium of information that was *good for them*, the newspapers that considered themselves serious and respectable struggled to regain their footing and define their role in a world in which democracy, reason, the power of truth, the status of traditional elites, the understanding of the average citizen, and their own journalistic integrity had all been found wanting. Some papers wilted under the challenges, while others underwent radical changes of identity. In New York, old stalwarts such as the *World*, the *Sun*, the *Herald*, and the *Tribune* changed owners, merged, or died off altogether, while the Scripps-Howard and Hearst chains went on cross-country buying sprees, and syndicate arrangements pressed even the remaining independent newspapers into looking more and more like each other. The new thrills afforded by radio and the movies, meanwhile, were bewitching audiences away in droves.

No one in the newspaper world knew quite how to respond. In the decades on either side of the turn of the twentieth century, a hearty declaration against faking had gone far toward identifying a newspaper as serious. In the post–Great War world, however, newspaper claims about repudiating the fake seemed much less credible, even as spiraling economic and political crises were making credible journalism all the more essential. In their various efforts—whether desperate, improvised, clueless, or crafty—to define their place, some previously sensational newspapers claimed a new authority, and some previously authoritative papers did serious damage to their reputations.

One of the first papers to remake itself in the postwar world was the *Chicago Defender*. Founded in 1905 by Robert S. Abbott, it had quickly become the flagship of the growing African American press. In the early years, many other Black-run papers had followed Abbott's decision to court attention with activist fare cast in a voice much more sensational than Ida B. Wells's had been, featuring strident stories that emphasized and sometimes exaggerated the most gruesome details of interracial violence, incendiary rumors, brash editorials, pointed political cartoons, and huge banner headlines printed in red. Abbott made his paper into what Carl Sandburg called the "single promotional agency" for the Great Migration, painting Chicago and other northern cities as promised lands brimming with freedom and opportunity. The sensational tone thrilled readers hungry for a newspaper that recognized and validated their everyday experience of grotesque violence—an everyday experience that the mainstream press routinely either distorted or ignored—but it also offered all the more ammunition for opponents eager to dismiss everything the Black press said as exaggerated or faked, as they had with Wells's work on lynching. White southerners, especially those who feared losing their workforce to the North, fought back with pressure, violence, efforts to halt the local distribution of the paper, wartime surveillance of it by the federal government, and fierce denunciations of its coverage as, in the words of one Mississippi senator, "a tissue of lies."[51]

But after the shattering Chicago race riots of 1919 that killed thirty-eight people (and deeply undermined the *Defender*'s gleaming vision of the city), the sensationalism of both Black-run and white-run papers came in for a share of the blame. The twelve prominent citizens, six Black and six white, who were named to the governor's Commission on Race Relations stated clearly in their report that some of the white papers in Chicago "made relations more difficult, fostering new antagonism and enmities and even precipitating riots by inflaming the public against Negroes," and included page after page of examples of bellicosity, bigotry, and rampant falsehood in those papers. The report acknowledged the importance of the Black press for morale and solidarity, but it also noted that some Black newspapers had "entered into a mad race with the most 'yellow' of yellow white journals in vitriolic race attacks, in this case upon all white people, in the attempt to meet the 'yellow' white press more than half way." In its conclusion, the report pressed white editors to cover Black Americans with sensitivity, fairness, and accuracy and urged Black editors to give up the sensational headlines, unfounded rumors, and exaggerated stories in favor of more educational and positive coverage. Abbott was one of the twelve commissioners, and by the time he put his name to the report in 1922, the *Defender* had begun moderating its yellow hue. The white Chicago press was much slower to drop out of that "mad race."[52]

Mainstream news organizations continued to find themselves caught in splashy, embarrassing deceptions, but the fallout could carry surprising messages about the meaning of professionalism. On August 16, 1924, a slow news day just five months after the ultrarespectable but unprofitable *New York Tribune* surprised the newspaper world by buying the louche, not entirely reliable, and also unprofitable *Herald*, its young reporter Sanford Jarrell tilted to the louche side with his front-page story "New Yorkers Drink Sumptuously on 17,000-Ton Floating Cafe at Anchor 15 Miles off Fire Island." Jarrell had distilled a clutch of vague rumors into the rollicking tale of his visit to the "floating cabaret," a luxurious "joy-giving steamship" that evaded Prohibition laws by holding its tipsy revels offshore. But as papers from Honolulu to Atlanta followed Jarrell's unfolding adventures on a ship that no one else, it seemed, could actually find, suspicions began to bloom, and he finally told his editors that he had fabricated the whole thing. On August 23, under the headline "Reporter Admits 'Sea Cabaret' Story Untrue," the new *Herald Tribune* took the honorable and now well-worn path of front-page public penance, confessing to the fake and announcing it had fired the reporter. Whether incidentally or with calculation, the statement made clear that the newly combined paper would plant itself, professionally speaking, on the side of the angels and the *Tribune* rather than on the dark side with the *Herald*: if it found itself publishing fake news, it would admit the error and apologize.[53]

Hardly anyone seemed to care about either the fake or the apology except the *Brooklyn Eagle*. Its columnist Nunnally Johnson griped on August 28 that "nobody does anything, so far as I can find out, but laugh over the whole affair," probably, he said, because nobody was hurt, no elections were compromised, and no reputations were damaged. (And nobody much minded taking a poke at the deeply unpopular idea of Prohibition.) Johnson's column, headlined "And, Strangely Enough, Twenty Years from Now the Jazz Ship Reporter Will Be Better Remembered Than the More Accurate News Writer of 1924," strangely enough turned out to be prescient. References to the "sin ship," nearly all affectionate, popped up periodically for decades and reemerged in force upon Jarrell's death in 1962. "The story remained and grew and was gilded," said his obituary in the *Herald Tribune*, his former paper, which at that point was seen as sprightly, humane, and doomed, incapable of matching the news-gathering resources of the distinctly unsprightly *Times*. (The *Herald Tribune* would close, deeply mourned, in 1966.) Jarrell's tale, the obituarist continued, "became—indeed, it still is—one of the first yarns a new man working on a paper in town hears."[54]

Half a century after Ralph Pulitzer told the students at Columbia's journalism school that the profession recognized no such thing as a harmless fake, a newspaper trying desperately to compete with the most "professional" paper in the country recalled Jarrell's old prank not as a firing offense but as a creative model for newbies to aspire to: a nostalgic shout-out to the raffish journalistic bohemianism of yore and the hallmark of a transgressive professionalism all its own. Another fake was being exploited as the counterfoil against which to measure the sober and respectable. But this time, it was the sober and respectable *Times* that was seen to be coming up short against the yeasty pleasures of the good old-fashioned fake given one last hurrah by a paper on the verge of death.

Some of the papers struggling to figure out what the public wanted in those confusing times or to strike a balance between the authoritative and the companionable only found themselves misstepping on both ends. On the one hand, even the dowdy *New York Times* felt compelled to show a little leg in its softer Sunday edition, larding it with the occasional piece of whimsy, parody, or humor. Among the oddest was the long-running saga of the caraway-seed merchant Marmaduke M. Mizzle of Mincing Lane. Between 1920 and 1940, the paper published at least seventeen long stories by its shipping reporter, T. Walter Williams, chronicling Mizzle's adventurous journeys in exotic parts of the world and his encounters with singing spiders, dimbadamba hounds, a hazzamazazza bug, and a vengeful Amazon who relentlessly pursued him on yakback.[55]

Strictly speaking, the stories weren't fakes; it seems absurd to think anyone could possibly have taken them as anything other than fantastic pastiches, part H. Rider Haggard and part Dr. Dolittle. But they also weren't terribly successful. Throughout the two decades that the stories ran, they attracted not a single published letter to the editor and were only very rarely reprinted, quoted, or even mentioned in other publications. The humor was labored, to be sure; as one old-time journalist recalled later about the tale of the hazza-mazazza bug, "Well, it was pretty funny for *The Times* and funnier still to think that *The Times* thought it funny."[56] And the tales had neither the immediacy nor the élan of Jarrell's adventure. But it's also possible that in those decades the *Times* was too ensnared in its own carefully cultivated reputation as respectable, empirical, impartial, and gray to leave readers anything but baffled or even irritated by their encounter with something so obviously *not* intended to be truthful. It was a fake fake.

On the other hand, the *Times* racked up two spectacular failures in stories it *did* intend to be truthful, seriously undermining the profession's claims that scientific objectivity was its paramount value. In 1920, in a follow-up to *Liberty and the News*, Walter Lippmann and his coauthor, Charles Merz, savaged the *Times* for its coverage of the Russian Revolution. Having analyzed more than three thousand articles published between 1917 and 1920, the two ranked the paper's coverage as "nothing short of a disaster," relying too heavily on information accepted uncritically from self-interested official sources and deeply tainted by the anti-Bolshevik bias of both reporters and editors. Ninety-one times in 1917, 1918, and 1919 the paper had reported that the Bolsheviks were about to collapse, had collapsed, or would collapse soon. Each time, noted Lippmann and Merz wryly, it was "false news," and "it will not be true news if the Soviet regime should collapse late in 1920 or thereafter." The "news about Russia is a case of seeing not what was, but what men wished to see," the authors concluded. "The chief censor and the chief propagandist were hope and fear in the minds of reporters and editors." The solutions to the printing of false news were the same ones Lippmann had offered earlier: better-educated journalists, "supervision" from vigilant readers, and higher standards that were clearly defined and enforced by the press itself.[57]

The *Times* reportedly took the critique to heart and acted "vigorously" to improve its reporting.[58] But the vigor didn't stop the paper from perpetrating an even greater disaster in its Moscow coverage a decade later. The second time around, the incorrect story was driven by a reporter who again relied largely on information handed out by official sources and again was misled by his own arrogance and bias into reporting news that he understood was fake, but this one leaned too far *toward* the Soviet Union rather than against it.

By 1933, Josef Stalin's catastrophic scheme for forcing the collectivization of agriculture in the rich grainlands in and around Ukraine had blown up into a vast famine. As production at the state-run farms staggered into chaos and food supplies dwindled away, police and party officials moved in to confiscate anything remotely edible that was left and to arrest, deport, or execute the rebellious or simply unlucky. Forbidden to leave their home turf without permission, millions of Soviets starved to death, most of them Ukrainians.

Not so, said Walter Duranty, the *Times*'s Moscow correspondent. "Russians Hungry but Not Starving" was the headline of his article of March 31, 1933. Don't believe the "big scare story" recently circulated by a young Welshman named Gareth Jones, Duranty warned his readers; Jones's judgment was "somewhat hasty" and based solely on his forty-mile walk through some villages where conditions appeared "sad." Duranty's own "exhaustive inquiries" allowed him to say with confidence that although there was "a serious food shortage," there was "no famine."[59]

Jones's arduous wintertime hike that Duranty dismissed so glibly was in fact a journalistic coup, one that Duranty, who was pushing fifty and had lost a leg in 1924 in a railroad accident, probably could not have managed. The young Welshman, a former foreign-affairs adviser to David Lloyd George and a contributor to the *Cardiff Western Mail* and other papers, slipped into the famine region, which was closed to the foreign press, and tramped alone through villages and collective farms. He spoke in their own language to peasants who talked frankly about the mass arrests, the persecution, the terror, and, constantly, the hunger. "There is no bread. We are dying," was the story he heard at every hand. But his meticulous and accurate *reporting* was drowned out by the strident, self-assured stories Duranty churned out from his office chair in Moscow. After all, Duranty had already won a Pulitzer Prize for foreign reporting for his series of dispatches in 1931 about the beginning of the Five-Year Plan. Who wouldn't believe a reporter who had his kind of access—who had actually interviewed Josef Stalin himself?[60]

Of course, Stalin was the least likely person in the world to tell the truth about the devastation. It was Stalin who declared there would be no famine, and he had the power to fake the reality of his choice into being. (He decided; it was not reported.) Party officials and newspapers were forbidden to mention the mass starvation. Death certificates were doctored to obscure it. Letters were suppressed to conceal it. Bodies were heaped hastily into mass graves after they succumbed to it. And when the head of the census came up with an embarrassingly short population count because of it, he and his statisticians were swiftly dispatched by firing squad. Foreign journalists, who operated in the Soviet Union under strict controls, understood both the carrots and the sticks on offer for them: honest reporting would earn them only censorship and possible eviction, while cooperation bought special treatment and access. Many other Western journalists played down the famine, too, but Duranty, who seems to have been driven more by the desire for influence and attention than by any deep ideological commitment, cooperated particularly well. As his reward, he enjoyed two sets of perks: in Moscow a car and a mistress and in the United States a growing cachet among intellectuals and others who admired the Soviet experiment and were grateful to hear that it was succeeding.

Yet even as Duranty enjoyed the bilingual esteem, he came to understand that his stories were wildly untruthful. In fact, after finally traveling (by car) to see the famine regions for himself in the fall of 1933, he privately told the British embassy that "the Ukraine had been bled white," with as many as ten million people dead, and he quietly discussed those findings with other journalists, too. No such insights, however, ever made it into his correspondence, which continued to carry the *look* of on-the-ground reporting even as it relied heavily on information fed to him by the Soviets. Harrison Salisbury, who served as the *Times*'s Moscow bureau chief in the early 1950s, believed that by the time of Duranty's trip in the early 1930s, Duranty, whom Salisbury called "a calculating careerist," was too deeply invested in the story he had already created and in his own self-image as the premier journalistic expert on the enigmatic tyrant to publicly change his views.[61]

While the *Times*'s respectable readers were merely baffled by its "entertaining" and obviously fake stories about big black bugs with stupid names, the paper's self-conscious seriousness cast an aura of credibility over Duranty's articles on much more consequential public matters that turned out to be fake in their own way. In November 1933, based in large part on Duranty's fake journalism from Moscow, the United States formally recognized the Soviet Union.[62] The "real" journalist Gareth Jones, meanwhile, was murdered by bandits in 1935 while reporting in Japanese-occupied Mongolia. The circumstances are murky, but some researchers say they have found suggestions the Soviet secret police were involved.[63]

The failures of Duranty's work have been recognized for decades, enumerated in scholarly and popular books and in 1990 castigated by a member of the *Times*'s own editorial board, who called it "some of the worst reporting to appear in this newspaper." Critics have periodically invoked his example as a malign symbol of a fake journalist who disguised his personal preferences and convictions as rigorous reporting.[64] But we can only guess why the *Times*, in the 1930s no fan of the Soviet Union or its leader, continued to run Duranty's pieces even as some readers protested and some editors expressed growing misgivings about his integrity and accuracy. Salisbury, noting that "the struggle over Duranty was, to some extent, a reflection of the struggle in the United States over the Russian question," suggests the paper calculated that Duranty's popularity with readers on the left was fervent enough to balance out the dismay of those on the right.[65]

But in the aftermath of the devastating report issued in 1920 by Lippmann and Merz, another possibility presents itself. Already burned once for its pronounced anti-Bolshevik bias, the paper could have been hoping to salvage its reputation for objective and impartial reporting by listing too far in the opposite direction—by showing that it was not biased against Duranty's pro-Bolshevik bias. In any case, Duranty would not be the last single-minded but misguided fake journalist in an organization with more clout than courage to have an outsize influence on the course of human events.

THE JAZZ TABLOIDS LOSE THAT SWING

The *Graphic* was the first of the jazz tabloids to die. Its closure in 1932 was attributable to a multitude of ills: a slew of expensive libel judgments, a weak and skittish advertising base, sensation fatigue, the personal eccentricities of its erratic publisher. All of those problems, however, were exacerbated by the shifting tastes of readers mired in economic depression and spooked by global crisis, and when the naughty, the nutty, and the fake began to fall short as responses to the increasingly dire state of the world, the *Graphic* had little else to offer. The *Daily News*, in contrast, and to a more modest extent the *Mirror* did have an alternative: that formerly boring thing known as information. Although the two papers had always drawn the most attention (good and bad) for their photographs, contests, columnists, and juicy, often embellished stories about celebrities or crimes, they had also devoted at least some attention—that 10 percent, in the *Mirror*'s precise calculation—to more typical news about local politics, sports, and financial matters. And the *Daily News* had always included brisk items from the wire services it subscribed to.

Then, as the political and economic crisis deepened, the *Daily News* took a hard look at itself and, like the penny press, the yellow press, and some of the Black press before it, began to temper its sensationalism in deference to the changing times. "We're off on the wrong foot," the publisher reportedly told his staff in 1930. "The people's major interest is not in the playboy, Broadway, and divorces, but in how they're going to eat; and from this time forward, we'll pay attention to the struggle for existence that's just beginning."[66]

The *Daily News* continued to feature plenty of photographs and human-interest stories, but it also visibly embraced the traditional view of journalism as a public good, striving to give readers what they *needed* as well as what they enjoyed. By 1936, for instance, two years after the New York State health commissioner had a public spat with CBS radio over the network's refusal to let him use the word *syphilis* on the air, a number of newspapers, including such stalwarts as the *New York Herald Tribune* and the *St. Louis Post-Dispatch*, were breaking the taboo and running serious reports on social and medical issues surrounding venereal disease. It was, however, the upstart *Daily News*'s series that earned an honorable mention for public service from the Pulitzer Prize committee, which marked the first time the prestigious organization had recognized a tabloid for its reporting and tacitly welcomed the tab to respectability.[67] The contrast could not have been starker with the persistently garish *Graphic*, which with its failure to change with the times had faked itself to oblivion. In a newly sobered world, readers found good reason to prefer factual information, expertly gathered and authoritatively presented, to frivolous games in which no answers counted as wrong. In a newly sobered world, even a tabloid worked to claim its readers' trust. But in a newly sobered world, it turned out, the memory of the disillusionments of the Great War continued to distort relationships between readers and the political, religious, military, and journalistic figures who claimed the authority to present the world with news of itself.

7

"WHY DON'T YOU GUYS TELL THE TRUTH ONCE IN A WHILE?"

Even as journalists were struggling to repair the public's battered faith in their ability to get their responsibilities straight and their facts right, the brutal succession of economic, political, and military crises that wracked the world around midcentury placed more demands on journalism than ever before. The world seemed full of enemies, challengers, propagandists, and troublemakers, all wielding their own truths; government offices and military censors soon got into the act as well. Both fake news and fake journalism were often used by the "other side" as weapons, and journalists were supposed to expose those cases. Sometimes, however, they were used by "our side" the same way for the "greater good," and journalists were encouraged to collude in it. And when the world emerged at last from war, some members of "our side" began radically rewriting the relationship between journalism, government, and truth by turning the weapons of fake news and fake journalism against journalists themselves in the service of a good that seemed less great all the time.

THE MARTIANS ARE COMING

Everyone has heard the one about the Martian invasion and the national panic. Probably the most famous "fake-news story" in U.S. journalism, it has often been invoked as an emblem of popular gullibility in an anxious time. Its real lessons, however, are more complicated than that.

On the evening before Halloween in 1938, as supper dishes were being put away and children were readying for bed, an announcer broke into the CBS radio broadcast of tango music from the Meridian Room at the Park Plaza Hotel to describe atmospheric disturbances on the planet Mars. More music, more interruptions by men with important job titles, and the sober interviews with astronomers soon gave way to increasingly graphic and terrifying eyewitness reports.

A flaming rocket cylinder had plummeted to earth and dug itself into a pit on the Wilmuth farm in Grovers Mill, New Jersey, reported the network commentator who had rushed to the scene. Then a tentacled monster with gleaming black eyes and a mouth dripping saliva began to wriggle out of the cylinder. "Wait a minute, something's happening," the commentator panted. "A humped shape is rising out of the pit. I can make out a small beam of light against a mirror. What's that? There's a jet of flame springing from the mirror, and it leaps right at the advancing men. It strikes them head on! Lord, they're turning into flame!" Over screams in the background, the heart-breakingly courageous commentator stood his ground and continued to broadcast. "Now the whole field's caught on fire . . . it's spreading everywhere! It's coming this way now! Ab–about twenty yards to my right—." And then, abruptly, the microphone went dead.[1]

The *New York Times* reported what happened next. Panicked CBS listeners across America fled their living rooms, it said, and took to the roads and rails in desperate efforts to escape the invaders. Police stations and newspaper offices were swamped with frantic callers asking where to mobilize, begging for gas masks, pleading for casualty lists. Hospitals were sedating hysterical patients and college students were fainting in the crush to get to a telephone. A woman burst into a church shrieking that it was the end of the world and everyone should go home to die; another, found by her husband with a bottle of poison in her hand, screamed, "I'd rather die this way than like that."[2] So of course how silly they all felt when they finally caught on that the whole thing was not a genuine news report but simply a clever radio drama based on a forty-year-old science-fiction novel! What a sorry statement it all made about human credulity in the face of crisis, especially considering the many *genuine* crises going on at the time!

As a scripted performance that had been clearly identified at the top of the broadcast, the program never intended to manipulate people into believing a false account was actually true. But *fake news* is an apt label for another component of the *War of the Worlds* fiasco: the journalistic *response* to the allegedly faked news. The durable story of the mass hysteria described by the *New York Times* and dozens of other papers was extravagantly exaggerated.

People were undeniably frightened. Telephone switchboards were jammed, and police and newspapers fielded many more calls than usual. A historian who pored over some two thousand letters that listeners wrote to the Federal Communications Commission (FCC) or to CBS after the broadcast found that some audience members, most of whom had tuned in to the program too late to hear Orson Welles introduce the evening's installment of *Mercury Theater on the Air*, did indeed acknowledge having been taken in, at least briefly. Some letter writers vividly described physical symptoms they had experienced, such as fits of trembling and headaches, while others who phoned family and friends spread the misinformation and fear even farther. But that's about as far as the panic went. No credible eyewitness evidence survives of streets clogged with cars; no contemporary photographs show stampeding mobs; arrests and hospital admissions remained at normal levels. Only about a dozen of the letter writers confessed to having fled their homes. And although ten reported fearing or suffering heart attacks during the broadcast, no deaths were ever conclusively linked to the show.[3]

So although the program didn't trigger the mass panic of legend, it did affect its listeners more profoundly than did, say, the comedy patter of the ventriloquist Edgar Bergen and his snarky dummy, Charlie McCarthy, whose popular program was entertaining a far bigger audience on NBC at the same time. Most of the explanations for the surprising reaction posit some combination of the unfamiliar affordances of an evolving technology and the public mood of pervasive anxiety over political and economic conditions. Some point to Welles's skill at manipulating the familiar conventions of radio broadcasts—the male announcer's resonant voice, the conscientious identification of each new speaker and location, the colloquial and apparently spontaneous speech of the "ordinary" interviewees—that drew audience members in before they had a chance to think twice. Some suggest that by the late 1930s radio listeners had become so accustomed to authoritative-sounding announcers and imposingly titled experts bearing urgent news that the authoritative and imposing voices describing an invasion from Mars felt like more of the same. Some say that listeners still on edge from the European crisis of the previous month, when Nazi Germany threatened to take the Sudetenland from Czechoslovakia by force, sensed eerie parallels in a tale of all-powerful aliens invading an unoffending neighbor.[4] But other, less charitable explanations also surfaced. The *Chicago Tribune* was not alone in grousing that people who preferred radio listening to the brainier pleasures of reading just weren't very bright or were even "a trifle retarded mentally."[5]

The common denominator in all of these explanations is the belief that there was something about the way radio itself worked—something about the way the technology interacted with the human brain and heart—that gave it a particularly strong and possibly pernicious influence on human behavior and an especially tight connection to falsity and propaganda. In fact, the roots of the legend of the mass panic lay in the conviction that the reaction to the broadcast *must* have been profound. The myth did gain support from the sensationalized reporting by a large swath of the newspaper press. It was a hot story in any case, and given the often-contentious competition between newspapers and radio for the public's attention, lavishly covering the putative panic offered the press an opportunity to make their rival look heartless and its devotees silly. On October 31, the tabloid *Daily News* (New York), for instance, ran the huge front-page headline "Fake Radio 'War' Stirs Terror Through U.S.," backing it up with a photograph of Welles looming out of a shadow and looking both sepulchral and nervous. The *New York Herald Tribune* columnist Dorothy Thompson, who had been keeping an eye on the rise of Adolf Hitler, scorched the "incredible stupidity, lack of nerve and ignorance of thousands" who fell prey to a "mass delusion."[6]

But the journalists had help. The newspapers' false narrative was strongly buttressed by some Ivy League clout in the person of Hadley Cantril, a psychology professor at Princeton University, barely three miles down the road from the real and perfectly intact Grovers Mill (where today stands a historical marker commemorating the "Martian Landing Site" and the "landmark" broadcast that provoked "continuing thought about media responsibility, social psychology and civil defense"). Cantril seized

FIGURE 7.1 Grovers Mill, NJ, put up a marker on the "Martian Landing Site" where no Martians landed in October 1938.

Source: Wikimedia Commons.

on the Welles broadcast as a golden opportunity for an on-the-spot study of mass media and mass behavior. The 135 listeners interviewed about their experiences by the Radio Research Project, however, made up a highly unrepresentative sample: people who lived close to the alleged "ground zero" in New Jersey and who in most cases had already acknowledged that the broadcast had scared them.

Cantril, moreover, who had been a graduate student in Germany when Hitler was beginning his rise and who had coauthored *The Psychology of Radio* (1935), had convinced himself of the special power of the medium long before he began this research. Thus, the study, based on flawed data and driven by Cantril's own concerns about Americans' susceptibility to propaganda, seriously overestimated the extent and nature of the panic. It also offered its readers an opportunity to indulge in that perennial favorite, the Myth of the Clueless Other: "*I* wasn't so dumb as to fall for that

obvious fake—but, boy, that neighbor of mine. . . ." Even more significantly, it reinforced the anxieties of the many Americans who already
feared the power of the radio to delude and deceive—Americans such as
Dorothy Thompson, whose disgust at the "stupidity" of listeners to the
broadcast led her to conclude that "the immediate moral is apparent . . .
no political body must ever, under any circumstances, obtain a monopoly of radio."[7] With technology that was so easy to misuse, the human
mind was too easy to mislead.

THE TURBULENT PRIEST

In the 1930s, propaganda took a central role in U.S. public life. Even as
Edward Bernays and his fellow PR practitioners continued to argue that
good propaganda was healthy for a democracy, many Americans still felt
scarred by the undeniably bad propaganda of the Great War and expressed
real ambivalence about the power of the mass media. Americans did love
their radios. Entertainment shows continued to dominate, but news programming was gradually making a place for itself, with polls by the late
1930s consistently showing that people rated radio news as more trustworthy, more accurate, and less prejudiced than news in print.

That wasn't necessarily a strong endorsement of the quality of radio,
however; because the big newspapers tended to be more conservative, more
Republican, and more business-friendly than the general public, they were
contributing to their own displacement. And even though President
Franklin Roosevelt was exaggerating when he gloated that 85 percent of
U.S. newspapers were against him, he clearly preferred the medium that
he could control more closely. Radio allowed the president to sound warm,
fatherly, reassuring—and not incidentally reinforced an item of ongoing
news that was not so much faked as suppressed. Most Americans knew
the president had battled polio, but the White House's "gentlemen's agreement" with newsreel and newspaper photographers (an agreement
enforced by a vigilant press secretary backed by Secret Service agents) generally kept images of his wheelchair out of sight and concealed how severe
his disability really was.[8] The radio, in contrast, could not possibly betray
FDR's condition.

People were also increasingly concerned, however, about what *other* listeners were hearing on their radios, a fear confirmed by the audience's response to the scarily plausible science-fiction story and reinforced all the more by the response to the response. Alarmed conservatives saw Roosevelt's fireside chats as undemocratic abuses of power. In Germany and Italy, radio was becoming deeply entangled in the apparatus of fascism. And homegrown demagogues Huey "the Kingfish" Long of Louisiana and Father Charles Coughlin of Detroit were treating their rapt listeners to radio jeremiads that could make Fighting Bob Shuler sound like the vicar at the wedding.

In 1935, an assassin's bullet put an abrupt end to the Kingfish's ambitions, but for a time Coughlin, a Catholic priest who had first turned to radio in the hope of bulking up his tiny congregation, revived and amplified many of the same conundrums Shuler had posed about truth and falsehood over the airwaves. Hugely popular, with a mellow and persuasive radio voice dappled with the hint of a brogue, Coughlin supported FDR in 1932 but soon turned against the New Deal as ineffective and plutocratic. In 1934, he established a political organization of his own, the National Union for Social Justice, and thrilled millions of Depression-weary listeners with his fire-breathing populism and his loathing of Wall Street, the Federal Reserve, the gold standard, communism, internationalism, Prohibition, and a host of other targets.

For a brief moment, Coughlin and his populist allies seemed capable of mounting a "spoiler" challenge that could tip the 1936 election against Roosevelt. But Coughlin's ferocious and increasingly crude opposition to the popular president—calling FDR a "betrayer," a "liar," and a "double-crosser" earned the priest a rare rebuke from his bishop—was beginning to disillusion his followers and loosen their loyalties. By the late 1930s, the fanatical core of supporters who remained only encouraged his growing and venomous anti-Semitism, while his speeches were sounding more and more like Josef Goebbels's and drawing praise for their "courage" from the Nazi sheet *Der Stürmer*.[9]

Neither the networks nor the Federal Radio Commission and its successor the FCC nor Coughlin's political opponents nor the Catholic Church knew quite what to do with the turbulent but powerful priest. Fighting back could backfire. At the beginning of his radio career, CBS, nervous about his injection of politics into what were supposed to be purely religious talks, asked him to tone down his criticisms of President Herbert Hoover and government policy. In response, a defiant Coughlin postponed the sermon he had planned and mounted a pointed and provocative defense of free speech instead. Then when CBS refused to renew his contract and NBC declined to take him on, the priest started his own network of affiliate stations that quickly reached most of the country.[10] At the peak of his popularity, with tens of thousands of letters pouring into his offices every week, millions of listeners tuning in every Sunday, and significant (but not unanimous) support from church leaders, condemnations were toothless.

But after the 1936 election, as his bile intensified in tandem with the fascist threat in Europe, efforts to control or neutralize the priest grew more urgent. As in the fight over Shuler's license, questions of censorship and First Amendment protections heavily shadowed the debate. And as in the Shuler fight, partisans on both sides argued that it was not just permissible but necessary to take into account the truth or falsehood of the broadcasts in question. As Americans increasingly turned to their radios for fast and accurate news about the world political crisis, the ether seemed more than ever to require special protections against the further encroachment of fake news and propaganda into that vulnerable space.

Suggestions for how to deal with airborne lies could be creative. The League of Nations tried to do it by multilateral treaty. In 1936, twenty-eight members signed the International Convention Concerning the Use of Broadcasting in the Cause of Peace, which included an undertaking to prohibit or to halt and immediately correct any broadcast "likely to harm good international understanding by statements the incorrectness of which is or ought to be known to the persons responsible for the broadcast." Even leaving aside the unaddressed questions about how the agreement was to be enforced, however, the effort was quixotic. Italy did not sign it, and Germany and Japan had already withdrawn from the League, so the most worrisome propagandists of the day remained beyond the treaty's reach.[11]

As usual, the United States preferred voluntary tactics. In 1937, a former reporter then working at Columbia University's Teachers College established the Institute for Propaganda Analysis to fight misinformation in the news by teaching people, including children, how to recognize and challenge it. The institute, which had financial support from the Boston department-store magnate Edward A. Filene, published reports and news-letters and developed materials for use in schools. One of the institute's first reports, published in 1939, chose Coughlin's speeches as its case study for exploring "the fine art of propaganda" because they "represent a fairly typical borrowing of foreign anti-democratic propaganda methods by an American propagandist." With clinical precision, the pamphlet laid out the seven ABCs of propaganda or "tricks of the trade" that Coughlin used, including "Name Calling," "Glittering Generalities," and "Card Stacking," and described how people could recognize them and evaluate their accuracy. "Don't be stampeded," the pamphlet concluded. "Beware of your own prejudices. Suspend your judgment until more sides of the issue are presented. Analyze them."[12]

It was an admirably rational approach to a hugely irrational phenomenon, one of the earliest attempts at what might now be called media literacy, and in the late 1930s a million schoolchildren were said to be using its materials. But the institute also came under fire from conservative voices such as the Hearst press and Martin Dies of the House Un-American Activities Committee, who accused it of an unfair focus on the sins of the Right. The Institute for Propaganda Analysis closed down shortly after the war began, in part because it feared undermining the U.S. government's own efforts at "good" propaganda.

In Father Coughlin's case, however, ordinary citizens considered the most logical umpire of the problem to be not voluntary organizations but the government, and many wrote to the FCC either to support the priest's right to speak or to complain about the real harm his speech was causing. But letter writers on both sides also argued strongly that the FCC should take Coughlin's relationship with the truth into account in assessing his fitness to broadcast. In 1939, one Coughlin supporter, for instance, told the commission that any free American "has a right to talk their mind providing they are telling truths." Another insisted that the priest "tells us truths we should know, regardless of efforts to silence him"—efforts that other correspondents ascribed to the Jews who controlled the FCC or the networks or the White House. On the other side, letter writers worried that "any broadcast in which the truth is distorted or untruths are presented tends to foment differences among the American people" or wished that there were "some way of requiring that radio speakers have evidence for what they say." Both sides, pro-Coughlin and con, were marking a departure from the traditional "elite discourse" on free speech, which focused on the right to express one's opinion no matter whether it was based on truth and the importance of protecting robust debate even if the facts were false. For these ordinary citizens, broadcasters had the right to speak only if what they said was true. They had no right to free speech on the radio if their speech was false or fake.[13]

Later, when the Supreme Court got around to specifically addressing questions concerning the protection of knowingly false statements, its record would be mixed: in the case *Gertz v. Robert Welch, Inc.* (418 U.S. 323 [1974]), for instance, the justices found "no constitutional value in false statements of fact" (at 340) even as they also acknowledged that protecting some falsehoods was necessary so as not to deter true speech. But in the case *United States v. Alvarez* (567 U.S. 709 [2012]), involving a man who falsely claimed he had received the Medal of Honor, the justices essentially found a First Amendment right to lie.[14] Coughlin's case, however, followed a familiar pattern. Although both sides were hyperaware of the dangers of falsehood and propaganda and strongly protective of the airwaves, neither side believed that the other could judge what was true and what was not.

With war appearing inevitable, Coughlin's increasingly unhinged rants drew more and more protest. Individual stations were dropping his broadcasts. Advertisers were increasingly uncomfortable. Both Jewish and Catholic leaders were demanding action against him. Throughout the controversy, the FCC calmly—and accurately—replied that Congress had not given it the authority to intervene in program content or to pull individual broadcasters off the air. The FCC chair, however, was reportedly "known to believe that radio propagandists must be dealt with somehow," raising fears within the industry that if it didn't figure out on its own how to solve the problem, the commission might step in with new regulations of some sort. With that incentive, the National Association of Broadcasters (NAB), the industry's trade organization, voted to revise the provisions in its code of ethics governing discussions of "controversial issues." Stations still had a responsibility to provide time for "public forums," decided the NAB, but to ensure that access to the airwaves would be fair and open to all parties, beginning in October 1939 stations should not charge for the time. Since Coughlin had always pointedly refused to take free airtime because, he said, he would lose control over his content, the NAB's action was clearly intended to get him off the air. It worked.[15] The erstwhile radio priest, deprived of his resonant public voice, spent the next two decades ministering to his parish.

The NAB's action was a neat solution—except, of course, for Coughlin and his fans. The broadcast industry dodged the threat of additional government regulation by presenting a plot to quash a controversial troublemaker as if it were nothing other than a principled decision in the public interest. The FCC got the radio propagandist dealt with while remaining above the fray and avoiding the appearance of condoning censorship. The political establishment and the Catholic Church were freed from the pressure in some quarters to act against a polarizing figure who still had vocal supporters. The president was grateful for his liberation from a persistent critic. Messy questions of freedom of speech were laid aside, and no one was required to rule on whether falsehoods over the air were constitutionally protected. And as an added bonus, Coughlin's erasure *appeared* to have been accomplished professionally and voluntarily by a broadcast industry that could be trusted to police itself and cleanse the airwaves of propaganda and falsehood.

Then came the war.

ANOTHER WAR

This time things were going to be different. Like so many aspects of World War II, both journalistic and official plans for informing the public were designed in the fervent hope of avoiding the mistakes and disasters of World War I. No hyperactive George Creel here ostentatiously insisting that his propaganda wasn't "propaganda," no Committee on Public Information lustily spinning morale-boosting press releases, no falling for fake atrocity stories or crazy rumors.

Of course, it was more complicated than that—and not just because this war was even vaster in scale and more threatening in its enemies or because both radio and photography were now capable of bringing intimate, immediate news of war's agonies into everyone's home or because newspapers had by then been struggling for decades with declining trust and declining sales. In a total war, truth was both an ideal and a weapon. The democratic ideal of free and informed debate about the public good was one of the things "we" were fighting for, but the strategic manipulation of information and disinformation was one of the things we were fighting *with*. With the fate of freedom at stake on global fields of battle, what did "truth," "propaganda," and "fake news" even mean?

Even before the United States entered the war, organizations were making statements and staking claims about their commitments to telling the truth (the addendum "this time" was uttered sotto voce). In early August 1941, the AP put itself out front. Always conscious of its role as the pacesetter for hundreds of newspapers and always feeling the hot breath of its rival United Press (UP) and International News Service (INS) at its back, the AP launched a feature it called its "Rumor Deflator." The brief items, each just a sentence or two, were intended to debunk the "wild rumors, of the type not carried by the Associated Press, [that] flood the world almost daily." Throughout that August, the AP informed readers that Mussolini had *not* been shot, that Germany was *not* planning to sever relations with the United States, that the Germans had *not* bombed the Kremlin to bits, that presidential adviser Harry Hopkins had *not* stopped in Canada en route home from London, that British forces had *not* entered Iran.[16] The items included no context, no explanation, and no indication of the source of the rumor.

The effort was clearly intended to reassure readers—especially those who remembered the corpse factory—that they could trust the AP to be on the case, professionally tracking and evaluating the truth in a world full of bewildering and frightening news. Apparently, however, in the late summer of 1941 the news wasn't really that confusing. A search of the Newspapers.com database of nationwide newspapers reveals that in most cases the Deflator items circulated more widely in the press than the original rumors ever had. The papers that *had* printed the rumors in the first place, moreover, had almost always treated them with proper journalistic caution, describing where they had heard or read them and hedging them around with warnings that the information hadn't been substantiated; very few papers ended up looking gullible. The demonstration of general professional competence left the wire service's effort low on memorable gotchas—misplacing Harry Hopkins seems more a fumble than a "wild rumor"—and the AP Rumor Deflator deflated within a couple of weeks.[17]

The government, too, declared itself on the side of accuracy; its ideal would be a "strategy of truth." That was the coinage of Archibald MacLeish, poet and librarian of Congress, whom Roosevelt picked to lead the Office of Facts and Figures. Established by executive order in October 1941, the office had the stated mission of keeping the public informed about the administration's defense policies. With many Americans still undecided about entering the war or downright opposed to intervention, the reassuring title was intended to convey certainty, accuracy, and scientific disinterestedness, the very opposite of advocacy or persuasion. As MacLeish explained it in a luncheon speech to the AP in 1942, in a democracy the "strategy of truth" fills both practical and symbolic roles. It "is appropriate to our cause and to our purpose. . . . [It] opposes to the frauds and the deceits by which our enemies have confused and conquered other peoples the simple and clarifying truths by which a nation such as ours must guide itself. . . . The strategy of truth, in other words, has for the object of its strategy a truthful understanding by the people of the meaning of the war in which they fight."[18]

Six months after Pearl Harbor, in June 1942, amid complaints of disorganization and confusion in the various government information and intelligence agencies, the president folded most of them into a new central Office of War Information (OWI). "In recognition of the right of the American people . . . to be truthfully informed about the common war effort," as his executive order put it, the new agency was to devise "information programs designed to facilitate the development of an informed and intelligent understanding, at home and abroad, of the status and progress of the war effort and of the war policies, activities, and aims of the Government."[19] The OWI would produce propaganda (or, as the calculatedly benign official label called it, *information programs*), but the propaganda would supposedly be restrained, informative, and true.

Headed by Elmer Davis, a former reporter for CBS and the *New York Times*, the new office oversaw myriad initiatives but in a noticeably lower key than the Creel committee's operations. It disseminated carefully curated information about the progress of the war. It produced its own films and radio programs, including the popular Sunday-afternoon *Army Hour* on NBC featuring interviews, hometown stories, and round-ups from battlegrounds around the globe. It suggested patriotic plot lines for Hollywood movies and commercial broadcasts. It operated the short-lived

Rumor Project, which assigned volunteers across the country to gather and submit data on the scuttlebutt, gossip, and fake news they were hearing through the grapevine. It launched PR campaigns of the baldest kind. Obey rationing! Grow vegetables! Buy war bonds! Zip your lips! Go rivet with Rosie!

Other messages worked to strengthen morale and convey an inspiring view of why and how Americans had to defend democracy from fascism—sometimes a complicated case to make. The OWI film *Japanese Relocation* (1942) showed smiling Japanese Americans cooperating "cheerfully" and "whole-heartedly" as they were forced from their homes on the West Coast and sent to "pioneer communities."[20] And the booklet *Negroes and the War* (1942) began roundly with an essay by Chandler Owen, head of a Chicago PR firm, who had undergone a radical change of heart since his arrest under the Espionage Act for telling fellow African Americans they should not fight in World War I: "Some Negro Americans say that it makes no difference who wins this war. They say that things could not be any worse under Hitler. These are the people who emphasize liabilities; they never appraise their assets. They magnify the bad. They minimize the good. Without underestimating the Negro's liabilities, without denying the fact of handicaps and inequalities, I want to set down just what stake the Negro has in America—just what he has to lose under Hitler."[21]

Backing up the OWI was the Office of Censorship, directed by the former AP editor Byron Price. He didn't deal with the official censorship in the combat zones; that was left to the military commanders in each theater, who issued credentials only to reporters who had undergone background checks and pledged to submit all their material to the censors. Price focused mainly on the home front, working to ensure that no stateside print or broadcast journalists (or anyone else) revealed information that might help the enemy, whether about military movements and defense production or about the president's travel plans and the weather.

At a press conference, Davis and Price explained how they worked with the news media. "We tell them what they cannot print," said Price. "We give them stuff we hope they will print," said Davis.[22] But Price, a lifelong journalist and champion of press freedom, declined to require any kind of routine prepublication review and instead simply trusted journalists to voluntarily seek appropriate authorization before sharing any sensitive information. The code book of the Office of Censorship summed up the guiding principle: editors should "ask themselves with respect to any given detail, 'Is this information I would like to have if I were the enemy?' and then act accordingly."[23] Most news organizations were willing to do their bit. (We thought about it—and didn't report.)

The challenges inevitable to the task of informing the public from the fields of war were magnified in the biggest war the world had ever seen. Whether chastened by the catastrophic example of World War I or eager to prove that democratic values were superior to fascist ones or persuaded that trusting citizens (including journalists) with truthful information would best secure their cooperation and support, some officials continued to advocate for something as close as possible to a "strategy of truth." The government and the military, they said, should be as open and informative about the progress of the war as they could without compromising national security. People should be given news they could trust.

That strategy, however, often crashed headlong into counterforces: inconsistent messages coming from the alphabet soup of government agencies, vigorous disagreements over what *would* compromise security, concern for home-front morale, partisan rancor (fearful that the OWI was propagandizing for the New Deal, Congress cut its budget in 1943), quarrels about the seemliness of using propaganda and advertising tactics to "sell" a war. Journalists, too, were torn. Many felt a professional imperative to report fairly, scrutinize authority, and honor truth in the face of chaos and despite the censors; many believed that defending press freedom was another way of defending democracy against totalitarianism. The war coverage was also a chance to redeem their reputation after decades of accusations about sensationalizing, commercializing, faking, or slanting the news. Some of the reporting by the men and women in the field was in fact superb, a testament to their courage and humanity as well as to their professional skill, and the best work did help to repair Americans' faith in journalism as a public service—at least for a time.

But with the world in peril, democracy in jeopardy, and soldiers in danger, war correspondents—like most other Americans—also felt enormous pressure to "do their part," which could mean deciding for themselves to suppress or shade news that might hurt the war effort. As Walter Cronkite, who covered the war for the UP, put it in an interview near the end of his life, "In World War II everybody was on the team. We knew what we were fighting. We knew what the record of the enemy was. We were perfectly aware of the nature of the fight." Andy Rooney, who reported for *Stars and Stripes*, recalled later that "we were all Americans and we all wanted our side to win the war, so we did not want to do anything that could possibly damage our side. . . . [The military censors] very seldom took anything out, because we knew what we could write and what we couldn't write." One story he decided for himself that he couldn't write: descending into a cellar in a French farmhouse and finding five dead Germans lying in a pool of blood next to a gore-smeared white flag on a pole. The enemy soldiers had been trying to surrender, but the American troops had been moving too quickly to take any prisoners. "I don't think the American public would understand that," said Rooney. "They do not like to think of American soldiers doing that."[24]

News organizations often made their own deeply consequential choices about what to cover and what not to cover, exercises of self-censorship that could present distorted versions of reality. In 1940, Colonel Robert McCormick's *Chicago Tribune* did not run the scrupulously sourced reports by its Berlin bureau chief, Sigrid Schultz, about Nazi atrocities; the stridently anti-interventionist publisher was unwilling to do anything that might increase the pressure for the United States to enter the war.[25] The *New York Times*, fearful of being typecast as a "Jewish newspaper," ran only brief and vague reports about the Nazis' death camps.[26] The heroic Black navy mess assistant who grabbed an antiaircraft gun and fired it at the attacking Japanese at Pearl Harbor was described in the press only as "the unnamed Negro messman" for two months before the *Pittsburgh Courier*, an influential African American newspaper, finally unearthed and published Dorie Miller's name.[27]

Official military censors, too, made choices that could force even journalists who were "on the team" to feel they were pressured into faking news. Reporters complained that censors changed the rules all the time, that they just wanted to protect or glorify their officers, that they figured it was always less trouble to keep dubious stories out than to let them through, that they didn't know what they were talking about. John Steinbeck, who wangled a brief assignment covering England and the Mediterranean for the *New York Herald Tribune*, devised a cheeky retaliation against a censor who had "bruised" him: the novelist submitted

Herodotus's account of the battle of Salamis between the Persians and the Greeks in 480 BCE. "Since there were place names involved," he wrote, "albeit classical ones, the Navy censors killed the whole story."[28]

Even worse were the censors who actively distorted the news by blocking stories to spare someone embarrassment or to cover up someone's appalling blunder. Operation Husky began for the war correspondents on a note of surprising openness: General Dwight D. Eisenhower, in command of the Mediterranean theater, told them in a background briefing a month beforehand that the next target would be Sicily. The openness was both principled and strategic. As Eisenhower later explained, a pack of energetic reporters poking around North Africa for scoops might inadvertently tip the Germans off to where the activity was the hottest. "I decided to take [the reporters] into my confidence," Ike said, and "immediately placed upon every reporter in the theater a feeling of the same responsibility that I and my associates knew." Flattered as well as dutiful, the correspondents kept the secret.[29]

Soon, however, a different kind of secret loomed. On July 11, 1943, the second night of the Sicilian invasion, 144 American transport planes came roaring over the beachhead at Gela to drop hundreds of paratroopers from the Eighty-Second Airborne. Jittery U.S. antiaircraft gunners below opened fire on their own planes, shooting down 23 and badly damaging 37 more. At least 410 Americans were blasted out of the sky by their own comrades, picked off by friendly guns as they dangled from their chutes, drowned when they hit the sea. It was, Don Whitehead of the AP later recalled, "one of the most blood chilling sights I have ever seen." With Whitehead on the beach was Jack Belden of *Time* and *Life*, a veteran seen-it-all correspondent who had marched with General Joseph Stilwell on his legendary retreat from Burma to India. "Oh, God, No! No!" Belden screamed futilely at the gunners. "Stop, you bastards, stop! Stop shooting!"[30]

Witnessed by thousands, the catastrophe soon became an open secret, with the news rippling through the ranks of journalists and military brass alike. But officially secret it remained, the story blocked by military censors, who told Whitehead—later a two-time Pulitzer winner for his reporting in Korea—that revealing the friendly-fire carnage would have given "aid and comfort" to the enemy.[31] The story Whitehead turned in focused instead on a much more heroic story from the invasion, recounting "How Yanks Saved Bridgehead at Gela by Sheer Guts: Used Everything but Bare Hands to Stop Tanks, Then Attacked," as the *Boston Globe* headlined it on July 16, 1943, and quoting a colonel who said the Americans' successful defense against more than one hundred German tanks was "the greatest exhibition of guts and discipline in the history of the American Army."

Belden's two-part *Life* account of the invasion at Gela, told in the first person, included some requisite moments of terror but also piled on homey details: he comforted a seasick soldier in the landing craft; he met an Italian prisoner who knew his captor's Sicilian grandmother. One brief, poignant comment tugs at the attention. About to set off inland with a unit of Rangers, Belden and the others craned their necks as a pilot bailed out of a damaged Spitfire overhead and then struggled with a parachute that failed to open. "Helplessly we watched the pilot hurtling towards the ground. 'Poor devil,' said everyone."[32] The sad little vignette may have been Belden's clandestine acknowledgment of the much more terrible disaster he had been unable to stop and was forbidden to report—and a pointed reminder to the authorities that he knew what had really happened in the skies over Gela beach.[33]

The general public didn't. On the next page after Belden's first installment, *Life* ran an editorial bearing the jaunty headline "Our Army: With Its Allies It Achieved in the Sicilian Landing a New High in Military Science." The whole action, it crowed, "was a triumph in logistics."[34] Not only had a heart-breaking mistake been completely rubbed out of the picture, but the empty space had also been filled in with a bombastic—and fake— good cheer.

ENVISIONING WAR

For some correspondents, the chasm between what they knew and what they could say grew more and more troubling as the war dragged on. In his postwar memoir, the CBS correspondent Eric Sevareid wrote eloquently of the emotional ravages of rigid battlefield censorship on both the ordinary soldier and the conscientious journalist. He had gone to cover the war, he said,

with a deep desire to describe it all as it truly was—its glories and bru-
talities, its achievements and stupidities, its misery and luxury, happiness and heartbreak. I found I could not. . . . Nothing bolstered a soldier's
spirit more than evidence that the truth of the situation *was* being frankly
told; nothing gave him more confidence than to know that *somebody* was
aware of the things that were wrong. Few reporters had any desire to do
a "muckraking" job; but it was sometimes trying indeed to fight for hours
with the censors, then have some realistic combat soldier ask: "Why don't
you guys tell the truth once in a while?"[35]

Eight months later, in March 1944, the guys did in fact tell the truth
about Gela, but it took an oversight to allow that to happen. A *Stars and
Stripes* reporter mentioned the disaster in a speech at the Commonwealth
Club in San Francisco, apparently without rancor; he called it a "misunderstanding" caused by "lack of experience." Then an AP item about the
speech was cleared by an inattentive censor who was expecting no bomb-
shells in a three-inch-long home-front story about a talk at a civic club.
Reporters who knew about the incident pounced, hammering Secretary
of War Henry Stimson to provide a public explanation and then, when he
dithered, demanding a "more definite" one from the War Department.
Generally exculpatory statements from the department and the navy
oozed out for a week. When asked specifically why the incident had not
been made public before, an unnamed department spokesman replied that
"there was no reason why it should have been made public—it was an
unfortunate mistake of war, and steps had been taken to prevent a
recurrence."[36]

The revelation provoked a furious response. A notable one came from
Thomas E. Dewey, who was preparing for the Republican presidential primary in Wisconsin just two weeks away. In a nationally broadcast speech
to an organization of photojournalists, Dewey praised freedom of the press
in America as a "precious thing," especially compared to the "unashamed
falsehoods" most other people in the world were being fed. But the White
House, he said, was suppressing events "not . . . to keep information from
the enemy so much as to keep them from our own people."[37]

Dewey's comments were surely driven in part by political calculation,
and he went on to do well in Wisconsin, but his remarks also exemplify
some of the complexities of the public attitudes toward war news. The

report that four hundred lives had been wasted by a mistake didn't lead to outraged calls for investigating who was at fault, nor did it produce heart-rending newspaper interviews with bereft parents and grieving widows; both newspapers and the public understood their duty. A number of local editorialists, in fact, took pains to proclaim mistakes in wartime "unavoidable." After all, noted the *Daily Clarion* of Princeton, Indiana, "Incidents of mistaken identity have occurred in every war. Gen. 'Stonewall' Jackson, brilliant Confederate leader, was shot by his own men."[38]

The protests instead focused on the official dishonesty, with the blame placed squarely on failures by the government and the military, not the press. A Mississippi paper scorched the army for "forget[ting] the basic values of truth-telling" and "overlook[ing] the essential element of confidence which comes from knowing that failures and defeats are being reported as well as successes and victories." A paper from Idaho argued that since there was "no military justification" for suppressing the news of a "tragic" but "understandable" happening, it served only for "the protection of those responsible from criticism." The *Daily Clarion* seemed to sum up the general frustration. "The high command," it concluded, "still assumes that Americans cannot be trusted with unfavorable news."[39]

It was clear many Americans believed that the government was faking the news—sweetening, manipulating, and covering up what was going on in the war. An internal OWI survey showed that in July 1942—at a time when the dire situation in the Pacific was just barely beginning to turn around—28 percent of Americans believed the government was sugarcoating the news it released about the war; by June 1943, the month before the Sicily campaign began, the percentage had risen to 39.[40] The argument for more honest coverage was also made, eloquently and to a huge audience, in the February 22, 1943, issue of *Life* magazine, the middle-class bible for war coverage that was renowned for its vivid and humane photographs. Along with a seven-page spread of images of the battle of Buna in New Guinea and a spread-eagle piece about the death of one soldier they called "Bill," the editors pointed out that "LIFE cannot show any pictures of Bill. . . . It is against Army policy to show American dead." Nevertheless, they said, "we think that occasional pictures of Americans who fall in action should be printed. The job of men like [photographer George] Strock is to bring the war back to us, so that we who are thousands of miles removed from the dangers and the smell of death may know what is at stake. We think Bill would want that. . . . If Bill had the guts to take it, we ought to have the guts to look at it, face-to-face. Until we do, the home front will continue to be a mess."[41]

Photographs presented a particular challenge for the censors and the reading public. The tremendously popular *Life* and its rival *Look* along with the enterprise of brilliant professionals such as Robert Capa, Margaret Bourke-White, Dickey Chapelle, Carl Mydans, and W. Eugene Smith had made visual images central to the way the home front learned about the fighting. Photographs offered a new way to look at war, and Americans, balancing fascination with disquiet, took the realism and accuracy of war pictures with a faith they did not routinely extend to war news in print. The images seemed talismans direct from the front, arriving on the coffee tables of America still bearing the smoke of battle and the stamp of authority of the military censor on the scene.

In March 1943, Harrison Roberts of the AP, who was serving as the pool photographer on the Tunisia front, turned in a striking picture of soldiers under bombardment that was published in hundreds of newspapers, including on the front page of the mass-circulation tabloid *Daily News* (New York). Praised as "the picture that every news and military photographer dreams of getting," the image showed two medics tending a fallen soldier as exploding enemy bombs kicked up geysers of dirt around them. Although *Life* noted in an April issue that some "sharp-eyed experts on military tactics" had pointed to anomalies in the image—neither the soldiers nor the bomb bursts seemed to have been behaving quite as they should have—the magazine ran the picture anyway because, it explained, "the fact that it was taken by a top-flight Associated Press photographer and released by the War Department argues that the picture is authentic."[42]

It wasn't. And when the news got out that Roberts had faked the photograph, staging it and four others at a training ground because he had been unable to shoot the actual bombardment, the response was fierce. The AP suspended him, the War Department investigated him, and General Eisenhower issued a statement disavowing the pictures. Many of the publications that had used any or all of Roberts's images treated the revelation as almost a personal betrayal, reporting it under headlines that made plentiful use of the words *fake* and *phony*.[43] "The American people will take their war news straight, thank you," scolded the *Abilene (TX)*

Reporter-News, while the *New York Herald Tribune*, rumbling that "the integrity of photographic, as of verbal, reporting is far too precious to be jeopardized," went on to reassure readers that *most* photographers were honest and accurate.[44]

In large part because viewers trusted photographs from the front so implicitly, the censors had from the very beginning taken the view that images had to be handled with particular care. If they were real, so were the suffering and pain they showed, packing an emotional punch for stateside civilians living in constant dread over the safety of their soldiers, sailors, airmen, and marines. No one could imagine, and everyone could fear, what would happen if some reader on the home front shook open the newspaper, glanced at a photograph, and recognized the legless casualty as her husband or the crumpled corpse as his son. It was that fear that drove the censors' ban on photographs or films showing the bodies of dead American soldiers. (Dead enemies, however, were perfectly acceptable.) Also prohibited were images of gruesome wounds, soldiers with mental-health problems, and anything that might upset the viewers at home—a huge category encompassing such possible morale threateners as soldiers fraternizing with local women. All such photographs were hustled into a secret file at the War Department that initiates referred to as the "Chamber of Horrors."[45]

The problem with the war reporting was not just that people felt they weren't being told bad news; the falsely optimistic news they did read was also shaping their opinion in worrisome ways. Other OWI polls taken in July 1943, as the Sicily campaign raged, revealed that Americans were feeling complacent, even cocky, about the progress of the war, with nearly 60 percent of them predicting a German defeat within a year.[46] The complacency was a disquieting prospect for officials who knew that a hard slog still lay ahead, that many further sacrifices would be asked and many further griefs endured. Thus, even as some military and government authorities insisted on hiding bad news because they feared upsetting people, other officials were afraid of not upsetting people enough.

All along, some commanders had been more willing than others to allow the occasional release of dispiriting news, and the persistent buzz from journalists arguing for more freedom to report honestly was becoming a rumble. In the spring of 1943, with Roosevelt's backing, the OWI took action, formally encouraging a rougher-edged, more realistic depiction of war. Hollywood producers were urged to tell stories that were less saccharine, while military censors were requested to permit the "judicious" use of confirmed stories about Japanese atrocities against Allied prisoners of war (though rarely about Nazi atrocities, lest the war appear to be about rescuing Jews) and to actively seek out photographs that showed the grimmest aspects of battle.[47] In its September 20 issue, *Life* was finally able to publish Strock's seven-month-old portrait *Three Dead Americans on the Beach at Buna*, one of them the "Bill" who "had the guts to take it." The photograph was, to be sure, a landmark in the portrayal of the costs of war. But it was also, considered purely objectively, a beautiful picture, clear, perfectly composed, and skillfully processed. The three bodies, sprawled but not distorted or mangled, trace a graceful arc on the sand, with not a wound, a speck of blood, or an identifying feature visible. Americans who shook open the newspaper and had the guts to look at it face-to-face were still not seeing the face of "Bill" or the worst of war.

The results of the new policy were mixed. Even after Chief of Staff George C. Marshall reinforced the message, some military officials could not bring themselves to release harsh photographs. Some publications declined to use the ones they were offered. Some used them for less-than-admirable purposes of their own; a New Jersey paper headlined the Buna beach picture "Victims of Jap Treachery," a pointed reminder of Pearl Harbor, and in the caption offered false information about how the soldiers had been shot down.[48] Some readers who did see the grim pictures protested in letters to the editor.[49] Some of the most disturbing images remained immured in the Chamber of Horrors.

In the desperate early days of the Battle of the Bulge, as reporters began to sense the extent of the shocking casualties, the censors retreated into their customary obduracy and imposed a total news blackout on stories originating from the front. In a rowdy news briefing at the Allied Supreme Headquarters in Paris days before Christmas, the frustrated OWI news bureau chief called the policy "stupid," and other correspondents argued that since Germans at home were hearing radio news about the battle, the Allied home front ought to be able to hear it, too. Although the ban was loosened slightly, it remained essentially intact until Patton's tanks relieved the siege of Bastogne, and there was finally some good news to report.[50] The civilians in the OWI could recommend and encourage and urge,

reporters could negotiate and complain, but in the end the military officials on the ground determined how bad—and how accurate—the news
that Americans heard would be. (They decide; we can't report.)

The end of the war brought, as Byron Price had promised, an immediate end to censorship; most restrictions were lifted on V-E Day and the
rest after the announcement of the Japanese surrender, though General
MacArthur retained tight control over reporters in Occupied Japan.
Although the OWI was shut down in September, unloved and unmissed,
its Voice of America section, founded to broadcast to the Soviet Union
and other countries around the globe, did survive, moving over into the
State Department and eventually to the U.S. Information Agency.

As the United States settled into a postwar order of widespread economic prosperity at home and existential insecurity about threats from
abroad, many mainstream journalists looked back on their wartime service with a sense of accomplishment. They had not been lapdogs, they
believed; with their periodic protests over censorship and suppression,
they had demonstrated professional responsibility and redeemed some of
the failures of journalism in the previous war. But they had also done their
part for a great cause that transcended politics and partisanship.

That sense of participating in and upholding a national consensus
underlay what Daniel C. Hallin has called the "high-modernist" style
that characterized mainstream midcentury journalism. Dominated by
the "quality" newspapers in New York, St. Louis, Washington, Los
Angeles, and other cities and soon joined by the network-news broadcasts, journalism understood itself as a respected and socially responsible profession rooted in norms of objective verification, fairness, neutrality, and rationality. Mainstream journalists generally stood apart
from the political system and "above politics," but in the anxious atmosphere of the Cold War—where national unity in the face of the Soviet
threat was celebrated, dissent marginalized, political institutions generally trusted, and the superiority of white middle-class values taken for
granted—they felt themselves to be "powerful and prosperous and at the
same time independent, disinterested, public-spirited, and trusted and
beloved by everyone, from the corridors of power around the world to
the ordinary citizen and consumer," writes Hallin. "Politically, it seemed
possible for journalism to be independent of party and state, and yet
fully a part of the 'Establishment.'"[51]

As it turned out, however, the Establishment was not a safe space for journalists. Some of its members became very good at manipulating or exploiting the proudly held standards and values of professional journalism in order to elicit the coverage they preferred or of producing their own fake journalism. Rather than being "trusted and beloved," some journalists found themselves cast as enemies and maligned as un-American by powerful politicians or institutions with agendas of their own. And in a paradoxical twist, journalists found that the very professional conventions that they had embraced as a way to distinguish themselves from the fakers and the propagandists—objective verification, fairness, neutrality, rationality—could be their undoing.

8

"SO GODDAMN OBJECTIVE"

Much of what Senator Joseph R. McCarthy of Wisconsin said about himself was embellished, exaggerated, or fake, starting with his nickname (although "Tailgunner Joe" had avidly volunteered for a number of aerial combat missions during World War II, his official assignment was as a deskbound marine intelligence officer) and his heroic stories about the "war wound" that he had actually sustained in a shipboard hazing ritual.[1] Most of what the Republican said about Communists overrunning the State Department, the army, the Democratic Party, and the press was recklessly fabricated out of whole cloth, solely to exploit Cold War fears and earn himself power, attention, and reelection. Most of what he claimed about immense conspiracies and decades of treason was a purposeful lie. But his nearly five years' worth of vicious assaults, verbal and occasionally physical—in the cloakroom of an exclusive Washington club, he either slapped the muckraking columnist Drew Pearson in the face or kneed him in the groin—represented not just a low point for the U.S. Senate but also for parts of the U.S. press. And it posed an essential question: What happens when one side plays by the old rules and the other side simply fakes it?

Senator McCarthy was a cunning thug. His deployment of innuendo, ridicule, and contempt, his blithe trampling of legal and constitutional constraints, his gaudy bullying, and his crass exploitation of his public office made it impossible for journalists to ignore him, and the conventional wisdom holds that journalists actively enabled his rise with coverage that was both overlavish and uncritical. In fact, however, the journalistic landscape was more varied than that story suggests.

Plenty of news people and organizations—including Colonel Robert McCormick's ultraconservative *Chicago Tribune*, the *San Diego Union*, the Hearst press, and Hearst's widely syndicated columnist Westbrook Pegler—supported McCarthy openly until the end, or near to it. Plenty of others—Dorothy Schiff's *New York Post*, the *Milwaukee Journal*, Edward R. Murrow of CBS, James Reston, Richard Rovere, Drew Pearson, the syndicated columnists Stewart Alsop and Joseph Alsop, the cartoonist Herblock, and others among the nation's most powerful journalistic voices—could be equally open with their dismay, in editorials if not in news columns. Established journals of opinion such as the *Progressive*, the *Nation*, and the *New Republic* did not hesitate to weigh in against the senator, and even some smaller newspapers, notably the *Capital Times* of Madison in the senator's home state, routinely ran critical pieces. Thus, another bit of conventional wisdom, that no journalist dared stand up to McCarthy until the heroic Murrow showed the world what television could do, pays tribute to the wallop of the new visual medium, but it doesn't stand up to scrutiny.

But many news organizations did cover McCarthy with the carefully balanced, fact-centered, disinterested approach characterized as "objectivity" afforded to all their coverage of Establishment institutions, often relying uncritically on information from official sources and treating anything related to national security with marked deference. It was the adherence to those traditional professional values, as critics argued at the time and afterward, that was exactly the problem. Reporters, they said, were failing in other important professional duties: to exercise skepticism, to point out contradictions and correct lies, to bring their own knowledge and experience to bear in their analysis. Journalists, they argued, were not supposed to let themselves be used as a politician's personal PR machine, mindlessly transcribing everything and challenging the accuracy of nothing. And they were failing at their most basic task of *informing* people. The American journalistic tradition of "straight reporting," wrote Richard Strout in the *Christian Science Monitor* in 1950, meant that "the writer takes the statement of one man, tries to find the reply of another man, puts them competently together in one story, adds a little color and goes home to his wife and three children in the happy satisfaction of a day's work well done." The poor reader, meanwhile, "has no possible way of weighing what is said and is therefore simply confused."[2] Decades earlier, the new breed of professional journalists had begun embracing a carefully balanced neutral voice as a way to earn their readers' trust. Now, critics such as Strout were complaining, the both-sideism was just befuddling everyone.

The dominance of the major wire services in the news columns of the local and regional press only exacerbated the problem. In the month after McCarthy's breakout "I have here in my hand a list" speech in Wheeling, West Virginia, in February 1950, 75.5 percent of the items about him in the newspaper press came from the AP, 16.5 percent from the UP, and 5 percent from the INS, while nearly all the news on the radio came from these same three sources.[3] Wire services, with their far-flung and varied client lists, were even more likely than other mainstream news organizations to embrace "straight" reporting lest they offend any client by offering it an opinion it didn't share or an interpretation it disagreed with. Decades later, when the former *Milwaukee Journal* journalist Edwin Bayley interviewed wire-service reporters who (like him) had covered McCarthy, some of them claimed that they still bore the scars. It was "the most difficult story" they ever had to cover, they said; they "let Joe get away with murder"; they lost weight on the McCarthy beat; they "felt trapped. . . . That feeling of powerlessness was terrible." All three of the wire services, said one veteran, "were so goddamn objective that McCarthy got away with everything, bamboozling the editors and the public."[4]

Not every journalist got a stomachache from the senator; some of them actively sought to keep *good* relationships with McCarthy, relationships that had benefits for both sides. Reporters and the senator drank together; they bet on the horses together; they even made money together, as when ten photographers banded together with the senator as a silent partner in a dodgy land deal.[5] In keeping with the chummy conventions of the time, reporters rarely published what they knew about his personal peccadilloes— his frequent bouts of mean drunkenness, his violent outbursts of temper, his transparently clumsy attempts to "prove" unprovable assertions— while McCarthy returned the favor by feeding them "exclusive" stories and obliging them with juicy quotes on deadline.

There's nothing new about politicians who appeal to the dark side. There's nothing new about politicians who exploit reporters and manipulate the conventions of professional journalism in their own favor. What *was* new about McCarthy was that he was as dedicated a press baiter as he was a Red baiter. In the eyes of some critics, no other politicians in that era, not even Richard Nixon, made the demonization of journalists and the discrediting of journalism so central and calculated a part of their modus operandi.[6] The senator's bile toward the press stood out as a particularly egregious violation of what Daniel Hallin calls the "high-modern" norms that valued disinterest and consensus in the relationships between public figures and the journalists who covered them. McCarthy was essentially branding the journalistic work of those who disagreed with him as illegitimate—as fake.

McCarthy's tactic was a twisted variation of Hallin's famous model of journalistic "spheres," which posits that journalists use different standards to cover issues depending on how contentious they are. Issues in the Sphere of Consensus—the "mom and apple pie" category of ideas seen to be widely accepted by the mainstream public—invite support or even celebration rather than the disinterested presentation of opposing views. Issues in the Sphere of Legitimate Controversy, which are settled through elections and legislative debate, are addressed through the professional values of objectivity and balance. And the Sphere of Deviance is the home of views considered so far outside the mainstream that journalists feel safe dismissing, undermining, or even ridiculing them.[7] This time, however, it wasn't the journalists who were directing McCarthy's ideas into one sphere or another—it was McCarthy who claimed the authority to do the sorting and the journalists who were treated as the subjects, with friendly reporters welcomed into the Sphere of Consensus and those who opposed him shoved into the Sphere of Deviance. The professional boundaries marking acceptable journalism were being drawn by a politician.

McCarthy did not simply express his disagreements with the press over policy or politics; he attacked the honesty and competence of the profession as a whole and of individual journalists, too, even as he relied on the press to fulfill its obligation to honestly and competently inform people of the terrible things he was saying about it. He insisted that the press was riddled with Reds and treasonous at heart. He urged boycotts. He threatened to sue papers over unfavorable coverage and actually did so if the target was soft enough—as was the *Syracuse (NY) Post-Standard*, circulation less than eighty thousand, when it made several minor misstatements in an editorial.[8] He pulled fantastic accusations out of the air, claiming, for instance, to know of 126 "dues-paying Communists" working for the Sunday *New York Times*, even though its entire staff numbered only ninety-three.[9]

McCarthy exploited his official position to retaliate against his critics; after the *New York Post* editor James Wechsler ran a scorching seventeen-part series in September 1951 called "Smear Inc." about McCarthy's authorship of "the most fabulous hoax of the century," the senator hauled the editor before a closed session of his investigating committee for questioning.[10] Some of his assaults were deeply personal. Ronald May, who teamed with the muckraker Jack Anderson on a critical (and not entirely accurate) biography of the senator, was attending a banquet in Milwaukee where McCarthy was to speak. Noticing May among the diners, McCarthy dumped his prepared speech and launched instead into a complaint that he was being harassed by Communist spies, one of whom, he said, was sitting right there in the audience. Called out by name, May reluctantly stood up. "Pandemonium broke loose," the journalist wrote later, and when he tried to escape, he was blocked by the senator's bodyguard and jostled and heckled by the crowd. McCarthy's taunts often had all the finesse of a second-grade bully's, but they could stick. "Hey, there's Bob Fleming of the *Milwaukee Daily Worker*," he would tell the crowd, referring to a tenacious reporter for the *Milwaukee Journal*. "Hell of a guy. He's quoted a lot in *Pravda*, you know."[11]

The senator clearly intended his assaults not just to intimidate the "left-wing" press but also to undermine its authority and credibility in the public's eyes. In a maneuver that has only grown more familiar since the 1950s, readers were being given permission, by a public figure who spoke their language, to dismiss legitimate coverage of controversial issues as nothing more than politically motivated lies. They were being invited to trust false and deceptive news as long as it came from a source they found congenial and to treat news they disagreed with as fake.

Some news organizations cooperated avidly in the creation of news that was both fake and congenial, appealing to the large clutch of Americans who admired McCarthy as a scourge of the intelligentsia and a patriot who fearlessly spoke his mind. Colonel McCormick, once dubbed "the greatest mind of the fourteenth century," ran his *Chicago Tribune* as a throwback to the old American tradition of the newspaper as the personal voice of a strong-minded editor, and his strong mind embraced

McCarthy for most of the senator's career.[12] In 1951, the paper ran a truc-
ulent series on the "left-wing" press by William Fulton. The reporter was
well prepared for that assignment, having in 1943 turned in an eight-part
screed relating in vivid detail how the eastern press, the international
press, the AP, the New Deal, and "official Washington" were out to "get"
the *Tribune*.[13] No more temperate (or less conspiratorial) this time around,
the new series included, for instance, "Capital Sheet Defends Reds, Rails
at Foes" (February 19, 1951), which claimed that the *Washington Post*
"defend[ed] Reds and pinkos" and accused the AP's Washington bureau
of a "bias" that was "anti-McCarthy" because it devoted only eight or
nine paragraphs to the senator's six-hour speech in Congress. In "12
Spew Out Propaganda of Many Hues" (March 18, 1951), Fulton trotted
out a dozen columnists for personal ridicule, including Walter
Winchell, the Alsops, and Eleanor Roosevelt. Chortling that McCarthy
had "refuse[d] to be cowed" by the "unprincipled liar and fake" Drew
Pearson, he reminisced fondly about the time "McCarthy slapped the
columnist around."

Paradoxically, McCormick's *Chicago Tribune* may have come closest
in spirit to what the critics of objectivity wanted. The colonel's paper was
no mere stenographer of events; its reporters were not going home to their
families blandly satisfied with having balanced one man's comments with
another's. It was bringing its experience and judgment, such as they were,
to bear on its reporting. It was pointing out what it saw as contradictions
and errors. It was skeptical. It was challenging. It rarely left its readers
"simply confused," as columnist Strout had complained, about how they
should weigh competing claims.

It's undeniable that the carefully neutral approach embraced by the wire
services and some other news organizations often produced heavily distorted coverage of the Red-baiting senator. It's also undeniable that the
general dismay over the failures of journalism in the face of thuggery
helped spark the gradual (and then not-so-gradual) shift by many newspapers away from the blandly even-handed approach traditionally called
"objectivity" and toward a more interpretive, contextual, even adversarial
approach to reporting the news.[14] Yet no one who believed that objectivity warped accuracy was pressing for the replacement of objectivity with
hyperbolic pro-McCarthy partisanship; no one was advocating that the
bland and uninformative "he said, she said" approach should give way to
"he said, and she's a dirty rotten Commie!" They were instead tacitly

asserting their faith that coverage in a more interpretive and less rigidly "balanced" vein would inevitably lead readers to share their own critical view of the senator—that readers would see the truth. That is one of the reasons the myth of how the heroic and appropriately opinionated Edward R. Murrow finally brought the senator down by giving him room to reveal his own his ugliness took such strong hold.

The deeply subjective *Chicago Tribune*, however, was not just supporting McCarthy's berserker brand of anti-Communism but also sharing his belligerence, his glee in violating Establishment norms, his aggrieved victimhood at the hands of the liberal elite, and his insouciance about facts, asserting as true whatever it preferred to believe was true. In fact, the *Tribune* organization did more than merely *assert*; in at least one case it *acted* to summon into being the truths it believed. It also recognized, however, that its transgression of what had become generally accepted boundaries between politics and mainstream journalism and its production of a fake publication were things to keep quiet about, not to bruit as any kind of bold principle.

THE ODIOUS COMPOSITE

In 1950, the four-term Democratic senator Millard Tydings of Maryland was appointed to head a special subcommittee to investigate McCarthy's charges about Soviet spies in the State Department. Over the loud dissent of the two Republican members, the Democrats on the committee found that McCarthy's tactics represented "perhaps the most nefarious campaign of half-truths and untruths in the history of this Republic" and employed "the totalitarian technique of the 'big lie.' "[15] The full Senate adopted the report in July by a strict party-line vote after a pyrotechnic debate featuring shouting matches, profanity, and at least one narrowly averted fistfight.[16] The findings of the report, however, were overshadowed by contemporary events—notably North Korea's invasion of South Korea and the arrest of Julius Rosenberg on suspicion of espionage—that only fueled McCarthy's argument for stronger measures to fight Communist aggression.

When Tydings ran for reelection that fall, the *Washington Times-Herald*, owned by Colonel McCormick and edited by his favorite niece,

Ruth McCormick Miller, clandestinely involved itself in a dirty-tricks campaign to tip the contest to Tydings's opponent, an obscure Republican lawyer named John Marshall Butler who had never held elected office. Apparently with the colonel's blessing, McCarthy's staff worked closely with Ruth Miller and a *Times-Herald* editorial writer to finance, produce, and distribute just days before the election an anti-Tydings tabloid that it attributed to a front organization called Young Democrats for Butler—an example of fake journalism created with the collusion of journalists. Its most notorious feature was a photograph that showed Tydings having what appeared to be a friendly chat with Earl Browder, the former leader of the Communist Party USA. Tydings had in fact met Browder only once, when he came to testify before the senator's subcommittee, and the image was really a composite stitched together from two genuine but completely separate photographs taken years earlier.

After Tydings lost the race, a special senatorial subcommittee set up to investigate possible election fraud found a string of ethical failures in the financing, leadership, and tactics of the campaign against him. The fake tabloid, it said, contained "misleading half truths, misrepresentations, and false innuendos" and "disregard[ed] simple decency and common honesty." But in yet another example of the special anxieties brought about by questions of the authenticity of a visual image, the Democrats on the subcommittee seemed most outraged by the fake photograph. In the public report, they argued that using the composite was unprincipled, even un-American, calling it "infamous," "odious," and a "shocking abuse of the spirit and intent of the first amendment [*sic*] to the Constitution." In private, they fretted about its potential as political dynamite. A senator attending a Democratic strategy session before the start of the subcommittee hearings warned his colleagues that if they didn't "do something about it," they could all be victimized by fake photographs. He had seen, said the senator, a photograph of a "very wonderful member of the United States Senate" wearing a brief bathing suit in the surf while on vacation. "It would be a simple process to take his outstretched hand," cautioned the senator, "and place the hand of a woman in his, against the backdrop of a South Sea isle. That's what this type of campaigning is coming to."[17]

As Democrats publicly protested the image on ethical grounds and privately fumed on political ones, Republicans and their supporters, who had been mired in the minority for most of the previous two decades, defended it in tactical terms that only lightly disguised their own partisan agenda. Some of them sounded as insouciant as Emile Gauvreau of the *New York Evening Graphic* had about his half-naked brides and tenors in togas: the caption had clearly labeled the image as a composite, so it wasn't really fake and hadn't been intended to deceive anybody. Tydings's anger, the *Chicago Tribune* editorialized, simply betrayed his arrogant belief that "the voters of Maryland don't know the meaning of the word [*composite*]"—a clever argument that flattered voters even as it ignored the reality that a picture always punches harder than a verbose caption in tiny type.[18]

Republican senators refused to condemn the fake picture. Herman Welker of Idaho argued in the chamber that there was nothing new about composites; such pictures "have been used in political campaigns ever since man knew how to snap a shutter or to draw."[19] A week later several other Republican senators hijacked the floor debate on a draft bill, turning it into an hour-and-half-long round robin on why the Tydings composite was nowhere near as bad as the "phony photography" in which the New Dealers had been "experts." Many of the Depression-era images purporting to show the anguish of life in the Dust Bowl, asserted Senator Bourke Hickenlooper of Iowa, had been "deliberate fakes." Senator Karl Mundt of South Dakota was still harboring bitterness about Pare Lorentz's documentary *The Plow That Broke the Plains*, which he called "the most malicious slander on the mid-West that has ever been portrayed by print or photograph."[20]

Hickenlooper was exaggerating, but he wasn't entirely wrong. In 1936, the Farm Security Administration photographer Arthur Rothstein acknowledged having photographed the same desiccated cow skull against several different backgrounds—all within an area of ten feet, the agency insisted—while shooting drought scenes in South Dakota. The admission set off a frenzy of screaming headlines about "fake" photography (and, perhaps inevitably, "skullduggery," as a Topeka paper put it). Senator Mundt had made very similar complaints about Lorentz's film from the Senate floor after it was first released. It was "propaganda," he said back in 1939, that showed that "seeing is deceiving" and gave a wildly inaccurate picture of the people of his home state, and he demanded it be withdrawn from distribution. In both cases, however, railing about the inauthenticity of the images had been in large part an excuse to air an even greater partisan grievance: the use of government money to finance cultural projects and support the New Deal.[21] Rather than debating the ethics or

FIGURE 8.1 Arthur Rothstein's wandering cow skull reappears in 1950, fourteen years after its original publication, to complicate the debate over the Tydings-Browder composite.

Source: Farm Security Administration/Office of War Information Collection, Library of Congress Prints and Photographs Division.

appropriateness of using false images, these politicians were using the falsity of images to brand their opponents as liars.

For Senator Hickenlooper (who had been a minority member of Tydings's subcommittee investigating McCarthy's charges) and Senator Mundt (a former member of the House Un-American Activities Committee and now a consistent McCarthy ally), the controversy over the fake Tydings photograph revived the old argument, providing a welcome opportunity to yet again taunt Roosevelt's party and Roosevelt's successor regarding big-government spending. (Both the *New York Times* and the *Washington Post*, by the way—two of the papers McCarthy targeted most vigorously as unfair and biased—conscientiously cited some of Hickenlooper's sharp remarks about the New Deal, the *Post* quoting him on the front page and at length.[22] Oddly, the choleric and opinionated *Chicago Tribune*, darling of the right, did not.) McCarthy's own comments on the fake photograph were typically sophistical. "In general," he told the subcommittee, composites are "improper" in campaigns. But, he continued slyly, "fortunately, in this particular instance . . . the composite photograph of Tydings and Browder did not as a matter of fact misrepresent the attitude of the former Senator from Maryland toward the notorious Communist leader."[23] It wasn't a fake if it told a larger truth—as long as that truth benefited *your* side.

The Senate subcommittee investigating the Tydings–Butler campaign eventually acknowledged it had not found enough evidence to take the grave step of overturning the election. The Democrats' anxiety over the power of fake photographs, however, and the impulse to do *something* to control them remained. According to one Washington correspondent, they were particularly wary of how the brand-new technology of television might be co-opted by their political opponents. No one knew yet what it was capable of, but anyone could imagine the possibility that visually arresting composites would end up on the air and thus reach millions of viewers.[24]

So over the next months Democrats offered a flurry of remedies for fake images. As one of their recommendations for cleaning up political campaigns, the majority members of the subcommittee urged the Senate to outlaw all composite pictures, recordings, or motion pictures "designed to misrepresent or distort the facts regarding any candidate." The chair of the subcommittee announced he would look into setting up a bipartisan Fair Elections Commission, one of whose tasks would be to "discourage scurrility in any campaign for Federal office." The U.S. attorney general proposed tightening federal election laws to cut down on "defamatory and scurrilous campaign literature"; the "very use of composite pictures," he said, "is morally indefensible."[25] All of the proposed remedies would have raised serious concerns about First Amendment rights, but the inevitable partisan maneuvering ensured that the debate over rights never got far enough to matter. Congress went Republican in the 1952 elections, and with the ascension to power of the party that had already found profit in the use of fake images, the efforts to legislate against them soon faded away.

As did McCarthy. The giant-killer effect of the new medium of television has been exaggerated. Neither Murrow's CBS programs in March and April 1954 nor the 187 televised hours of the army–McCarthy hearings between April and June attracted the huge audiences that myth has endowed them with.[26] In a classic response to the entrance of any new technology into the world of politics, even some who were no fans of McCarthy had reservations about the way Murrow was wielding "the newest and most powerful form of mass media" in the absence of any "ground rules" to ensure its fair use. The newsman's highly selective editing, wrote the cultural critic Gilbert Seldes, "became the equivalent of the partial truth and the innuendo" that were McCarthy's own weapons of deceptiveness. "In the long run," he argued, "it is more important to use our communications systems properly than to destroy McCarthy."[27] Still, television was less essential to the dimming of the senator's star than were his own increasingly unhinged public statements, which began to dismay even his Republican colleagues and which fed President Eisenhower's decision to finally move against him behind the scenes. McCarthy fell because his own party was no longer protecting him.

For many of those Americans who did curl up on the living-room sofa to watch McCarthy in action, however, the stark visual contrast between the grotesque figure he cut—the heavy jowls and beetling brows, the thinning hair apparently filled in with shoe-polish, the juvenile needling and bombastic cruelty—and the mild, respectable-looking civil servants and uniformed soldiers he was bullying exposed his cruelty as real, his accusations as fake, and himself as belonging in the Sphere of Deviance. After his censure by the Senate in December 1954, he was essentially ignored by both the press and his colleagues. Within three years, he had drunk himself to death.

To this day, McCarthy continues to haunt the imagination. Few other politicians have given their names to an entire era, and the sturdy survival of "McCarthyism" in the public discourse is just one testament both to the enduring fascination with how the United States went so far off the rails and to the persistent suspicion that it's doing so again now. The lessons to be drawn, however, are unclear. True, much of the mainstream objective press and particularly the wire services clung for a long time to a deeply conservative professionalism rooted in cozy gentlemen's understandings about the social performance of authority, stability, rationality, and accuracy. The Establishment was to be respected; its boats were not to be rocked. And the conviction lingers that the press brought a rulebook to a knife fight: that journalists who were simply trying—even if unsuccessfully—to fairly and disinterestedly describe what was happening in the world inhabited by McCarthy were doomed from the start of their unequal battle against a shameless and devious opponent who delighted in violating norms.

But from another perspective, "McCarthy versus the press" was mostly a fake battle. From the point of view of the senator and his supporters, it didn't particularly matter *what* a given news organization said about him. It didn't matter how objective or not the organization was trying to be. It didn't matter that, say, the *Washington Post* had followed the rulebook in dutifully quoting without further comment Hickenlooper's comparison of the maliciously doctored campaign photograph to a hoary and over-hyped controversy over the bones of a dead cow. Nuance meant capitulation: the *Washington Post* had "defend[ed] Reds and pinkos"; therefore, it was the enemy, and even happening to hit on an accidental truth now and then rendered it no less illegitimate. McCarthyism set the terms that retain their power to this day: truth is about partisan advantage, not reality. Those who can control the journalists control the truth. And proving your opponents to be fake is a longer-lasting and more devastating tactic than proving them to be simply wrong.

CLOAKS AND DAGGERS

The anxieties and cruelties of the Cold War continued to inspire extreme responses that led to epic entanglements between fake journalism and the Establishment. A two-decade-long endeavor involved one of the most powerful, secretive, and unaccountable institutions in the western world— the Central Intelligence Agency (CIA)—which carried out some of the most egregious acts of fake journalism in U.S. history.

Some elements of the endeavor sound more like a UNESCO wish list than a CIA plot. The *Paris Review*, founded in 1953, was the archetype of the smart literary magazine. Run mainly out of a Left Bank café, it was edited by bright young men who skewed Ivy League and hosted legendary parties *everyone* attended. The quarterly journal published fiction, poetry, essays, and interview coups with the likes of William Faulkner, Dorothy Parker, Ralph Ellison, and Françoise Sagan. And it was fake journalism, the magazine having been "invented" by its cofounder Peter Matthiessen as "cover" for his own brief career as a CIA officer. At least one of the other founders hadn't been told about the connection and was "sore as hell" and "hurt" when he found out years later. He asked that his name be taken off the masthead.[28] In the case of the *Paris Review*, the agency's influence was minimal. The CIA left the editors alone most of the time, Matthiessen quit the agency early on, and the *Review* survives, presumably agency free, to this day, having maintained its Bohemian-inflected name even after it left Paris for a ritzy neighborhood in Manhattan.

Another of the agency's soft-power propaganda efforts, a front organization called the Congress for Cultural Freedom (CCF), toiled for twenty years to demonstrate the superiority of "the American way" over socialist thought. With CCF offices in thirty-five countries, the agency secretly funded magazines, musical and theatrical performances, and art exhibitions. It sponsored conferences and lectures. It commissioned translations of American literature—everything from Ernest Hemingway to Laura Ingalls Wilder to Ellery Queen—and subsidized the publication of hundreds of works of fiction, poetry, history, philosophy, and more.[29] But the CIA didn't stop at fictional literature: it fictionalized the news, too, creating fake news organizations staffed by fake journalists, placing its own fake journalists in real news organizations, and using real journalists overseas as real undercover agents.[30]

To an agency rooted in the credo that any weapon was justified in the battle against the worldwide Communist threat, the rationale made practical sense: because journalists could openly travel anywhere and ask questions of anyone, who would be better positioned to carry out a little intelligence work along the way? Journalists operated on the currency of trust, so why not take advantage of that trust and divert it to the service of a greater cause? In the agency's earliest years, it wasn't terribly difficult to find recruits; the same kind of Cold War deference toward national security that discouraged journalists from challenging McCarthy's extremist crusades also encouraged some of them to get "on the team" with the nation's foremost intelligence agency.

The CIA also set up front organizations with innocuous names to carry Radio Free Europe and Radio Liberty broadcasts to eastern Europe and the Soviet Union. From 1966 to 1975, it ran its own fake-journalism operation, Forum World Features. The news service "provided the United

States with a significant means to counter Communist prop [*sic*]," according to an anonymous internal memo written to the director of Central
Intelligence in 1968, "and has become a respected feature service well on
the way to a position of prestige in the journalism world." Among the many
bland features it distributed every week, however, could be stories giving
a distinctly American take on hot-button topics such as the war in Vietnam or wildly overstating the number of fighter-bombers sold to Somalia
by the Soviets. The forum's first titular head was John Hay Whitney, chair
of the *International Herald Tribune*. Its second was Richard Mellon Scaife,
who would later make a name as the "Funding Father of the Right" by
pumping hundreds of millions of dollars into conservative think tanks,
academic institutions, political campaigns, and publications, including
some doing opposition research on Bill Clinton.[31]

As the CIA came under increasing fire in the 1960s and 1970s for its
long record of dirty tricks, illegal tactics, and complicity in political
assassinations and coups, word of its secret dealings with the press began
to leak out, too. Among the most damning take-downs was Carl Bernstein's report in *Rolling Stone* in October 1977 that more than four hundred journalists from many of the nation's most powerful news
organizations—including, he said, ABC, CBS, NBC, Time Inc., the *New
York Times*, AP, Reuters, and Hearst—had worked for the agency over the
years with the full knowledge and approval of their top executives. Most
of those executives immediately denied knowing anything, or at least
knowing very much, and others claimed Bernstein's count was vastly exaggerated (the *New York Times* later reported it had identified "more than
70" working journalists with some sort of CIA connection), but it was clear
that the alliance between reporters and spooks had been both strong and
unholy.[32]

By their very nature, the reach and effects of the CIA-generated news
items are hard to assess. But in a three-part series published in December 1977, the *New York Times* offered an abundance of examples of bogus
news that it said the CIA had planted in the foreign press: an interview
with a Russian defector that included fabricated quotes; a doctored version of Nikita Khrushchev's off-the-record speech denouncing Stalin; a
false report that Chinese troops were en route by ship to aid Vietnamese
Communists fighting the French; "favorable" slants on the incursion by
American forces into Cambodia in 1970; a "stream" of stories attacking

and undermining Salvador Allende, the elected Marxist president of Chile who was eventually overthrown in a military coup abetted by the CIA. Agency officials insisted they had never consciously attempted to influence the U.S. press, and, indeed, the agency was supposedly prohibited from engaging in domestic operations—though that hadn't stopped it from spying on counterculture and antiwar groups in the United States. But several unnamed agency sources told the *Times* that there had been nothing to stop American correspondents abroad or news organizations at home from unknowingly picking up the bogus stories and using them in good faith in U.S. publications. In fact, the agency had recognized that what it called "blowback" or "fallout" in the United States from fake foreign sources "is inevitable and consequently permissible."[33]

The agency wasn't at all sorry, at least in public. The *Times* series ran just as a subcommittee of the House Intelligence Committee was opening hearings to examine the relationships between the CIA and the media. The new director of Central Intelligence, Admiral Stansfield Turner, was on hand to discuss his revised regulations that "unequivocally" barred the agency from using U.S. journalists in intelligence work.[34] But the hearings began with a bang when the former director, William Colby, told the committee members that the CIA's past efforts "should not dismay us today, but should rather give us pride that our Nation met those challenges with the weapons of ideas, and in fact won that ideological battle without recourse to bloodier weapons."[35] The longtime intelligence official Ray S. Cline made the hard-headed case in his prepared statement that in the brutal reality of Cold War politics there was—there should be—no difference between journalists and spies.

At this historical moment, the American news media, which have so successfully wrapped themselves in the First Amendment as if there were no other Constitutional obligations, constitute the only relatively unfettered espionage organizations in the country. Reporters investigate all leads to good stories, pay sources whose secrecy they preserve, and receive—and print—stolen documents from inside our own government. That is exactly what U.S. intelligence agencies do except that they concentrate exclusively on penetrating foreign governments and institutions, not our own. . . . It is only the extravagant post-Watergate pretension to purity and morality that suggests to some journalists that they should preserve a reputation for "cloistered and fugitive virtue" at the expense of a healthy relationship with the parallel profession of newsgatherers in CIA.[36]

In the war with the communist foe, there was no room for sentiment or idealism—or virtue.

Journalists appeared at the hearings, too, to protest against the CIA's exploitation of their colleagues, but they had another audience in mind as well: it was an opportunity to defend their tattered professionalism and reinforce its boundaries before a mistrustful public. Even the suspicion that reporters were being used to promote government policies, they said, was fatal to the credibility of all media. It was personally dangerous, too; if *some* journalists were known to be spies, then *all* journalists in overseas postings could be at risk. (Neither Cline nor Colby had any patience with that argument. Foreign nations always assumed U.S. journalists were undercover intelligence agents anyway, they said, so *not* using them wouldn't change a thing, and they might as well be put to good use.[37]) In a ringing statement, Eugene Patterson, the editor of the *St. Petersburg Times* and then president of the American Society of Newspaper Editors, fought back against Cline's cynicism and on behalf of honorable journalism. "It is essential," he said, "that the Central Intelligence Agency be brought to recognize that it must not destroy the validity of American institutions in order to save them. . . . The United States unilaterally disarms itself in its ideological conflicts when it abandons its beliefs and adopts its opponents'. The wound is self-inflicted when we rush to fall on our adversary's knife."[38]

As it turned out, Patterson's eloquent plea not to compromise the independence of the press did not sway the agency. Nineteen years later, journalists and others were appalled to discover that those revised regulations of Turner's that "unequivocally" banned the CIA from collaborating with U.S. journalists were equivocal after all. Turner had, it turned out, quietly included a provision allowing the director to waive the ban if he believed that extraordinary circumstances so required.[39] The CIA's promise to never again use fake journalists was fake. The long shadow it cast on the credibility of the press (and the government, too) was much more real.

9

"THE BASTARDS ARE MAKING IT UP!"

The hearing in 1977–1978 on the CIA's secret involvement with the media was just one sign of the passing of the journalistic era Hallin calls "high modernism." Journalists' and citizens' traditional trust in the credibility and goodwill of political and civic leaders had undergone a parade of shocks since McCarthy's rise and fall: the sometimes violent resistance of large swaths of the country to the expansion of civil rights; the embarrassments of the U-2 incident and the Bay of Pigs; the buzz of conspiracy theories surrounding everything from John F. Kennedy's assassination to Area 51; the war in Vietnam, launched by a lie and supported by a scaffolding of falsehoods; the sordid revelations from the Pentagon Papers; the low dishonesty of Watergate; the years of "research" from Big Tobacco assuring smokers that their habit wouldn't kill them. Poll after poll showed Americans' faith in the institutions of public life in a prolonged skid.[1]

Among those institutions were and continue to be journalism and the very idea of objective truth. Beginning in 1972, Gallup began questioning Americans about how they regarded news organizations. Four years later, shortly after the end of the "long national nightmare" that was Watergate, the proportion of respondents who trusted the news media a "great deal" or a "fair amount" to report fully, accurately, and fairly hit a peak of 72 percent, and it's been going downhill ever since.[2] Contributing to the decline has been a string of journalistic failures ranging from malpractice by rogue reporters to whopping errors of judgment by top editors. Also contributing has been a string of journalistic *successes* by reporters increasingly willing to be aggressive—tough stories about power, wealth, injustice, and war that presented readers and viewers with disturbing facts they were sometimes unwilling to entertain. Journalism also found itself in the crosshairs of the larger cultural shift that in its scholarly form was summed up (often with a sneer) as "postmodernism." But whereas in the 1970s and 1980s it became fashionable to blame academics, intellectuals, and liberals for having destroyed the very idea of truth and for promoting an impotent relativism, plenty of Americans who had never heard of Lyotard or Jameson had no trouble finding evidence from their own experience living in a diverse and fractious late-capitalist society that truth was contingent, language manipulative, and subjectivity paramount. From there, it was a short leap for many to the conclusion that journalism was little more than a collection of prejudices and personal points of view.

It's both a cause and a consequence of the fading faith in journalism that the past half century or so has brought both the broad disengagement of traditional objectivity from professionalism and the mass weaponization of journalistic faking (including the weaponization of *accusations* of faking) as tactics of political life, especially on the right. The danger to the public's understanding has more and more come from *fake journalism* and the often deliberate entanglement of fake objectivity with real partisanship.

TRUST NO ONE?

Already damaged by the McCarthy era and the revelations about the CIA's fake journalism, the traditional neutral-voiced, Establishment-sourced, "objective" brand of reporting was increasingly seen by readers and reporters alike as inadequate and outmoded, and many journalists, especially on the flagship newspapers, were redefining their own job descriptions. The McCarthy-inspired trend toward an interpretive, "contextual," even aggressive approach to reporting—which not incidentally also offered readers something deeper and more complete than television and the

218 "THE BASTARDS ARE MAKING IT UP!"

popular news magazines could supply—continued to grow. A recent study of front-page articles in the *New York Times*, the *Washington Post*, and the *Milwaukee Journal* shows that the percentage of "contextual" stories rose from 8 percent in 1955 to 45 percent in 2003.[3] Especially for a younger generation of journalists, deeply skeptical of the institutions of power and eager to pursue the big stories about government and the military, being "on the team" was a fading goal. David Halberstam of the *New York Times*, whose reporting from Vietnam grew steadily more critical over his two years there, later recalled spending some time in the field with Richard Tregaskis, an INS correspondent during World War II who was legendary for his coverage of the Battle of Guadalcanal. After meeting some of Halberstam's sources, Tregaskis turned on the younger journalist. "If I were doing what you are doing," he snapped, "I'd be ashamed of myself."[4]

Following a familiar pattern, clashes over the changing role of journalism both shaped and were shaped by partisan politics. Many on the right, Richard Nixon among them, saw the growing journalistic scrutiny of the powerful as confirmation that most reporters tilted left, and Nixon's White House systematically amplified and exploited that dismay, delighting supporters with slashing assaults on "the media" as elitist, un-American, deceitful, and reeking with liberal bias. As Nixon told his speechwriter, William Safire—proud creator of Spiro Agnew's immortal slap at journalists as "nattering nabobs of negativism"—the press was an enemy that must be "effectively discredited."[5]

The Nixon administration devoted immense energies to spinning the news in its favor, centralizing all news management and PR functions in the new Office of Communications, whose mandate was to orchestrate good news and, when necessary, rebut or undermine "hostile" journalistic coverage of White House actions and policies. Strategies included pushing out a "line of the day" that officials hoped would dominate the nightly news broadcasts, encouraging sympathetic interest groups to bombard journalists and politicians with pro–White House messages, and even secretly colluding with the influential public-opinion researchers Gallup and Harris to produce poll results favorable to the president.[6]

In the end, of course, it all fell apart. Not even the fake news, the fake grassroots surges, the fake public opinion, and the genuine efforts to "use the available federal machinery to screw our political enemies," as White

House counsel John Dean put it in a memo in 1971, prevailed over the combined efforts of whistleblowers, members of Congress, the FBI, the courts, and "real" journalists of the *Washington Post* and elsewhere to expose the president's corruption.[7] In this case, the "real" journalism—combining investigative *reporting* that was mulishly aggressive with a *voice* that was cool, dispassionate, even plodding—embedded in its style and tone a strong defense of the values of the kind of journalism increasingly being seen as old-fashioned. The *Washington Post* intended its approach to persuade readers that even on an intensely political story, its reporters were operating according to the professionally accepted conventions of impartial observation and rigorous verification—in other words, that the White House claims of media bias were biased for effect and that the *Post* reporters were not out simply to screw the president.

Other reporters, however, particularly those identified with the New Journalism, were much more unruly and much less demure. That squishy label encompassed a sprawling genre that appeared mainly in book form and in magazines such as *Esquire, New York, Rolling Stone*, and the *New Yorker*, where it was liberated from the daily deadline pressures, the stylistic conventions, and—some thought—the commitment to factual accuracy of the mainstream newspaper. Like the penny press of the 1830s, the yellow press of the 1890s, and the tabloid press of the 1920s, the New Journalism was driven in part by a sense that mainstream journalism as it stood wasn't serving readers, in part by a search for profitable new markets, in part by the pleasure of experimentation, and in part—a large part—by a rebellious desire to rattle the Establishment. The label generally referred to intensively reported stories aiming to connect more intimately with readers through a more personal voice, a more interpretive approach, and a more novelistic style that incorporated techniques such as deep description, verbatim dialogue, and close attention to the narrative arc. Strongly influenced by the self-focused, antiauthoritarian values of the counterculture, New Journalists embraced subjectivity and individuality as their hallmarks.

They also made the explicit rejection of objectivity a centerpiece of their identity. Given that journalistic work was deeply imprinted with the experiences, values, and biases of its authors, New Journalists argued, readers who didn't know anything of the "concrete details and particular sweat of [the journalists'] own inner life" had no real reason to trust them.

Because the ostensibly "value-free," nonjudgmental approach required of objective journalism, moreover, discouraged challenges to the social and political status quo, it tended to reinforce existing (mainly white and male) institutions of power. The performance of impartiality and neutrality, New Journalists and their allies insisted, was simply inadequate to address the urgent moral issues of the times; war, women's rights, civil rights, corporate malfeasance, and political corruption required something deeper than "on the one hand . . . on the other." Objectivity, wrote the *Village Voice* editor Jack Newfield, "is not shouting 'liar' in a crowded country."[8]

Other New Journalists, however, seemed more interested in style than in moral issues. They delighted in experimenting with the expressive possibilities of the personal voice and doing away with what Tom Wolfe called the "pale beige tone" of the traditional newspaper. That tone was, he said, the signal "that a well-known bore was here again, 'the journalist,' a pedestrian mind, a phlegmatic spirit, a faded personality, and there was no way to get rid of the pallid little troll, short of ceasing to read."[9]

The emphasis on literary art and personal vision wasn't, of course, particularly new; nearly a century earlier, "New Journalism" was the label for the human-interest stories that were the specialty of Pulitzer's *World*. And some critics carped that the new approach wasn't even journalism. Wolfe himself, however, insisted in his seminal three-part essay for *New York* magazine in 1972 that it was both, and given that one early critic defined the genre as "it's what Tom Wolfe writes," Wolfe's word carried weight.[10] As a young newspaper reporter, Wolfe recalled, he had been thrilled by his "discovery" that "it just might be possible to write journalism that would . . . read like a novel. *Like* a novel, if you get the picture." He did insist that even if the new kind of journalism *sounded* like fiction, it always adhered to fact. "The really unique thing" about it, he wrote, was the meticulous, often immersive reporting that undergirded even stories of ordinary day-to-day life. Wolfe said that in reading Gay Talese's *Esquire* story on Joe Louis published in 1962, which began with a quoted conversation between the boxer and his wife about his missing necktie, at first he "really didn't understand how anyone could do reporting on things like the personal by-play between a man and his fourth wife at the airport." His "instinctive, defensive reaction was that the man had piped it, as the saying went . . . winged it, made up the dialogue. . . . Christ, maybe he made up whole scenes, the unscrupulous geek. . . . The funny thing was, that was precisely the reaction that countless journalists and literary intellectuals would have over the next nine years as the New Journalism picked up momentum. *The bastards are making it up!*"[11]

The even funnier thing, however, was that for most of his career, the instinctive reaction of some readers to his work was that the bastard named Wolfe was making it up. They were not entirely wrong. Many of the New Journalists were (and are) conscientious reporters who remained committed to the ideal of accuracy and the professional discipline of verification even as they experimented with voices that were more personal and interpretive. Thoughtful in their craftsmanship, they were skillful at drawing insights from the deep excavation of events large and small—as in Terry Southern's piece in *Esquire* in 1963 about the Dixie National Baton Twirling Institute that turned into a meditation on the integration of the university widely known as "Ole Miss," or Joan Didion's bravura explorations of modern anomie through her immersion in California's countercultures. New Journalists vastly expanded the idea of the kind of topic that was worthy of journalistic attention—just think of John McPhee and the orange.

But some enfants terribles among the New Journalists seemed to be breaking the wrong rules of professional practice, not just the hoary ones about style and voice but the essential ones about factuality, too, as their looser narrative styles seemed to encourage, or at least allow for, looser relationships with accuracy. Much of this criticism of them came from mainstream journalists and from intellectuals in the literary world, the sort of people who saw themselves as guardians of tradition and who worried that the old standards and conventions, even with all their problems, were too valuable to toss away—that journalistic credibility would be even further eroded if the boundaries between journalism and other kinds of writing became too blurry. If the stylistic cues that everyone knew and agreed on were changed or missing, if readers were being offered work called "creative nonfiction" and "nonfiction novels" and "history as a novel, the novel as history," how would they know how or what to believe? If *some* New Journalists were casual about accuracy, would that raise suspicions about *all* New Journalists? If the loudest antagonists of objectivity were also the ones most often found to have shaded the truth, had "subjectivity" become synonymous with fakery? If reporters could choose to stop following *some* of the rules, who could say they were honoring *any*?

The critics had plenty of examples to worry about. One of Wolfe's most notorious pieces was the mischievous two-part series on William Shawn and the *New Yorker*, published in April 1965 in the *New York Herald Tribune*'s Sunday magazine, which purported to reveal the deepest secrets of that literary sanctum and its eremitic editor. Rich detail after outré detail, however, turned out to have simply been made up; Shawn did not, for instance, owe his reclusive nature to a close childhood brush with the thrill-killers Leopold and Loeb.[12] A story by Gail Sheehy in *New York* magazine in 1971 explored the city's sex trade through the experiences of a prostitute named "Redpants," who was quickly revealed to be a composite character. "So the story was true, sort of, but then again it wasn't," the *Wall Street Journal* grouched.[13] Truman Capote often boasted about the years' worth of research, the thousands of pages of notes, and the highly trained memory undergirding his "nonfiction novel" *In Cold Blood*, an elaborately detailed, dramatically structured, and "immaculately factual" tale of murder and justice in Kansas that originally appeared in the *New Yorker* in 1965. Over the years, however, readers and critics have pointed out any number of inaccuracies, misinterpretations, romanticized details, and inventions running through Capote's account, including the closing scene, a valedictory encounter in a cemetery that is both exquisitely poignant and entirely invented.[14]

All three pieces and many more drew both plaudits and derision. Some readers loved when New Journalists included themselves as characters in their own work or swanned their outsize personalities in real life: the dapper Wolfe in year-round white suits, the flamboyant Capote, the pugnacious Norman Mailer, the gonzo Hunter S. Thompson, and Nora Ephron, whose barely disguised roman à clef about her explosive divorce from Carl Bernstein left it up to the reader to decide whether it was Ephron's celebrity-journalist husband or her fictional heel who was "capable of having sex with a venetian blind."[15] For others, however, questions of personality blurred the lines even more between the real and the fake, raising questions about whether the journalists were reporting or navel-gazing, watching events or directing them for theatrical effect. Pallid little trolls obviously had their limitations, but how much more credible was a troll who was dancing on stilts and rocking a spray-on tan?

Many of these writers and others were heavily covered in the press by New Journalists and old ones alike, thus guaranteeing that any debates and doubts over journalistic veracity were also heavily covered—new revelations about Capote's *In Cold Blood* are still attracting attention fifty years later[16]—which has complicated their credibility all the more. But most of the New Journalists who came under challenge for fabricating details tended to respond with the blithe excuse that it wasn't faking—it was technique. Wolfe said later that his pieces about Shawn and the *New Yorker* had been parodies, but given that his normal style was already a parody of itself, it's difficult to understand how he expected anyone to know.[17] Sheehy's editor (and later husband) Clay Felker confessed in 1995 that he had deleted her paragraph explaining Redpants as a composite character "because I felt that it slowed the story down." But Felker—widely praised as a "visionary editor" who left a huge imprint on American magazine journalism—also went on to say that he hadn't seen a problem with using a composite at the time because the revered *New Yorker* writer Joseph Mitchell had done the same thing.[18] Capote simply dismissed all doubts as "silly question[s]" from "suspicious" people.[19]

Unlike mainstream journalists for whom the ritual of public acknowledgment, correction, and recommitment to standards serves the classic function of paradigm repair, the New Journalists' Wolfean wing generally refused to acknowledge that anything needed repairing in the first place. Rather than seeking to earn or restore readers' trust with a declaration of professional standards, they simply leaned on the ample liberties of subjectivity, asserting their *personal* authority and their *personal* right to transcend the normal standards. (We write what we please; you read what you please.) Many of the New Journalists of the 1960s and 1970s, having rejected the old rules, saw no reason to constrain themselves with new ones. Their professional boundary work consisted of vocally rejecting boundaries completely. And the massive popularity they often enjoyed—*In Cold Blood* reportedly earned its author $2 million from magazine, book, and film deals even before the book hit the streets[20]—suggested there was little reason for them to change. A large swath of the public was evidently willing to make its own peace with the ambiguities and to accept the existence of two categories of journalism: the kind you believed was true and the kind you knew was fun. It was the Pulitzers' you-can-have-it-all team of the serious "Senior" and four-o'clock-lizard-loving "Junior" all over again.

The most cogent critique in the standoff between the fuddy-duddies and the brats came from John Hersey, the author of the long piece

"Hiroshima" published in the *New Yorker* in 1946. Sometimes called a pioneering example of New Journalism, Hersey's meticulously reported, artfully structured, and stylistically ascetic piece about six survivors of the atomic bomb routinely tops lists of the best journalism ever. Writing in 1980 about recent work by Capote, Mailer, and Wolfe, he denounced Capote's term *nonfiction novel* as an "appallingly harmful phrase" that "may be mortal to journalism." There was, he said, "one sacred rule of journalism."

> The writer must not invent. The legend on the [journalist's] license must read: *NONE* OF THIS WAS MADE UP. . . . The moment the reader suspects additions, the earth begins to skid underfoot, for the idea that there is no way of knowing what is real and what is not real is terrifying. . . . [In *The Right Stuff,*] Wolfe is the paradigm of the would-be journalist who cannot resist the itch to improve on the material he digs up. The tricks of fiction he uses dissolve now and then into its very essence: fabrication. The notice on the license reads: THIS WAS NOT MADE UP (EXCEPT FOR THE PARTS THAT WERE MADE UP).[21]

Hersey's rejection of fakery was both eloquent and uncompromising, but his invocation of a metaphorical license to practice journalism left important questions unanswered. Who gets to issue those licenses? Who has the authority to police the profession and decide which sins are unforgivable? And what happens if no one trusts the licensing authority either?

Then in 1980 came Janet Cooke.

JANET'S WORLD

She wasn't a New Journalist. She wrote for the *Washington Post*, which was still enjoying bragging rights over its (mainly) rigorous investigation of a venal U.S. president, carried out in the cool impersonal voice of that despised "pallid little troll" as the most credible way to perform a version of objectivity. But as expectations about journalism continued to change, as newspaper circulations slid, as television news veered toward entertainment and television entertainment soaked up the public's attention, pressure was building in newspaper newsrooms to apply bronzer to the cheek of the troll.

Janet Cooke's "Jimmy's World" was exactly the kind of story editors were looking for. In early 1980, the *Post*, which was working to bring more diversity to its newsroom, had snapped up the promising young African American reporter from Toledo and assigned her to the staff of its District Weekly section. That September, after nine months of covering mainly routine local stories, Cooke turned in an article about the Washington drug trade told from an unusual angle. The lede was unusual, too, taking a tone that was strikingly dramatic for an article that shared the front page in a national newspaper with news about Iraq's drive into Iran and the campaign tactics of Carter and Reagan.

"Jimmy is 8 years old and a third-generation heroin addict," Cooke's 2,300-word story began, "a precocious little boy with sandy hair, velvety brown eyes and needle marks freckling the baby-smooth skin of his thin brown arms." Interviews with social workers, law enforcement officials, and medical experts were interwoven with matter-of-fact descriptions of Jimmy's daily life with his mother and her lover, a drug dealer who had hooked the boy on heroin when he was five. Jimmy, born after his mother was raped by his grandmother's boyfriend, didn't like school and rarely went. But when he did, "I pretty much pay attention in math," he said, "because I know I got to keep up when I finally get me something to sell."[22]

The story caused a national furor. City officials, appalled by Jimmy's plight but also shocked that a reporter had apparently stood "idly" by while a child was endangered, demanded the boy be produced for his own safety. The *Post*, with a touch of sanctimoniousness unsurprising in the paper that gave the world Deep Throat, insisted its reporter had the right to keep her sources confidential, and Woodward, who had left the underground parking garage behind to become the editor of the Metro section, promoted Cooke to his staff.[23] After a seventeen-day police search for the boy came up dry, the mayor called off the effort. "I've been told the story is part myth, part reality," he said.[24] The *Post* nominated the story for a Pulitzer anyway, and the following April Cooke's story was awarded the prestigious prize in the feature-writing category. Within two days, however, she was confessing that Jimmy was a fake: she had invented him from snippets of information picked up in conversations around town, and on top of that she had lied on her résumé about her educational background. She resigned and has not worked in journalism since. The *Post* returned the prize amid an even bigger national furor.

Just three days after the paper reported the fraud, its exhausted ombudsman posted an intensive multipage investigation into what had gone wrong. The *Post's* unseemly lust for prizes had made its editors careless. The *Post* had been lax in allowing Cooke to keep her sources secret even from her direct supervisors. *Post* reporters and editors who had harbored doubts about the story all along felt uncomfortable pressing the issue up the chain of command. The Pulitzer advisory committee had rigged the results by moving Cooke's story into the feature category and then overruling the jurors for that category to give it the prize. As a young African American reporter, Cooke had confronted impossible pressures that new white reporters did not face. The ferocity of Cooke's ambition had driven her to betray her editors and her profession. And a betrayal it was seen to be: the *Post* columnist Haynes Johnson wrote that the affair had left "a grievous open wound that will be long in healing and never, I believe, forgotten. Nor should it be."[25]

Thirty-five years later, some were still feeling the ache. A *Post* reporter who had worked with Cooke wrote in a retrospective of the affair that the young reporter's transgressions had forever changed the public's perception of journalism. "Suddenly, the institution known for bringing down liars and shining light on injustice was itself revealed to be a transgressor against the truth," he wrote. "As a reporter at the time, at the *Post* or anywhere else, you could feel the door slam. . . . After Cooke, it was still cool to be a reporter, but it was also a little tainted. One of us had flown too close to the sun. All had been burned."[26]

Even though no one called Cooke a New Journalist, mainstream journalists leaped to blame the fiasco on the entire edifice of New Journalism with an alacrity that suggested they had been looking for the opportunity to make that case. The National News Council, a foundation-supported organization that investigated complaints about journalistic inaccuracy or unfairness (though cooperation by any news organization in question was purely voluntary), asked more than thirty editors how they would prevent another "Jimmy's World." Among the suggestions: "Guarding against a blurring of the line between fact and fancy. Guarding against such techniques of the New Journalism and docudrama as tampering with or inventing quotes, rearranging events, and guessing what goes on in the recesses of people's minds."[27] Haynes Johnson was just one of many who invoked Sheehy's "Redpants" composite as a deplorable turning point; the specious defense of the composite as "a way to a greater truth," he said, had helped lead to the "eroding [of] public trust in the reliability of reporting."[28]

And the *New York Times*, the *Post*'s hottest rival, lamented the "permissiveness" about factuality that since the late 1960s had been creeping from *Esquire* and *New York* into the pages of the daily press. Some newspaper writers, it said, "felt they had a license to rearrange details to suit literary necessity, to 'polish' quotations, to combine biographical details from three or four people into one composite and pseudonymous character." The scandal, said the *Times*, had impelled some papers to issue formal guidelines about such matters as creating composite characters and using anonymous sources. "In some cases," the paper ventured cautiously, "they have published the guidelines, an action that both informs the public of the papers' policies and, presumably, encourages the public to trust the paper."[29] The idea here was an old one that went back to the *Boston Globe* and its extravagant apology for maligning Lizzie Borden: transparency, confession, and repentance would demonstrate professional responsibility and repair credibility.

This time, they didn't. When New Journalists such as Tom Wolfe and Truman Capote fiddled with the details in stories in glossy magazines or between hard covers, they were criticized in some quarters but not ostracized; there was no authority in a position to pull their licenses. These journalists' stature and their own refusal to acknowledge any wrongdoing deprived punishments and reproofs of their sticking power. And the readiness of many of their readers to agree that the disruptive originality of the New Journalism earned it leniency in the matter of factuality—that higher truths could emerge from lower bars of accuracy and that readers could decide for themselves where to set their own bars—further insulated the New Journalists from serious backlash. Subjectivity meant never having to say you were sorry.

When Janet Cooke faked a story in one of the most powerful papers in America, in contrast, the *Post* cranked up the apparatus of paradigm repair, ejecting her from the profession as brusquely as if she had carried bubonic plague into the newsroom. The paper had no other choice than to yank her license. Given the *Post*'s commanding reputation in investigative reporting, said an Arizona editor whose paper had won a Pulitzer that year for an investigative story of its own, the episode was "degrading to the whole industry."[30] In front of the whole industry, the *Post* had to prove it had not been tainted by the looseness of New Journalism. It had to reembrace the rules, reject the fake, and vow to reform.

But the reputation of traditional journalism was already too tattered to be easily repaired by an explanation and a penance, and the *Post*—the paper that was still preening itself over Watergate, whose young reporters had parlayed their scoop into two best-selling books and had been portrayed on the big screen by A-list stars with great hair—was too rich a target. Several commentators raised pointed questions about whether Deep Throat had been any more real than Jimmy, while others found evidence of partisan imbalance in the media coverage of Cooke's infractions. In the right-leaning *National Review*, Joseph Sobran argued that *Post* editors had been blinded by their desire to "*improve*" their readers with reportage "shaped by liberal mythology, by the imperative to show forth the suffering of society's victims, with the ultimate goal of remaking society." The press, he wrote, "even when accurate, gets what it's looking for. In this case, it was looking for the liberal victim par excellence. Miss Cooke served him up, and brinky though her offering was, not too many questions were asked."[31]

Sobran was not the only commentator to argue that editors were interested only in satisfying the stereotypes they already held. But that argument wasn't the unique possession of the Right, either. The left-leaning New York *Newsday* columnist Murray Kempton pointed out that Cooke had been driven by her yearning to move from the *Post*'s District Weekly section, which covered Washington's mainly Black neighborhoods and looked for stories that celebrated Black success, into the more prestigious Metro section, whose mostly white editors preferred stories of "black disasters." So "when she was struck down," he wrote, "she was busy contriving a 14-year-old black prostitute. She was, in other words, delighting her editors by bringing them back tales from a zoo."[32] The editor and columnist William O. Walker argued in the *Cleveland Call and Post*, an African American weekly, that Cooke's ambition to win a prize drove her to invent a story "about Black people [that] fit the mold the white press reserves for Blacks."[33]

If your coverage is making *everybody* angry, goes the newsroom cliché, you must be doing something right. In this case, though, everybody was angry because the coverage was doing everything wrong. But it wasn't merely the perennial "eroding of public trust" that was problematic. People seemed to have lost trust in the possibility of an *objectively credible* journalism—in the possibility that statements could be made about the world that were based on facts rather than on interest, identity, or partisanship and that would be acceptable across a broad spectrum of readers. Sobran, Kempton, and Walker, proxies for their very distinct audiences, singled out Cooke's editors, not Cooke herself, for the blame. Each argued that her editors misdirected her based on their own biases. Each perceived the editors' biases differently; Cooke's fake story was not an ethical or practical problem but an ideological one, proof for an increasingly cynical public that journalists would bend any fact in the service of their idea of truth. And debates over whether objectivity was possible or valid grew increasingly entangled with concerns about the flourishing of fakery.

The door was open for the routine weaponization of fake news in what used to function as the Sphere of Legitimate Controversy. In 1992, Bill Clinton walked right through it.

A PRETTY BIG RIGHT-WING CONSPIRACY

Hillary Clinton was roundly mocked when she claimed on January 27, 1998, in an interview on NBC's *Today* show that a "vast right-wing conspiracy" was attempting to destroy her husband's presidency. She wasn't wrong. Not all of the opposition came from the right and not all was conspiratorial, but the first Baby Boomer president (and the first Democrat to unseat a duly elected Republican incumbent since FDR beat Hoover) did unleash, among a sizeable chunk of the population, a focused antagonism so fierce that pundits were calling it Clinton Derangement Syndrome. Opponents objected to his politics, his morals, his slickness, his brainy wife, his youth, his "Dogpatch" background, his saxophone, and the personal charisma that somehow survived despite everything, even those "too-short jogging shorts, revealing an expanse of soft, milky thigh."[34] After Representative Newt Gingrich of Georgia drove the Republicans to a smashing victory in the 1994 midterm elections, the GOP took control of both houses of Congress for only the third term since 1933 and entered into a constant state of war with the White House. The former minority

party won important legislative battles, but missteps such as twice shut-
ting down the federal government during the impasse over the budget—to
the astonishment of many Republican lawmakers, Americans missed their
government when it was gone and blamed Gingrich and his crew for
hijacking it—only increased the Derangement.

So did the continuing ripples from regulatory changes such as the
Reagan administration's abolition of the Fairness Doctrine, the FCC
rule of 1949 with roots reaching back to the Shuler controversy, which
had been designed to make broadcasters serve the public interest by
devoting a "reasonable" amount of time to important questions while
"insur[ing] [sic] fair presentation of all sides of any controversial issue."[35]
So did the passage in 1996 of the Telecommunications Act, which only
hastened the wave of mergers and acquisitions of media companies by a
handful of sprawling conglomerates that were more focused on the bottom line than on the public good. So did the slew of new media struc-
tures, practices, and technologies—video cassettes, fax blasts, twenty-
four-hour cable news, MTV, incendiary talk-radio hosts newly liberated
from the mandate to be "fair," and the brand-new information and
communication system called the World Wide Web—that were allowing private citizens to follow or enter the public conversation more easily, often at head-snapping speed. An elderly reclusive billionaire, a political consultant who had masterminded the malignant "Willie Horton"
ad against Michael Dukakis in 1988, and a young former convenience-
store clerk were among the many actors who were supporting or producing a stream of extravagant alarms and accusations in forms that *looked
like* journalism, at least to anyone willing to squint. Supported by technological and policy changes, fed by *and* feeding off an all-consuming
culture of hyperpartisanship, fake news and fake journalism ran rampant throughout the years of Clinton's campaign and his presidency,
changing the terms of political coverage.

To be sure, Clinton had his (substantial) share of flaws, and one of the
most important media triggers for his travails came directly from the generally mainstream *New York Times*. Beginning in March 1992, as Clinton
campaigned for the Democratic nomination, stubborn reporting by the
Times's Jeff Gerth (sometimes working with Stephen Engelberg or other
reporters) posed insistent questions about a web of possible conflicts of
interest, favor trading, and obscure criminal activity involving an invest-
ment by the Clintons and their dodgy partner in 1978 in a money-losing

real estate deal in the Arkansas Ozarks. The stories were byzantine, even "incomprehensible" at times, as at least one fellow journalist complained.[36] Coming as they did from the nation's most influential paper, however, they commanded attention, often uncritical, from other news outlets while fattening the anti-Clinton narratives circulated by his opponents.

In early 1994, the mounting pressure over the so-called Whitewater deal finally drove Clinton to ask the U.S. attorney general to appoint a special counsel to examine the matter. Multiple investigations turned up no evidence sufficient to charge the Clintons with anything related to Whitewater, though more than a dozen associates and peripheral figures were convicted of various crimes. Gerth's reporting came under criticism for relying on sources who were obvious enemies of the Clintons, for misdirecting readers with muddled timelines, and for using what a persistent Gerth critic called a combination of "prosecutorial bias and tactical omission to insinuate all manner of sin and skullduggery."[37] (In 1999 Gerth would go on to coauthor several of the articles in the notorious *New York Times* series falsely accusing the Los Alamos scientist Wen Ho Lee of stealing nuclear secrets for the Chinese.[38]) Meanwhile, however, in August 1994 a new independent counsel had taken over the investigation begotten by Gerth's Ahab-like tenacity and lumpy prose. Kenneth Starr's inquisition was soon wandering far from the Ozarks, following Clinton into Little Rock hotel rooms and closing in on a former White House intern named Monica Lewinsky.

The right wing, delighted as it was by the Whitewater scandal, was not about to leave the thrill of exposure to the *Times* alone. Floyd Brown—the Willie Horton mastermind, founder of the hard-right advocacy group Citizens United, and author of the book *"Slick Willie": Why America Cannot Trust Bill Clinton* (1992)—blasted out a monthly print newsletter and a near-daily fax bulletin to keep hundreds of media organizations up-to-date on the latest anti-Clinton tips, scandals, and dirt. The media showed their gratitude. In an examination of two hundred stories in major news outlets published from November 1993 to March 1994, the *Columbia Journalism Review* found in mid-1994 "an eerie similarity between the Citizens United agenda and what has been appearing in the press, not only in terms of specific details but in terms of omission, spin, and implication." Rarely if ever did those stories say where the information had come from, obscuring the fact that the ostensibly independent press was being strongly driven by the Right.[39]

Another key figure was the billionaire Richard Mellon Scaife, an heir to the Mellon family oil, banking, and aluminum fortune in Pittsburgh. As a longtime angel of such right-leaning institutions as the Heritage Foundation, the American Enterprise Institute, and the Pepperdine School of Law, he wielded a potent but largely hidden influence on the burgeoning national conservative movement. As the former head of Forum World Features, the CIA's news-and-propaganda service, he had some experience in the dark arts of both fake journalism and front organizations. He also owned a paper of his own, eventually known as the *Pittsburgh Tribune-Review*, which he routinely used as his personal Rottweiler. Staffers said he frequently demanded they spin their stories to discomfit his enemies, suppress views that opposed his, and never, ever put anything about the Pittsburgh Pirates on the front page. (He didn't like the baseball team's owner.)[40]

Scaife had an "obsession" with Clinton, said a reporter who covered the mogul for years, because the president "represent[ed] what, for the right, ha[d] become the successor to the Soviet Evil Empire—cultural deterioration."[41] And Scaife put his money where his obsession was. He hired Christopher Ruddy, a former investigative reporter for Rupert Murdoch's *New York Post*, to cover Clinton's presidency for the *Tribune-Review*. For the newspaper and then later in a book, Ruddy turned the sad suicide of a depressed and overwhelmed Clinton friend into a lurid epic of murder and cover-up. Something was fishy, he insisted, about the death of deputy White House counsel Vincent Foster, whose body was found in July 1993 in a park outside Washington with a gunshot wound to the head. Brandishing scientific-sounding factoids about the amount of blood loss and muttering darkly about missing files and botched forensics, Ruddy made it easy for his readers to conclude that someone very, very high up had offed Foster to keep him quiet about . . . something.

Scaife also ginned up the conservative magazine the *American Spectator* into what he hoped would be a Clinton scandal factory. The billionaire had been giving money to the *Spectator* since the early 1970s, when it was a scrappy alternative paper run by Indiana University students whose raison d'être was making fun of the Left. By the 1990s, however, it had developed a name as a right-wing muckraker—a rare focus at the time among conservative magazines, most of which emphasized opinion and punditry over reporting. Two recent *Spectator* pieces by David Brock stood out. In March 1992 came "The Real Anita Hill," with its notorious put-down of Clarence Thomas's accuser as "a little bit nutty and a little bit slutty," which earned an enormous boost when the pugilistic right-wing talk-radio host Rush Limbaugh read excerpts on the air to his huge audience of "dittohead" fans. That was followed in January 1994 by "Living with the Clintons," a blockbuster alleging that as governor Clinton had routinely used Arkansas state troopers to procure women for him. Sharply criticized in many mainstream and liberal quarters, the "Troopergate" issue of the magazine reportedly sold nearly 300,000 copies, more than twice as many as the December number had.[42]

Not long after Foster's suicide, the *Spectator*'s editor in chief, R. Emmett Tyrrell, and a tight little team including a corporate lawyer, a PR man, and the owner of a bait shop secretly launched the "Arkansas Project," funded by grants from Scaife that would eventually total 2.4 million tax-deductible dollars. (Like other advocacy publications on both the left and the right, the *Spectator* had established itself as a charitable foundation.) Their plan was to dig up and publish what they were sure would be a huge trove of further Clinton scandals and thereby achieve Scaife's openly stated goal: to "get that goddamn guy out of the White House." The team, with the assistance of a private detective who had a history of segregationist ties, lavished Scaife money on chasing the latest leads into the Whitewater "fraud" and Foster's "murder." They poured it into searches for evidence that Clinton used cocaine, that he had fathered a Black baby, that as governor he had been implicated in the CIA's use of the tiny airport in Mena, Arkansas, for a gun-running and drug-smuggling operation in and out of Central America.[43]

From the outside, the Arkansas Project looked like a fiasco, brought down in large part by fake news run amok. Byron York, one of the *Spectator*'s investigative reporters during the Clinton era, wrote in a post mortem article that by 1994 "it seemed increasingly clear that nothing of any real consequence would come out of the Arkansas Project." Tyrrell's fixation on the flimsily sourced Mena story appalled some staffers, who argued that pursuing it would make the magazine a "laughingstock." When Tyrrell persisted, following up two portentous editorials with a long "investigative" story in August 1995, the assistant managing editor resigned.[44]

Everything began to collapse. After the *Spectator*'s Troopergate boom, circulation fell by one-third over the course of 1995, and advertisers leaked away.[45] The publisher was fired after he questioned the profligate and largely unmonitored spending on the Arkansas Project. After the magazine published a dismissive review of Ruddy's book on Vince Foster, a furious Scaife cut the *Spectator* off completely. Then the Department of Justice investigated Scaife and the magazine for more than a year on suspicion they had used some of the project's money to pay a potential federal witness against the president in the Whitewater case. No formal charges were brought. Even the Troopergate story was spattered when David Brock declared in *Esquire* magazine in July 1997 that he was no longer a "rightwing hit man." He apologized to the president for having ignored serious red flags concerning the troopers' credibility and having swallowed his own qualms about reporting on private sexual behavior.[46] Broke, the *Spectator* was sold in 2000.

Yet while genuine journalists may want to take a sneaky satisfaction in the apocalypse of the *Spectator*, the legacy of the Arkansas Project lingered. A private citizen with unlimited wealth and a personal vendetta against a duly elected president spent years secretly shoveling money at an all-out effort to dig up enough dirt to get him impeached and removed from office. The diggers were zealots with endlessly lurid imaginations and no experience in investigative journalism, and most of the "news" they pursued was fake. Their obsession was embraced and amplified by a large network of right-wing organizations, many of which were intricately connected through shared funders, supporters, and leaders. And the work was overseen by an editor in chief who "never saw the *Spectator* solely as a journalistic enterprise," York wrote of Tyrrell, but rather "as an adjunct to a political movement."[47] It was opposition research disguised as journalism or perhaps opposition disguised as research. It was certainly fake journalism.

The magazine did, moreover, have sporadic success with one of its main goals: getting its anti-Clinton material into the mainstream press. To be sure, the conventional media sometimes debunked and ridiculed the *Spectator* stories, but at least those stories were garnering attention. In late December, as galleys of the *Spectator*'s Troopergate piece began to circulate through the ranks of journalists and administration officials and as the White House struggled to wave reporters off of the story, CNN became the first mainstream news organization to address the affair. Reporter Bob Franken, however, seems to have done little original reporting other than trying to phone a few people, whom he said he was "unable to reach," and extracting a dismissive comment from a "senior administration official"; most of the segment simply cited Brock and the *Spectator* and repeated its allegations. (The segment also included a statement by the troopers' attorney and footage he provided of comments by his clients.)[48]

But once a member of the establishment media had taken the plunge to air its iffy take on an iffy story, other news organizations—including all three major networks news programs as well as NPR, the *Washington Post*, the *New York Times*, and the AP—stampeded to cover it, too, some of them "whipsawed," a *New Republic* columnist sniped, into repeating Brock's dubious yet damaging material just to keep up with the pack. (The columnist then obligingly repeated some of Brock's most dubious and damaging material yet one more time.) The *Los Angeles Times*, meanwhile, had been competing behind the scenes with the *Spectator* for months after receiving a tip from the same attorney for the troopers—and notorious Clinton nemesis—who had also pointed Brock to the story and who was hoping that coverage in a more mainstream publication would lend the accusations more clout. He needn't have worried. The paper's editors held their story back for days' worth of internal debate and further checking, finally publishing it only after the *Spectator* went public with its own version. Although the *Times*'s story left out most of Brock's lurid details and focused more on whether Clinton had offered the troopers jobs for their silence, it, too, reinforced attention to the *Spectator*. The widely circulated AP piece was often topped with loaded headlines such as "2 Say Clinton Used Cops to Cheat on Wife" or "2 Troopers Say They Knew of Clinton Trysts." The story faded quickly from the mainstream press after some errors came to light as well as news of the troopers' previous involvement in an insurance scam. But reminders continued to bubble on the right.[49]

The *New York Times Book Review* also strained to demonstrate its impartiality even when dealing with voices from the fringe. It could simply have declined to allot any of its limited space to Ruddy's *Strange Death of Vincent Foster*, especially since the book appeared right about the same time Kenneth Starr released his official report concluding—just as all the other official investigations into the death had—that Foster had unquestionably committed suicide. The *Times* instead assigned the book to Richard Brookhiser of the *National Review*, whose assessment was much more measured than the *Spectator*'s own review would be.[50]

In any case, beliefs are sticky, and given the powerfully partisan tilt to the *Spectator*'s coverage, loyal readers picked up the magazine knowing exactly what they would find and predisposed by their confirmation bias to believe that what they found was true. They would not easily have changed their minds about Clinton's dark deeds simply because the publication that fed their convictions got into financial trouble or suffered infighting among the staff. Tyrrell did not change his. In 1998, shortly after the release of the final Starr report, he published a celebratory round-up of the magazine's six years' worth of Clinton investigations, in which he insisted that Foster's death was still unresolved (which is not what the police, the FBI, the Justice Department, Congress, or either of the two independent counsels had concluded), that no "significant error" had been found in the Troopergate story (except that its own author had disowned the piece), and that no one had managed to "discredit" the Mena story, either—perhaps because everyone was ridiculing it instead. Even the *Weekly Standard*, another stalwartly conservative opinion magazine, used "Mena" twice in its "Parody" pages as a shorthand for daffy conspiracy theories.[51]

So the lessons from the *American Spectator* are mixed. The editor in chief's obsessive pursuit of evidence for his wish list of scandals weighed heavily in the collapse of the magazine. Even so, it also played a large part in normalizing—even requiring—the public discussion of Clinton's most personal failings, and it encouraged the wide circulation of fake scandals among those who preferred their facts untainted by contradictory evidence: truth as a matter of just deserts. And in something of a cosmic joke, it was a one-word copyediting mistake in the ever-contentious Troopergate story—the failure to delete the single name "Paula" along with the names of the other women who were reported to have had consensual sex with Clinton—that set in motion Paula Jones's sexual harassment lawsuit and led directly to the impeachment of the president.

EVERYONE IS A REPORTER

The screech of the computer modem was the mood music of the Clinton sex scandal. Unknown to most Americans when they went to the polls in

November 1992, the World Wide Web had just begun insinuating itself into their everyday lives when they first heard the name "Monica Lewinsky."

Among the first to grasp the populist potential of the web was a young former 7-Eleven clerk named Matt Drudge. Bored with his job at the CBS gift shop in Los Angeles and piqued by his father's gift of a computer, in 1995 Drudge began emailing and posting online snippets of gossip and entertainment news he picked up at work, eventually broadening into politics (and quitting his job) as his circle of readers and tipsters grew. Strenuously cultivating an air of bad-boy iconoclasm, he celebrated the web for democratizing the press and depriving the elites of their traditional control over information. "We have entered an era vibrating with the din of small voices," he said in a speech to the National Press Club in 1998. "Every citizen can be a reporter, can take on the powers that be. . . . The Net gives as much voice to a 13-year-old computer geek like me as to a CEO or Speaker of the House. We all become equal."[52]

Except that Drudge was more equal than others, hyperactive in his search for scoops, tips, and scandal. The original aggregator, he gathered much of his material from other sites and filled the home page of his *Drudge Report* (really his only page, with a design that to this day is firmly rooted in the web's Neolithic age) with dozens of links. Those he supplemented with some "exclusive" reports of his own—some based on legwork, some on gossip and guesswork—and with material from newspapers and wire services that he was able to access, often from insiders, before it was published.[53]

He was also more incendiary than others. Insisting he was carrying on the "great tradition of freedom of the press in this country, unpopular press," he prided himself on not having a journalism degree (or even a college diploma) and delighted in smashing all the contemporary rules of journalism.[54] At a bar association panel in 1999 on privacy and the press, he spoke freely about how he worked. He thought the best topic was scandal because it sold the most advertising. He saw nothing wrong in paying for information or using material that might have been gotten illegally. He had no problem with revealing the names of confidential sources. Sometimes he didn't bother looking for confirmation of things he knew for himself. And sure, he said, he had given information to the FBI; that was any citizen's "civic duty." When an attorney praised a magazine for delaying a story to check it further, Drudge challenged him: "So you're the type that would hold back information from the American people?" "Absolutely not," the attorney replied. "I would just advise people to form a belief in the truth of the information before they put it on their Web site."[55]

Not surprisingly, Drudge's rules-are-for-suckers approach and his preference for speed and provocation led to frequent errors, most of which he simply ignored. In 1998, when the media-watchdog magazine *Brill's Content* reviewed the fifty-one archived stories Drudge had run under the headline "Exclusive" during the first nine months of the year, it found that only thirty-one actually deserved that label. Of those, ten were untrue and/or never happened, eleven were true, and the remaining ten were of "debatable or still unknown" accuracy. That gave him an error rate possibly as high as 65 percent for the material that was actually original (and nearly 40 percent just for his claims of exclusivity). His most notorious flub was a report—sourced to "one influential Republican" referring vaguely to "court records"—that the White House aide Sidney Blumenthal had abused his wife. Even though Drudge retracted the item the next day, Blumenthal brought a $30 million defamation suit, one of the first legal actions to confront the meaning of free speech and free press on the anarchic frontier of the web. The suit was eventually settled, and a Scaife-funded foundation paid Drudge's legal expenses.[56]

Although much of the time Drudge was simply acting out the role of journalist, insisting he was upholding the freedom of the press while casually flouting the most basic standards for gathering, corroborating, and verifying evidence, some of his scoops turned out to be solid, and the "exclusive" that made his name and earned him national attention was generally accurate. But Drudge's report early on the morning of January 18, 1998, that *Newsweek* had "killed" an explosive story about Clinton's sexual affair with a White House intern (in fact, magazine staffers were still fighting over whether the story was sound enough to run) kicked off some of the worst journalism ever committed by the national press. The screech of the computer modem carried much—though not all—of the blame.

With the *New York Times* having established its website just two years earlier and the *Washington Post* a year and a half earlier, mainstream news organizations and news consumers alike were still figuring out what the internet was all about and what relationship it might have to journalism. A Pew survey taken in late 1998 showed that 43 percent of American adults owned a computer and 41 percent used the Internet, but only 15 to 26 percent visited online news sites at least once a week. The most popular topic for nearly two-thirds of those news consumers was the weather, while fewer than half visited sites about politics, mainly the websites of traditional broadcast or print media. Email use was heavy, online shopping was catching on, and a modest but visible community was using the web not just to get information but also to share it, through Usenets, chat rooms, forums, discussion lists, and the first stirrings of what would become the blogosphere.[57]

Both the vague promises and the murky perils of the web loomed large in the imaginations of the elite media scrambling to handle the hottest political story most of them had ever faced in a landscape none of them had ever inhabited. The new networked world seemed fast, and it seemed lawless. It harbored no editors or gatekeepers and required little more than a pair of deft hands at a keyboard to instantly launch stories, rumors, and gossip into the world. It could beat your scoop by hours. It could step on your editorial judgment, pushing you into publishing before you nailed down every fact. It could zing word of your own errors out into the world before you even noticed you made them. The whole affair turned into a classic media echo chamber, with anxious journalists writing for and against each other rather than for the public—which wasn't, it turned out, either terribly interested or terribly impressed. In the week after the sex scandal broke, nearly three-quarters of Americans surveyed in a CNN/*USA Today*/Gallup poll said there was too much coverage about it in the media. Only 37 percent said news organizations were acting responsibly, and 55 percent said they had been irresponsible.[58]

The poll's responders were right. Misjudgments and mistakes abounded in the press and often went uncorrected. No "second intern" ever came forth with more stories of sex, no steamy messages from the president were found on Lewinsky's answering machine, and on none of the tapes secretly made by Lewinsky's treacherous friend Linda Tripp did the young woman say that either Clinton or his adviser Vernon Jordan had told her to lie. On January 26, Larry King interrupted his conversation with his guests on his live CNN talk show to read the AP bulletin he had just been handed. It said the *Dallas Morning News* was reporting that a Secret Service agent was preparing to testify he had seen Clinton and Lewinsky together in a "compromising position." Ninety minutes later the paper pulled the item off its website; a source had called to say the story was wrong, and no agent ever testified to any such episode.

Brill's Content traced the item on its long and winding path back to its source. King told his viewers that the AP reported that the Dallas paper was reporting a story it had heard from a Washington lawyer who had heard his wife talking to a friend of someone who had talked to someone who said he had seen the president with Lewinsky. ("IMPORTANT IF TRUE!") By the time King decided (with the backing of CNN's chair) to read the bulletin on the air, it had become a seventh-hand version of a one-source story. And like many stories let loose into the media network, it was as immortal as a holiday fruitcake, continuing to surface in other outlets even after the Dallas paper retracted it.[59] News organizations were losing control over that classic tactic of responsible professionalism, the correction of their own errors.

Covert partisanship ran rampant. Many news organizations were basing their coverage on information from sources they did not name who had strong partisan agendas of their own. Kenneth Starr and the office of independent counsel were allegedly leaking like a sieve—a possibly illegal sieve, as questions arose about whether some of the information had come from grand-jury proceedings. (Starr denied revealing anything he should not have.) And the assortment of anti-Clinton activists, provocateurs, and book-deal seekers who had pushed the story to *Newsweek* and Drudge in the first place continued to peddle their talking points. Only rarely did journalists who used the information warn their audiences of its tendentious origins. In a study of 1,565 statements and allegations made by major news outlets about the scandal, a group calling itself the Committee of Concerned Journalists found that only 1 percent of them met the gold standard of citing two or more named sources. One-quarter relied on one named source; more than 40 percent were "analysis, opinion, speculation or judgment"; and the rest cited only anonymous sources or the reporting of other media.[60]

After Drudge burst on the scene with his *Newsweek* scoop, some journalists agonized over how to deal with his disruptive approach. Was he a fresh new voice who would reinvigorate a tired profession or a bomb thrower about to blow it up? Should the professional boundaries be redrawn to include him or was that a gerrymander too far? Tim Russert, host of NBC's Sunday-morning talk show *Meet the Press* and an acknowledged Bigfoot of the Washington media, caused a ruckus in some quarters when he invited Drudge to appear in a round-table segment with the journalists William Safire, Michael Isikoff, and Stuart Taylor. "You've been covering this rather aggressively on the Internet," Russert began. "What's your take?" After some back-and-forth, Drudge held up a copy of the *New York Post*, Rupert Murdoch's tabloid, with its front-page headline screaming that "hundreds!" of other women had been involved with the president. There's a "whole psychosis taking place in the White House," Drudge said knowingly. Russert simply turned to the next guest.[61]

The acerbic *Washington Post* television critic Tom Shales, for one, was indignant. Russert, he said, had "committed a moral if not journalistic sin" by hosting the "sleazy-looking character" who had "no credentials whatever to serve on a panel with professional journalists or even professional pundits." Russert later explained that he viewed his program as an op-ed page. "And Matt Drudge was a big player—*the* big player—in breaking this story," he said. "We can pretend that the seven to ten million Americans who were logging on to him don't have the right to see him, but I don't agree."[62] But Russert didn't invite his guest to the roundtable merely to be "seen." He treated him like a fellow journalist, referring to Drudge's gossipmongering and rumor peddling as "covering" the story. And he accepted without question an obviously extreme and thinly sourced claim ("There are hundreds of women!," Murdoch's tabloid said Lewinsky said Clinton said) quoted by a man already facing a $30 million lawsuit instigated by his nonchalance about sources. The longtime anchor evidently realized the paradoxical appeal of inviting a bad boy who blithely disrespected the establishment and the media onto a program that embodied the media establishment. That week's installment of *Meet the Press* (which also included an interview with Lewinsky's lawyer and with Clinton's staunch defender James Carville) earned its highest ratings since the Persian Gulf War.[63]

It was a perfect encapsulation of the way many mainstream news organizations behaved during the whole miserable affair. They were not producing fake news; the reporting wasn't *purposefully* wrong. It was something very close to *fake journalism*, work that carried both the look and the imprimatur of professional news organizations but that in the heat of competition shattered the rules and norms they purported to follow. When a year later Matt Drudge flaunted his operating principles—or lack of them—at the bar association panel, he could almost have been describing the charter for the mainstream coverage of the Clinton sex scandal. And when in February 1999 the Senate failed to convict Clinton on either of the articles of impeachment adopted by the House and his personal approval ratings soared, the press looked every bit as feckless as the president's adversaries did. A survey taken for *Newsweek* on the eve and the day of Clinton's acquittal asked respondents whether their opinion of the national media had changed over the previous year. Five percent said it had become "more favorable," and about a third said it had stayed the same. More than half reported their opinion had fallen.[64]

"FAIR AND BALANCED"

Another new entrant into the media landscape approached the Clinton scandal with laudable caution—at first. The Fox News channel, part of Rupert Murdoch's international empire of newspapers, satellite networks, magazines, television stations, book publishers, and movie studios, was just fifteen months old when the scandal burst. Murdoch, eager to expand his reach into American television, had hired Roger Ailes in 1996 to create a twenty-four-hour news channel that would compete with the maturing CNN and the brand-new MSNBC, a collaboration between NBC and Microsoft that had gone live only three months before Fox News. (Microsoft would later sell its stakes in the enterprise to NBC.) Ailes had made his name in politics by persuading Richard Nixon he needed a media adviser to orchestrate his comeback in 1968 and had gone on to help elect the likes of Senator Mitch McConnell of Kentucky, President Ronald Reagan, and President George H. W. Bush.

The presence of so aggressively partisan an animal at the head of a television news division broke precedent. But at Ailes's insistence the new channel was branding itself as straightforward and nonpartisan. "Fair and balanced," the famous slogan went; "we report, you decide." The strategy was to portray the network as standing in principled contrast to the many other news organizations that routinely and often unconsciously tilted left, while allowing viewers the illusion that they—not elites, not even right-wing elites—were the ultimate authorities on what was true. Ailes told the *Columbia Journalism Review* in early 1998 that he made "no apology for trying to be fair and objective and reaching out to points of view the mainstream media probably will ignore. . . . We work very hard bending over backward to present more than one point of view."[65] Artfully, the news chief was *not* telling his audience he would give them news with a conservative bias. He was promising them news free of a liberal bias. Normal news.

So for the first days of the scandal coverage, with rumors popping everywhere, Ailes ordered caution. He told John Moody, the senior vice president for news, to be sure he had multiple sources for anything that was said on the air. The message for everyone, said a staffer in the Washington bureau who took part in a conference call with Moody, "was—given Ailes's reputation and because of his Republicanism—as a news channel, we don't want to be first unless we have it dead right. We have to be sure."[66] But as soon as the *Washington Post* and other mainstream media ran their own stories, Fox News joined in with saturation coverage of the scandal, proudly trotting out an interview with Gennifer Flowers, who had roiled the 1992 primary with her announcement that she had had a twelve-year affair with Clinton. Fox also launched a short-lived show for Drudge (inspired by his star turn on *Meet the Press*) and a more successful nightly six o'clock program with Brit Hume that devoted five producers and correspondents to the Starr investigation.[67]

Despite the slogans, Fox News's conservative slant was clear from the outset. In 1998, the news segments tended to be generally straightforward, according to an analysis by the *Columbia Journalism Review*, though the choice of topics covered (and not covered) could be telling. But straight news took up very little of the twenty-four-hour day, and the chat and opinion programs featured many more guests on the right than on the left, lavished attention on Clinton scandals both real and imagined, and, said *CJR*, tended to use the phrase "fair and balanced" as "a marketing device and a fig leaf for Fox staffers who are otherwise perfectly candid (as they were in interviews for this article) about their right-of-center convictions."[68] The network's conservative tilt grew only more noticeable as it went on to cover a series of politically polarizing events: the bitter fight over the results of the 2000 presidential election, the response to the terror attacks on September 11, 2001 (9/11), the invasion of Iraq and its catastrophic aftermath, the hotly contested presidential election of 2004, the devastation of Hurricane Katrina in New Orleans, the global financial crisis, the election of the nation's first Black president, the rise of the Tea Party. Fox News's viewership was homogenous demographically as well as politically: it was overwhelmingly white; it skewed heavily male and older; and a smaller percentage than CNN's or MSNBC's viewership was college educated.[69]

That a news channel features partisan opinion does not, of course, make its offerings fake news. MSNBC, after gradually shedding such early hires as Oliver North, Laura Ingraham, and Ann Coulter, went on to solidify its own strongly partisan identity on the left, in part to distinguish itself from Fox News. A compelling argument could be made that having two robust networks with opposing voices serves the classic journalistic ideal of nourishing well-informed debate over public issues, just as if they were, say, the *Nation* and the *National Review*.

But that was never what Ailes had in mind. With his ostentatious embrace of fairness and balance, he was manipulating the outward forms of journalism for his own purposes, essentially using Fox News as a front. The network presented itself as acting in the public interest even as it defined a large chunk of the public as unworthy and deluded; it cloaked its opinionated views in the familiar language of fairness and objectivity, insisting that *it* was fully capable of upholding the ideal that was humanly impossible for any other media organization; it co-opted the traditional gatekeeping function to hold the gate against news it disagreed with. It was, in short, practicing fake *journalism* as a cover for its real work of partisan activism.

The myth of Fox News's impartiality was lethally undercut on the wild election night of November 7, 2000, as George W. Bush, the Republican governor of Texas, wrestled Vice President Al Gore for the presidency. Around eight o'clock, John Ellis, who was heading Fox News's "decision desk," reluctantly joined the other networks and the AP in projecting Gore as the winner in Florida, a victory that seemed likely to capture the tight election for the vice president. About two hours later, however, some questionable numbers prompted the news outlets to reverse course and return Florida to the "too close to call" column. Just after two o'clock in the morning, with about 3 percent of the state's precincts outstanding and Bush

ahead by half a whisker, Fox News became, at Ellis's urging, the first network to call Florida—and the presidency—for Bush. When the other networks quickly echoed Fox's projection, Gore called to congratulate Bush,
climbed into his limousine, and set out into the rainy night for the War
Memorial in Nashville to make his concession speech. As the numbers
continued to churn, however, frantic aides intercepted Gore before he
could step onstage, and the vice president called Bush again to take back
his congratulations. At four o'clock, the networks rescinded their projection for the second time. Only after thirty-six days of battles, bitterness,
and hanging chads did the Supreme Court put an end to the suspense with
its five-to-four decision for Bush. But the momentum from Ellis's original call helped keep the media narrative tipped in Bush's favor as the right-
ful winner throughout, with Gore cast as the sore loser.[70]

John Ellis was not just the high-level Fox News consultant hired by Ailes
whose premature call anointed a president. John Ellis was also the first
cousin of George W. Bush, the man he had rushed to anoint. No mainstream news organization would have allowed a close relative of a candidate for president anywhere near the unit where exit-poll numbers were
crunched and outcomes projected, and in fact the previous summer Ellis
had announced that he was recusing himself from writing about the campaign in his twice weekly *Boston Globe* column because he could not be
impartial. "I am never going to write a column about my cousin that is
not sympathetic," he told his readers. "He's family, and I'm for him today,
I'm for him tomorrow, I'm for him as long as he's running for office. If for
some reason he doesn't make it and decides to get out of politics, then I'm
for his brother Jeb from that day forward." Nor was Ellis's professional
stature enhanced by the giddy interview he gave Jane Mayer of the *New
Yorker* the morning of November 9, when he casually divulged that he had
been discussing numbers over the phone throughout the night of the election with George W. and "Jebbie," a.k.a. the governor of Florida. Exit-poll
results were supposed to be kept strictly confidential within the
network.[71]

But Ailes was unperturbed. Called with other network-news heads to
testify at a congressional hearing into the election-night fiasco, he worked
his characteristic jujitsu, turning the challenge to his own advantage. "We
at Fox News do not discriminate against people because of their family
connections," he said in his prepared statement. "Obviously, through his

family connections, Mr. Ellis has very good sources. I do not see this as a fault or shortcoming of Mr. Ellis. Quite the contrary, I see this as a good journalist talking to his very high level sources on election night."[72] No Congress member pressed Ailes to say what information Ellis could possibly have been seeking *from* the candidate and the governor that could inform his work at the decision desk. The only high-level source that night was Ellis himself, a political operative disguised as a journalist.

Having done its bit to put Bush into the White House, Fox News continued to serve the president. From his Fox News office, Ailes advised Bush Jr. just as he had Bush Sr., Nixon, and his other clients, counseling him on policy as well as on image; according to some senior editorial staffers, "Roger was on the phone every day with Bush. . . . He gave Bush the same kind of pointers he used to give George H. W. Bush—delivery, effectiveness, political coaching." And after 9/11, Ailes sent a memo to Bush's adviser Karl Rove urging the president to strike back hard at the attackers because Americans wanted revenge. Rove shared the memo not just with Bush but also with the national security adviser and other senior White House staff.[73]

Fox News personnel understood clearly what kind of coverage was acceptable. Accounts by current and former employees, disgruntled and not, anonymous and not, abound with instances when they felt pressured into changing stories, headlines, or placement in a more Republican-friendly direction. During the impeachment investigation, Ailes reportedly gave Brit Hume a "laundry list" of anti-Clinton stories he wanted the unit to do, some of which Hume resisted. Rupert Murdoch, too, sometimes weighed in with his preferences. Catherine Crier later said she had been told to temper her coverage of Hong Kong's transfer from Britain to Beijing so as not to endanger Murdoch's efforts to expand his empire into China. She soon left Fox News for Court TV.[74]

The pressure could be quite specific, as demonstrated by a trove of documents leaked to a filmmaker who was funded in part by progressive advocacy groups. (Fox News did not disown the documents.) For a period around 2003–2004, John Moody issued daily internal memos with instructions on how stories were to be spun. Staffers who covered the growing number of American war dead in Iraq, said one memo, should not "fall into the easy trap of mourning the loss of U.S. lives." The coverage of Bush's efforts toward peace in the Middle East should note his "political courage and tactical cunning." And when the independent 9/11 Commission investigated the administration's failure to prevent the attacks, Moody cautioned the staff, "This is not 'What did he know and when did he know it?' stuff. Do not turn this into Watergate. Remember the fleeting sense of national unity that emerged from this tragedy. Let's not desecrate that."[75]

Throughout it all, Ailes insisted that Fox was a traditional news network operating according to professional standards—and honoring them, too, unlike all the other news media that betrayed them instead. After the 2004 election, an independent research foundation found that 41 percent of Fox News viewers identified themselves as Republican (compared to 29 percent who said they were Democrats), and 52 percent said they were conservative. But when the *New York Times* cited the report in a question to Ailes about a rightward tilt at the network, the chief scoffed. That was "a totally fraudulent survey done by a bunch of liberals," he said. So protective was the network of its image that in October 2004 it successfully pressured the *Wall Street Journal* to issue a correction to its story about media strategies in the Bush and Kerry campaigns. "NEWS CORP.'S Fox News was incorrectly described in a page-one article yesterday as being sympathetic to the Bush cause," the *Journal* confessed.[76]

Ailes's refusal to acknowledge the obvious was in part a marketing strategy; in the network's early days, it wasn't yet clear whether advertisers might feel squeamish associating themselves with strongly opinionated programming. But it was also a brilliant political strategy. Viewers didn't want to think they were watching "conservative" news or "biased" news or "Republican" news; they wanted to think they were watching *true* news. And if their news was unbiased and true, then everything they saw on other networks was biased and wrong.

The strategy worked. Fox News surpassed CNN in viewership in January 2002 and led consistently thereafter. Ratings for the older network, which had made its name with its urgent, on-the-ground coverage of the first Gulf War, lagged behind Fox's even during the Iraq invasion.[77] And the Fox news division was bringing in spectacular profits—according to one report, higher than those of the other cable networks and the Big Three broadcast evening news programs *combined*. Ailes earned $23 million in 2009.[78]

MSNBC, meanwhile, was struggling with its persistent identity crisis. On what terms should it compete with Fox News? As the news network that offered real journalism instead of fake or as the cable network that offered a progressive bias instead of a conservative one? It had some notable successes with commentators who were opinionated, some of them operatically so. Keith Olbermann, whose highly rated *Countdown* program aired on MSNBC from 2003 to 2011, was famous for, among other things, his incendiary rivalry with Fox's Bill O'Reilly, who often "won" Olbermann's regular "Worst Person in the World" segment. But Olbermann's career highlighted the dilemma of a new-news cable network that unlike Fox had an old-news parent. In November 2010, Olbermann acknowledged that he had donated to the campaigns of three Democratic candidates. Like most traditional news organizations, MSNBC's corporate owner, NBC, does not allow employees to contribute money to (or participate in) partisan campaigns without approval from the head of news. So MSNBC's president, "mindful of NBC News policy and standards," briefly suspended the *Countdown* host. Some fans believed that Olbermann's violation played a part in the abrupt and unexplained cancellation of his program just two months later (though others, pointing to Comcast's pending purchase of NBC, speculated that the new corporate owner saw Olbermann as too liberal or at least too controversial. Comcast denied it had meddled).[79]

After the suspension, some argued that commentators, whose audiences after all tuned in expressly to hear feisty political opinions, should not be bound by the rigid rules of impartiality crafted for employees of network-news divisions that identified themselves with traditional journalistic values and strove to serve broad general audiences. But MSNBC intended its suspension of Olbermann to send a clear message: unlike Fox News, where commentators such as Sean Hannity donated unrebuked, MSNBC considered itself a journalistic organization with journalistic standards. Nevertheless, the boundaries could be difficult to maintain. Watching the coverage of the 2012 Republican nominating convention, the *New York Times* television critic Alessandra Stanley noted the uneasy ping-ponging between the "arch sarcasm and partisan brio" of the MSNBC hosts and the studied neutrality of the NBC anchors, who managed to "keep their opinions to themselves." MSNBC, she concluded, was "Fox's Liberal Evil Twin."[80]

Not quite. MSNBC's existential confusion over whether it was a news or a cable network could and did lead to confusion for its viewers. Fox

News's disingenuous but unwavering insistence that it offered only straight news, in contrast, confused only people who were not its loyal watchers. The real accomplishment of Fox News's brand of programming was that it helped to forge a large and devoted community bound not only by the political views that its members held in common (and those they despised in common) but also by their shared ideas about their precarious place in public life. Those ideas included a sense of being under assault by the liberal establishment; polls in 2004 showed, for instance, that among Fox News viewers 38 percent thought the media were strongly biased toward the Democrats, and just 14 percent saw their bias as favoring Republicans. People who got their news mainly from newspapers, CNN, or network news, in contrast, were about evenly balanced in their perceptions of where bias lay.[81] Fox News viewers were also more cynical about the mainstream media than other news consumers were, and, unlike CNN and network-news viewers, they said they preferred news that reflected their own point of view.[82] One consequence was that they tended to be less well informed about what was going on in the world than people who didn't pay attention to news at all, as measured in a survey and quiz administered in 2011.[83]

But if Fox wasn't preparing its viewers to ace a current-events exam, it was giving them something they found more useful, what the sociologist Arlie Hochschild has called a "deep story"—a story "that *feels as if* it were true." It was a story about the liberal elites' dismissiveness and condescension toward the white Christians who dominate Fox's audience—about their feeling of being under siege in an increasingly diverse and demanding world. Beginning in the early 2010s, Hochschild spent five years living in the largely conservative, working-class, and racially mixed community around Lake Charles, Louisiana, and talking with people about their lives. Many of her interviewees spoke about Fox News with a reverence and affection no other mere news organization could claim; it felt like "family," they told her, and, Hochschild wrote, it seemed to stand as "an extra pillar of political culture all its own," telling viewers "what to feel afraid, anxious, and angry about."[84]

Fox News was not just serving as a covert wing of the Republican Party; it was also fulfilling many of the functions of a traditional fundamentalist church. It offered comfort, community, identity, and validation. Its dicta were accepted as absolute truth. And anyone who questioned its truth could be—at least metaphorically—damned. The network was calling what it did "journalism" that provided the information "you" needed to "decide"; it claimed to be rooted in the empirical conventions of traditional reporting. But its fake journalism allowed Fox to tacitly claim a sort of extrajournalistic authority that few other news organizations could or would sustain: it was asserting biblical inerrancy. That made its hyper-partisan fake news undebatable in the public square.

10

"FAKE BUT ACCURATE"

In a nation beset by polarizing contentions and crises—a minority president seated by Supreme Court fiat, an appallingly lethal terrorist attack, a pair of endless wars fed by deceptive intelligence and marked by human-rights abuses, the election of an "alien" president—a parade of journalistic mistakes, misinterpretations, and manipulations kept the mainstream press poised in an almost constant state of agitation and apology. Not all of the errors were *fakes* according to any classic definition: not all were conscious efforts to deceive readers or viewers for reasons of the journalists' own. Some seem to have reflected the journalists' deception of themselves in the service of some other belief. Some were mischievous or half-serious. Others were legitimate news items that were branded as fakes by actors with other goals in mind. Their creators shared no specific agenda; the efforts conveyed no single message or lesson and suggested no obvious solution. But the ugly atmosphere of exploitation and pervasive mistrust made clear that something about the way journalism worked—and public life worked—was broken.

It didn't help that mainstream news organizations kept shooting themselves in the foot and undermining their own trustworthiness. Janet Cooke, it was becoming obvious, had not been an aberration, and a series of spectacular personal infractions, each of them a strong contender for the title of "worst journalistic scandal ever," confronted some of the nation's most elite news organizations again and again with troubling questions—not just what went wrong and why, not just *how* to repair the damage, but also whether repair was even possible. Was the decades-old professional practice of acknowledging and correcting mistakes still an effective way to restore readers' trust, or did it merely make the press look incompetent—or, worse, malicious, manipulative, or fake?

An element almost of vaudeville characterized the career of Stephen Glass, whose dozens of concoctions for the *New Republic* between 1995 and 1998—teenage master hackers, collectors of Monica Lewinsky memorabilia, drunken debauchery at a young conservatives' convention—were no less fanciful than his efforts, after he fell under suspicion, to fabricate supporting evidence ranging from forged reporter's notebooks to fake business cards to fictitious websites. Glass was fired in May 1998, and the magazine published two editors' notes about the discredited articles.[1]

More sobering was the case of Jayson Blair, whom the *New York Times* had accepted as an intern and promoted up the ladder to reporter despite a long record of errors and carelessness. As a staffer on the national desk, Blair turned in datelined stories about the spate of "Beltway Sniper" attacks in and near Washington, DC, about the families of soldiers missing or killed in Iraq, about hospitalized marines, and other topics—all complete with interview quotes and local-color details. When he wrote those stories, however, he had not been on the road in Texas or West Virginia or Maryland or Ohio; he was instead holed up in his Brooklyn apartment, inventing scenes, making up quotes, and lifting details from other newspapers he read online. In May 2003, the *Times*, acknowledging that at least thirty-six of the seventy-three stories Blair had written for the national desk contained plagiarized or fabricated elements, published an exhaustive 7,300-word examination into what it called "a low point in the 152-year history of the paper."[2] Blair resigned.

Jack Kelley, *USA Today*'s star foreign correspondent, was nominated for a Pulitzer five times during his two-decade-long career of offering exotic, often hair-raising glimpses into the world's crisis spots. In early 2004, however, the paper reported that a panel of staffers and outside journalists found that Kelley had copied at least one hundred passages from other publications and had invented chunks of at least twenty stories going back as far as 1991. His visit to two of Osama bin Laden's abandoned terrorist training camps shortly after 9/11 never happened, nor had he accompanied a Jewish extremist group in the West Bank as they fired at "blood-sucking Arab" passengers in taxis or endured gunfire on a trek through the mountains with the Kosovo Liberation Army. Kelley resigned and eventually issued an apology for "serious mistakes that violate the values that are most important to me as a person and as a journalist."[3]

It seemed an epidemic: during those same years, Patricia Smith resigned from the *Boston Globe*, the contributing writer Michael Finkel was dismissed by the *New York Times Magazine*, and Christopher Newton was fired by the AP after each was found to have used composite or fabricated characters or quotes. But no shared quality linked the fakers, no common explanation sufficed. Both Blair and Glass were ambitious young men striving to make their way at prestigious but hypercompetitive publications, and Blair, an African American hired into a newsroom working to promote diversity, carried an additional and complicated burden of others' expectations both high and low. But Kelley, a middle-aged white family man and devoted churchgoer who did not smoke, drink, or curse, belied the stereotype of the hard-charging, hard-living reporter.[4] Both Glass and Kelley relished their reputations as masters of the "How on earth did he get that?" story, the kind that deftly served up the perfect quote, the brilliant anecdote, the telling aside that they were in exactly the right place to overhear—which of course kept them under pressure to "find" ever-more perfect moments. But Blair's inventions seem to have been intended mainly to cover up his reporting failures.

Each case set off a tempest of mortified soul searching, apologies, ritualistic public penance, and attempts at paradigm repair by the publications involved, while journalists struggled to explain the epidemic. Did the internet make faking too easy? Did the internet make it easier to discover that reporters in fact faked all the time? Were journalists less ethical? Was *society* less ethical?[5] Editors resigned under pressure; professional organizations held panel discussions; columnists wrote editorials; the *New York Times*, after decades of arguing that its own editors rather than outside ombudsmen were the right people to represent readers' interests and investigate their complaints, appointed a "public editor" to do just that. The position was eliminated in 2017 during a round of cost cutting, but the publisher also insisted that social media and internet users could be more effective watchdogs.[6]

Executives at all three publications acknowledged they had been guilty of sloppy editing and fact-checking practices, and all had protected the reporters in question for reasons of their own while ignoring persistent warnings from readers, subjects, and other staffers. They all pledged to do better: to strengthen and publicize their standards, to more carefully hire and mentor young reporters, to reform their newsroom cultures, to foster better communication from and between editors. And all three pedaled vigorously to distance themselves from their problematic reporters and to present themselves as having been victimized by their own trusting natures; like Pulitzer's *World* after the kaiser's interview, they made the obvious choice to be seen as dupes rather than as frauds. They made sure everyone knew they had done the right thing and thrown the bums out.

It's true that Glass, Blair, Kelley, and the others got away with so many fakes in part because no one wanted to believe that the likable colleague at the next desk—the words *charming* and *charismatic* popped up strikingly often in their coworkers' descriptions of them—was capable of a sociopathic deception that betrayed the essence of what journalism was all about. Long accustomed to the fragile state of the public's trust in their profession, journalists were stunned and demoralized by the undermining of their own trust in each other.

But it's also true that the fakers were enabled by structural failures in the newsroom and by grievous lapses by their editors. The *Times*'s stature and its contested reputation as a "liberal" paper made Blair's transgressions a particularly irresistible topic for other journalists, for pundits, for writers of letters to the editor, for people who disliked the paper, for late-night comedians. For weeks after the revelations, the press and the airwaves resounded with commentary on the case, most of it negative. Just as with the *Washington Post* in the Cooke affair, people saw the *Times* as cocky, elitist, unaccountable, self-exempted from ordinary values of decent conduct. Although some newspaper readers weren't concerned by the scandal—one roundtable group told the editor of the *Indianapolis Star* to "get over [the] news industry buzz" about "a New York Times problem" and focus on its own accuracy and fairness—others felt the ripples far beyond Times Square. A writer for the *Cleveland Plain Dealer* who had left two sources unnamed in her column for their own protection was shaken when dozens of readers left angry voicemail messages accusing her of making up the quotes. It had not occurred to her, she said, that the scandal would reverberate outside the tight media circles of New York, but "every single message had Jayson Blair's name in it."[7]

For some readers, the mistakes betrayed not merely arrogance but mendacious ill will. When the Blair scandal broke, the Ukrainian Congress Committee of America had already decided to commemorate the seventieth anniversary of the Great Famine by mounting a new campaign to have Walter Duranty's Pulitzer Prize revoked and to "expose [him] as a disgrace to journalism." The committee gleefully seized the opportunity to remind the world of the *Times*'s past transgressions and demanded a meeting with the paper's publisher. "With everything that's happened at the *New York Times* recently," the committee's executive director said, "they need to set the record straight. Jayson Blair wasn't the first *Times* journalist to lie." But he was, she said, "the best thing that's happened to our campaign."[8]

In the end, of course, he wasn't; Duranty still has his prize. But the members of the Ukrainian Congress Committee were not the only ones to use the *Times*'s scarred record as a "scarlet L" for *liar*. Writing in the *Nation* a month after the revelations about Blair, the caustic Alexander Cockburn excoriated the *Times* for so floridly condemning Blair's "timid" and unambitious use of the "faker's arts" even as it was uncritically publishing the reports of Judith Miller, then hot on the hunt for weapons of mass destruction in Iraq. Miller "has been," wrote Cockburn, "a major, interested player in one of the greatest disgraces in the history of American journalism—to wit, its complicity in the fomenting of pretexts to invade Iraq." An unsigned editorial in the broadsheet *New York Sun*, founded in 2002 as a conservative challenger to the *Times* (and soon thereafter reduced to a modest online presence), ridiculed the latter for calling Blair's fraud a "low point" in its history given its far more "egregious . . . sins," among them Duranty's coverage of the Soviet famine and Herbert Matthews's favorable reporting on Fidel Castro in 1958. It was easy enough, the editorialist wrote, "for the Times to apologize to those harmed by Mr. Blair's reporting. At least they are still alive, which is more than one can say for the victims of Stalin, Castro, and the Iranian mullahs."[9] To this day, the Blair scandal continues to be invoked as the ultimate symbol of knowing journalistic fakery, which Google searches of "another Jayson Blair" or "the next Jayson Blair" or "Jayson Blair fake" will quickly confirm. The former reporter's name has become a convenient shorthand for "the constant failures of elite journalism."

As far back as the era of the *Boston Globe*'s Lizzie Borden whoppers, news organizations have held as an article of faith that if they get something wrong, acknowledging their mistakes and publicly setting the record straight are both a professional obligation and the best way to restore their readers' or viewers' trust. "Errors can be forgiven, but confession is required," as the American Society of Newspaper Editors put it in 2000 in its report on a project to build credibility.[10] But true forgiveness generally requires the forgiver to accept the sinner's confession as having been made in good faith. The string of scandals seemed instead merely to harden many readers' conviction that the sinners were unforgivable and reflected a general cynicism about journalistic accuracy.[11] In a widely discussed nationwide email survey of three thousand readers taken in 2003 by the Associated Press Managing Editors, some of those readers reported that they didn't bother trying to get their local paper to correct its mistakes. Their reasons were both varied and world-weary: some said that the paper offered no convenient way to reach an editor or that they didn't believe the paper would take them seriously. And some assumed the paper had embellished the facts on purpose to boost circulation.[12]

The problem goes deeper than the general conviction that newspapers often get things wrong. News organizations that identify themselves as professional accept the obligation to publicly correct their lapses, but publicly correcting lapses is screaming proof that they have acted unprofessionally. In an atmosphere of intense partisanship, an organization that admits errors offers to its ideological opponents an often irresistible opportunity to claim that the offender got things wrong on purpose—that it faked. Meanwhile, fake journalistic organizations that only pretend to honor professional standards are free to present their substandard work as blemish free and themselves as more credible than the hypocritical Bigfeet media who mess up in front of everyone's eyes. That's some catch, that Catch-22.

MISSION TEMPORARILY ACCOMPLISHED

"Truthiness" was already a pervasive phenomenon in search of a name when in 2005 Stephen Colbert came up with his masterful coinage.

"Something that seems like truth—the truth we want to exist," as the host of Comedy Central's satirical *Colbert Report* defined it, seemed to describe much of the media landscape.[13] Information, misinformation, disinformation, hoaxes, satires, fakes, attacks, and lies, some of which looked very much like journalism, clamored for attention in the public square. Apparently innocuous forms and genres were often more (or less) than they seemed. Wildly popular reality-TV shows insisted they were offering fly-on-the-wall glimpses into whatever spontaneous, real-life she-nanigans the islanders or housemates or apprentices were up to even as producers stirred up conflicts, played favorites, edited their "raw" foot-age, and hid their scriptwriters in the credits as "story editors."[14] Oprah embraced James Frey on her program when his book *A Million Little Pieces* was a memoir, then called him back to yell at him on the air when it turned out to be a novel instead. Ordinary citizens with camera phones scooped the mainstream press with photographs of a passenger plane landing safely in the Hudson River—incredible!—and with equally incredible pictures of a shark swimming through hurricane-flooded city streets. Michael Moore's film *Bowling for Columbine* (2002), which blamed a toxic U.S. gun culture for the mass shootings at Columbine High School in Colorado in 1999, used techniques that even favorable reviewers described as manipulative, exhibitionistic, tendentious, and deceptive; its very title incorporated a lie.[15] It won the Academy Award for Best Documentary Feature anyway. With all the boundaries between reality and fiction and between journalism and everything else contested territory, truth and falsehood seemed infinitely flexible, matters of per-sonal preference, commercial profit, or partisan advantage.

No one was more adept than George W. Bush and his advisers at creat-ing their own reality. A president who was elected, as the bitter joke went at the time, by one vote—having lost the popular poll, he was installed when Justice Sandra Day O'Connor's swing vote stopped the recount in Florida—Bush chose to assert his legitimacy not with humility but by fiat. Not only did the White House routinely ignore, marginalize, or spurn mainstream journalists and favor Fox News, the *Wall Street Journal*, and other reliable backers. Not only did it regularly dismiss scientific evidence about the dangers of climate change, the hazards of secondhand smoke, and even the origin of the universe as "the spin of experts" who were cap-tive to their own prejudices. But when spinning real journalists wasn't

enough, it also made unprecedented use of a traditional PR tactic to create fake journalists of its own. Federal agencies including the Departments
of Education, Defense, Agriculture, State, and Health and Human Services
regularly produced "video news releases" that looked like ordinary news
reports and that were delivered by people identifying themselves as journalists ("I'm Karen Ryan reporting") but that carried pointed political
messages. Local television broadcasts around the country folded these vid-
eos into their lineups without saying (and sometimes without knowing)
who was behind them.[16]

The administration's most consequential "truth" rested on virtually no
facts at all. Much of the mainstream coverage of the invasion of Iraq in
2003 and the subsequent insurgency has been amply and justifiably criticized for a multitude of failures; this isn't the place for yet another lengthy
rehearsal of the resort to pack journalism, the uncritical deference to official sources, the tendency for news organizations to put "patriotism" before
professional skepticism.[17] But another factor was the disinformation born
of a combustible combination: the peculiarly fact-free fake information
distributed by the Bush White House and the news organizations' practice of something very close to fake journalism, treating the fake facts as
if they were true. (We pretend to report about the stuff they make up.)

Shortly after the 9/11 terror attacks and the invasion of Afghanistan,
Bush and a cluster of powerful administration insiders—Vice President
Dick Cheney, Secretary of Defense Donald Rumsfeld, National Security
Adviser Condoleezza Rice—moved quickly to exploit the public anger and
fear, launching a propaganda blitz that called for the removal of Saddam
Hussein. It was bad enough, they said, that Saddam had links to al-Qaeda.
It was bad enough that he already had stockpiles of chemical and biologi-
cal weapons. But it was truly terrifying that the Iraqi leader had also
resumed his nuclear program and was on the verge of acquiring the most
horrific weapon of all. Deploying an artful phrase crafted by speechwriter
Michael Gerson, administration officials warned repeatedly that "the first
sign of a 'smoking gun' might be a mushroom cloud." All those claims,
too, were false; any number of international agencies, weapons inspectors,
and intelligence experts were stating publicly that there was no evidence
Saddam was producing or gathering any kind of weapon of mass destruction (WMD) and that the connection to al-Qaeda was illusory. But that
didn't matter to Bush and his White House (or to his staunch ally, Prime

Minister Tony Blair of the United Kingdom). Many insiders and close observers said later that the decision to overthrow Saddam came first; the rationale was created afterward.[18]

The claims that launched the war did, however, have the support of the two sources Bush trusted most: his gut and his God. In October 2004, a year and a half after the start of the war, the *New York Times Magazine* ran a profile by Ron Suskind of Bush's "faith-based presidency." Suskind quoted an anonymous adviser widely believed to have been Karl Rove, who spoke disdainfully about what he called "the reality-based community" and its belief that "solutions emerge from [the] judicious study of discernible reality. . . . We're an empire now, and when we act, we create our own reality." The president often spoke of operating on his "instincts," serene in the certainty that they were God blessed, correct, and superior to any facts. Bruce Bartlett, who had served in the Reagan and George H. W. Bush administrations, told Suskind that the second president Bush had a "weird, Messianic idea of what he thinks God told him to do. . . . Absolute faith like that overwhelms a need for analysis. The whole thing about faith is to believe things for which there is no empirical evidence. But you can't run the world on faith."[19]

A responsible and vigilant press could have supplied that missing empirical evidence and challenged the president's guts with actual facts. With rare exceptions, however—notably the Washington bureau of the now-defunct Knight-Ridder chain—it did not. No one was surprised when Fox News broke out the pompoms to cheer the administration's determination to oust Saddam, but few mainstream news organizations were much more critical or distanced in their coverage of the WMDs-that-weren't. Most defaulted to the traditional journalistic deference toward the White House on issues of national security, a stance that not only asserted their "patriotism" in a time of high anxiety but also relieved some of the pressure on their budgets in an era of economic calamity for legacy journalism.

Some influential journalists also apparently shared the president's faith in his version of the truth and actively stoked it with facts they refused to see as fake. Leading the journalistic pack in backing the administration's claims about the WMD program was Judith Miller of the *New York Times*, who had covered the Middle East and national security issues for decades and was part of the team that in 2002 won a Pulitzer Prize for a series on the global terror network. But her coverage of the weapons program relied heavily and uncritically on information from often anonymous administration insiders or from self-interested Iraqi defectors, exiles, and opposition leaders whose fervent goal was regime change in their homeland.[20] Miller's approach was strikingly similar to that which Walter Duranty had earlier used and Fox News was also using at the time. It was yet another black eye for the credibility of the mainstream press.

The White House's gurus of news management were meticulous planners highly accomplished in the sort of concocted PR spectacle that Daniel Boorstin called the "pseudoevent," which generates what might be called "pseudonews." The aircraft carrier bedecked with the huge "Mission Accomplished" banner was close enough to shore that the president could easily have flown there aboard his Marine One helicopter, but outfitting him in a rakish green flight suit and swooping him in by navy jet made for much better television.[21] But Bush's people were also poised to immediately exploit whatever opportunities fell into their laps. In the first weeks of the ground war, the news—the real news—was surprisingly dispiriting. As many as ten of the eighteen marines who died in an action on the fourth day of combat were killed by friendly fire from U.S. warplanes. A helicopter that crashed on a stateside training mission killed nearly a dozen soldiers before they ever set foot in Iraq. Americans guarding a checkpoint near Najaf shot up a van packed with women and children.

Then suddenly a new narrative emerged, one that perfectly symbolized the White House's strategy of opportunistic news management: Rambo of Sunnybrook Farm. The starring role belonged to the teenage Private First Class Jessica Lynch, a supply clerk in a maintenance unit who was traveling with her company near Nasiriyah when their convoy rolled into an ambush. Badly wounded but "fighting to the death [because] she did not want to be taken alive," as one anonymous official gushed later to the press, Lynch was captured only after emptying her rifle at her attackers.[22] Reportedly imprisoned and tortured in an Iraqi hospital, she was rescued nine days later in a daring night-time helicopter raid by special-operations forces.

News organizations swarmed and the American public swooned over the story of the captured innocent with the mean M-16. (One of the swarm of reporters was the *New York Times*'s Jayson Blair, who pretended he had visited her hometown and interviewed her family and friends for his coauthored story "Rescue and a 'Big Stir' in West Virginia" published on April 3, 2003—a fake story squared.) That the captured innocent in the hands of the dark brutes was both a woman and a white person was a critical part of her story's popularity. None of the five other captured soldiers who were rescued later without fanfare (including a Panamanian-born Black woman who had suffered gunshot wounds) and none of the eleven killed (among them a member of the Hopi Tribe who was the first U.S. servicewoman to die in Iraq) garnered the same enraptured attention as the wispy blonde from the West Virginia woods. *People* magazine's lavish cover story of April 21, 2003, headlined "Saved from Danger," even anointed her with a touch of the divine. It opened with a colonel describing a white-knuckle moment when a rescue helicopter almost crashed. "God smiled on us," he told *People*. "He also," *People* beamed, "smiled on Jessica Lynch."[23]

Very soon, however, the saga began to unravel. Lynch's doctors reported that her injuries had come not from gunfire or torture but from the crash of her vehicle during the ambush. Her rifle had never been fired. Her Iraqi guards had fled long before the rescuers arrived, leaving the hospital undefended for more than a day. The military's news-management efforts, meanwhile, were increasingly obvious. Having sent a camera crew along with the rescue mission, the Pentagon had already edited and released a five-minute video showing phosphorescent-green night-vision footage of helmeted men with big guns sidling around corners before bearing a fragile young woman away in a stretcher. And the dramatic details about Lynch's heroic stand with her M-16 had been leaked by military officials from battlefield intelligence that had not yet been confirmed.[24]

U.S. allies, expressing exasperation with the Pentagon's heavy hand, leaped to expose more deceptions surrounding the story. The BBC, the *Guardian*, the *Toronto Star*, and others were reporting that the young woman had been treated with generosity and tenderness by the Iraqi hospital staff and that the Americans' rescue mission had been staged for the cameras in the full knowledge that the raiders would meet no resistance. The story they told, in fact, had elements of opéra bouffe. The day before Lynch's rescue, Iraqi doctors had reportedly bundled her into an ambulance and set out to return her to her people, but after nervous American troops shot at the approaching vehicle, the doctors quickly turned around and raced her back to the safety of the "enemy" hospital. According to the

Toronto Star, an American medical officer visited the hospital three days after the rescue to thank the staff for the excellent care they had given the wounded private. It was their pleasure, one of her doctors told the officer, but "you do realize," he went on, "you could have just knocked on the door and we would have wheeled Jessica down to you, don't you?" Years later the House Oversight Committee, after a cursory investigation, concluded there had been nothing fake about the rescue. But whether the Pentagon had staged a chest-thumping (and pricey) raid it knew to be unnecessary or not, it had vigorously exploited Lynch's story, turning it into a tale of high drama that much of the press swallowed whole as an irresistible distraction from what was going wrong in the war.[25]

The problem with high-level news management is that when reality does intrude, it can leave both the managers who fed fake news to the press and the journalists who swallowed the fakes with their credibility in shreds. Reality intruded when Lynch, testifying before the Oversight Committee "to set the record straight," confessed herself "confused as to why they chose to lie and tried to make me a legend when the real heroics of my fellow soldiers that day were legendary." Reality intruded when the growing insurgency in Iraq made a mockery of the president's boastful banner, inevitably inviting taunts such as the cover of *Time* magazine on October 6, 2003, that blared "Mission Not Accomplished." And reality intruded when the WMDs so confidently sought by the military and so ardently reported by journalists turned out not to exist. In May 2004, more than a year after the invasion began, the *New York Times* published an apology for "coverage that was not as rigorous as it should have been. . . . Looking back, we wish we had been more aggressive in re-examining the claims as new evidence emerged—or failed to emerge." That August the *Washington Post* weighed in as well with an article confessing it had too often played down dissenting voices or failed to push back against what Bob Woodward called the "groupthink" of the intelligence community, which he said made journalists fearful of writing anything that might look silly later if the WMDs were eventually found in Iraq.[26] As usual, these news outlets' public acknowledgments of their failures invited fierce public criticism.

Reality, however, can intrude only into the reality-based community. In 2014, more than a decade after the invasion—and six years after the Senate Intelligence Committee issued the last of a series of unsparing reports cataloging dozens of White House claims about the dangers in Iraq that were false—a survey by Fairleigh Dickinson University showed 42 percent of respondents overall believed it was "probably true" or "definitely true" that the United States had found WMDs in Iraq. Among the people who said they got their news from MSNBC, the percentage dropped to 14. Among those who reported getting their news from Fox, more than half—52 percent—believed the American military had found weapons of mass destruction that had been produced by Saddam Hussein.[27] Reality can't hurt and credibility can't suffer in the well-barricaded precincts where fake news triumphs.

THE WICKED WITCH IS DEAD

Like its predecessor, the presidential election of 2004 was roiled by the shrewd manipulation of a new information format, but this time the links between fakery and bias in the mainstream media were made explicit through the exploitation of a set of artifacts central to the affair that by coincidence almost certainly *were* fake. Accusations and counteraccusations of partisanship, conspiracy, and fraud flew wildly in the media and online, shrouding the story in a thick atmosphere of intrigue that suggested nothing was what it seemed. That may have been the most accurate aspect of the whole murky affair.

On September 8, just two months before President Bush and his Democratic challenger, Senator John Kerry of Massachusetts, would face the voters, CBS News's *60 Minutes Wednesday* aired a segment investigating a cluster of persistent rumors about Bush's service in the Texas Air National Guard (TANG) during the Vietnam War. Bush's family, the story went, had pulled strings to land him a spot in the TANG's so-called champagne unit, a fighter wing that was understood to be safe from combat and overseas duty and that was heavily populated with privileged young men. Once enrolled, moreover, Bush had supposedly dodged his duties with impunity. The segment was produced by Mary Mapes, an experienced journalist who was among the first to report on the abuses at Abu Ghraib prison, and anchored by Dan Rather, the network's most recognizable face and a longtime target of the Right.

It was a hot story, one that had had mainstream news organizations in on-and-off pursuit for years. It also had taken on new relevance in the face of the brutal ad campaign targeting John Kerry's navy service that had been launched the previous month by a group calling itself "Swift Boat Veterans for Truth," an ostensibly grassroots organization actually funded by wealthy and politically connected Texas Republicans. Mindful of Kerry's distinguished service under fire in the war Bush was accused of dodging, the group fought back by falsely claiming that Kerry had lied about his record and had not deserved the Bronze and Silver Stars he had received. The group also criticized Kerry's antiwar activism upon his return home as a betrayal of his fellow soldiers.[28]

Over Labor Day weekend, Mapes obtained what she considered evidence clinching the TANG story: faxed copies of a set of documents criticizing Lieutenant Bush's conduct, several of which carried the signature of Bush's commanding officer, Lieutenant Colonel Jerry B. Killian. The memos had come to Mapes through a retired Texas Army National Guard officer and longtime Bush antagonist who did not want to be named on the air. Pulling the segment together with breakneck speed, Mapes's team celebrated what at first looked like a triumphant scoop: USA Today's story, based on the same batch of documents, straggled into print the day after their broadcast.[29]

By then, however, a swarm of bloggers was already challenging the documents. Some of the typographic features in the documents could have been produced only by a computer, they argued, not by any typewriter available in the early 1970s, so the memos must be fakes. As mainstream media outlets joined in investigating the sourcing and conclusions of the segment, new holes began to open in the story. Among them were anachronistic details in the content of the memos, the admission by the retired officer who had provided the documents that he had lied about their provenance, and a statement by Killian's secretary that she hadn't typed the documents and didn't think they were authentic, even though, she said, they did reflect her boss's thinking at the time. (Her parsing led on September 15 to the memorable New York Times headline "Memos on Bush Are Fake but Accurate, Typist Says.")[30]

After steadfastly defending the segment for nearly two weeks, CBS News finally crumbled under the weight of evidence against the documents and issued a statement acknowledging that it couldn't prove they were authentic. "We should not have used them," the statement said. "That was a mistake, which we deeply regret."[31]

To examine the segment, the network commissioned a panel of independent investigators, who in January 2005 issued a report that managed the rare task of sounding both scalding and noncommittal. The panel declined to take a stand on whether the documents were genuine—experts unanimously insisted that because they were copies, not the originals, it was impossible to say for sure—but it did note "a number of issues that raise serious questions" about their authenticity. Nor would the panel say definitively that Mapes and Rather had been driven by a political agenda, but it did not dismiss the possibility, either. Dan Rather, insisting to the panel that he was just doing what investigative journalists do, listed tough stories he had reported on presidents from both parties. But the panel cited several dubious actions by the CBS team, including the ambiguous incident that some of Mapes's colleagues called "outrageous" and "incredibly stupid" in which the producer helped her confidential source connect with a senior adviser in the Kerry campaign. The panel also identified serious deficiencies in the reporting process as well as the "fierce conviction of some at CBS News that the story was true" and the "refusal by some to consider that it might be false." The report concluded that the producers in their "competitive zeal" and "rush to air" had failed to follow CBS News standards.[32] A plausible interpretation of the whole affair was that the CBS team, in its eagerness to legitimize "evidence" that was in fact fake, had indulged in journalism that was in fact fake, too. Mapes was fired, three other senior staffers resigned under pressure, and Dan Rather retired from the *Evening News* anchor desk earlier than planned.

The episode introduced to the public a new set of heroes: the scrappy citizen watchdogs of the blogosphere, a realm at that point so new that the panel's report included a footnote explaining what a "blog" was. (Calling it a "website that contains an online personal journal, often with reflections, comments, and hyperlinks provided by the writer," the panel emphatically did not categorize blogs as traditional journalism—a distinction also embraced by most bloggers, who tended to think of themselves as activists or polemicists.[33]) After the election, Ronald Reagan's former speechwriter Peggy Noonan exulted in the *Wall Street Journal* that "every time the big networks and big broadsheet national newspapers tried to pull off a bit of pro-liberal mischief, [such as] CBS and the fabricated

Bush National Guard documents . . . the yeomen of the blogosphere and AM radio and the Internet took them down. . . . It was Agincourt. It was the yeomen of King Harry taking down the French aristocracy with new technology and rough guts. God bless the pajama-clad yeomen of America."[34] A new era had dawned, said the Noonans of the world—or rather another new era, vibrating with the din of even more of the "small voices" Matt Drudge had celebrated in the early years of the web. In that miraculous time, the elite media would never again hold a monopoly over information, and a Goliath of the press could be humbled by ordinary citizens armed with nothing more than homemade websites with names such as "Little Green Footballs" and an Everyman's commonsensical ability to know the truth. The authority of the expert was dead—or, worse, just plain unnecessary.

It certainly looked like a spontaneous uprising of the grass roots against the establishment—a "blogswarm," in the new parlance. It was also a heavily partisan one. According to one scholar's calculation, conservatives talked about the memos much more and for much longer; posts about the National Guard segment on conservative blogs outnumbered those on liberal ones by a ratio of seventeen to three in the three weeks following the broadcast, and their arguments were quickly picked up and amplified by conservative opinion magazines and other publications.[35] A large swath of the blogosphere was becoming a refuge—and a hothouse—for right-wingers who felt their views were disdained and excluded by mainstream media.

Some of the bloggers couched their arguments in civil terms; some were simply flaunting their detective skills for an admiring audience. But in a pattern increasingly familiar in political debate, much of the blogosphere instantly ascribed the direst of partisan motives to its opponents-in-arms, erecting the episode into yet another emblem of the moral fraudulence of the liberal elite while presenting itself as just a bunch of ordinary folks motivated solely by a populist yearning for the truth. After a professor at a state university posted a report questioning the consensus about the anachronistic typography, his inbox filled with hate mail, and callers to the university demanded that he be fired. Wizbang, one of the first bloggers to challenge the professor's posting, later apologized for the intemperate language but maintained that the professor's methods were unethical.[36] Others circulated conspiracy theories, claiming, for instance, that the Kerry campaign had planted the documents on CBS in order to inject them into the mainstream.[37]

For many bloggers, however, the main target was CBS and the journalistic establishment. Some invoked the ultimate bogeyman, likening CBS News to Jayson Blair to make the implicit argument that the program was guilty not of stupid slips but of calculated frauds. A *Columbia Journalism Review* story in the issue for January–February 2005 started with the blunt acknowledgment "Yes, CBS screwed up badly in 'Memogate'" before moving on to scrutinize the bloggers' arguments. It generated "well over 100 e-mails, almost all of them unhappy," the magazine's editors wrote in the next issue. *CJR* published a selection from the letters, including one crowing that "this movement is bigger than the left's domination of the universities, the newspapers, and the film industry; it's bigger than anything that has occurred since you wormed into power in the 1960s." The writer concluded with a flourish: "It doesn't matter," he said, "what the people at Harvard and Berkeley have to say about [the *CJR* article]. It will be dragged into the light by honest people with philosophical disagreement, and it will be flogged to death for every lie, every misrepresentation, and every exaggeration that it contains. It's over, you clowns. Now, when you lie, we will report it, every time."[38] Other bloggers went beyond writing about the broadcast to call for direct action: demanding Rather's resignation, boycotting the network, insisting on a criminal investigation. Some also asked for donations.[39]

Unlike in the romanticized old vision of the public sphere as a place where people gathered for civil face-to-face debate on issues of the day, in the new digital world bloggers often wrote under pseudonyms that left their faces invisible, their names illegible, and all the guardrails of civility down. Insiders may well have known who was behind which URL, but casual online web surfers would not have realized that some of the bloggers who pounced on the typographic anomalies were more likely to be sporting bow ties than pajamas. Among the most active blogs was one registered to a firm with ties to the powerful right-wing fund-raiser Richard Viguerie. A blogger who went by the screen name "Buckhead" and whose post on the popular conservative web forum Freerepublic.com raised the accusation of forgery less than four hours after the broadcast ended turned out to be an Atlanta lawyer affiliated with the Federalist Society and deeply engaged with conservative legal causes. The executives of the PR firm

Creative Response Concepts, promoters of the allegedly grassroots Swift Boat group that even then was continuing to pump out disinformation about John Kerry's military service, claimed credit for similarly framing the exposure of the memos as both spontaneous and nonpartisan. They crowed to an industry publication that they had immediately rounded up typographical experts to express skepticism and had pushed the story out to news sites as well as to bloggers "to make sure they know it isn't just Rush Limbaugh and Matt Drudge who are raising questions."[40]

The murkiness clouding the faces in the blogosphere never cleared. Some of the bloggers bristled at the suggestion they had colluded with the conservative establishment, and several, denying they had been contacted by Creative Response Concepts, accused the professionals of stealing credit for breaking the story.[41] Paradoxically, the anonymity afforded by the web didn't just complicate the bloggers' efforts to prove the *non*existence of another vast right-wing conspiracy. It also gave defenders of the CBS segment (or opponents of Bush) an opening to counter, if feebly, with conspiracy theories of their own, suggesting that the president's famously Machiavellian adviser Karl Rove, perhaps with the help of the arch-dirty trickster Roger Stone, had planted the forged memos to trap CBS in controversy and divert attention from the dangerous topic of Bush's sketchy service. Even Mapes, however, dismissed that one. In her bitterly defensive book about the broadcast, she offered the back-handed compliment that although Rove was "capable of that kind of dirty trick," if he had really been behind it, the resolution of the dispute would have been "more unequivocal."[42]

Who was telling the truth? Whomever you chose. Accusations of bias, falsehood, and conspiracy lurked at every turn, and if it's permissible to call the memos at the center of the affair "genuine fakes"—artifacts consciously fabricated with deceptive intent—the odor of their fraudulence seeped everywhere and tainted everything. When the CBS News team fell for the forgeries and then refused for two weeks to entertain even valid criticism of their authenticity, it made itself look partisan whether liberal partisanship had anything to do with the coverage in the first place or not. Well-connected and well-funded bloggers used the affordances of their new platform (with backup framing from sympathetic "old" media such as the *Wall Street Journal*) to present partisan information, misinformation, and opinions as if they were the collective wisdom of the grass roots.

In their effort to critique as fake CBS's journalism about a fake, they essentially created *fake citizen journalism*. And in the process, they tightened the association of political bias with calculated fakery, branding as illegitimate any disagreement that was rooted in partisan differences and sometimes ganging up or issuing threats to discourage opponents from speaking out.

In the end, the set of fake documents—which to this day no author has claimed—served as little more than a MacGuffin. The blogosphere's aggressive focus on the forged memos distracted voters' attention from the genuine questions about the real holes and anomalies in Bush's service record, even as other right-wingers were circulating fake stories smearing the genuinely distinguished service record of Bush's opponent. The bloggers' insistence that a powerful news organization routinely and purposefully committed fraud tainted the mainstream press as a whole, even as they delivered to their followers an aggressively *non*mainstream (and often inaccurate) confirmation of their preferred vision of the world. And they claimed a long-desired scalp. The *Atlanta Journal-Constitution* reported that on the day of Rather's final *Evening News* broadcast, the lawyer known as "Buckhead" attended a celebratory watch party with fifty guests, many of them local Republicans prominent in legal and government circles. Dan Rather, the lawyer said at the party, had been viewed as "a black beast" and "an enemy" by conservatives. Now, Buckhead said at the festive gathering, "the wicked witch is dead."[43] The pajama-clad yeomen had been on a partisan witch hunt after all.

SOMETHING "VERY STRANGE"

Barack Obama was a radical socialist. An anti-Semite. A thug. An extremist with ties to everyone from Louis Farrakhan to the Weather Underground. The anti-Christ.

Not to mention a Muslim terrorist born in Africa who had ascended illegitimately to the presidency.

Beginning as soon as Obama launched his unprecedented campaign for the presidency in 2007 and continuing on and off throughout both of his terms, a cluster of durable falsehoods like these about his family, his religion, his education, his name, his associates, his politics, and his birthplace swirled around the first Black person to become president of the United States. None gained more traction than the "birther" lie, a lunatic scenario of conspiracy and cover-up whose roots reached all the way back to August 13, 1961.[44] On that date, according to the scenario, some mysterious plotter had placed a fake announcement in the "Births, Marriages, Deaths" column of the *Honolulu Advertiser*—an announcement falsely declaring that a baby boy who half a century later would happen to run for president had been born in a hospital in Hawaii when in fact his actual birthplace was Kenya, his father's native country. According to the birthers' (incorrect) reading of constitutional law, that meant he was not a "natural-born citizen," and therefore was ineligible to serve as president. Because his father was a Muslim, Barack Jr. must be one, too. And because Barack Jr. was a Muslim, he was also undoubtedly a terrorist. It all added up.

The story reached its peak in March and April of 2011 with a giant push from Donald Trump, who was at that point considering a run for president in 2012. The real-estate mogul and reality-TV star began spicing his appearances and interviews with ponderous hints that there was something "very strange" about Obama's origins and something fake about the standard short-form Hawaiian birth certificate the Obama campaign had released in 2008 in the futile hope of putting the matter to rest. Trump soon found plenty of support from a reliable stable of talk-show hosts and fake journalists. Especially helpful was Fox News, where Sean Hannity pounded the story and the potential candidate was given a soapbox of his own, a weekly call-in segment called "Monday Mornings with Trump" on the chatty morning program *Fox & Friends*. Obama was certainly not the first candidate or president to inspire batty conspiracy theories, but in previous campaigns those theories tended to lurk on the fringes of public discourse. Now they took a central place, floated by a potential major-party rival, openly abetted by some of the most powerful figures in the national media, and amplified by vigorous social media campaigns.

Another tenacious supporter of the birther claim brought with him long experience in the fake journalism of chicanery and conspiracy. The far-right web periodical *WorldNetDaily* (*WND*) was launched in the late 1990s by Joseph Farah, whose Western Journalism Center had earlier received funding from Richard Mellon Scaife to promote Christopher Ruddy's coverage of the Vincent Foster "murder."[45] *WND* published a years-long torrent of online articles under aspirational headlines such as "Americans Demanding Obama's Birth Certificate" (August 4, 2009), "We're Making Progress on Birth Certificate" (January 6, 2011), "Mathematical 'Proof' Obama Birth Certificate a Phony" (July 5, 2011), "Now More Than Ever: 'Where's the Birth Certificate?'" (July 19, 2012), and "Israeli Science Website: Obama Birth Certificate Forged" (September 10, 2012). One of *WND*'s writers, Jerome Corsi, who had made his name with a book published in 2004 promoting the Swift Boat smear against John Kerry, produced a new splash in May 2011 with *Where's the Birth Certificate? The Case That Barack Obama Is Not Eligible to Be President.* Offering brazen falsehoods and positing baroque skullduggeries involving Obama's birth and background, Corsi demanded that Obama release the "long-form" version of his birth certificate—a more detailed document that Hawaii does not normally make public—to prove his eligibility. It scarcely mattered to Corsi's followers that by the time *Where's the Birth Certificate?* hit the shelves, the birth certificate was already right *there* for all to see at https://www.slideshare.net/whitehouse/birth-certificatelongform, where the White House had posted it three weeks earlier. "We're not going to be able to [solve our problems] if we just make stuff up and pretend that facts are not facts," Obama said in releasing it. "We do not have time for this kind of silliness."[46]

Obama was clearly gambling that making the certificate public—offering a lofty, cerebral response to an absurd argument—would put a definitive end to the drama. But Corsi's book went on to spend two weeks in June on the *New York Times*'s hardcover nonfiction best-seller list anyway, while Corsi and *WND* busied themselves for months more "proving" that the long-form certificate was a fake, too. (Visitors to the *WND* website could signal their approbation by buying bumper stickers, lawn signs, signed copies of Corsi's book, and other themed merchandise.) The publication of the certificate did carry some persuasive power, at least at first; some polls taken before and after its release registered significant spikes in the percentage of respondents who said they believed Obama was born in the United States. But by the time YouGov carried out a follow-up survey nine months later, the spike had subsided noticeably, and among Republicans the number who believed

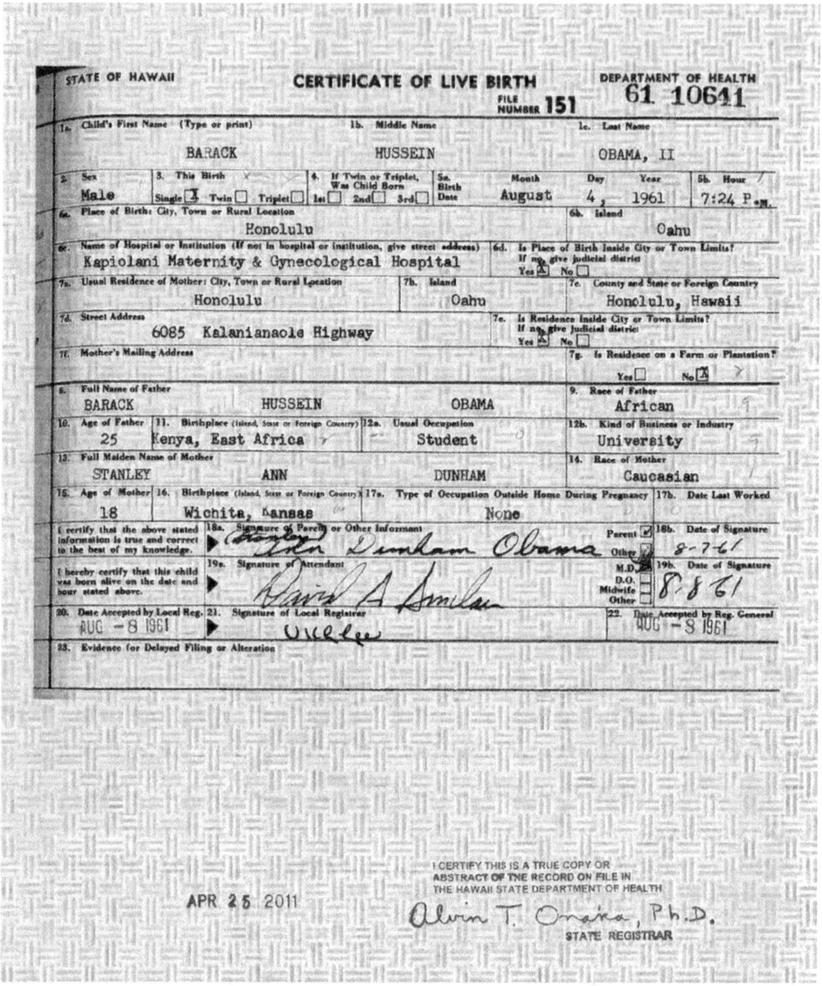

STATE OF HAWAII
CERTIFICATE OF LIVE BIRTH
FILE NUMBER 151
DEPARTMENT OF HEALTH
61 10641

1a. Child's First Name (Type or print): BARACK
1b. Middle Name: HUSSEIN
1c. Last Name: OBAMA, II
2. Sex: Male
3. This Birth: Single [X] Twin [ ] Triplet [ ]
4. If Twin or Triplet, Was Child Born: 1st [ ] 2nd [ ] 3rd [ ]
5a. Birth Date: Month August, Day 4, Year 1961
5b. Hour: 7:24 P.M.
6a. Place of Birth: City, Town or Rural Location: Honolulu
6b. Island: Oahu
6c. Name of Hospital or Institution (If not in hospital or institution, give street address): Kapiolani Maternity & Gynecological Hospital
6d. Is Place of Birth Inside City or Town Limits? If no, give judicial district. Yes [X] No [ ]
7a. Usual Residence of Mother: City, Town or Rural Location: Honolulu
7b. Island: Oahu
7c. County and State or Foreign Country: Honolulu, Hawaii
7d. Street Address: 6085 Kalanianaole Highway
7e. Is Residence Inside City or Town Limits? If no, give judicial district. Yes [X] No [ ]
7f. Mother's Mailing Address
7g. Is Residence on a Farm or Plantation? Yes [ ] No [X]
8. Full Name of Father: BARACK HUSSEIN OBAMA
9. Race of Father: African
10. Age of Father: 25
11. Birthplace (Island, State or Foreign Country): Kenya, East Africa
12a. Usual Occupation: Student
12b. Kind of Business or Industry: University
13. Full Maiden Name of Mother: STANLEY ANN DUNHAM
14. Race of Mother: Caucasian
15. Age of Mother: 18
16. Birthplace (Island, State or Foreign Country): Wichita, Kansas
17a. Type of Occupation Outside Home During Pregnancy: None
17b. Date Last Worked
I certify that the above stated information is true and correct to the best of my knowledge.
18a. Signature of Parent or Other Informant: Ann Dunham Obama
Parent [X] Other [ ]
18b. Date of Signature: 8-7-61
I hereby certify that this child was born alive on the date and hour stated above.
19a. Signature of Attendant: David A Sinclair
M.D. [X] D.O. [ ] Midwife [ ] Other [ ]
19b. Date of Signature: 8-8-61
20. Date Accepted by Local Reg.: AUG -8 1961
21. Signature of Local Registrar
22. Date Accepted by Reg. General: AUG -8 1961
23. Evidence for Delayed Filing or Alteration

I CERTIFY THIS IS A TRUE COPY OR ABSTRACT OF THE RECORD ON FILE IN THE HAWAII STATE DEPARTMENT OF HEALTH
APR 25 2011
Alvin T. Onaka, Ph.D.
STATE REGISTRAR

FIGURE 10.1 In April 2011, President Obama posted his nonfake, long-form birth certificate on the White House website in the hope of ending the "birther" controversy.

Source: White House.

that Obama was a U.S. citizen had dropped to three percentage points *below* what it had been before the certificate was released.[47] In the opposition party, more people than ever were choosing to believe the fake journalists over the real president. (We report what you want to hear; you swallow it.)

Obama's appeal to reason failed because reason had nothing to do with birtherism. As with so many other American conspiracy theories involving everything from depraved Jesuits to power-mad Trilateral Commissioners to doctors injecting babies with autism, literal accuracy and rationality were just impediments for people striving to devise explanations that *felt* true for the baffling or baneful or bad things that happened in what was supposed to be a land of opportunity and plenty. Especially for people who felt powerless in their own lives, to blame disappointments, whether personal or political, not on random misfortune or individual shortcoming but on the focused malevolence of secret groups of all-powerful actors made sense.

In the birther claims, another characteristic often associated with conspiracy believers came into play: racial animus and resentment. That a Black man could achieve spectacular successes of a sort that eluded so many (white) Americans who considered themselves more "normal" and more deserving was, it seemed, a clear sign that nefarious hidden forces must have been at work on his behalf.[48] It was never clear exactly *what* people thought Obama's motives were for having gone to such lengths to conceal his true identity as an African Muslim terrorist or what sinister use of his fraudulent position they imagined he was plotting to make. But the goal was not precision; the goal was emotional satisfaction. For media and voters alike, birtherism was a masterful way to air suspicion and fear about Obama's Blackness without actually talking about Obama's Blackness.

The story began to lose steam in much of the press after Trump turned away from a run in 2012 and no longer commanded the center stage in the campaign. Yet even though some of his political advisers, television associates, and others had expressed quiet concerns that questioning Obama's citizenship would be seen as either racist or simply ineffectual, Trump continued to drop random birther taunts into his Twitter feed.[49] The claim that dark forces were working in secret against decent, honest, "real" Americans assured swaths of voters that the fault was not in themselves but in their stars, while the suggestion that only Trump was bold enough to uncover and defeat those forces ingeniously manipulated their anxieties in ways that no other candidate, potential or actual, could keep up with. The conspiracy theory that *felt* true for many voters also proved to be both popular and profitable for Trump's devoted allies in the right-wing empire of fake journalism. It was a potent combination whose effectiveness both the mogul and the media would remember.

TRY FAKING IT

In the first decades of the new millennium, "fake news" reentered the public conversation. More than one hundred years after respectable newspapers such as Adolph Ochs's *New York Times* turned the term into a denunciation of everything unprofessional and false about journalism, "fake news," so called, was back. This time around, though, the term was not a denunciation but an accolade. Even as the fakest of conspiracy theories grew to dominate a large chunk of the media landscape, "fake news" remained most closely associated with Jon Stewart, not a newsman but a comedian, and his popular news-parody program the *Daily Show*, which he hosted from 1999 to 2015 on the Comedy Central cable channel. It was Stewart's unprofessionalism—his position outside the boundaries of conventional mainstream journalism—that in the eyes of many empowered his special ability to tell the truth.

The *Daily Show* bore some surface similarities to the fake journalism of, say, Fox News in that it imitated the styles and forms of mainstream professionalized journalism—the earnest anchor in jacket and tie, the correspondents doing stand-ups in locations identified as remote, the studio interviews with prominent people, the overall attitude of (self-)importance—in order to subvert them. The difference, of course, was that Fox viewers fervently believed they were watching the real thing, whereas *Daily Show* viewers understood perfectly well that imitation was the sincerest form of mockery. Stewart consistently maintained he was not a journalist; when the Jayson Blair scandal broke, for instance, he joked that "as the fake anchorman of a fake news show, I have a pretend obligation to inaccurately report news. I'm proud to say our commitment to journalistic falsehood is catching on."[50] But as a professed nonjournalist, Stewart was free to buck professional conventions and offer satirical takes on politics, politicians, the media, and other institutions that were often more pointed and in their own way more informative than anything coming from news organizations following journalistic norms. At the time that some mainstream reporters were treating the Swift Boat group's smears against John Kerry as valid news, for instance, a *Daily Show* segment featured the correspondent Rob Corddry telling Stewart that the Kerry campaign was going to "spin" the story by pointing out that the senator's official military records had been undisputed for thirty-five years. "That's not a spin thing, that's a fact. That's established," Stewart responded.

> **Corddry:** Exactly, Jon, and that established, incontrovertible fact is one side of the story.
> **Stewart:** But isn't that the end of the story?. . . What's your opinion?
> **Corddry:** I'm sorry, "my opinion"? I don't have opinions. I'm a reporter, Jon, and my job is to spend half the time repeating what one side says, and half the time repeating the other. Little thing called "objectivity"— might want to look it up.
> **Stewart:** Doesn't objectivity mean objectively weighing the evidence and calling out what's credible and what isn't?
> **Corddry:** Whoa-ho! Listen, buddy: Not my job to stand between the people talking to me and the people listening to me.[51]

The segment offered not just a pointed indictment of the Swift Boaters' fake claims but also the perfect summation of the widespread public disdain for what was seen as mindless "balance." A fake-news program savaged the way politics worked by satirizing the way real news worked.

Stewart's insurrectionary approach held a special appeal for young people. In 2004, the Pew Research Center sowed consternation among traditionalists when it reported that 21 percent of people ages eighteen to twenty-nine said they "regularly learned something" about the presidential campaign from comedy shows—very nearly the same number who got news about the campaign from daily newspapers (23 percent) and a leap from the 9 percent who had learned from comedy programs four years earlier.[52] But others in the journalistic and political establishment lent a certain legitimacy to Stewart's program by treating it like real news. In both 2000 and 2004, the program's election coverage won a prestigious Peabody Award ("Boy, you think it's hard to *be* a news organization," Stewart told the august audience in his acceptance speech in 2000, "try faking it"), and Democrats and Republicans alike credentialed *Daily Show* correspondents for their nominating conventions.[53] Everyone from Madeleine Albright to Newt Gingrich to the president of Liberia sat for interviews.

The establishment's embrace of the program was in part a calculated bid to reach out to younger audiences and present itself as knowing and up-to-date about pop culture. When in 2003 Senator John Edwards, Democrat of North Carolina, chose Stewart's program for his announcement that he was running for president, he was clearly positioning himself as the hip candidate, and the show seemed a natural home for the über-cool Barack Obama, who made three appearances during his 2008 campaign and then became the first sitting president to come on the program. Some mainstream journalists expressed admiration and even envy of Stewart's approach. As Peter Jennings, the longtime anchor of ABC's *World News Tonight*, told the *New York Times*, Stewart "does stuff on the broadcast that we're dying to do and can't, just because that's not what we do." Stewart had an answer for that kind of comment, too. "I can't tell you," he told the journalist Bill Moyers in 2003, "how many times we'll run into a journalist [who] go[es], 'Boy that's—I wish we could be saying that. That's exactly the way we see it and that's exactly the way we'd like to be saying that.' And I always think, 'Well, why don't you?'"[54]

A century after it galumphed into the debate over how journalism worked, the term *fake news* had come full circle. Coined to describe the jaunty, casual, crowd-pleasing approach to journalism that disdained mathematical precision and declined to follow rules, it had been co-opted by serious journalists for use as a brand of shame against practitioners who did not merit a place within the boundaries of professional journalism. Now, however, with all the boundaries dilapidated and the traditional gatekeepers discredited, with mathematical precision dismissed as unattainable, with rules invoked mainly to prove transgressions by rivals, with the very idea of professionalism ridiculed as elitist, obsolete, and ineffective, "fake news" was once again seen as a bold and transgressive means to do what the professionals could not: tell the truth.

That vision would not last long.

CONCLUSION

"A Degenerate and Perverted Monstrosity"

Rudolph Giuliani, President Trump's personal lawyer: And when you tell me that, you know, [the president] should testify because he's going to tell the truth and he shouldn't worry, well, that's so silly because it's somebody's version of the truth. Not the truth . . .

Chuck Todd, host of NBC's *Meet the Press*: Truth is truth. I don't mean to go like—

Giuliani: No, it isn't truth. Truth isn't truth.

—*Meet the Press*, August 19, 2018

Donald Trump's presidency and its Götterdämmerung made it impossible for any sentient journalism historian to avoid the urgent queries: Isn't fake news worse now than it's ever been? Isn't it posing unprecedented dangers to democracy and public life?

Yes.

Trump did not invent either the term *fake news* or the tactic of blaming the news media for his own errors. Nor was he the first public figure to manipulate journalists and journalistic conventions to his own advantage or to measure truthfulness by the yardstick of ideology or to exploit new technologies in devious ways their inventors never intended. Other political operators have also purposefully undermined citizens' faith in civic and journalistic institutions or forged symbiotic relationships with congenial news organizations that only pretended to be independent or slapped the label *fake* on reporting they found unflattering or embarrassing. Fake news and fake journalism have been part of the American media landscape for as long as there's been an American media landscape and have shown a disturbing ability to innovate and adapt, to camouflage their intentions, to complicate and confound civic life. No history of American journalism is complete without an accounting of the many ways that the information system of democracy—the critical but unsecurable infrastructure of civic life—has been invaded and exploited over the years by hoaxers, humbuggers, propagandists, puffers, partisans, blusterers, scandalmongers, and fraudsters with motives of their own. The relationship between journalism and truth has always been more fragile than many of us realize.

But the president who made more than thirty thousand "false or misleading claims" in public during his four years in office—generally to the delight of his loyal base of right-wing supporters—focused and accelerated the historical trends as never before.[1] Add to that the corrosive political partisanship, decades in the making, that came to a head during his administration; the stark polarization of the citizenry into factions that barely speak the same language; and the routine demonization of experts, expertise, and the very idea of truth as anything other than someone else's opinion. Pile on the rejection of science and specialized knowledge, even in the midst of a lethal pandemic, as elitist and untrustworthy; the widespread embrace of loony, apocalyptic conspiracy theories; the vast, cryptic, and unaccountable apparatus of social media, with its seemingly limitless capacity for hackery, fakery, and disinformation; and the mutually expedient contract binding the world of right-wing politics and the empire of right-wing media. The result has been a public life awash in toxic mendacity on an unprecedented scale, with disinformation and misinformation co-opted into service as its essential instrument and "truth" seen as a matter of just deserts. Anything that *should* be true *can* be true. Anything that supports one's political opponents *must* be fake.

Journalism historians are also besieged by the plea: Can't anything be learned from the history of fake news that might help us in this current crisis? Historians are rightly wary of treating the past as a sort of Tarot deck that will offer portentous insights into the path ahead, but, even so, that may be the wrong question—and certainly the Trump administration's ostentatious overuse of the term *fake news* muddled and besmirched any possible answers. More useful, perhaps, is the question: What can we learn from the history of *fake journalism* and its increasingly cancerous relationship with political partisanship?

For two centuries after the first American newspaper flickered to life in Boston and immediately died, newspapers were almost as apt to play with the truth as to investigate it, and neither fake journalism nor its real counterpart bore distinct shapes. Responsible news organizations have always been willing to recognize an obligation to provide the public with trustworthy information, and responsible readers and viewers have always expected journalism to pay serious attention to serious matters. But in the free-for-all world of the early newspaper, the responsible were in constant competition with the mischievous, the zealous, the greedy, and the dim. And since the nineteenth-century newspaper—as well as the photograph album, the fin-de-siècle motion-picture palace, and the realm of the ether—was widely understood to include plenty of content that wasn't, in the strictest sense, informative, readers did not expect everything they heard or read in the public square to be truthful. The choice of what to accept as true was theirs.

It was the combined pressures of two stakeholders that eventually imposed a measure of order on the practice of journalism: readers who saw the social and economic value of information they could trust to be reliable and relevant, and journalists who saw usefulness, prestige, and commercial advantage in claiming the status of *the people who told the public the truth.* The label *fake* was an essential foil for their construction of their status as truth tellers. In the 1880s, when reporters first began talking about "faking," many of them meant it as a compliment, the signal of something cheerful and reader-friendly. Soon, however, the professionalizing class of journalists co-opted the term as a shibboleth, in the process relieving readers of the responsibility (or the opportunity) of deciding what public information they should believe.

Thus, it was only when mainstream journalists began to claim the investigative method eventually known as objectivity as their professional lodestar, factuality as their creed, and "the truth" as their particular possession that faking in a newspaper took on the odor of what Ralph

Pulitzer in 1912 called "a degenerate and perverted monstrosity."[2] Although the professionalizing journalists themselves sometimes fell short of the standards they set, they were making a clear statement about the kind of work they deemed acceptable, the kind of journalist they were willing to welcome into their ranks, and the kind of service they were responsible for performing for the public. Their principle was clear: truth was what looked like journalism, and journalism looked like truth.

Yet rather than putting a stop to fakery, stigmatizing the fake turned it instead into a weapon that could be used against the stigmatizers. The word *fake* gradually faded out of the discourse about journalism, too breezy for such serious matters. But as journalists rooted their claims of authority and special status ever more deeply in impartiality and accuracy, *accusations* of partiality and inaccuracy became ever more powerful weapons. Citizens and public figures alike wielded them to undermine the credibility of information they did not want to accept as true.

Sometimes those accusations were valid criticisms of reporting that truly was bad: lurid tales of corpse factories, Walter Duranty's tendentious take on the Soviet famine, the fabrications by Janet Cooke and other journalists. Sometimes, as with Senator McCarthy's assaults on the "Red" press or with Big Tobacco's challenges to scientifically based coverage of the hazards of smoking, the accusers were making ideological or factually unsound arguments *disguised* as valid criticisms of reporting that was in fact accurate as it stood.

Sometimes other disguises came into play. Essentially impossible before the emergence of "real," professionalized journalism, fake journalism dressed itself up in its counterpart's conventions, pretended to embrace its standards, and often by its very presence undermined the credibility of good-faith journalistic work. Fake journalism was more and more looking like truth, and fake truth like journalism.

The periodic attempts by mainstream journalists to defend the boundaries of their profession have often been further complicated by the difficulties of explaining to the public at large (and sometimes to themselves) exactly why the fakes weren't, in fact, real. New communications technologies and new practices were constantly reshaping the media landscape, but did they even count as journalism? What needed correction from journalists? Where were the lines to be drawn between fake journalism and the stuff that happened to share some of the qualities of journalistic work but never claimed an allegiance to truth? Was it really so bad, after all, that in 1898 the pioneering filmmakers Albert Smith and J. Stuart Blackton presented their canvas tabletop tub as Santiago Bay as long as most people had a pretty good idea they weren't really seeing Cuba? When journalism entangled itself with entertainment, which values prevailed—and how much did readers and viewers care?

As the media grew ever more massive and ever more deeply entwined in the political system, so did fake journalism, which remained generally impervious to efforts by politicians, reformers, educators, and others to root it out. After the shameful excesses of Great War propaganda, the League of Nations tried to ban fake news by treaty. It was a noble undertaking to get everyone just to agree not to spread lies over the air, but the world's worst propagandists blithely ignored the whole thing. Nor did the idealistic U.S. attempt at education fare much better in the long run: after barely half a decade of teaching children and grown-ups how to check their prejudices, the Institute for Propaganda Analysis was shuttered to make room for wartime propaganda that was officially sanctioned. During the McCarthy era, Democrats in the Senate opened an abortive and constitutionally dubious effort to outlaw willfully distorted campaign material, but the attempt died after they lost their majority and the newly empowered Republicans chose not to banish what had become an effective weapon for them.

By the 1970s, the traditional authority of the journalistic establishment to police itself or to credibly criticize the journalistic tactics of others was in tatters. Rebellious New Journalists aggressively dismissed objectivity, the decades-old foundation of professional journalism, as inadequate or uninformative, but at the same time they forced new questions about whether subjectivity encouraged inaccuracy. Young reporters at some of the most prestigious news organizations brought humiliation after humiliation down on bosses who seemed powerless to control them. Embarrassing errors on critical stories of war and foreign affairs further eroded the public's faith that the press could be trusted to get anything right. Doing the honorable thing by issuing public acknowledgments and corrections often seemed merely to invite even more scathing criticism. As that famous "din of small voices" grew ever more clamorous on the internet, any attempts at rational conversation were increasingly doused by filter bubbles, lost in echo chambers, and overwhelmed by trolling, flaming, hacking, scamming, sock-puppeteering, algorithm manipulating, and other online misbehaviors. Legacy news organizations struggling with the unprecedented financial challenges of the new digital world stretched themselves thinner and thinner, which only helped drive more and more dissatisfied consumers away.

Fake journalism has now solidified its status as an essential driver of the political polarization of public life, rooted in a burgeoning ecosystem of right-wing media activists and organizations that exploit the swift, lightweight affordances of the online world and embrace the Fox News tactic of presenting its hyperpartisan fare as professionally verified, accurate, and unbiased. Often flaunting the rhetoric of democracy and press freedom, these organizations explicitly claim to be operating according to the standards of professionalized journalism and frequently denigrate the national press and the "liberal media" for failing to do the same thing.

In 2018, for instance, dozens of news anchors in local markets served by the conservative Sinclair Broadcast Group were required to read a script deploring "the troubling trend of irresponsible, one-sided news stories plaguing our country." National news outlets publish "fake stories" they pull from social media "without checking facts first," the script ran, and "are using their platforms to push their own personal bias and agenda to control 'exactly what people think,'" which is "extremely dangerous to our democracy."[3] Meanwhile, as more and more local newspapers go under, a shadowy network has established some 1,300 online sites throughout all fifty states that operate under benign-sounding names such as *Ann Arbor Times* and *Des Moines Sun* and routinely describe their approach as "provid[ing] objective, data-driven information without political bias." The sites rarely acknowledge that many of their articles have in fact been ordered and paid for by Republican political operatives, corporate PR firms, and conservative advocacy groups, which dictate the content, the sources, and the pronounced rightward slant.[4]

The Breitbart News Network, whose then executive chair Steve Bannon boasted to a reporter in 2016 during the Republican National Convention that it was "the platform for the alt-right," describes itself on its website as "one of America's leading news organizations," founded on the idea that "truthful reporting and the free and open exchange of ideas is [sic] essential to maintain a robust democracy."[5] James O'Keefe's Project Veritas has often used ethically or legally dubious undercover techniques and editing practices regularly denounced as deceptive in its "investigation[s]" (as the group's website calls them) of mainstream news organizations, Democratic politicians, labor unions, and liberal advocacy groups. The *New York Times* reported in 2020 that a security contractor closely allied with the Trump White House was involved with an initiative by former U.S. and U.K. spies to train Project Veritas operatives in espionage tactics and intelligence-gathering techniques. Asked for comment, O'Keefe told the *Times* that his group was a "proud independent news organization."[6]

Over at InfoWars.com, Alex Jones, who has pushed conspiracy theories ranging from Pizzagate to white genocide and has been sued for defamation by parents of first-graders killed in a school massacre that he has called a hoax, has described himself as a "tenacious journalist" whose organization "wear[s] our bias—the truth—openly and proudly on our sleeve."[7] The Gateway Pundit blogger, who has numbered among his many whoppers the claims that Hillary Clinton was deathly ill, that COVID-19 vaccines were killing thousands, and that Joe Biden had called for a Muslim jihad, was suspended from Twitter in early 2021 after spreading weeks' worth of disinformation about voter fraud. He boasted on his homepage for months in 2019 and 2020 that his site was "More Accurate than The New York Times, Washington Post, CNN and MSNBC for Two Years and Counting!"[8]

And the stridently white-nationalist and anti-immigrant Daily Caller website, which cofounder Tucker Carlson left in June 2020 to focus on his top-rated primetime Fox News program, makes a point of inviting readers to report any errors, which it promises will be "hastily" corrected "so that our readers can get the real story." Publicly accepting and correcting one's mistakes is, of course, usually understood as a prime signal of professional integrity, and the extent of a news organization's willingness to do so honestly offers a yardstick for measuring just how serious its commitment is to factual accuracy. The Daily Caller, however, doesn't quite work that way. When in January 2020 I used the site's search engine to retrieve uses of the word *correction* and its variants, the first one hundred returns included only three that addressed errors made by the Daily Caller itself, one of which involved the "hotness" of the actor and swimsuit model Kate Upton. Most of the rest shared giggles about "major" or "embarrassing" or "stunning" or "MASSIVE" or "HUGE" corrections that other news organizations or experts had had to make or allegedly should have made—the lion's share by the *New York Times*, the *Washington Post*, and CNN.[9]

The message was clear: the Daily Caller's interest in professional integrity was confined to exploiting professional conventions in order to undermine the news organizations that adhered to them. The tactic is clear: the fake journalists are defining the practice of journalism to mean the way *they* carry it out. The fake journalists are drawing their own professional boundaries to undermine, delegitimize, and defenestrate the genuine ones. The fake journalists are claiming control of what truth looks like.

To say that journalism has reached a crisis point sounds tiresomely familiar—What, again?—but the assaults by Trump and his allies on journalists and on truth itself have been unparalleled, and given the power as well as the wealth at stake, they are unlikely to subside quickly. And there's only so much that even the best-intentioned journalists can do on their own to repair the damage to public life, to restore people's battered trust in public institutions, or to atone for the profession's own record of consequential mistakes. Journalists can try to bridge the chasms of political polarization with information, can investigate the grievances and resentments that have produced those chasms, but they can't force the aggrieved and resentful to accept or act on or even pay attention to what they have to say. Journalists can attempt to clarify how the world works, but they can't—*shouldn't*—succumb to their audiences' (very human) desire for validation that the world works exactly the way they wish it did. Journalists can't stop public figures from lying or force people to recognize when they are. Journalism looks like truth only to those who allow themselves to accept its authority. For everyone else, truth doesn't look like journalism.

I wish I had a solution. So do most people who care about the quality of civic life; journalists, news executives, public figures, scholars, and ordinary people alike continue to float suggestions for combatting the flood of fake news and disinformation. Maybe education in media literacy will help. Maybe stepped-up institutionalized fact checking. Maybe a labeling system for dodgy posts on social media. Maybe transparency. Maybe public shaming, boycotts, or pressure campaigns. Maybe some kind of official credentialing for journalists. Maybe the regulation of Facebook and other immensely powerful and unaccountable platforms. Measurable successes have been elusive.

Then there's the decades-long argument, pressed even more urgently now, that reporters must ditch the frayed straitjacket of journalistic objectivity for good, reveal their own subjectivity more transparently, denounce misbehavior by public figures more forthrightly, even become activists.[10] The Trump presidency was, after all, an entertainment juggernaut that smashed all the standards journalism had tried for more than a century to impose on itself and on the public's understanding of reality. Trump tweeted the term *fake news* 931 times between his inauguration in 2017 and the suspension of his Twitter account on January 8, 2021, most of the time referring to news or news media he disliked. He routinely referred to journalists as "enemies of the people" and reportedly told his national security adviser that reporters who published leaks or protected anonymous sources should be jailed or even "executed."[11]

Close aides and advisers spoke breezily of Trump's fabrications as "alternative facts" and unblushingly asserted that "truth isn't truth." Disinformation became literally life threatening, with some studies showing that people who are regular Fox News viewers seemed to exhibit riskier behavior during the COVID pandemic, to put less faith in medical experts and more in conspiracy theories, and to suffer higher infection rates. The relentless lies by the president and his right-wing media enablers about the "stolen" 2020 election led directly to a lethal assault on the U.S. Capitol building by a furious mob under the carefully fostered delusion that they could overturn Trump's defeat. It's understandable many mainstream journalists felt compelled to say it was time to take a side and take a stand.[12]

It's true that the traditional journalistic norm known as objectivity has long been under attack, understandably so, for hypocrisy, for remoteness, for inadequacy, for positing false equivalences, for blindly reinforcing the default "neutral" values of white- and-male-dominated institutions, for simply being humanly impossible. Long before Trump, as the preceding chapters made clear, misplaced or mishandled attempts at objectivity by the professionalized press had already been implicated in the production of fake news.

Yet it's also true that by now the word *objectivity* has become next to meaningless and the ideal itself is carrying blame it doesn't quite deserve. Everyone has a favorite example of journalistic inertia to bran-dish, and concerns are real and urgent that the rote performance of "balance" can have perniciously unbalancing effects, whether it's favor-ing spokespeople from the Establishment or legitimizing extreme ideas. The *New York Times* was criticized for doing both at once when during the massive racial-justice protests in June 2020 the paper ran an op-ed by a Republican senator advocating the sending of military troops against the "nihilist criminals" and "cadres of left-wing radicals like antifa" he said were running wild in the streets. Amid the widespread condemnation of this op-ed that followed, the paper ran an "Editors' Note" saying that it had published the piece because the senator's comments, "however objectionable people may find them," represented "a newsworthy part of the current debate." But, the editors went on to say, the essay contained unsubstantiated allegations, was "needlessly harsh" in tone, and should not have been run.[13]

Even as incidents of this sort continue to seize attention, however, the routine performance—successful or not—of what was supposed to be even-handed neutrality in mainstream journalism continues its decades-long decline, elbowed aside by the rise of more contextual and interpre-tive reporting and weakened by ever-increasing competitive pressures from the sassier, snarkier, and economically woollier world of digital media.[14] The unprecedented democratic emergency of the Trump era, moreover, impelled many mainstream journalists to mount unusually aggressive investigations into alleged presidential misconduct. A number of those investigations produced important new information, but others shaded over from "aggressive" to downright eager—and when that over-eager reporting turned out to be downright wrong, as some of it was about such stories as Trump's alleged "conspiracy" with the Kremlin to manip-ulate the 2016 election, many saw the misreporting as proof that the main-stream media were downright biased against the president. Amid some-times passionate debate within and beyond the newsroom during his presidency, journalists often couched their reporting in language of unprecedented intensity. Front-page stories routinely called out Trump's "lies," referred to "racist" behavior, and openly deliberated about whether to use the term *coup* or *attempted coup* in describing the Capitol riot. (The AP, whose reputation for strenuous neutrality has prevailed for more than a century and a half, did advise against using the term—but so did a "liberal messaging guru" in her comments to a group of progressive organizers and activists, lest it make Trump seem stronger than he was.)[15]

Yet although the term *objectivity* may be hopelessly compromised by now—and its implication in the perpetuation of dominant social norms rightly under scrutiny—there's still a case to be made for taking a fresh look at the original meaning of that battered ideal and to reconsider how it relates to fake journalism. An inhuman impassivity was never what Walter Lippmann had in mind and never what serious professionals have argued for since then. Objectivity does not refer to the futile contortions of journalists attempting to deny they have emotions. Objectivity does not mandate allowing equal time to both an antivaccination activist and the Centers for Disease Control or lending equal credence to both the rants of a Capitol Hill rioter and the chants of a social-justice protester. Objectivity did not require abject deference to officially sanctioned fabrications about communists in the State Department or about WMDs in the Iraqi desert.

It would be hyperbole to say that objectivity was invented to stamp out fake news—but not by much. The roots of the idea reach back more than a century to the nascent professional community whose civic obligations aligned neatly with its market incentives: to tell the truth and expose the false. In its ideal form, it meant the disciplined *practice* of journalism, in which facts were investigated and verified with a scientific rigor sufficient to recognize one's inevitable personal biases and keep them from compromising the essential accuracy of the story.[16]

The point is that objectivity is a social *process*, a cog in the great self-correcting mechanism that a democratic society is supposed to be. Power has its levers, and politicians have their leverage. But journalists—mostly middle-class people who live on modest salaries, when they can land a job at all—have a time-consuming and expensive process that can sift through evidence and assert a claim to truth based on evidence and source material. Objective journalism is not a contest for standing or for outcomes. Rather, it is a procedural questioning—pursued in public, checked factually, commented on by the relevant parties, and paid for indirectly by advertising—of those who have standing and the outcomes they support. Objective journalists test and evaluate all evidence with intellectual honesty and an openness toward following that evidence wherever it leads—even if that's in a direction they would rather not go toward a conclusion they personally disagree with—and share with their readers and viewers whatever that evidence reveals.

This version of objectivity is just one aspect of the collection of strategies, values, understandings, and goals that has been under construction ever since journalism began to professionalize. Removing the problematic term *objective* and simply describing the best practices of professionals at work are less controversial. Professionals endeavor to be transparent about their methods, which includes publicly admitting and correcting their errors as well as calling out the errors of their colleagues. They work to describe events in ways that scrupulously recognize the experiences of a diverse populace. They are capable of *both* carrying out tough-minded, adversarial investigations *and* conveying their commitment to fairness and accuracy in the modulation of their voice. And they acknowledge that it's hard to be fair and balanced and that they don't always get it right. These tactics may register as too temperate now for an era that feels perpetually in crisis mode. But then their goal is temperate, too: to produce statements about the world that are based on evidence rather than on preference, are confirmed by professional practice, and can be recognized as truthful by a broad community.

If that's not enough, let's consider another reason to recognize some value in straightforward, objective journalism: because objective journalism is what the fake journalists so vigorously pretend to be doing. Fox News and other "news" organizations that are deeply entrenched in partisan politics routinely use their platforms as propaganda arms to boost favored political leaders and to smear opponents. They regularly spread conspiracy theories, fake news, and fringe beliefs. They "[differ] categorically from the rest of the media environment," as three Harvard scholars put it, in that they are "much more susceptible . . . to disinformation, lies, and half-truths." Their strategy is to offer their "family" of readers and viewers a sense of validation and value in a world they portray as predatory and dismissive while giving their consumers only and exactly the picture of the world those consumers want and expect.[17] The fake journalists are writing the end of their stories first.

But fake journalists also routinely claim, without caveat or exception, that they're presenting "objective, data-driven information without political bias," that their "truthful reporting" is "essential to maintain a robust democracy," that they produce "proud independent" journalism, that their only "bias" is truth, that they are more accurate than CNN and the *New York Times*, that it's those *other* media pushing "their own personal bias and agenda" that are dangerous to democracy. They follow the playbook of the organization that defiantly, unshakably insisted for years in the face of all evidence to the contrary that its news-division programming was "fair and balanced." (Fox decided to drop the legendary motto after Roger Ailes, its coiner, was forced to resign over multiple allegations of sexual misconduct, but the network has experimented with new slogans, including "Real News. Real Honest Opinion."[18]) Objectivity *does* work, after all, these news organizations insist—as long as it's the Right that's claiming it. Anyone else is merely peddling stuff that is partisan, biased, and not "real news"—in other words, fake.

Objectivity, neutrality, impartiality—whatever its label, the concept is still obviously fraught, the practice is still flawed, and the task of earning and keeping the trust of a leery public is as challenging as ever. Nor will objectivity have a chance of working fairly without newsrooms that are populated with a wide and diverse range of voices capable of forging responsible professional communities with room for both agreement and disagreement.

But for all its flaws, when it's carried out correctly, genuine professional objectivity still offers news consumers an alternative increasingly rare in the chaotic, hyperpartisan scrum that is today's media landscape: a declaration that the truth is contingent not on emotion or individual whim or partisan mandate but on evidence tested through the use of dedicated processes and tools. Objective journalists who truly follow their obligation to fairly weigh and analyze a range of plausible viewpoints, even those they disagree with, have no alternative but to recognize room for debate— for democratic deliberation—in finding the truth. Fake journalists prefer to slam the door to that room.

It would be both ironic and sad if the tactic that was devised a century ago to stamp out fake news in fact ends up being killed by fake journalism. But for mainstream journalists to wholly succumb to the canard that *genuine* professional objectivity is impossible rather than to undertake the hard but hopeful work of reclamation, explication, and repair may be another way of failing at it. If the sole measure of credibility for responsible professional journalists becomes their willingness to openly express attitude, be "transparent" about their individual convictions, and embrace activism, then Fox News and the whole empire of fake journalism that insists it is the only source for unbiased and impartial news will have won the day. If the media landscape is divided between a mainstream side that flaunts its subjectivity and a right-wing side that denies its own, all hope is gone that the two sides can ever offer a common place for news consumers to stand. If the right-wing media machine is left as the sole owner of "objective" journalism, Fox and friends will be more empowered than ever to use accusations of "fake" as their foil in carrying out their pseudoprofessional boundary work.

And if fake journalism is left in so strong a position to define what genuine journalism is, then Rudy Giuliani will be right. Truth will never be truth.

NOTES

INTRODUCTION

1. Ralph Pulitzer, *The Profession of Journalism: Accuracy in the News: An Address Before the Pulitzer School of Journalism, Columbia University, New York, Delivered at Earl Hall December 16, 1912* (New York: World, 1912), 5.
2. William H. Hills, "Advice to Newspaper Correspondents IV: 'Faking,'" *Writer* 1 (November 1887): 154.
3. See, for instance, Claire Wardle, "Fake News: It's Complicated," Firstdraftnews.org, February 16, 2017, https://firstdraftnews.org/latest/fake-news-complicated/, which posits seven different types of mis- and disinformation; Maria D. Molina, S. Shayam Sundar, Thai Le, and Dongwon Lee, "Fake News Is Not Simply False Information: A Concept Explication and Taxonomy of Online Content," *American Behavioral Scientist*, October 2019, doi:10.1177/0002764219878224.
4. Andie Tucher, "Why Journalism History Matters: The Gaffe, the 'Stuff,' and the Historical Imagination," *American Journalism* 31, no. 4 (2014): 432–44.
5. On textual analysis, see Susan J. Douglas, "Does Textual Analysis Tell Us Anything About Past Audiences?," in *Explorations in Communication and History*, ed. Barbie Zelizer (London: Routledge, 2008), 66–76. See also Tucher, "Why Journalism History Matters."
6. The best-known journalistic code of ethics is the one first adopted by the Society of Professional Journalists in 1926 and periodically updated. The latest version, revised in 2014, identifies four foundational principles: "seek truth and report it"; "minimize harm"; "act independently"; and "be accountable and transparent." See Society of Professional Journalists, "SPJ Code of Ethics," https://www.spj.org/ethicscode.asp.
7. The question was part of a larger study by the *Columbia Journalism Review*, in partnership with Reuters/Ipsos, in which 4,214 adults were asked about how they view "the

makings of journalism." The top nine organizations clustered closely together as being considered "mainstream": CBS (76 percent), NBC (75 percent), ABC (75 percent), CNN (73 percent), the *New York Times* (70 percent), the *Washington Post* (66 percent), the *Wall Street Journal* (66 percent), Fox News (66 percent), and MSNBC (65 percent). Whether the latter two earned their places from their fervent partisans defending them as mainstream, from viewers who considered partisanship to *be* mainstream, or from viewers of the supposedly more straightforward daytime TV news programming is impossible to tell. At the bottom of the list of nineteen organizations were the *Daily Show* (24 percent), the *National Enquirer* (23 percent), Vice News (22 percent), and BillOReilly.com (19 percent). "Poll: How Does the Public Think Journalism Happens?," *Columbia Journalism Review*, Winter 2019, https://www.cjr.org/special_report/how -does-journalism-happen-poll.php.

8. Pulitzer, *Profession of Journalism*, 16.

1. "FALSE REPORTS, MALICIOUSLY MADE"

1. 3 Edw. I c. 34; David A. Copeland, *The Idea of a Free Press: The Enlightenment and Its Unruly Legacy* (Evanston, IL: Northwestern University Press, 2006), 37–38.

2. James Sutherland, *The Restoration Newspaper and Its Development* (Cambridge: Cambridge University Press, 1986), 15 (quoting the royal proclamation of May 17, 1680, on "Lyes"), 21 (quoting the divine Robert South on the "great business"); John Nerone, *The Media and Public Life: A History* (Cambridge: Polity, 2015), 19–22.

3. The *Monthly Recorder* is quoted in Sutherland, *Restoration Newspaper*, 48.

4. William David Sloan, "Chaos, Polemics, and America's First Newspaper," *Journalism Quarterly* 70 (1993): 666–81; Victor Hugo Paltsits, "New Light on 'Publick Occurrences': America's First Newspaper," *Proceedings of the American Antiquarian Society* 59 (1949): 75–88.

5. The full text of Harris's newspaper is available at the National Humanities Center site, http://nationalhumanitiescenter.org/pds/amerbegin/power/text5/PublickOccurrences .pdf.

6. The sole copy of *Publick Occurrences Both Forreign and Domestick* is in the archives of the Public Record Office in London. The council's judgment is quoted in Charles E. Clark, *The Public Prints: The Newspaper in Anglo-American Culture, 1665–1740* (New York: Oxford University Press, 1994), 73.

7. Sewall's diary quoted in Paltsits, "New Light," 77.

8. Hugh Amory, *Bibliography and the Book Trades: Studies in the Print Culture of Early New England*, ed. David D. Hall (Philadelphia: University of Pennsylvania Press, 2005), 117.

9. George Henry Payne, *History of Journalism in the United States* (New York: Appleton, 1920), 12, 21.

10. Antonia Fraser, *Love and Louis XIV: The Women in the Life of the Sun King* (New York: Doubleday, 2006), 175–76, 232; Guy Rowlands and Julia Prest, introduction to *The Third*

Reign of Louis XIV c. 1682–1715, ed. Julia Prest and Guy Rowlands (London: Routledge, 2017), 14.

11. Sutherland, *Restoration Newspaper*, 186–93.

12. Robert Darnton, *The Forbidden Best-Sellers of Pre-revolutionary France* (London: Fontana, 1997), 210.

13. On Campbell and the *News-Letter* generally, see Clark, *Public Prints*, 77–102.

14. Clark, *Public Prints*, 92–93; Richard D. Brown, "The Shifting Freedoms of the Press in the Eighteenth Century," in *A History of the Book in America*, vol. 1: *The Colonial Book in the Atlantic World*, ed. Hugh Amory and David D. Hall (Cambridge: Cambridge University Press, 2000), 367–68.

15. For older periodical publications referenced in chapters 1–7, my main sources were the databases Accessible Archives, America's Historical Newspapers (Readex), Chronicling America (Library of Congress), Newspaperarchive.com, Newspapers.com, and ProQuest Historical Newspapers. I also used proprietary databases for individual newspapers and magazines. I do not cite individual articles in the notes as long as the item is sufficiently identified in the text by publication title and date.

16. Carol Sue Humphrey, *The American Revolution and the Press: The Promise of Independence* (Evanston, IL: Northwestern University Press, 2013), 33.

17. Stephen Botein, " 'Meer Mechanics' and an Open Press: The Business and Political Strategies of Colonial American Printers," *Perspectives in American History* 9 (1975): 127–225; Benjamin Franklin, "Apology for Printers," *Pennsylvania Gazette*, June 10, 1731, available online at the National Archives Founders Online site, https://founders.archives .gov/documents/Franklin/01-01-02-0061.

18. Statistics cited in Stephen Botein, "Printers and the American Revolution," in *The Press and the American Revolution*, ed. Bernard Bailyn and John B. Hench (Boston: Northeastern University Press, 1980), 41, 32.

19. Botein, "Printers."

20. Albert Matthews, "The Snake Devices, 1754–1776, and the *Constitutional Courant*, 1765," *Transactions of the Colonial Society of Massachusetts* 11 (1906–1907): 421–46.

21. Benjamin Franklin, "Supplement to the *Boston Independent Chronicle* [Before April 22, 1782]," in *The Papers of Benjamin Franklin*, vol. 37: *March 16 Through August 15, 1782*, ed. Ellen R. Cohn (New Haven, CT: Yale University Press, 2003), available at the National Archives website, https://founders.archives.gov/documents/Franklin/01-37-02-0132.

22. Marcus Daniel, *Scandal and Civility: Journalism and the Birth of American Democracy* (Oxford: Oxford University Press, 2009), 12–18; *Philadelphia Aurora*, December 23, 1796, 2; *Porcupine's Gazette*, November 16, 1797, 3; *Independent Chronicle* (Boston), October 16, 1797, quoted in Carol Sue Humphrey, *The Revolutionary Era: Primary Documents on Events from 1776 to 1800* (Westport, CT: Greenwood, 2003), 260.

23. Ron Chernow, *Alexander Hamilton* (New York: Penguin, 2004), 364–70, 529–42; Jacob Katz Cogan, "The Reynolds Affair and the Politics of Character," *Journal of the Early Republic* 16 (Autumn 1996): 389–417.

24. Geoffrey R. Stone, *Perilous Times: Free Speech in Wartime from the Sedition Act of 1798 to the War on Terrorism* (New York: Norton, 2004), 36–43; statistics from Wendell Bird,

Criminal Dissent: Prosecutions Under the Alien and Sedition Acts of 1798 (Cambridge, MA: Harvard University Press, 2020), 7, 361, 374–85.

25. Michael Durey, *"With the Hammer of Truth": James Thomson Callender and America's Early National Heroes* (Charlottesville: University Press of Virginia, 1990), 119–20; James T. Callender, *The Prospect Before Us*, 2 vols. (Richmond, VA: Jones, Pleasants, and Lyon for the author, 1800–1801), 2:119.

26. *Richmond Recorder*, September 1, 1802, 2.

27. On the rise of the penny press generally, see Andie Tucher, *Froth and Scum: Truth, Beauty, Goodness, and the Ax-Murder in America's First Mass Medium* (Chapel Hill: University of North Carolina Press, 1994); and Michael Schudson, *Discovering the News: A Social History of American Newspapers* (New York: Basic, 1978), 12–60. Historical literacy rates are notoriously hard to pin down and interpret, but in the 1840 census only 4 percent of the residents of New York State reported they could not read; see David M. Henkin, *City Reading: Written Words and Public Spaces in Antebellum New York* (New York: Columbia University Press, 1998), 21.

28. Tucher, *Froth and Scum*, 46–61; Karen Halttunen, *Confidence Men and Painted Women: A Study of Middle-Class Culture in America, 1830–1870* (New Haven, CT: Yale University Press, 1982), 33–55; Neil Harris, *Humbug: The Art of P. T. Barnum* (Chicago: University of Chicago Press, 1973), 70–79.

29. On the penny-press coverage of the Robinson–Jewett affair, see Tucher, *Froth and Scum*, 21–84.

30. Tucher, *Froth and Scum*, 42–43.

31. Ray Allen Billington, "Maria Monk and Her Influence," *Catholic Historical Review* 22, no. 3 (1936): 283–96; Richard Hofstadter, "The Paranoid Style in American Politics," *Harper's*, November 1964, https://harpers.org/archive/1964/11/the-paranoid-style-in-american-politics/.

32. Maria Monk, *Awful Disclosures, by Maria Monk, of the Hotel Dieu Nunnery of Montreal, Revised, with an Appendix . . . Also, a Supplement . . .* (New York: Maria Monk, 1836), 217. The mother also said Monk had never been a nun, but Monk's partisans dismissed the mother as intemperate and erratic.

33. Tucher, *Froth and Scum*, 99–190, explores the changing tone manifested in the coverage of the murder of a tradesman by the brother of Samuel Colt in 1841.

2. "IMPORTANT IF TRUE"

1. Hazel Dicken-Garcia, *Journalistic Standards in Nineteenth-Century America* (Madison: University of Wisconsin Press, 1989), 136–39.

2. John Nerone, "History, Journalism, and the Problem of Truth," in *Assessing Evidence in a Post-modern World*, ed. Bonnie Brennen (Milwaukee: Marquette University Press, 2013), 14.

3. Andie Tucher, "Reporting for Duty: The Bohemian Brigade, the Civil War, and the Social Construction of the Reporter," *Book History* 9 (2006): 131–57.
4. T. Campbell-Copeland, *The Ladder of Journalism: How to Climb It* (New York: Forman, 1889), 37 (drinking), 107 (gifts), 108 ("big head"), 94 (church). *Neat* and *neatness* also appeared several times in the advertisements at the back of the book for Pears Soap, which touted cleanliness as "the interviewer's most valuable stock in trade."
5. In *American Journalism, a History: 1690–1960*, 3rd ed. (New York: Macmillan, 1962), Frank Luther Mott notes that in the 1860–1872 era four-page weekly papers used much more feature material than the dailies did, sometimes devoting "most of page one to selected essays, articles, stories, humorous paragraphs, and poetry" (391). The equivalent of another page or even more was generally given over to advertisements. The Batchelor's ads appeared, with occasional minor changes in wording, in hundreds of papers in the 1860s, 1870s, and 1880s.
6. On the origins of the newspaper exchange, see Richard B. Kielbowicz, "Newsgathering by Printers' Exchanges Before the Telegraph," *Journalism History* 9, no. 2 (Summer 1982): 42–48.
7. Tim Vos and Teri Finneman, "The Early Historical Construction of Journalism's Gatekeeping Role," *Journalism* 18, no. 3 (2017): 265–66.
8. *Ontario Repository* (Canandaigua), October 10, 1809, quoted in Milton W. Hamilton, *The Country Printer: New York State, 1785–1830*, 2nd ed. (Port Washington, NY: Ira J. Friedman, 1964), 165.
9. *Gettysburg (PA) Star & Banner*, July 19, 1831, 3.
10. Ronald J. Zboray and Mary Saracino Zboray, *Everyday Ideas: Socioliterary Experience Among Antebellum New Englanders* (Knoxville: University of Tennessee Press, 2006), 268–69.
11. Originally published in early October by a paper in Bowling Green, Kentucky, this item about Mrs. Blankenship was frequently reprinted; see, for instance, *Manitowoc (WI) Pilot*, October 18, 1867, 1; *Gold Hill (NV Terr.) Daily News*, October 29, 1867, 2; and *Edgefield (SC) Advertiser*, November 27, 1867, 1. I have been unable to identify the Widow Blankenship or confirm her existence.
12. Carolyn S. Brown, *The Tall Tale in American Folklore and Literature* (Knoxville: University of Tennessee Press, 1987), 33–38, 58–63.
13. Gary Scharnhorst, *The Life of Mark Twain: The Early Years, 1835–1871* (Columbia: University of Missouri Press, 2018), 182–84.
14. E. D. Cope to De Quille, on *American Naturalist* letterhead, Philadelphia, September 18, 1880, and Thomas Donaldson to T. T. Orbiston, on U.S. Centennial Commission letterhead, Philadelphia, March 7, 1876, both in Dan De Quille Papers, BANC MSS P-G 246, Bancroft Library, University of California, Berkeley. See also C. Grant Loomis, "The Tall Tales of Dan De Quille," *California Folklore Quarterly* 5, no. 1 (January 1946): 26–71.
15. "Practical Jokes" and the column of letters headed "A Harmless Practical Joke," *New York Times*, November 10, 1874, 4.

16. Mark Wahlgren Summers, *The Press Gang: Newspapers and Politics, 1865–1878* (Chapel Hill: University of North Carolina Press, 1994), 2.

17. On the governor's stance on Tammany, see, for instance, "Gen. Dix and the Tammany Gang," *New York Times*, October 21, 1872, 1.

18. *The War of the Rebellion: A Compilation of the Official Records of the Union and Confederate Armies*, 70 vols. (Washington, DC: U.S. Government Printing Office, 1880–1901), series 1, vol. 36 (part II): 272–87.

19. *Biographical Dictionary of the United States Congress, 1774–Present*, s.v. "Schell, Richard," https://bioguide.congress.gov.

20. William Safire, *Safire's Political Dictionary*, updated and exp. ed. (Oxford: Oxford University Press, 2008), 630.

21. James L. Roberts II, "The Roorback Hoax: A Curious Incident in the Election of 1844," *Annotations* 30, no. 3 (September 2002): 16–17; see also the substantial coverage of the story in the *Albany Evening Journal*, beginning with "James K. Polk's Slaves Sold and Driven in Manacles!," September 16, 1844, 2.

22. On the conviction that the forgery harmed the Whigs, see, for instance, letters to Polk from J. George Harris of the *Nashville Union* and William E. Cramer of the *Albany Argus* in James K. Polk, *Correspondence of James K. Polk*, vol. 8: *September–December 1844*, ed. Wayne Cutler (Knoxville: University of Tennessee Press, 1993), 143, 149. On the campaign against Clay, see Robert V. Remini, *Henry Clay: Statesman for the Union* (New York: Norton, 1991), 649–52.

23. *Knoxville (TN) Register*, January 6, 1863, quoted in J. Cutler Andrews, *The South Reports the Civil War* (1970; reprint, Pittsburgh: University of Pittsburgh Press, 1985), 534–35; Mary Chesnut, *Mary Chesnut's Civil War*, ed. C. Vann Woodward (New Haven, CT: Yale University Press, 1981), 121.

24. "The Telegraphic Seer" first appeared in the *Daily Missouri Republican*, April 10, 1861, 2, and was copied in, for instance, the *Arkansas State Gazette* (Little Rock), April 20, 1861, 2, and the *Tennessean* (Nashville), April 13, 1861, 2. Newspapers often cited the *Missouri Republican* as the *St. Louis Republican*.

25. J. Cutler Andrews, *The North Reports the Civil War* (1955; reprint, Pittsburgh: University of Pittsburgh Press, 1985), 88–101.

26. "The Press and the Government," *New York Times*, July 24, 1861, 4.

27. William Lusk to Elizabeth F. Lusk, August 5, 1861, in William Lusk, *War Letters of William Thompson Lusk: Captain, Assistant Adjutant-General, United States Volunteers, 1861–1863, Afterward M.D., LL.D.* (New York: W. C. Lusk, 1911), 69.

28. "Affairs in England," bylined "Our Own Correspondent, 26 October 1861," *New York Times*, November 7, 1861, 2.

29. Junius Henri Browne, *Four Years in Secessia: Adventures Within and Beyond the Union Lines* (Hartford, CT: O. D. Case, 1865); Thomas W. Knox, *Camp-Fire and Cotton-Field: Southern Adventure in Time of War, Life with the Union Armies, and Residence on a Louisiana Plantation* (New York: Blelock, 1865); Albert D. Richardson, *The Secret Service, the Field, the Dungeon, and the Escape* (Hartford, CT: American, 1865); Franc Wilkie, *Pen and Powder* (Boston: Ticknor, 1888). See also Tucher, "Reporting for Duty."

30. Browne, *Four Years in Secessia*, 15–16.

31. Browne, *Four Years in Secessia*, 16–20; Knox, *Camp-Fire*, 490–91; Wilkie, *Pen and Powder*, 369–70.

32. "The Great Battle of Sugar-Creek," *New York Tribune*, March 20, 1862, 6–7; "The New York Herald Vindicated," *New York Herald*, April 17, 1862, 4, citing the *St. Louis Democrat* (actually the *Missouri Democrat*).

33. Richardson, *Secret Service*, 271.

34. Wilkie, *Pen and Powder*, 129; see also Tucher, "Reporting for Duty," 144. Wilkie claimed that Browne's article "contain[ed] only a single fact or two of the battle" (126) and mentioned "not a single regiment of infantry or cavalry, or the name of a battery" (129), but those claims are untrue: although the order of battle that appears in the fifth paragraph of Browne's article, for instance, includes some inaccuracies, it does list plenty of units by name. Wilkie also unfurled a string of purple quotes purportedly drawn from Browne's article as "a specimen of what can be done by a vivid imagination" (126). The quotes, however, did not actually come from Browne's newspaper report; they were excerpted from a passage in his postwar memoir, *Four Years in Secessia*, 94–101.

3. "NOT EXACTLY LYING"

1. W. T. Stead, *The Americanization of the World; Or, The Trend of the Twentieth Century* (New York: Horace Markley, [1902]), 293.

2. Michael Schudson, "Question Authority: A History of the News Interview," in *The Power of News* (Cambridge, MA: Harvard University Press, 1995), 74, 91–93.

3. Richard Grant White, "Wedding, Interviewing, et Cetera," *Galaxy*, December 1874, 826–28.

4. See, for example, Nils Gunnar Nilsson, "The Origin of the Interview," *Journalism Quarterly* 48 (1971): 707–13, arguing for Bennett's primacy and suggesting some other interview-like reports he published even before the alleged one with Townsend.

5. Andie Tucher, *Froth and Scum: Truth, Beauty, Goodness, and the Ax-Murder in America's First Mass Medium* (Chapel Hill: University of North Carolina Press, 1994), 34–36. Given the prevalence of humbugs throughout the penny press in this era, the errors betrayed in Bennett's alleged report, and the editor's own well-known propensity for exaggeration and fabrication, the authenticity of all the conversations mentioned in Nilsson, "Origin of the Interview," is suspect.

6. The interview is reprinted in *A Treasury of Great Reporting: Literature Under Pressure from the Sixteenth Century to Our Own Time*, 2nd ed., ed. Louis L. Snyder and Richard B. Morris (New York: Simon and Schuster, 1962), 106–9.

7. Edgar White, "The Art of Interviewing," *Writer* 17 (March 1904): 33.

8. R. G. White, "Wedding, Interviewing," 827.

9.   Andie Tucher, "Reporting for Duty: The Bohemian Brigade, the Civil War, and the Social Construction of the Reporter," *Book History* 9 (2006): 133–34, 137–39, 141–42, 148–49.

10. George William Curtis, "Editor's Easy Chair," *Harper's New Monthly Magazine*, April 1871, 774.

11. George William Curtis, "Editor's Easy Chair," *Harper's New Monthly Magazine*, October 1876, 785.

12. E. White, "Art of Interviewing," 34.

13. Edwin L. Shuman, *Steps Into Journalism: Helps and Hints for Young Writers* (Evanston, IL: Evanston Press, 1894), 70, 71.

14. Theodore Dreiser, *Newspaper Days: An Autobiography*, ed. T. D. Nostwich (Santa Rosa, CA: Black Sparrow Press, 2000), 184.

15. Dreiser, *Newspaper Days*, 166–67.

16. A. F. Hill, *Secrets of the Sanctum: An Inside View of an Editor's Life* (Philadelphia: Claxton, Remsen, and Haffelfinger, 1875), 55–56.

17. Charles M. Sheldon, "The Daily Papers and the Truth," *New Outlook*, May 12, 1900, 117.

18. John Arthur, "Reporting, Practical and Theoretical," *Writer* 3 (February 1889): 36, 37.

19. Andie Tucher, "The True, the False, and the 'Not Exactly Lying': Making Fakes and Telling Stories in the Age of the Real Thing," in *Literature and Journalism: Inspirations, Intersections, and Inventions from Ben Franklin to Stephen Colbert*, ed. Mark Canada (New York: Palgrave Macmillan, 2013), 100.

20. William H. Hills, "Advice to Newspaper Correspondents III: Some Hints on Style," *Writer* 1 (June 1887): 51.

21. William H. Hills, "Advice to Newspaper Correspondents IV: 'Faking,'" *Writer* 1 (November 1887): 154, 155.

22. Shuman, *Steps Into Journalism*, 122, 123.

23. "The Spectator," *Outlook*, February 23, 1901, 438; George Grantham Bain, "Newspaper 'Faking,'" *Lippincott's Monthly*, August 1894, 274–75.

24. "The Spectator," 437.

25. H. R. (Harriette Robinson) Shattuck, "Reporters' Ethics," *Writer* 3 (March 1889): 57–58; on the serious papers' repudiation of faking, see Tucher, "The True, the False," 102–6.

26. "No Yellow Fever at Memphis," *Chicago Tribune*, August 28, 1893, 3.

27. Most of the papers that carried the denial printed only abbreviated versions that left out Dr. Rogers's name and the specific accusation of having sent a "fake telegraph." Digital search engines are of course subject to error, but searches through ProQuest Historical Newspapers, America's Historical Newspapers (Readex), Chronicling America (Library of Congress), and Newspapers.com turned up no "fake" reports placing the fever in Memphis. Official mortality statistics showed no deaths from yellow fever in August 1893 in Memphis (or in any other reporting city in the state): Tennessee State Board of Health, *Bulletin* 9, no. 2 (September 20, 1893): 24. Dr. S. A. Rogers's name appears nowhere in the bulletin; Plunket appears throughout as president or director of the board.

28. H. Leon Prather Sr., *We Have Taken a City: Wilmington Racial Massacre and Coup of 1898* (Rutherford, NJ: Fairleigh Dickinson University Press, 1984), 9; 1898 Wilmington Race Riot Commission, *1898 Wilmington Race Riot Report* (Raleigh: North Carolina Department of Cultural Resources, 2008), 61, https://digital.ncdcr.gov/digital/collection /p249901coll22/id/5335; David Zucchino, *Wilmington's Lie: The Murderous Coup of 1898 and the Rise of White Supremacy* (New York: Atlantic Monthly Press, 2020), 65–76; Josephus Daniels, *Editor in Politics* (Chapel Hill: University of North Carolina Press, 1941), 295–96. See also, generally, Kathy Roberts Forde and Sid Bedingfield, eds., *Journalism and Jim Crow: White Supremacy and the Black Struggle for a New America* (Champaign: University of Illinois Press, 2021).

29. *Memphis Appeal-Avalanche*, April 23, 1893, quoted in Paula Giddings, *Ida, a Sword Among Lions: Ida B. Wells and the Campaign Against Lynching* (New York: Harper Collins, 2008), 268; "British Anti-Lynchers," *New York Times*, August 2, 1894, 4; "The New Campaign of Slander Against the South," *Baltimore Sun*, August 3, 1894, 4; "A Disgraceful Affair," *Clarion Ledger* (Jackson, MS), September 6, 1894, 4.

30. "Glad to Get Truth," *Atlanta Constitution*, July 29, 1894, 15.

31. The *Spectator*'s comment was appended to W. McKay, "Letter to the Editor," *Spectator* (London), July 28, 1894, 111, which quotes Governor Northen's denial. For the original piece that drew Northen's "correction," see "Lynch-Law in America," *Spectator* (London), June 2, 1894, 743–44 (McKay's letter misidentifies the date of that issue as June 16).

32. Edwin H. Porter, *The Fall River Tragedy: A History of the Borden Murders* (Fall River, MA: Buffinton, 1893), 154, 157; Joseph A. Conforti, *Lizzie Borden on Trial: Murder, Ethnicity, and Gender* (Lawrence: University Press of Kansas, 2015), 123; "Henry G. Trickey Dead," *Boston Daily Globe*, December 5, 1892, 1, 5; "Buried in Flowers," *Boston Daily Globe*, December 7, 1892, 8; and so on (the *Globe* ran tributes for a week).

33. Porter, *Fall River Tragedy*, 144.

34. On "paradigm repair," see Tim P. Vos and Joseph Moore, "Building the Journalistic Paradigm: Beyond Paradigm Repair," *Journalism* 21 (2020): 17–33.

35. "The Business of Faking," *Courier Journal* (Louisville), May 9, 1898, 4; "Yellow Papers Don't Make Yellow People," *Puck*, March 9, 1898, 7, referring to the yellow papers' coverage of the sinking of the *Maine*.

36. On the yellow papers' coverage of the Spanish-American War, see, generally, David R. Spencer, *The Yellow Journalism: The Press and America's Emergence as a World Power* (Evanston, IL: Northwestern University Press, 2007), 123–203; David Nasaw, *The Chief: The Life of William Randolph Hearst* (Boston: Houghton Mifflin, 2000), 125–42; James McGrath Morris, *Pulitzer: A Life in Politics, Print, and Power* (New York: Harper, 2010), 338–42; and Charles H. Brown, *The Correspondents' War: Journalists in the Spanish-American War* (New York: Scribner's, 1967).

37. W. R. Hearst, "Col. Laine's Reprisal on His Spanish Captives," *New York Evening Journal*, July 11, 1898, 3; Hearst insisted the error had arisen during the transcription of his cable.

38. Roosevelt's denials were widely published by AP member papers; see, for example, "Roosevelt Denounces St. Louis Fakes Coming Via New York," *St. Louis Post Dispatch*,

March 20, 1898, A2 (noting that the rival *St. Louis Republic* had fallen for the *New York Journal*'s interview).

39. "The Week," *Nation*, March 24, 1898, 215–16.

40. On the influence of the yellow press, see Spencer, *Yellow Journalism*, 123–51.

41. Michael Schudson, *Discovering the News: A Social History of American Newspapers* (New York: Basic, 1978), 93; *Boston Globe* editor quoted in Gerald J. Baldasty, *The Commercialization of News in the Nineteenth Century* (Madison: University of Wisconsin Press, 1992), 81.

42. The "professionalizing" turn as manifested in the embrace of scientific objectivity and in the separation of politics from journalism is well documented; see, for instance, Schudson, *Discovering the News*, 106–20; Michael Schudson, "Is Journalism a Profession? Objectivity 1.0, Objectivity 2.0, and Beyond," in *Why Journalism Still Matters* (Cambridge: Polity, 2018), 46–52; Kathy Roberts Forde and Katherine A. Foss, "'The Facts—the Color!—the Facts': The Idea of a Report in American Print Culture, 1885–1910," *Book History* 15 (2012): 123–51; Silvio Waisbord, *Reinventing Professionalism: Journalism and News in Global Perspective* (Cambridge: Polity Press, 2013), 19–42; and John Nerone, *The Media and Public Life: A History* (Cambridge: Polity, 2015), 143–74. On the wider cultural turn toward realism in the United States, see Miles Orvell, *The Real Thing: Imitation and Authenticity in American Culture, 1880–1940* (Chapel Hill: University of North Carolina Press, 1989); and David E. Shi, *Facing Facts: Realism in American Thought and Culture, 1850–1920* (New York: Oxford University Press, 1995).

43. See, for instance, Vos and Moore, "Building the Journalistic Paradigm"; and Matt Carlson, "Metajournalistic Discourse and the Meanings of Journalism: Definitional Control, Boundary Work, and Legitimation," *Communication Theory* 26 (2016): 349–68.

44. "Business Announcement," *New York Times*, August 19, 1896, 4.

45. See Matt Carlson, *Journalistic Authority: Legitimating News in the Digital Era* (New York: Columbia University Press, 2017), 29–93; and Christopher Anderson, "Journalism: Expertise, Authority, and Power in Democratic Life," in *The Media and Social Theory*, ed. David Hesmondhalgh and Jason Toynbee (London: Routledge, 2008), 248–64, which includes a useful historical survey of scholarship in the field of journalistic expertise. James W. Carey makes an explicit argument drawn from Walter Lippmann and Jürgen Habermas that the new professionalized approach to journalism transformed what had been a conversation between readers and their newspapers into "a journalism of fact without regard to understanding . . . that justifies itself in the public's name but in which the public plays no role, except as an audience" ("The Press, Public Opinion, and Public Discourse," in *Public Opinion and the Communication of Consent*, ed. Theodore L. Glasser and Charles T. Salmon [New York: Guilford, 1995], 391).

46. Tucher, "The True, the False," 102–6; Guenter B. Risse, *Plague, Fear, and Politics in San Francisco's Chinatown* (Baltimore: Johns Hopkins University Press, 2012), 157. See also, for instance, "Plague Fake Is Exploded: No Reason for Health Board's Alleged 'Suspicion,'" *San Francisco Chronicle*, March 9, 1900, 12.

47. Max Sherover, *Fakes in American Journalism* (Buffalo, NY: Buffalo Publishing, 1914), 3.

48. Ben Hecht, *A Child of the Century* (1954; reprint, New York: Primus, 1985), 133.

49. "'All the News That's Fit to Print,'" *New York State Journal of Medicine* 9 (December 1909): 483; the article in question was "Drug Habit Curable, Says Dr. Lambert," *New York Times*, October 7, 1909, 18.

50. The two interviews were described in "Offenses Against Good Journalism" and "Untrue and Impertinent," *New Outlook*, February 29, 1908, 479. The interview with Green first appeared in the *Boston Traveler* on February 14, 1908, and was widely quoted or reprinted—for example, as "Hetty Green Talks Cash and Politics," *New York Times*, February 15, 1908, 1. The Morgan interview by Alexander Ular appeared on the front page of the morning edition of the *World* (New York) on February 9, 1908, as "Morgan Predicts Starvation for Workingmen" and on the same day in its sister paper, the *St. Louis Post Dispatch*, as "Morgan Declares Workingmen Must Submit or Starve," sect. 3, 1. Morgan's repudiation of the interview as "a fake from start to finish" appeared on page 2 of the *World* the following day; see also, for example, "Denial by Mr. Morgan," *Washington Post*, February 10, 1908, 3, and "Morgan Quoted Correctly, Ular Makes Answer," *St. Louis Post-Dispatch*, February 16, 1908, sect. 3, 3. Nothing in the *World*'s surviving papers reveals any internal discussions: *World* (New York) Records, 1882–1940, Rare Book & Manuscript Library, Columbia University, New York.

51. Morris, *Pulitzer*, 273. The *Evening World*'s edge persists; the Library of Congress offers access to Junior's first thirty-five years in its free searchable database, but digitized issues of Senior are available only in limited runs and only to paying subscribers: the database Newspapers.com includes the years 1890 to 1899, and Newspaperarchive.com covers from 1860, before Pulitzer's purchase, to 1903, both with significant gaps.

52. Don C. Seitz, *Joseph Pulitzer: His Life and Letters* (New York: Simon and Schuster, 1924), 22–23.

53. Dreiser, *Newspaper Days*, 625; James Boylan, *Pulitzer's School: Columbia University's School of Journalism, 1903–2003* (New York: Columbia University Press, 2003), 3–4.

54. Theodore Roosevelt to Whitelaw Reid, January 6, 1909, in *The Letters of Theodore Roosevelt*, 8 vols., ed. Elting E. Morison (Cambridge, MA: Harvard University Press, 1951–1954), 6:1466–467.

55. The *Century*'s softened and suppressed version of the interview is reprinted in Peter Winzen, *Das Kaiserreich am Abgrund: Die Daily-Telegraph-Affäre und das Hale-Interview von 1908: Darstellung und Dokumentation* (Stuttgart, Germany: Franz Steiner, 2002), 348–59; this version was taken from the copy edited by the Foreign Office and preserved in the Politisches Archiv des Auswärtigen Amts (AA), Berlin. A fuller version published in 1934 by Hale's son (William Harlan Hale, "Thus Spoke the Kaiser: The Lost Interview Which Solves an International Mystery," *Atlantic Monthly*, May 1934, 513–23) also reprints the actual text of the edited article but in addition restores the inflammatory language that had been deleted by the Foreign Office, which he retrieved from his father's own extensive postinterview memorandum, reprinted in Winzen, *Kaiserreich*, 344–48. See also, generally, Ralph R. Menning and Carol Bresnahan Menning, "'Baseless Allegations': Wilhelm II and the Hale Interview of 1908," *Central European History* 16, no. 4 (December 1983): 368–97; and Robert Underwood Johnson, *Remembered Yesterdays* (Boston: Little, Brown, 1923), 229–37.

56. "The Kaiser's Suppressed Interview Criticised England, Praised America," *New York American*, November 20, 1908, 1; "Kaiser, in a Rage, Told Hale That King Edward Had Been Hounding Him," *World* (New York), November 21, 1908, 1. The *World*'s interview and its follow-up coverage ran only in the paper's flagship morning edition, not in the *Evening World*.

57. "Ein plumper Schwindel . . . eine grobe Mystifikation und von A bis Z erfunden." Bernhard Fürst von Bülow to Kaiser Wilhelm II, November 23, 1908, in Winzen, *Kaiserreich*, 262–63; Kaiser to von Bülow, November 23, 1908, quoted in Winzen, *Kaiserreich*, 262 n. 2. The extensive file on the matter preserved in Archive-volume R 17240, file Vereinigte Staaten von Amerika 6 Nr. 2: Journalisten, vol. 1, May 1908–December 1908, AA, Berlin, includes numerous clippings from English-language and other newspapers debating the episode.

58. "To the Editors of the *New York Times*," *New York American*, November 26, 1908, 16; "Mr. Hale Replies," *New York Times*, November 23, 1908, 1. Hale also claimed that a *World* reporter sent to ask him about the piece acknowledged that the paper knew it was fake.

59. "Hale Approved Kaiser Interview Printed in World," *World* (New York), November 22, 1908, 1; see also "Kaiser's Talk in World News Amazes Britain," *World*, November 23, 1908, 1; "Europe Deeply Moved by the World's Report of Kaiser Interview," *World*, November 24, 1908, 1.

60. William Harlan Hale, "Adventures of a Document: The Strange Sequel to the Kaiser Interview," *Atlantic Monthly*, June 1934. See also " 'The World' Retracts: Says 'Synopsis' of Hale Interview Was Unfounded," *New York Tribune*, November 30, 1908, 7. The accuracy of the *World*'s account of Hale's actions is difficult to assess. An internal *World* memo to the paper's business manager mentions an attempt to confirm the synopsis with Hale but leaves the result ambiguous: the piece, the memo said, did not appear in the day's earliest edition because "they were trying to find Dr. Hale to see that he would not deny it. Rather foolish to my mind, because Hale's attitude in the whole matter has been made perfectly plain before" (F. W. Knapp to Don C. Seitz, typescript, November 21, 1908, box 47, *World* Records).

61. Stewart Halsey Ross, *Propaganda for War: How the United States Was Conditioned to Fight the Great War of 1914–1918* (Jefferson, NC: McFarland, 1996), 137–42.

62. "Kaiser Interview 'Killed' to Postpone World War," *New York Tribune*, December 18, 1917, 2; see also "Kaiser's 'Killed' Interview Foretelling in 1908 World War Rises from the Sea," *New York Tribune*, December 17, 1917, 1, and "Kaiser Interview Diluted Before It Went to 'Century,' " *New York Tribune*, December 27, 1917, 14. The *Christian Science Monitor*, the *Chicago Tribune*, and the *Washington Post* were among the other major papers that followed the *Tribune* in covering the revelations.

63. "Roosevelt . . . bemüht gewesen ist ein Aufbauschen in den Zeitungen zu verhindern" (Roosevelt endeavored to keep things from blowing up in the newspapers): Hatzfeldt to the German Foreign Office, telegram, Washington, DC, November 23, 1908, Archive-volume R 17240, 72, AA, Berlin. In *Kaiserreich*, 84–85, Winzen cites (but does not quote) this telegram to argue that the Roosevelt administration applied "einen starken Druck" (strong pressure) to force the *World*'s apology.

64. Morris, *Pulitzer*, 4–5, 417–40, quote at 424.

65. "Hiesige Regierungskreise legen bis jetzt den Veröffentlichungen der als Skandalblätter bekannten World und New York American über Interview Herrn Hales keine grössere Bedeutung bei" (Hatzfeldt, telegram, November 23, 1908).

66. Hale's letter to Reick, which the *American* seems to have acquired, appears in Oscar King Davis, *Released for Publication: Some Inside Political History of Theodore Roosevelt and His Times* (Boston: Houghton Mifflin; Cambridge: Riverside, 1925), 81–83. The letter to Northcliffe, now preserved in the Public Record Office in London, is reprinted in Winzen, *Kaiserreich*, 343–44. Although the *World*'s version is more a paraphrase of the letter than a transcription, it makes most of the same points and seems to have lifted some notable phrases nearly verbatim—for instance, that war with England would come, "the sooner the better."

67. Frank I. Cobb, "Memorandum to Mr. Pulitzer in the Matter of the Kaiser Interview," November 25, 1908, signed typescript, box 47, *World* Records.

68. Cobb, "Memorandum."

69. Menning and Menning, "'Baseless Allegations,'" 387 n. 59; 378 n. 30, 387.

70. Ralph Pulitzer, *The Profession of Journalism: Accuracy in the News: An Address Before the Pulitzer School of Journalism, Columbia University, New York, Delivered at Earl Hall December 16, 1912* (New York: World, 1912), 5.

71. Pulitzer, *Profession of Journalism*, 3.

72. David Paul Nord, "Accuracy or Fair Play? Complaining About the Newspaper in Early Twentieth-Century New York," in *New Directions in American Reception Study*, ed. Philip Goldstein and James L. Machor (Oxford: Oxford University Press, 2008), 233–53.

73. H. N. Gardner to Isaac White, September 27, 1913, "Initial reaction" folder, box 55, *World* Records.

74. John Fay to Isaac White, September 26, 1913, and Peter Carroll to Isaac White, October 15, 1913, "Initial reaction" folder, *World* Records.

75. Lincoln Steffens, *The Autobiography* (New York: Grosset and Dunlap, 1931), 179.

76. Carroll to White, October 15, 1913.

77. Versions of the story also appeared in, for instance, the *New Castle (PA) News* under the headline "Gloom Owls Scared Him," March 28, 1913, 8, and the *Des Moines Evening Tribune* as "Hark to the Horror of Gloom Owl Stunt," March 27, 1913, 9. For years, it stuck in the mind of a shipping reporter as an example of the heavy-handedness of the Bureau of Accuracy, which, he said, had "wrestled" with the story for two months in an effort to confirm it. The reporter, however, was misremembering; the story was published six months before the bureau was established. See Jack Lawrence, *When the Ships Came In* (New York: Farrar and Rinehart, 1940), 26–28.

4. "I BELIEVE IN FAKING"

1. Bruce Hackett and Lauren Lutzenhiser, "The Unity of Self and Object," *Western Folklore* 44 (1985): 322.

2. Edgar Allan Poe, "The Daguerreotype," *Alexander's Weekly Messenger*, January 15, 1840, 2.

3. Barnum quoted in Louis Kaplan, *The Strange Case of William Mumler, Spirit Photographer* (Minneapolis: University of Minnesota Press, 2008), 67. On Barnum's distinction between humbug and fraud, see Neil Harris, *Humbug: The Art of P. T. Barnum* (Chicago: University of Chicago Press, 1973), 77–78.

4. Judge quoted in Kaplan, *Strange Case*, 27.

5. *New York World* [*sic*], May 4, 1869, 8, quoted in Kaplan, *Strange Case*, 207.

6. Debby Applegate, *The Most Famous Man in America: The Biography of Henry Ward Beecher* (New York: Three Leaves Press, 2006), e.g., 197–98, 302–5, 318–20.

7. Mia Fineman, *Faking It: Manipulated Photography Before Photoshop* (New York: Metropolitan Museum, 2012), 117–19; Miles Orvell, *The Real Thing: Imitation and Authenticity in American Culture, 1880–1940* (Chapel Hill: University of North Carolina Press, 1989), 73–102.

8. See, for example, H. H. Snelling, "Retouching Negatives," *Philadelphia Photographer*, March 1, 1872, 71.

9. W. J. Hickmott, "A Plea for Retouching," *American Annual of Photography and Photographic Times Almanac* 11 (1897): 82–83.

10. Before about 1885, no photographer was known to have specialized exclusively in news reporting; see Ulrich Keller, "Photojournalism Around 1900: The Institutionalization of a Mass Medium," in *Shadow and Substance: Essays on the History of Photography in Honor of Heinz K. Henisch*, ed. Kathleen Collins (Bloomfield Hills, MI: Amorphous Institute Press, 1990), 285. The term *photojournalism* came into use in the 1920s and 1930s with the advent of picture magazines such as *Life*; see Michael Griffin, "The Great War Photographs: Constructing Myths of History and Photojournalism," in *Picturing the Past: Media, History, and Photography*, ed. Bonnie Brennen and Hanno Hardt (Urbana: University of Illinois Press, 1999), 122.

11. Kevin G. Barnhurst and John Nerone, *The Form of News: A History* (New York: Guilford, 2001), 111–39; Neil Harris, "Iconography and Intellectual History: The Halftone Effect," in *Cultural Excursions: Marketing Appetites and Cultural Tastes in Modern America* (Chicago: University of Chicago Press, 1990), 304–17.

12. Bates Lowry and Isabel Lowry, "Simultaneous Developments: Documentary Photography and Painless Surgery," in *Young America: The Daguerreotypes of Southworth and Hawes*, ed. Grant B. Romer and Brian Wallis (New York: International Center of Photography, 2005), 75–88; William A. Frassanito, *Gettysburg: A Journey in Time* (New York: Scribner's, 1975), 187–92.

13. A. Horsley Hinton, "Faking and Control in Principle and Practice," *Photographic Times* 30 (1898): 70; Morris Burke Parkinson, "The Idiosyncrasies of the Customer and a Word About 'Faking,'" *American Amateur Photographer*, November 1902, 522, 523. On the rise and fall of photographic faking, see, generally, Andie Tucher, "'I Believe in Faking': The Dilemma of Photographic Realism at the Dawn of Photojournalism," *Photography and Culture* 10, no. 3 (June 2017): 195–214.

14. Gilson Willets, "News-Photography," *American Annual of Photography and Photographic Times Almanac* 14 (1900): 53.

15. Willets, "News-Photography," 54.

16. Arthur W. Page, "Adventures of Daring Photographers: The Camera's Part in Making Current Literature," *World's Work* (New York ed.), May 14, 1907, 8837; "Experiences of a Newspaper Photographer by One of Them: Part IV," *Photographic Times* 37 (May 1905): 203, 205.

17. Martin Loiperdinger, "Lumière's 'Arrival of the Train': Cinema's Founding Myth," *Moving Image* 4 (Spring 2004): 89–118. See also Stephen Bottomore, "The Panicking Audience? Early Cinema and the 'Train Effect,'" *Historical Journal of Film, Radio, and Television* 19, no. 2 (1999): 177–216, which complicates Loiperdinger's argument with the suggestion that some rural, less worldly, and non-Western viewers might well have felt panic.

18. David Nasaw, *Going Out: The Rise and Fall of Public Amusements* (New York: Basic, 1993), 174–78; Daniel J. Czitrom, *Media and the American Mind from Morse to McLuhan* (Chapel Hill: University of North Carolina Press, 1982), 39–43.

19. John Wertheimer, "Mutual Film Reviewed: The Movies, Censorship, and Free Speech in Progressive America," *American Journal of Legal History* 37, no. 2 (April 1993): 160, 166; Stephen Hilgartner and Charles L. Bosk, "The Rise and Fall of Social Problems: A Public Arenas Model," *American Journal of Sociology* 94, no. 1 (July 1988): 53–78.

20. Homer Croy, *How Motion Pictures Are Made* (New York: Harper, 1918), 74.

21. Elizabeth Ezra, *Georges Méliès: The Birth of the Auteur* (Manchester, U.K.: Manchester University Press, 2000), 91.

22. "Widow Jones's Kiss Forty-Two Feet Long," *World* (New York), April 26, 1896, 21.

23. Tom Gunning, "An Aesthetic of Astonishment: Early Film and the (In)Credulous Spectator," in *Film Theory and Criticism: Introductory Readings*, 7th ed., ed. Leo Braudy and Marshall Cohen (New York: Oxford University Press, 2009), 750.

24. Albert E. Smith, with Phil A. Koury, *Two Reels and a Crank* (Garden City, NY: Doubleday, 1952), 53, 51. Although Smith gives 1896 as the founding date of Vitagraph (38), other evidence puts it at 1897. See Charles Musser, "American Vitagraph: 1897–1901," *Cinema Journal* 22, no. 3 (Spring 1983): 9.

25. Ezra, *Georges Méliès*, 66–67.

26. Raymond Fielding, *The American Newsreel: A Complete History, 1911–1967*, 2nd ed. (Jefferson, NC: McFarland, 2006), 25.

27. Kristen Whissel, "Placing the Spectator on the Scene of History: The Battle Re-enactment at the Turn of the Century, from Buffalo Bill's Wild West to the Early Cinema," *Historical Journal of Film, Radio, and Television* 22, no. 3 (2002): 225–43, quoting a "Buffalo Bill's Wild West" program from 1896 at 228.

28. Bonnie M. Miller, *From Liberation to Conquest: The Visual and Popular Cultures of the Spanish-American War of 1898* (Amherst: University of Massachusetts Press, 2011), 87–88.

29. This drawing, published in the *Charleston News and Courier* on July 24, 1898, is reproduced in Miller, *From Liberation to Conquest*, 97.

30. On the challenges of photographing the war, see, generally, John C. Hemment, *Cannon and Camera: Sea and Land Battles of the Spanish-American War in Cuba, Camp Life, and the Return of the Soldiers* (New York: Appleton, 1898).

31. The estimate of five hundred comes from Michael S. Sweeney, *The Military and the Press: An Uneasy Truce* (Evanston, IL: Northwestern University Press, 2006), 1; on local correspondents, see Michael Robertson, *Stephen Crane, Journalism, and the Making of Modern American Literature* (New York: Columbia University Press, 1997), 153.

32. Stephen Crane, "Roosevelt's Rough Riders' Loss Due to a Gallant Blunder," in Stephen Crane, *Reports of War; War Dispatches; Great Battles of the World*, ed. Fredson Bowers (Charlottesville: University Press of Virginia, 1971), 146. See also Robertson, *Stephen Crane*, 153–54, 159–60.

33. Michael Schudson, *Discovering the News: A Social History of American Newspapers* (New York: Basic, 1978), 61–65; *New York Journal*, February 12, 1897, 2.

34. Richard Harding Davis, "The Battle of San Juan," *Scribner's*, October 1898, 402; see also John Seelye, *War Games: Richard Harding Davis and the New Imperialism* (Amherst: University of Massachusetts Press, 2003), 34–36.

35. Robertson, *Stephen Crane*, 159.

36. G. W. Bitzer, *Billy Bitzer: His Story* (New York: Farrar, Straus and Giroux, 1973), 34.

37. Ezra, *Georges Méliès*, 65–66. *Divers at Work* is the only one of Méliès's five films on the *Maine* that survives.

38. Fielding, *American Newsreel*, 19–21; Edison film catalog entries quoted in Library of Congress, "The War in Cuba," in *Collection: The Spanish-American War in Motion Pictures*, https://www.loc.gov/item/00694305/, https://www.loc.gov/item/00694185/, https://www.loc.gov/item/98501105/.

39. "A Large Audience Was Present," *Tyrone (PA) Daily Herald*, December 8, 1898, 6; "The Warograph [*sic*] Tonight," *St. Joseph (MO) Gazette-Herald*, May 24, 1898, 5; "Edison Wargraph," *Washington Evening Star*, December 3, 1898, 24; "At the Funke," *Lincoln (NE) Journal Star*, May 26, 1898, 4.

40. Gerald J. Baldasty, *The Commercialization of News in the Nineteenth Century* (Madison: University of Wisconsin Press, 1992), 70–74.

41. Smith, *Two Reels*, 54.

42. Smith, *Two Reels*, 65–68. I have found little evidence to support Smith's claim that "almost every newspaper in New York carried an account of the showings, commenting on Vitagraph's remarkable feat in obtaining on-the-spot pictures" of battle.

43. Smith, *Two Reels*, 62–63.

44. The George Eastman House journal *Image* reproduces two stills showing soldiers standing on the "chow line" that it says were taken from *Fighting with Our Boys* (see "Pioneer Newsreels," *Image*, September 1953, 39), but Louis Pizzitola notes that "no copyright has been located for a film with this title" (*Hearst Over Hollywood: Power, Passion, and Propaganda in the Movies* [New York: Columbia University Press, 2002], 67), and I have been unable to find an actual copy.

45. Some scholars argue that legal and other evidence places the pair in New York at the time in question and note that Blackton's daughter denied that either her father or

Smith ever went to Cuba. See, for instance, Stephen Bottomore, "Filming, Faking, and Propaganda: The Origins of the War Film, 1897–1902," PhD diss., Utrecht University, 2007, chaps. 5, 10, https://dspace.library.uu.nl/bitstream/handle/1874/22650/?sequence=6; and Musser, "American Vitagraph," 16. Arguing for the truth of Smith's claim are, for instance, Donald Dewey, *Buccaneer: James Stuart Blackton and the Birth of American Movies* (Lanham, MD: Rowman and Littlefield, 2016), 48–50, and Pizzitola, *Hearst Over Hollywood*, 67–68, citing the memoir of a soldier who said he saw Blackton with the troops.

46.   Arthur Edwin Krows, "Motion Pictures—Not for Theatres Part 2," *Educational Screen*, October 1938, 250. Krows was promoted to assistant scenario editor at Vitagraph in 1919: "Krows Made Assistant Vitagraph Editor," *Motion Picture News*, September 6, 1919, 2061.

47.   *Sun* (New York), June 12, 1898, 12.

48.   *Chicago Tribune*, June 5, 1898, 36.

49.   *Detroit Free Press*, October 30, 1898, A7.

50.   *Atlanta Constitution*, December 11, 1898, 52.

51.   *New York Times*, December 4, 1898, 17; Charles Musser, "The Eden Musee in 1898: The Exhibitor as Creator," *Film & History* 11, no. 4 (December 1981): 80.

52.   *Los Angeles Times*, September 26, 1898, A1.

53.   Siegfried Kracauer, "Cult of Distraction: On Berlin's Picture Palaces," trans. and ed. Thomas Y. Levin, *New German Critique* 40 (Winter 1987): 92, 96.

54.   On the whoppers, see "Yellow Journals and Yellow Readers," *New York Times*, March 18, 1898, 6; Godkin's comments in the *New York Evening Post*, February 19, 1898, quoted in Frank Luther Mott, *American Journalism, a History: 1690–1960*, 3rd ed. (New York: Macmillan, 1962), 532.

55.   Erik Barnouw, *Documentary: A History of the Non-fiction Film*, 2nd ed. (New York: Oxford University Press, 1993), 36–47; Louis Menand, "Nanook and Me," *New Yorker*, August 9, 2004, https://www.newyorker.com/magazine/2004/08/09/nanook-and-me; Dean W. Duncan, "*Nanook of the North*," On Film/Essays, January 11, 1999, Criterion Collection, https://www.criterion.com/current/posts/42-nanook-of-the-north.

56.   Hackett and Lutzenhiser, "Unity of Self and Object," 322.

57.   Susan J. Douglas, *Inventing American Broadcasting 1899–1922* (Baltimore: Johns Hopkins University Press, 1987), 190–92.

58.   Alvin F. Harlow, *Old Wires and New Waves: The History of the Telegraph, Telephone, and Wireless* (New York: Appleton-Century, 1936), 469.

59.   See, for example, "To Check Wireless Anarchy," *Louisville Courier Journal*, June 30, 1912, C6; "The Wireless Pirates," *Washington Post*, April 17, 1912, 6; "False Titanic News to Be Investigated," *New York Times*, April 18, 1912, 1, quoting the *Times* of London on Lloyd's and on the bogus messages; and "Rigid British Inquiry," *Washington Post*, April 19, 1912, 4. On the role of wireless in the *Titanic* disaster, see Douglas, *Inventing American Broadcasting*, 226–36.

60. U.S. Department of Commerce, Bureau of Navigation, Radio Service, *Radio Communication Laws of the United States and the International Radiotelegraphic Convention: Regulations Governing Radio Operators and the Use of Radio Apparatus on Ships and on Land* (Washington, DC: U.S. Government Printing Office, 1914), 11, 14.

5. "WE DID NOT CALL IT PROPAGANDA"

1.   Jonathan Auerbach and Russ Castronovo, "Introduction: Thirteen Propositions About Propaganda," in *The Oxford Handbook of Propaganda Studies*, ed. Jonathan Auerbach and Russ Castronovo (Oxford: Oxford University Press, 2013), 2, 5.

2.   "Kaiser Set Aside $30,000,000 for Propaganda Here," *New York Times*, July 10, 1918, 1, 4; U.S. Senate, Subcommittee on the Judiciary, *Brewing and Liquor Interests and German and Bolshevik Propaganda: Report and Hearings . . .*, 3 vols., 66th Cong., 1st sess. (Washington, DC: U.S. Government Printing Office, 1919), 2:1453–455; Phillip Knightley, *The First Casualty: The War Correspondent as Hero and Myth-Maker from the Crimea to Kosovo*, rev. ed. (Baltimore: Johns Hopkins University Press, 2000), 85–87.

3.   See, for instance, the *Baltimore Sun*, May 1, 1915, 15. Many newspapers also published articles drawing attention to the ads.

4.   Will Irwin, *The Making of a Reporter* (New York: Putnam, 1942), 245.

5.   Quoted in Raymond Fielding, *The American Newsreel: A Complete History, 1911–1967*, 2nd ed. (Jefferson, NC: McFarland, 2006), 68.

6.   Emmet Crozier, *American Reporters on the Western Front 1914–18* (New York: Oxford University Press, 1959), 39–41.

7.   Crozier, *American Reporters*, vii–viii. Since Crozier rarely cites sources, his own credibility is hard to judge; I have not found the item about the bayonet jab in any searchable database.

8.   Richard Harding Davis, "Horrors of Louvain Told by Eyewitness; Circled Burning City," *New York Tribune*, August 31, 1915, 1, 4.

9.   "Alleged Cruelty of Germans Untrue, Statement of Tribune War Correspondents," *Chicago Tribune*, September 7, 1914, 1. The telegram was also signed by one reporter from the *Chicago Daily News*, one from the Associated Press, and one, the widely beloved Irvin S. Cobb, from the *Saturday Evening Post*.

10. Committee on Alleged German Outrages, *Report of the Committee . . . Appointed by His Britannic Majesty's Government and Presided Over by the Right Hon. Viscount Bryce* (London: His Majesty's Stationery Office, 1915).

11. Trevor Wilson, "Lord Bryce's Investigation Into Alleged German Atrocities in Belgium, 1914–15," *Journal of Contemporary History* 14 (1979): 369–83. See also Susan A. Brewer, *Why America Fights: Patriotism and War Propaganda from the Philippines to Iraq* (Oxford: Oxford University Press, 2009), 51–52; Joachim Neander, *The German Corpse Factory: The Master Hoax of British Propaganda in the First World War* (Saarbrücken, Germany: Saarland University Press, 2013), 28–31.

12. "The Bryce Report," *New York Tribune*, May 13, 1915, 8.

13. George Creel, *How We Advertised America: The First Telling of the Amazing Story of the Committee on Public Information That Carried the Gospel of Americanism to Every Corner of the Globe* (New York: Harper & Brothers, 1920), 4, 5.

14. Creel, *How We Advertised America*, 4; Wolfgang Schivelbusch, *The Culture of Defeat: On National Trauma, Mourning, and Recovery*, trans. Jefferson Chase (New York: Picador, 2004), 215.

15. David Greenberg, *Republic of Spin: An Inside Story of the American Presidency* (New York: Norton, 2016), 108–9; Richard Hofstadter, *The Age of Reform from Bryan to F.D.R.* (New York: Vintage, 1955), 186–98.

16. Creel, *How We Advertised America*, 3.

17. Creel, *How We Advertised America*, 74. See also Stewart Halsey Ross, *Propaganda for War: How the United States Was Conditioned to Fight the Great War of 1914–1918* (Jefferson, NC: McFarland, 1996), 230–31; John Maxwell Hamilton, *Manipulating the Masses: Woodrow Wilson and the Birth of American Propaganda* (Baton Rouge: Louisiana State University Press, 2020), 107–15.

18. Eugene Debs is quoted from *Debs v. United States*, 249 U.S. 214 (1919). See also Jeffery A. Smith, *War and Press Freedom: The Problem of Prerogative Power* (New York: Oxford University Press, 1999), 131–33; and Brewer, *Why America Fights*, 70–71.

19. Knightley, *First Casualty*, 132–33; Brewer, *Why America Fights*, 72–73; Smith, *War and Press Freedom*, 140–41.

20. Richard Kluger, *The Paper: The Life and Death of the "New York Herald Tribune"* (New York: Knopf, 1986), 196–98; Richard O'Connor, *Heywood Broun: A Biography* (New York: Putnam, 1975), 63–64; Heywood Broun, "American Censors in France Doubt Courage of American People," *New York Tribune*, January 6, 1918, 3; Heywood Broun, "French Render First Aid to Our Unprepared Army," *Tribune*, January 10, 1918, 1.

21. George Creel, "Aid and Comfort to the Enemy," including indictments against several other reporters and papers besides Broun and the *New York Tribune*. The *New York Tribune* ran the article on March 13, 1918, under the heading "Official Propaganda Reprinted from the *Independent*," and included the subheadline "The Sixth Message from the United States Government to the American People, Presented Every Week in 'The Independent,' by George Creel," 8.

22. The most thorough analysis of the corpse-factory affair is in Neander, *German Corpse Factory* (though Neander misdates the Arthur Post story discussed in this chapter to 1921 instead of 1920 [285]). See also Randal Marlin, *Propaganda and the Ethics of Persuasion* (Peterborough, Canada: Broadview, 2002), 71–76.

23. Neander, *German Corpse Factory*, 17–19; Peter Putnis, "SHARE 999: British Government Control of Reuters During World War I," *Media History* 14, no. 2 (2008): 154; Lord Northcliffe, "How the World Shall Kill Its Prussian Cobra," *New York Tribune*, May 27, 1917, 1, reprinted the same day by such influential papers as the *St. Louis Post Dispatch*, the *Chicago Tribune*, and the *Baltimore Sun*.

24. U.S. Federal Census, 1920, Los Angeles, CA, roll T625_116, 4B, National Archives, Washington, DC, available on the subscription database Ancestry.com at https://tinyurl

.com/ydhnmq6m. For Arthur Post's lectures, see, for instance, "To Tell of Prison Camps," *Courier Journal* (Louisville), April 8, 1919, 5 ("physical wreck"); "Man Tells of Horrors and Cruelties by the Germans," *Logansport (IN) Pharos-Tribune*, April 18, 1919, 5 (bandages); "Rotarians Hear How Germans Mistreated Men in Camps," *Muncie (IN) Star Press*, April 18, 1919, 9; and the advertisement "Coming to Mystic . . . 5 Acts Real Pep Vaudeville 5," *Rushville (IN) Daily Republican*, April 30, 1919, 6, which lists a program of entertainment by discharged soldiers that also included "the Famous Arthur V. Post account of Germany's Soap Factory, where soap was made of human flesh from the battle fields. Full account of the crucifixion of Arthur V. Post." The talk at Logansport was advertised in the *Pharos-Tribune* on April 17 (p. 3) as for men only.

25. The most complete investigation of this episode is Stefan Maechler, *The Wilkomirski Affair: A Study in Biographical Truth*, trans. John E. Woods (New York: Schocken Books, 2001).

26. During the war, the *Los Angeles Times* had offered stories on both sides. It ran the widely reprinted report by the respected syndicated correspondent Philip Gibbs challenging the factory story: "Nothing to Stop British," October 6, 1918, I2. But nine days later it ran a brief paragraph headed "The Callous Hun," October 15, 1918, II4, purporting to reprint a letter by an unnamed officer who claimed to have seen bundles of headless German bodies salted for preservation and ready for transport to the factory.

27. "Charteris Denies Propaganda Story," *New York Times*, October 25, 1925, 24; see also "Tells of British War Propaganda," *New York Times*, October 20, 1925, 10; Neander, *German Corpse Factory*, 291–306.

28. See "Germans Using Bodies of Dead to Make Fertilizer," *Public Opinion* (Chambersburg, PA), April 23, 1917, 5; "[Hor?]rible—and Worse," *San Bernardino County (CA) Sun*, May 16, 1917, 4; and "Gruesome Story Confirmed," *Billings (MT) Gazette*, May 16, 1917, 10.

29. The Orwell piece, first published on March 31, 1944, as one of his "As I Please" columns in the left-wing British newspaper *Tribune*, is reprinted in George Orwell, *Orwell in "Tribune": "As I Please" and Other Writings 1943-7*, comp. and ed. Paul Anderson (London: Politico's, 2006), 118–21, quote at 120; Gallup cited in Deborah E. Lipstadt, *Beyond Belief: The American Press and the Coming of the Holocaust 1933–1945* (New York: Free Press, 1986), 240–41; Cavendish-Bentinck quoted in David Reynolds, *The Long Shadow: The Legacies of the Great War in the Twentieth Century* (New York: Norton, 2014), 281; see also Neander, *German Corpse Factory*, 8–10.

6. "NOTHING THAT IS NOT INTERESTING IS NEWS"

1. Greg Mitchell, *The Campaign of the Century: Upton Sinclair's Race for Governor of California and the Birth of Media Politics* (New York: Random House, 1992), 423–24, 499–501, 561.

2. Daniel Pope, *The Making of Modern Advertising* (New York: Basic, 1983), 202–20 (quote at 205).

3. *United States v. Johnson*, 221 U.S. 488 (1911); "A Pure Food Indictment," *Kansas City (MO) Star*, November 5, 1909, 20.

4. Edward L. Bernays, *Propaganda* (New York: Liveright, 1928), 50, 9.

5. Edward L. Bernays, *Crystallizing Public Opinion* (New York: Liveright, 1923), 18–19. See also Sue Curry Jansen, "Semantic Tyranny: How Edward L. Bernays Stole Walter Lippmann's Mojo and Got Away with It and Why It Still Matters," *International Journal of Communication* 7 (2013): 1094–111.

6. Ernest Gruening, "The Higher Hokum," *Nation*, April 16, 1924, 450.

7. Silas Bent, *Ballyhoo: The Voice of the Press* (New York: Boni and Liveright, 1927), 21, 123; "Sees the Ballyhoo in Our Press but Misses the News," *Hartford Courant*, November 20, 1927, E6. This reviewer refused to condemn ballyhoo outright, pointing out, tongue in cheek, that "of course there is ballyhoo in the press. It would not be a mirror to American life if there was not."

8. Walter Lippmann, *Liberty and the News* (New York: Harcourt, Brace and Howe, 1920), 5; the essays included in the volume were first published in the *Atlantic Monthly* in 1919.

9. Lippmann, *Liberty and the News*, 72–76.

10. Lippmann, *Liberty and the News*, 82.

11. Michael Schudson, *Discovering the News: A Social History of American Newspapers* (New York: Basic, 1978), 151–59; Michael Schudson, "Is Journalism a Profession? Objectivity 1.0, Objectivity 2.0, and Beyond," in *Why Journalism Still Matters* (Cambridge: Polity, 2018), 50–52.

12. Simon Michael Bessie, *Jazz Journalism: The Story of the Tabloid Newspapers* (1938; reprint, New York: Russell and Russell, 1969), 25.

13. Frank Luther Mott, *American Journalism, a History: 1690–1960*, 3rd ed. (New York: Macmillan, 1962), 668.

14. Andie Tucher, *Froth and Scum: Truth, Beauty, Goodness, and the Ax-Murder in America's First Mass Medium* (Chapel Hill: University of North Carolina Press, 1994), 14–15, 25, 76–79.

15. Tim P. Vos and Teri Finneman, "The Early Historical Construction of Journalism's Gatekeeping Role," *Journalism* 18, no. 3 (2017): 274–75.

16. Quoted in Bessie, *Jazz Journalism*, 139.

17. William M. Kunstler, *The Hall–Mills Murder Case: The Minister and the Choir Singer* (New Brunswick, NJ: Rutgers University Press, 1964), viii.

18. Kunstler, *Hall–Mills Murder Case*, 317–34. The drawing of Mrs. Hall's brother Willie, which had also run in the *New York Journal*, appeared on November 9, 1926, in a six-panel strip (p. 4) and purported to show "Some of the Points scored by the State."

19. Kunstler, *Hall–Mills Murder Case*, 309; Stanley Walker, *City Editor*, foreword by Alexander Woollcott (1934; reprint, Baltimore: Johns Hopkins University Press, 1999) 202–4. The Hall family's hometown newspaper was just about the only publication to pay much attention to the settlement: see "Big Settlement Made by Hearst to Hall Family," *Central Jersey Home News* (New Brunswick, NJ), December 24, 1928, 1, 5. The short and widely used AP story appears in, for instance, the *New York Times*, December 25, 1928, 20.

20. *Graphic* quoted in Bessie, *Jazz Journalism*, 187; Macfadden quoted in Oswald Garrison Villard, "Sex, Art, Truth, and Magazines," *Atlantic Monthly*, March 1926, 396.

21. "Dead!," *Daily News* (New York), January 13, 1928, 1.

22. Frank Mallen, *Sauce for the Gander* (White Plains, NY: Baldwin Books, 1954), 30; Walker, *City Editor*, 72.

23. Elizabeth M. Smith-Pryor, *Property Rites: The Rhinelander Trial, Passing, and the Protection of Whiteness* (Chapel Hill: University of North Carolina Press, 2009). The headline "RHINELANDER'S COLORED BRIDE" appeared in late editions of the *Daily News* (New York) on November 14, 1925 (quoted in Smith-Pryor, *Property Rites*, 27), and the phrase was widely used in the press throughout the trial.

24. Frank J. Dolan, "Alice Tears Her Pride to Shreds to Hold Her Man," *Daily News* (New York), November 24, 1925, 3.

25. Mallen, *Sauce*, 29, illustration following 36.

26. Surviving copies of the *Evening Graphic* are rare, but legible reproductions of the front page of this issue appear as the frontispiece to Bent, *Ballyhoo*, and on the website of the Charlie Chaplin Archive, http://www.charliechaplinarchive.org/en/collection/cerca/rudy-meets-caruso-tenors-spirit-speaks-by-natacha-rambova/search/search:caruso/page/1/view_as/grid.

27. Helen MacGill Hughes, *News and the Human Interest Story* (1940; reprint, New Brunswick, NJ: Transaction, 1981), 239.

28. Emile Gauvreau, *Hot News* (New York: Macaulay, 1931), 40; "Graphic's Shocking Picture," *Editor & Publisher*, November 28, 1925, 34.

29. S. Elizabeth Bird, *For Enquiring Minds: A Cultural Study of Supermarket Tabloids* (Knoxville: University of Tennessee Press, 1992), 119–37.

30. Bird, *Enquiring Minds*, 122.

31. Louise M. Benjamin, *Freedom of the Air and the Public Interest: First Amendment Rights in Broadcasting to 1935* (Carbondale: Southern Illinois University Press, 2001), 1–7; Paul Starr, *The Creation of the Media: Political Origins of Modern Communications* (New York: Basic, 2004), 327–39; Tim Wu, *The Master Switch: The Rise and Fall of Information Empires* (New York: Vintage, 2011), 74–85.

32. Quoted in Benjamin, *Freedom of the Air*, 84.

33. Erik Barnouw, *A History of Broadcasting in the United States*, vol. 1: *A Tower in Babel* (New York: Oxford University Press, 1966), 68–70.

34. Edward G. Lowry, "Radio's Part in Politics," *Popular Science Monthly*, July 1924, 112; the ad is on page 1 of the magazine.

35. Norman Brokenshire, *This Is Norman Brokenshire: An Unvarnished Self Portrait* (New York: David McKay, 1954), 48–49.

36. Brokenshire, *This Is Norman Brokenshire*, 49–52.

37. Erik Barnouw, *A History of Broadcasting in the United States*, vol. 2: *The Golden Web* (New York: Oxford University Press, 1968), 109.

38. E. P. H. James, "Reminiscences" (1963), 9, 11, Radio Pioneers Project, Oral History Archives, Rare Book & Manuscript Library, Columbia University, New York; William L. Shirer, *20th Century Journey: A Memoir of a Life and the Times*, vol. 2: *The Nightmare*

Years: 1930–1940 (New York: Little Brown, 1984), 321. See also Sally Bedell Smith, *In All His Glory: The Life and Times of William S. Paley, the Legendary Tycoon, and His Brilliant Circle* (New York: Touchstone, 1991), 174–75.

39.   Smith, *In All His Glory*, 174, citing Smith's interviews with Paley and with the longtime CBS executive Blair Clark; Shirer, *20th Century Journey*, 2:322; Michael Biel, "The Making and Use of Recordings in Broadcasting Before 1936," PhD diss., Northwestern University, 1977, 593–98.

40.   Federal Radio Commission (FRC), "In re Application of Trinity Methodist Church, South (Station KGEF), for Renewal of Station License: Statement of Facts, Grounds for Decision, and Order of the Commission," in *Trinity Methodist Church, South v. Federal Radio Commission (D.C. Cir. 1931): Transcript of Record*, vol. 1, 1932, 969, https://archive.org/details/dc_circ_1931_5561_trinity_methodist_church_s_v_fed_radio_commn/page/n977/mode/2up. On the Shuler case generally, see Benjamin, *Freedom of the Air*, 97–107.

41.   "Champion 'Ag'inner' of Universe Is Shuler," *Los Angeles Times*, June 1, 1930, A2.

42.   See, for instance, "Shuler Jury Reports That It Stands Eight to Four After Six Hours of Deliberation," *Los Angeles Times*, May 5, 1929, B2 (plaintiff was the Knights of Columbus); "Shuler Verdict Favors Pastor," *Los Angeles Times*, November 18, 1929, A1 (plaintiff was the former mayor).

43.   Robert Shuler, testimony, in "Appendix A: Abstract of Testimony at Hearing Held at Los Angeles, Cal., January 8, 1931 to January 24, 1931, Before Chief Examiner Ellis A. Yost of the Federal Radio Commission," in *Trinity Methodist v. FRC*, 77, 50.

44.   "Judge Collier Assails Shuler," *Los Angeles Times*, January 14, 1931, A1.

45.   R. B. Von Kleinsmid, testimony, in "Appendix A," in *Trinity Methodist v. FRC*, 411–12.

46.   Shuler cited in "Examiner's Report No. 241," and Shuler, testimony, in "Appendix A," both in *Trinity Methodist Church v. FRC*, 924–25, 147–49.

47.   FRC, "In re," in *Trinity Methodist v. FRC*, 969–70.

48.   Louis G. Caldwell, "Freedom of Speech and Radio Broadcasting," *Annals of the American Academy of Political and Social Science* 177 (1935): 190, 203; Starr, *Creation of the Media*, 365–67.

49.   Charley Orbison, "'Fighting Bob' Shuler: Early Radio Crusader," *Journal of Broadcasting* 21, no. 4 (1977): 462–65.

50.   Benjamin, *Freedom of the Air*, 117.

51.   Rodger Streitmatter, *Voices of Revolution: The Dissident Press in America* (New York: Columbia University Press, 2001), 142–56 (Sandburg quoted at 152, the senator at 155); Gene Roberts and Hank Klibanoff, *The Race Beat: The Press, the Civil Rights Struggle, and the Awakening of a Nation* (New York: Knopf, 2006), 17–18; James Grossman, "Blowing the Trumpet: The *Chicago Defender* and Black Migration During World War I," *Illinois Historical Journal* 78, no. 2 (1985): 82–96; Ethan Michaeli, *The Defender: How the Legendary Black Newspaper Changed America, from the Age of the Pullman Porters to the Age of Obama* (Boston: Houghton Mifflin Harcourt, 2016), 77–79.

52.   Chicago Commission on Race Relations, *The Negro in Chicago: A Study of Race Relations and a Race Riot* (Chicago: University of Chicago Press, 1922), 520, 556–57, 650–51;

Streitmatter, *Voices of Revolution*, 154–57; Roi Ottley, *The Lonely Warrior: The Life and Times of Robert S. Abbott* (Washington, DC: Regnery, 1955), 197–99.

53. Neil Henry, *American Carnival: Journalism Under Siege in an Age of New Media* (Berkeley: University of California Press, 2007), 118–19; Richard Kluger, *The Paper: The Life and Death of the "New York Herald Tribune"* (New York: Knopf, 1986), 216–18.

54. "Sanford Jarrell Dies, Hoax Story Reporter," *New York Herald Tribune*, January 31, 1962, 8. See also Westbrook Pegler, "Fair Enough: Grandiose Hoax," *Washington Post*, May 3, 1940, 15, calling the hoax "a sort of gem" in the "jewel case of literary journalism"; and John D. Tierney, "The Days When Reporters Wrote Real Stories," *Wall Street Journal*, April 3, 1982, 20.

55. Stories naming Mizzle in a peripheral role appeared in 1917, 1918, and 1919, but the first entry in the exotic adventure series was "Finds an Old Friend Behind Circus Bars," *New York Times*, April 11, 1920, sec. 2, p. 6; the last, "Egad! M. Mizzle Shows Up Again," ran on May 26, 1940, sec. 1, p. 37.

56. Andie Tucher, "Why Marmaduke Mizzle and the Good Ship *Wabble* Fooled No One: Fake News and Metajournalistic Discourse in the Era of Journalistic Professionalism," in *Journalists and Knowledge Practices: Histories of Observing the Everyday in the Newspaper Age*, ed. Hansjakob Ziemer (New York: Routledge, forthcoming); John Ferris, *The Winds of Barclay Street: The Amusing Life and Sad Demise of the* New York World-Telegram and Sun (Bloomington, IN: Author House, 2013), 93.

57. Walter Lippmann and Charles Merz, "A Test of the News: An Examination of the News Reports in the *New York Times* on Aspects of the Russian Revolution of Special Importance to Americans, March 1917–March 1920," *New Republic*, supplement, August 4, 1920, 3, 10, 3, 42.

58. Sue Curry Jansen, "'The World's Greatest Adventure in Advertising': Walter Lippmann's Critique of Censorship and Propaganda," in *Oxford Handbook of Propaganda Studies*, ed. Jonathan Auerbach and Russ Castronovo (New York: Oxford University Press, 2013), 312.

59. Walter Duranty, "Russians Hungry but Not Starving," *New York Times*, March 31, 1933, 13.

60. Anne Applebaum, *Red Famine: Stalin's War on Ukraine* (London: Allen Lane, 2017), 304–7, 316–25, quoting Jones at 320–21. See also Ray Gamache, "Breaking Eggs for a Holodomor: Walter Duranty, the *New York Times*, and the Denigration of Gareth Jones," *Journalism History* 39, no. 4 (Winter 2014): 208–18; S. J. Taylor, *Stalin's Apologist: Walter Duranty, the* New York Times's *Man in Moscow* (New York: Oxford University Press, 1990), 215–40.

61. Taylor, *Stalin's Apologist*, 221 (quoting Duranty), 231 (citing Taylor's interview with Salisbury on Duranty's self-image). Salisbury's harsher comments about Duranty appear in his own history of the *Times*; the correspondent was not just a "calculating careerist" but also a "cynical man-on-the-make" who had no interest in communism but saw Stalin as a "winner." See Harrison E. Salisbury, *Without Fear or Favor: An Uncompromising Look at the* New York Times (New York: Ballantine, 1980), 460, 462.

62. Applebaum, *Red Famine*, 324–25.

63. See, for instance, the documentary *Hitler, Stalin, and Mr. Jones*, aired on BBC Four's Storyville strand in 2012; Neil Prior, "Journalist Gareth Jones' 1935 Murder Examined by BBC Four," BBC.com, posted July 5, 2012, https://www.bbc.com/news/uk-wales-south-east-wales-18691109.

64. Karl E. Meyer, "The Editorial Notebook: Trenchcoats, Then and Now," *New York Times*, June 24, 1990, E20.

65. Salisbury, *Without Fear or Favor*, 462–63.

66. John D. Stevens, *Sensationalism and the New York Press* (New York: Columbia University Press, 1991), 122; Joseph Medill Patterson quoted in Mott, *American Journalism*, 669. See also Bird, *For Enquiring Minds*, 19–24; and Hughes, *News and the Human Interest Story*, 222–55.

67. Allan M. Brandt, *No Magic Bullet: A Social History of Venereal Disease in the United States Since 1880*, exp. ed. (New York: Oxford University Press, 1987), 122, 141. The *Daily News* (New York) won a Pulitzer outright the same year for editorial cartooning. According to the Pulitzer Prize office (personal communication, September 30, 2020), the organization has rarely if ever announced "honorable mentions" (and did not cite "finalists" until the 1980s), but internal documents confirm the designation. The move in this case may have reflected some disagreement among the jurors over the quality or appropriateness of the series.

7. "WHY DON'T YOU GUYS TELL THE TRUTH ONCE IN A WHILE?"

1. *The War of the Worlds, Mercury Theater on the Air*, CBS, first aired October 30, 1938; available at the Internet Archive's Wayback Machine site, https://archive.org/details/OrsonWellesMrBruns, with the quote starting at 18.00.

2. "Radio Listeners in Panic, Taking War Drama as Fact," *New York Times*, October 31, 1938, 1, 4.

3. A. Brad Schwartz, *Broadcast Hysteria: Orson Welles's "War of the Worlds" and the Art of Fake News* (New York: Hill and Wang, 2015), 7–11, 65–94 (statistics at 82).

4. Schwartz, *Broadcast Hysteria*, 172–86; Susan J. Douglas, *Listening in: Radio and the American Imagination, from Amos 'n' Andy and Edward R. Murrow to Wolfman Jack and Howard Stern* (New York: Random House, 1999), 165–66; Jefferson D. Pooley and Michael J. Socolow, "Checking Up on *The Invasion from Mars*: Hadley Cantril, Paul F. Lazarsfeld, and the Making of a Misremembered Classic," *International Journal of Communication* 7 (2013): 1919–947; Robert J. Brown, *Manipulating the Ether: The Power of Broadcast Radio in Thirties America* (Jefferson, NC: McFarland, 1998), 197–239, which uncritically accepts much of the misinformation about the panic.

5. "The Gullible Radio Public," *Chicago Daily Tribune*, November 10, 1938, 16, quoted in Schwartz, *Broadcast Hysteria*, 140.

6. Dorothy Thompson, "On the Record: Mr. Welles and Mass Delusion," *New York Herald Tribune*, November 2, 1938, 21.

7.   Schwartz, *Broadcast Hysteria*, 171–84; Michael J. Socolow, "The Hyped Panic Over 'War of the Worlds,'" *Chronicle of Higher Education*, October 24, 2008, B16, B17; Thompson, "On the Record."

8.   William Stott, *Documentary Expression and Thirties America* (Chicago: University of Chicago Press, 1986), 78–84; Graham J. White, *FDR and the Press* (Chicago: University of Chicago Press, 1979), 69–72; Hugh Gregory Gallagher, *FDR's Splendid Deception* (New York: Dodd, Mead, 1985), 91–95.

9.   Irving E. Fang, *Those Radio Commentators!* (Ames: Iowa State University Press, 1977), 100–101; Alan Brinkley, *Voices of Protest: Huey Long, Father Coughlin, and the Great Depression* (New York: Vintage, 1982), 257–68; David Goodman, "Before Hate Speech: Charles Coughlin, Free Speech, and Listeners' Rights," *Patterns of Prejudice* 49, no. 3 (2015): 199–224.

10.   Brinkley, *Voices of Protest*, 99–101.

11.   League of Nations, International Convention Concerning the Use of Broadcasting in the Cause of Peace, No. 4319, Geneva, September 23, 1936, 309, https://treaties.un.org/doc/Publication/UNTS/LON/Volume%20186/v186.pdf; Elizabeth A. Downey, "A Historical Survey of the International Regulation of Propaganda," *Michigan Yearbook of International Legal Studies* 5, no. 1 (1984): 343–45 (this journal is currently known as the *Michigan Journal of International Law*).

12.   Institute for Propaganda Analysis, *The Fine Art of Propaganda: A Study of Father Coughlin's Speeches*, ed. Alfred McClung Lee and Elizabeth Briant Lee (New York: Harcourt, Brace, 1939), x, 134; Anya Schiffrin, "Fighting Disinformation with Media Literacy—in 1939," *Columbia Journalism Review*, October 10, 2018, https://www.cjr.org/innovations/institute-propaganda-analysis.php; David Greenberg, *Republic of Spin: An Inside History of the American Presidency* (New York: Norton, 2016), 209–13.

13.   Letters quoted in Goodman, "Before Hate Speech," 215–16, 219, and "elite discourse" comment from Goodman, 213.

14.   Erwin Chemerinsky, "The First Amendment and the Right to Lie," *ABAJournal*, September 5, 2012, https://www.abajournal.com/news/article/the_first_amendment_and_the_right_to_lie.

15.   James A. Brown, "Selling Airtime for Controversy: NAB Self-Regulation and Father Coughlin," *Journal of Broadcasting* 24 (1980): 199–224, quote from FCC chair James L. Fly at 208.

16.   Newspapers.com shows dozens of papers that ran each of the "Rumor Deflator" items from the AP between August 6 and August 25, 1941; many of them included the "wild rumors" explanation. See, for instance, *Baltimore Sun*, August 7, 1941 (Mussolini, 2); *Battle Creek (MI) Enquirer*, August 7, 1941 (severing relations, 2); *Tallahassee (FL) Democrat*, August 8, 1941 (Kremlin, 1); *Grand Junction (CO) Weekly Sentinel*, August 22, 1941 (Iran, 1). See also the comments on the deflator by AP news editor Charles Honce in "News Gathering in War Times: An Address Before the Fall Convention of the New York State Publishers Convention," typescript, September 8, 1941, 13, available at the subscription database Associated Press Collections Online, https://www.gale.com/primary-sources/associated-press-collections-online.

17. I am grateful to Lisa Gibbs of the AP for directing me to the Rumor Deflator.

18. Archibald MacLeish, "The Strategy of Truth," in *A Time to Act: Selected Addresses* (Boston: Houghton Mifflin, 1943), 28–29.

19. Franklin D. Roosevelt, "Executive Order 9182 Establishing the Office of War Information," June 13, 1942, American Presidency Project, https://www.presidency.ucsb.edu /node/210709. See also Allan M. Winkler, *The Politics of Propaganda: The Office of War Information 1942–1945* (New Haven, CT: Yale University Press, 1978), 38–72.

20. The film is available at https://archive.org/details/Japanese1943.

21. U.S. Office of War Information, *Negroes and the War* (Washington, DC: U.S. Government Printing Office, 1942), [1], https://transcription.si.edu/project/10156.

22. Quoted in Susan A. Brewer, *Why America Fights: Patriotism and War Propaganda from the Philippines to Iraq* (Oxford: Oxford University Press, 2009), 100; see also Jeffery A. Smith, *War and Press Freedom: The Problem of Prerogative Power* (New York: Oxford University Press, 1999), 149–54.

23. U.S. Office of Censorship, *Code of Wartime Practices for the American Press* (Washington, DC: U.S. Government Printing Office, June 15, 1942), 1.

24. "Walter Cronkite" and "Andy Rooney," in *Reporting America at War: An Oral History*, comp. Michelle Ferrari, with commentary by James Tobin (New York: Hyperion, 2003), 29, 58–59.

25. Richard Norton Smith, *The Colonel: The Life and Legend of Robert T. McCormick, 1880–1955* (Boston: Houghton Mifflin, 1997), 390–91.

26. Deborah E. Lipstadt, *Beyond Belief: The American Press and the Coming of the Holocaust 1933–1945* (New York: Free Press, 1986), 169–71.

27. "Mess Attendant Turned Machine Gun on Japanese," *Pittsburgh Courier*, March 14, 1942, 1.

28. John Steinbeck, *Once There Was a War* (New York: Viking, 1958), xiv–xv.

29. Eisenhower quoted in Merle Miller, *Ike the Soldier: As They Knew Him* (New York: Putnam, 1987), 517–18.

30. Steven Casey, *The War Beat, Europe: The American Media at War Against Nazi Germany* (New York: Oxford University Press, 2017), 157–58; Don Whitehead, *Combat Reporter: Don Whitehead's World War II Diary and Memoirs*, ed. John B. Romeiser (New York: Fordham University Press, 2006), 168 (quoting Belden); statistics from Rick Atkinson, *The Day of Battle: The War in Sicily and Italy, 1943–1944* (New York: Holt, 2007), 106–10. See also Charles R. Schrader, *Amicide: The Problem of Friendly Fire in Modern War*, Combat Studies Institute Research Survey no. 1 (Fort Leavenworth, KS: U.S. Army Command and General Staff College, 1982), 66–68.

31. Don Whitehead, *"Beachhead Don": Reporting the War from the European Theater, 1942–1945*, ed. John B. Romeiser (New York: Fordham University Press, 2004), xxvii.

32. Jack Belden, "Troop Landings at Gela in Sicily," *Life*, July 26, 1943, 32–33; Jack Belden, "Adventure in Sicily," *Life*, August 9, 1943, 82–89 (quote at 82).

33. I spent some time with Jack Belden in 1985, four years before his death. I don't recall that he spoke of Gela—and at that point, unfortunately, I didn't know to ask—but a defiant gesture like that would, I think, have been very much in character for him.

34. "Our Army: With Its Allies It Achieved in the Sicilian Landing a New High in Military Science," editorial, *Life*, July 26, 1943, 34.

35. Eric Sevareid, *Not so Wild a Dream; with a New Introduction by the Author* (1946; reprint, New York: Atheneum, 1979), 81–82.

36. Stories based on the original AP item and a similar one from the UP were published in hundreds of papers—appearing, for instance, as "23 U.S. Planes Shot Down in Mistake: 410 Yanks Lost: Sicily Tragedy," *Chicago Daily Tribune*, March 17, 1944, 1; and "410 Paratroopers, Mistaken for Foe, Killed in Battle," *Los Angeles Times*, March 17, 1944, 1. For the War Department explanations, see, for example, "Americans Felled Own Planes, Killed 410 Paratroopers in Sicily," *New York Herald Tribune*, March 17, 1944, 1; "Stimson Explains Why U.S. Guns Shot Down U.S. Planes in Sicily," *New York Herald Tribune*, March 24, 1944, 3.

37. Dewey quoted in "News Suppression by Administration Charged by Dewey" and "Text of Dewey Charge of News Suppression," *New York Times*, March 25, 1944, 1, 10.

38. "War's Unavoidable Mistakes," *Princeton (IN) Daily Clarion*, May 4, 1944, 4.

39. "But There Is the Public," *Greenwood (MS) Commonwealth*, May 3, 1944, 4; "Another Black Eye," *Twin Falls (ID) Times-News*, March 26, 1944, 4, reprinted from the *Nampa (ID) Free Press*; "War's Unavoidable Mistakes."

40. George H. Roeder Jr., *The Censored War: American Visual Experience During World War Two* (New Haven, CT: Yale University Press, 1993), 11.

41. "The Guts to Look at It," *Life*, February 22, 1943, 24; Strock's photographs are at 81–87. See also the first installment of "The Battle of Buna" with more photographs, *Life*, February 15, 1943, 17–29.

42. "Ground Action: 'Greatest War Picture' from Africa Puzzles Experts on Military Tactics," *Life*, April 12, 1943, 30–31. Roberts took five photographs that day, but the one with the medics was the most widely used; it appeared in the *Daily News* (New York) on March 30, 1943. The praise from the photo editor of *Editor & Publisher* is quoted in the UP's story—see, for example, "Army Reveals 'Prize' Tunisia Pictures Faked by Photographer at Training Center," *Dayton (OH) Herald*, April 7, 1943, 15—which also names the photographer. The AP's more widely circulated story does not.

43. See, for instance, "Phony Photos," *Time*, April 19, 1943, 54; "General Terms Photo a Fake," *Pittsburgh Press*, April 7, 1943, 38; and "Appropriate Action Taken on Fake War Pictures," *Bloomington (IN) Pantagraph*, April 9, 1943, 4.

44. "Apologies to All," *Abilene (TX) Reporter-News*, April 9, 1943, 11; "The Camera as Reporter," *New York Herald Tribune*, April 10, 1943, 14.

45. Roeder, *Censored War*, 1.

46. Casey, *War Beat*, 164–65.

47. Roeder, *Censored War*, 9–14; Sweeney, *Military and the Press*, 117–19; Brewer, *Why America Fights*, 124–25 (on atrocities).

48. "Victims of Jap Treachery," *Central New Jersey Home News* (New Brunswick), September 17, 1943, 23. The caption stated that the enemy had fired from a hiding place inside the half-sunken barge offshore—which could be interpreted as strategic rather than

"treacherous" in any case—but *Life* (September 20, 1943, 34) reported that the Americans had been cut down by a machine-gun nest on the shore.

49. *Life* published six letters about Strock's photograph, only one of which was unfavorable; "Letters to the Editor," *Life*, October 11, 1943, 4+.

50. James F. McGlincy for the UP, "War News 'Blackout' Held Stupid," published, for example, in *Arizona Republic*, December 20, 1944, 1; Casey, *War Beat*, 308.

51. Daniel C. Hallin, "The Passing of the 'High Modernism' of American Journalism," *Journal of Communication* 42 (Summer 1992): 16, 14. See also James Boylan, "Declarations of Independence," *Columbia Journalism Review*, November–December 1986, 29–33; and John Nerone, *The Media and Public Life: A History* (Cambridge: Polity, 2015), 180–83.

8. "SO GODDAMN OBJECTIVE"

1. Larry Tye, *Demagogue: The Life and Long Shadow of Senator Joe McCarthy* (Boston: Houghton Mifflin Harcourt, 2020), 17–21, 49–57.

2. Richard L. Strout, "Ordeal by Publicity: McCarthy Hearings Prove Once More the Distorting Effects of 'Straight Reporting,'" *Christian Science Monitor*, May 27, 1950, WM5; for other contemporary critiques, see, for example, Douglass Cater, "The Captive Press," *Reporter* 2 (June 6, 1950): 17–20, and "Job for the Readers?," *Time*, January 25, 1954, 81.

3. Edwin R. Bayley, *Joe McCarthy and the Press* (Madison: University of Wisconsin Press, 1981), 66.

4. Bayley, *Joe McCarthy*, 67.

5. Haynes Johnson, *The Age of Anxiety: McCarthyism to Terrorism* (Orlando, FL: Harcourt, 2005), 140–41.

6. Both Johnson, *Age of Anxiety*, 139, and Bayley, *Joe McCarthy*, 217, make the comparison to Nixon.

7. Daniel C. Hallin, *The "Uncensored War": The Media and Vietnam* (Berkeley: University of California Press, 1986), 116–17.

8. Bayley, *Joe McCarthy*, 170–73.

9. Marquis Childs, "Campaign Against Press," *Washington Post*, May 9, 1953, 11, citing the reporting of the *Great Falls (MT) Tribune*.

10. Oliver Pilat and William Y. Shannon, "The One-Man Mob of Joe McCarthy," part 1, *New York Post*, September 4, 1951, 3.

11. Quoted in David M. Oshinsky, *A Conspiracy so Immense: The World of Joe McCarthy* (New York: Free Press, 1983), 183–84.

12. The sobriquet is widely quoted but rarely attributed; the entry "McCormick, Robert Rutherford" in *Encyclopedia of American Journalism*, ed. Steven L. Vaughn (New York: Routledge, 2008), 297, credits the *Tribune*'s drama critic Burton Rascoe.

13. Published each day in the *Chicago Tribune* from January 11 to January 18, 1943, and carrying headlines such as "New Deal Jumps at Every Excuse to 'Get *Tribune*': Here's How

Sleuths Failed in 3 Other 'Probes'" and "International Set Active Foe of the *Tribune*: Thunders at Paper for Its Editorial Policy," the stories in the series by Fulton were a response to the White House's effort to prosecute the *Tribune* under the Espionage Act for a story about the Battle of Midway that revealed the navy had broken the Japanese codes.

14. Matthew Pressman, *On Press: The Liberal Values That Shaped the News* (Cambridge, MA: Harvard University Press, 2018), 27–36.

15. U.S. Senate, Subcommittee of the Committee on Foreign Relations, *State Department Employee Loyalty Investigation. Report . . . Pursuant to S. Res. 231 . . .* , 81st Cong., 2nd sess. (Washington, DC: U.S. Government Printing Office, 1950), 168.

16. Oshinsky, *Conspiracy so Immense*, 169–70.

17. U.S. Senate, Committee on Rules and Administration, *Maryland Senatorial Election of 1950: Report*, S. Rep. 647, 82nd Cong., 1st sess. (Washington, DC: U.S. Government Printing Office, 1951), 4, 6, 4; senator quoted in Drew Pearson, "Campaign Photo Rouses Ire," *Washington Post*, January 9, 1951, B13.

18. "An Old Issue Revived," *Chicago Tribune*, February 23, 1951, 16.

19. Quoted in AP, "Senator Urges Ending 'Silly' Tydings Probe," *Chicago Tribune*, March 1, 1951, A4.

20. Senators quoted in Dewey L. Fleming, "Senator Knowland Demands Truman End Vacation to 'Clean House' in D.C.," *Baltimore Sun*, March 7, 1951, 1, 8.

21. On Rothstein, see Errol Morris, "The Case of the Inappropriate Alarm Clock," in *Believing Is Seeing (Observations on the Mysteries of Photography)* (New York: Penguin, 2011), 128–33, 169–73 (citing the Topeka paper at 132); on Mundt, see Robert L. Snyder, *Pare Lorentz and Documentary Film* (Reno: University of Nevada Press, 1994), 89–90.

22. Clayton Knowles, "Republicans Score Tydings Vote Case," *New York Times*, March 7, 1951, A39; Edward F. Ryan, "'Clean House,' Truman Told; GOP Attacks Butler Probe," *Washington Post*, March 7, 1951, A1.

23. U.S. Senate, Committee on Rules and Administration, *Maryland Senatorial Election*, 46.

24. Gerald Griffin, "Congressmen Consider New Campaign Laws," *Baltimore Sun*, March 18, 1951, 1.

25. U.S. Senate, Committee on Rules and Administration, *Maryland Senatorial Election*, 8; "Fair Election Group Studied," *Baltimore Sun*, February 17, 1952, 18; William Knighton Jr., "Tighter Election Laws Are Urged," *Baltimore Sun*, September 15, 1951, 1 (quoting the attorney general).

26. Brian Thornton, "Published Reaction When Murrow Battled McCarthy," *Journalism History* 29, no. 3 (Fall 2003): 133–46; Michael Gauger, "Flickering Images: Live Television Coverage and Viewership of the Army–McCarthy Hearings," *Historian* 67, no. 4 (Winter 2005): 678–93.

27. Gilbert Seldes, "Murrow, McCarthy, and the Empty Formula," *Saturday Review*, April 24, 1954, 26–27.

28. Peter Matthiessen, interview, *Charlie Rose*, PBS, May 27, 2008, video and transcript at https://charlierose.com/videos/26524, with quoted comments beginning at 15:55; Joel Whitney, *Finks: How the CIA Tricked the World's Best Writers* (New York: OR Books,

2016), 1–2; H. L. Humes to George Plimpton, Oxford, March 4, 1966, original in the Harold Humes Archives, Pierpont Morgan Library, New York, and available online at the Doc Humes Institute website, https://sites.google.com/a/dochumes.com/www /aletterfromdoc.

29.   Frances Stonor Saunders, *The Cultural Cold War: The CIA and the World of Arts and Letters* (New York: New Press, 1999), 1–23, 244.

30.   John M. Crewdson, "The CIA's 3-Decade Effort to Mold the World's Views," *New York Times*, December 25, 1977, 1.

31.   Bernard D. Nossiter, "CIA News Service Reported," *Washington Post*, July 3, 1975, A26, quoting the CIA memo; Robert G. Kaiser and Ira Chinoy, "How Scaife's Money Powered a Movement," *Washington Post*, May 1999, A1, in the *Post's* digital database under the title "Scaife: Funding Father of the Right," https://www.washingtonpost.com/wp -srv/politics/special/clinton/stories/scaifemain050299.htm.

32.   Carl Bernstein, "The CIA and the Media," *Rolling Stone*, October 20, 1977, available on Bernstein's website, http://www.carlbernstein.com/magazine_cia_and_media.php. See also John M. Crewdson, "News Organizations Say They Find No Evidence Their Employees Maintained C.I.A. Relationships," *New York Times*, September 13, 1977, A29; John M. Crewdson, "C.I.A. Established Many Links to Journalists in U.S. and Abroad," *New York Times*, December 27, 1977, A1, A40.

33.   Crewdson, "C.I.A.'s 3-Decade Effort"; the other two parts of the series were John M. Crewdson, "Worldwide Propaganda Network Built by the C.I.A.," December 26, 1977, A1, A37, and Crewdson, "C.I.A. Established Many Links."

34.   U.S. House of Representatives, Subcommittee on Oversight, Permanent House Select Committee on Intelligence, *The CIA and the Media: Hearings*, 95th Cong., 1st and 2nd sess. (Washington, DC: U.S. Government Printing Office, 1978), 294.

35.   William Colby, statement, in U.S. House, Subcommittee on Oversight, *CIA and the Media*, 5–6.

36.   Ray S. Cline, statement, in U.S. House, Subcommittee on Oversight, *CIA and the Media*, 65–67; see also John M. Crewdson, "Colby Acknowledges U.S. Press Picked Up Bogus C.I.A. Accounts," *New York Times*, December 28, 1977, A1.

37.   Colby and Cline, statements, U.S. House, Subcommittee on Oversight, *CIA and the Media*, 6, 66.

38.   Eugene Patterson, statement, U.S. House, Subcommittee on Oversight, *CIA and the Media*, 242.

39.   Tim Weiner, "C.I.A. Chief Defends Secrecy, in Spending and Spying, to Senate," *New York Times*, February 23, 1996, A5.

9. "THE BASTARDS ARE MAKING IT UP!"

1.   See, for example, Pew Research Center, "Beyond Distrust: How Americans View Their Government," November 23, 2015, https://www.people-press.org/2015/11/23/1-trust-in

-government-1958-2015/; Gallup Organization, "In Depth: Confidence in Institutions," n.d., showing statistics from 1973 through 2021 as of September 2021, https://news.gallup .com/poll/1597/confidence-institutions.aspx; Gallup, "Americans' Confidence in Institutions Stays Low," June 13, 2016, https://news.gallup.com/poll/192581/americans -confidence-institutions-stays-low.aspx.

2. Gallup, "In Depth Topics: Media Use and Evaluation," n.d., showing statistics through July 2021 as of September 2021, https://news.gallup.com/poll/1663/Media-Use-Evalu ation.aspx.

3. Matthew Pressman, *On Press: The Liberal Values That Shaped the News* (Cambridge, MA: Harvard University Press, 2018), 184–218; Katherine Fink and Michael Schudson, "The Rise of Contextual Journalism, 1950s–2000s," *Journalism* 15, no. 1 (2014): 3–20. See also James Boylan, "Declarations of Independence," *Columbia Journalism Review*, November–December 1986, 31–33; and Daniel C. Hallin, "The Passing of the 'High Modernism' of American Journalism," *Journal of Communication* 42 (Summer 1992): 16–18.

4. "David Halberstam," in *Reporting America at War: An Oral History*, comp. Michelle Ferrari, with commentary by James Tobin (New York: Hyperion, 2003), 120.

5. William Safire, *Before the Fall: An Inside View of the Pre-Watergate White House* (1975; reprint, New York: Routledge, 2017), 323, 360.

6. David Greenberg, *Republic of Spin: An Inside History of the American Presidency* (New York: Norton, 2016), 396–401; Lawrence R. Jacobs and Robert Y. Shapiro, "Presidential Manipulation of Polls and Public Opinion: The Nixon Administration and the Pollsters," *Political Science Quarterly* 110, no. 4 (Winter 1995–1996): 519–38.

7. John Dean's memo, dated August 16, 1971, is quoted in U.S. Senate, Select Committee on Presidential Campaign Activities, *The Senate Watergate Report*, 2 vols. (New York: Dell, 1974), 1:59.

8. Seymour Krim quoted in Ronald Weber, "Some Sort of Artistic Excitement," in *The Reporter as Artist: A Look at the New Journalism Controversy*, ed. Ronald Weber (New York: Hastings House, 1974), 19; Jack Newfield, "Is There a New Journalism?," in *Reporter as Artist*, ed. Weber, 304 (first published in *Columbia Journalism Review*, July–August 1972).

9. Tom Wolfe, "The New Journalism," in *The New Journalism: An Anthology*, ed. Tom Wolfe and E. W. Johnson (New York: Harper and Row, 1973), 15.

10. Weber, "Some Sort of Artistic Excitement," 13.

11. Wolfe, "New Journalism," 9, 11, all ellipses in the original.

12. Wolfe's articles "Tiny Mummies! The True Story of the Ruler of 43d Street's Land of the Walking Dead" and "Lost in the Whichy Thickets: The New-Yorker—II" were reprinted in his anthology *Hooking Up* (New York: Farrar Straus and Giroux, 2000), 255–87. The *Herald Tribune*'s Sunday supplement would later become the stand-alone magazine *New York*. Commentary on the pieces includes Dwight Macdonald, "Parajournalism, or Tom Wolfe & His Magic Writing Machine" and "Parajournalism II: Wolfe and the *New Yorker*," *New York Review of Books*, August 26, 1965, and February 3, 1966 (page numbers unavailable); Leonard C. Lewin, "Is Fact Necessary?," *Columbia Journalism Review*,

Winter 1966, 29–34, including a long letter from Renata Adler and Gerald Jonas; and John Hersey, "The Legend on the License," *Yale Review* 70 (Autumn 1980): 1–25.

13. Gail Sheehy, "Wide Open City, Part II: Redpants and Sugarman," *New York*, July 26, 1971, 27–36; W. Stewart Pinkerton Jr., "Believe It or Not: The 'New Journalism' Is Sometimes Less Than Meets the Eye," *Wall Street Journal*, August 13, 1971, 1.

14. *In Cold Blood* was first published in four parts in the *New Yorker* in September and October 1965 and issued in book form by Random House in 1966. For Capote's own claims, made in an interview originally published in the *New York Times Book Review* in 1966, see George Plimpton, "Truman Capote: An Interview," in *Reporter as Artist*, ed. Weber, 188–206. Critics include Phillip K. Tompkins, "In Cold Fact," *Esquire*, June 1966, https://classic.esquire.com/article/1966/6/1/in-cold-fact; Van Jensen, "Writing History: Capote's Novel Has Lasting Effect on Journalism," *Lawrence (KS) Journal-World*, April 3, 2005, https://www2.ljworld.com/news/2005/apr/03/writing_history_capotes/; Kevin Helliker, "Capote Classic 'In Cold Blood' Tainted by Long-Lost Files," *Wall Street Journal*, February 9, 2013, A1.

15. Nora Ephron, *Heartburn* (1983; reprint, New York: Vintage, 1996), 13.

16. See, for example, Kevin Helliker, "The Memoir of an Infamous Murderer: 'In Cold Blood' Killer's Long-Lost Manuscript Raises Questions About His Motive," *Wall Street Journal*, March 18, 2017, A1.

17. Tom Wolfe, "The Virtues of Gutter Journalism," *San Francisco Chronicle*, December 17, 2000, https://www.sfgate.com/magazine/article/THE-VIRTUES-OF-GUTTER-JOUR NALISM-Tom-Wolfe-on-2771418.php.

18. Deirdre Carmody, "Clay Felker: He Created Magazines by Marrying New Journalism to Consumerism," *New York Times*, April 9, 1995, https://timesmachine.nytimes.com /timesmachine/1995/04/09/876095.html?pageNumber=162; Deirdre Carmody, "Clay Felker, Magazine Pioneer, Dies at 82," *New York Times*, July 2, 2008, https://www .nytimes.com/2008/07/02/business/media/02felker.html.

19. Plimpton, "Truman Capote," 202.

20. Harry Gilroy, "A Book in a New Form Earns $2-Million for Capote," *New York Times*, December 31, 1965, https://www.nytimes.com/1965/12/31/archives/a-book-in-a-new -form-earns-2million-for-truman-capote-he-put-6.html.

21. Hersey, "Legend on the License," 1, 2, 5.

22. Janet Cooke, "Jimmy's World: 8-Year-Old Heroin Addict Lives for a Fix," *Washington Post*, September 28, 1980, https://www.washingtonpost.com/archive/politics/1980/09/28 /jimmys-world/605f237a-7330-4a69-8433-b6da4c519120/.

23. Lewis M. Simons, "D.C. Authorities Seek Identity of Heroin Addict, 8," *Washington Post*, September 30, 1980, https://www.washingtonpost.com/archive/politics/1980/09 /30/dc-authorities-seek-identity-of-heroin-addict-8/38c10641-c029-441e-a7d3-bff515 f9a32b/.

24. Quoted in Bill Green, "The Publication: 'Jimmy' Hit Washington Like a Grenade, and Bounced," *Washington Post*, April 19, 1981, A13.

25. Bill Green, "Janet's World: The Story of a Child Who Never Existed—How and Why It Came to be Published," *Washington Post*, April 19, 1981, A1, plus additional articles on

A12–A15 (this source is a collection of articles, including the summary story "Janet's World" and a number of other reports—including Green, "The Publication" cited in note 24—with each inside article on pages A12–A15 having a different headline; my own summary draws on the whole five-page package, not just "Janet's World"); Haynes Johnson, "A Wound That Will Be Long in Healing and Never Forgotten," *Washington Post*, April 19, 1981, A3. See also David L. Eason, "On Journalistic Authority: The Janet Cooke Scandal," *Critical Studies in Mass Communication* 3 (1986): 429–47.

26. Mike Sager, "The Fabulist Who Changed Journalism," *Columbia Journalism Review*, Spring 2016, https://www.cjr.org/the_feature/the_fabulist_who_changed_journalism.php.

27. National News Council, "Report," *Columbia Journalism Review*, September–October 1981, 84.

28. Johnson, "A Wound."

29. Jonathan Friendly, "Disclosure of Two Fabricated Articles Causes Papers to Re-examine Their Rules," *New York Times*, May 25, 1981, https://www.nytimes.com/1981/05/25/us/disclosure-of-two-fabricated-articles-causes-papers-to-re-examine-their-rules.html.

30. William Woestendiek, executive editor of the *Arizona Daily Star*, quoted in Jonathan Friendly, "Falsification of Prize Article Puts a Spotlight on How Newspapers Check Stories," *New York Times*, April 17, 1981, https://www.nytimes.com/1981/04/17/nyregion/falsification-of-prize-article-puts-a-spotlight-on-how-newspapers-check.html.

31. Joseph Sobran, "The Party of Compassion," *National Review*, June 26, 1981, 722. For the Deep Throat/Jimmy comparison, see, for example, Richard Brookhiser, "Book Arts & Manners: Yellow Journals, Black Faces," *National Review*, August 21, 1981, 965; and Philip F. Lawler, "A Great Pair of Eggs," *American Spectator*, June 1981, 24–26.

32. Murray Kempton, "A Newspaper Ghetto That Let a Reporter Invent a Story," *Newsday*, April 21, 1981, 49.

33. William O. Walker, "Down the Big Road: A Black Woman Shakes Up the White Press and Reveals Its Bias," *Cleveland Call and Post*, May 2, 1981, 8A.

34. Jill Gerston, "Code Blue," *Los Angeles Times*, January 15, 1993, E1.

35. Victor Pickard, "The Strange Life and Death of the Fairness Doctrine: Tracing the Decline of Positive Freedoms in American Policy Discourse," *International Journal of Communication* 12 (2018): 3441, quoting the FCC.

36. Ted Gup, "Eye of the Storm: Why Jeff Gerth, a Most Accomplished Investigator, Is Also Most Controversial," *Columbia Journalism Review*, May–June 2001, 35.

37. Gene Lyons, *Fools for Scandal: How the Media Invented Whitewater* (New York: Franklin Square Press, 1996), 30–56 (quote at 31); James Stewart, *Blood Sport: The President and His Adversaries* (New York: Simon and Schuster, 1996), 183–220; Anthony Lewis, "Abroad at Home: Smears and Facts," *New York Times*, April 1, 1996, https://www.nytimes.com/1996/04/01/opinion/abroad-at-home-smears-and-facts.html.

38. The first in the series was James Risen and Jeff Gerth, "Breach at Los Alamos: A Special Report: China Stole Nuclear Secrets for Bombs, U.S. Aides Say," *New York Times*, March 6, 1999, https://www.nytimes.com/1999/03/06/world/breach-los-alamos-special-report-china-stole-nuclear-secrets-for-bombs-us-aides.html. See also "From the Editors:

The Times and Wen Ho Lee," *New York Times*, September 26, 2000, https://www
.nytimes.com/2000/09/26/us/from-the-editors-the-times-and-wen-ho-lee.html.

39. Trudy Lieberman, "Churning Whitewater," *Columbia Journalism Review*, May–
June 1994, 26–30 (quote at 28).

40. Kimberly Conniff, "All the Views Fit to Print," *Brill's Content*, March 2001, 105–7, 152–
55. See also Jane Mayer, *Dark Money: The Hidden History of the Billionaires Behind the
Rise of the Radical Right* (New York: Doubleday, 2016), 60–86; Karen Rothmyer, "Unindicted Co-conspirator?," *Nation*, February 23, 1998, 19–24; Karen Rothmyer, "Citizen
Scaife," *Columbia Journalism Review*, July–August 1981, 41–50.

41. Rothmyer, "Unindicted Co-conspirator?," 24.

42. Byron York, "The Life and Death of the *American Spectator*," *Atlantic*, November 2001,
https://www.theatlantic.com/magazine/archive/2001/11/the-life-and-death-of-the
-american-spectator/302343/. The actual quote from the article "The Real Anita Hill"
was "a bit nutty, and a bit slutty," but I am quoting the better-known version, which
appeared in David Brock, *Blinded by the Right: The Conscience of an Ex-conservative*
(New York: Crown, 2002), 100.

43. Joe Conason and Gene Lyons, *The Hunting of the President: The Ten-Year Campaign to
Destroy Bill and Hillary Clinton* (New York: St. Martin's, 2000), 107–15, 168–74, with
Scaife quote at 111; York, "Life and Death."

44. York, "Life and Death," quoting Christopher Caldwell on making the magazine a
"laughingstock." See R. Emmett Tyrrell, "Mena Spirited," *American Spectator*,
December 1994, 14; "Moving on Mena," *American Spectator*, May 1995, 14; and "The
Arkansas Drug Shuttle," *American Spectator*, August 1995, 16–18. Not only was the
Mena story factually dubious, but allegations had also swirled for years that a CIA-
backed drug-trafficking operation had been part of the Reagan administration's illegal
secret scheme to arm right-wing rebel groups in Nicaragua, and many fellow conservatives vainly warned Tyrrell that pursuing the story had the potential to tarnish
both Reagan and Oliver North, whom the Right saw as a hero for his Central American swashbuckling.

45. York, "Life and Death."

46. David Brock, "Confessions of a Right-Wing Hit Man," *Esquire*, July 1997, 52–57; David
Brock, "The Fire This Time," *Esquire*, April 1998, 60–64. See also Brock, *Blinded by the
Right*, 140–59; and Ken Gormley, *The Death of American Virtue: Clinton vs. Starr* (New
York: Crown, 2010), 116–17.

47. York, "Life and Death."

48. CNN's story "'American Spectator' Alleges Clinton Had Affairs" aired at 5:57 p.m. on
December 19, 1993; a transcript is available on Lexis Nexis.

49. Stewart, *Blood Sport*, 347–65; Michael Kinsley, "TRB from Washington: F-Troop," *New
Republic*, January 10–17, 1994, 4; *Chicago Tribune*, December 20, 1993; *Cleveland Plain
Dealer*, December 20, 1993.

50. Richard Brookhiser, "Body Politics," *New York Times Book Review*, September 28, 1997,
https://www.nytimes.com/1997/09/28/books/body-politics.html; John Corry, "Vince
Foster Redux," *American Spectator*, December 1997, 56–57. Starr's report on Foster's

death was officially released on October 11, 1997, but his conclusions had been common knowledge for several months.

51. R. Emmett Tyrrell Jr., "From Troopergate to Monicagate," *American Spectator*, November 1998, 18–22; "Parody," *Weekly Standard*, November 6, 1995, 48; "Parody," *Weekly Standard*, January 22, 1996, 40.

52. David McClintick, "Town Crier for the New Age," *Brill's Content*, November 1998, 114–15; Matt Drudge, "Speech to the National Press Club on Media and the Internet," June 2, 1998, Washington, DC, https://www.americanrhetoric.com/speeches/mattdrudge nationalpressclub.htm.

53. McClintick, "Town Crier," 117.

54. Matt Drudge and Doug Harbrecht, "Q&A at the Washington Press Club," June 2, 1998, https://www.americanrhetoric.com/speeches/mattdrudgepressclubquestionans wer.htm.

55. Quoted in Cynthia Cotts, "Libel Bible," *Village Voice*, February 9, 1999, https://www .villagevoice.com/1999/02/09/libel-bible/.

56. McClintick, "Town Crier," 114, 117–18; *Blumenthal v. Drudge and America Online*, U.S. District Court for the District of Columbia, Civil Action No. 97-1968, April 22, 1998, available online at Electronic Privacy Information Center, https://epic.org/free_speech /blumenthal_v_drudge.html. Citing section 230 of the Communications Decency Act, the court dismissed the suit against AOL.

57. Pew Research Center, "The Internet News Audience Goes Ordinary," posted January 14, 1999, https://www.people-press.org/1999/01/14/the-internet-news-audience-goes-ordin ary/. Online audiences varied significantly in size from month to month.

58. "Poll: Too Much Lewinsky Coverage," allpolitics.com, posted January 29, 1998, http:// www.cnn.com/ALLPOLITICS/1998/01/29/poll/.

59. Steven Brill, "Pressgate," *Brill's Content*, July–August 1998, 142–43.

60. Brill, "Pressgate," 131–32; Gormley, *Death of American Virtue*, 502–3; Pew Research Center, "The Clinton Crisis and the Press," February 18, 1998, https://www.journalism.org /1998/02/18/the-clinton-crisis-and-the-press-2/, summarizes the committee's report and attaches a PDF.

61. *Meet the Press*, NBC News, January 25, 1998, available on the Proquest database Alex-anderstreet.com, quoted comments starting at 31:25.

62. Tom Shales, "TV Pundits in Bed with Tabloids? Say It Ain't So," *Washington Post*, January 26, 1998, C1; Russert quoted in Brill, "Pressgate," 139.

63. William Cash, "The News That's Unfit to Print," *Globe and Mail*, February 7, 1988, C9.

64. Drew Desilver, "Clinton's Impeachment Barely Dented His Public Support, and It Turned Off Many Americans," Pew Research Center, October 3, 2019, https://www .pewresearch.org/fact-tank/2019/10/03/clintons-impeachment-barely-dented-his -public-support-and-it-turned-off-many-americans/; *PSRA/Newsweek # 9904: Getting Past Impeachment*, question 3, USPSRNEW.021399.R02A, Princeton Survey Research Associates (Cornell University, Ithaca, NY: Roper Center for Public Opinion Research, 1999), data set.

65. Quoted in Neil Hickey, "Is Fox News Fair?," *Columbia Journalism Review*, March–April 1998, 33. See also Gabriel Sherman, *The Loudest Voice in the Room: How the Brilliant, Bombastic Roger Ailes Built Fox News—and Divided a Country* (New York: Random House, 2014), 196.

66. Quoted in Sherman, *Loudest Voice in the Room*, 229–30.

67. Hickey, "Is Fox News Fair?," 32; Sherman, *Loudest Voice in the Room*, 230–32.

68. Hickey, "Is Fox News Fair?," 35.

69. Reece Peck, *Fox Populism: Branding Conservatism as Working Class* (Cambridge: Cambridge University Press, 2019), 133–39; Derek Thompson, "The Twilight of Fox News," *Atlantic*, posted August 29, 2016, https://www.theatlantic.com/business/archive/2016/08/the-twilight-of-fox-news/497684/.

70. Christopher Hanson, "All the News That Fits the Myth," *Columbia Journalism Review*, January–February 2001, 50–53; Alicia C. Shepard, "How They Blew It," *American Journalism Review*, January–February 2001, 20–27; Sherman, *Loudest Voice in the Room*, 244–56; Charles L. Zelden, *Bush v. Gore: Exposing the Hidden Crisis in American Democracy*, 3rd ed. (Lawrence: University Press of Kansas, 2020), 1–4.

71. John Ellis, "Why I Won't Write Anymore About the 2000 Campaign," *Boston Globe*, July 3, 1999, A11; Jane Mayer, "Dept. of Close Calls: George W.'s Cousin," *New Yorker*, November 20, 2000, 38.

72. Roger Ailes, testimony, U.S. House of Representatives, Committee on Energy and Commerce, *Election Night Coverage by the Networks, Hearing, 14 February 2001* (Washington, DC: U.S. Government Printing Office, 2001), 117.

73. Tim Dickinson, "How Roger Ailes Built the Fox News Fear Factory," *Rolling Stone*, May 25, 2011, https://www.rollingstone.com/politics/politics-news/how-roger-ailes-built-the-fox-news-fear-factory-244652/; Sherman, *Loudest Voice in the Room*, 267.

74. Sherman, *Loudest Voice in the Room*, 237–38.

75. Robert Greenwald used Moody's memos in his film *Outfoxed: Rupert Murdoch's War on Journalism* (2004). Selections from the memos are quoted in a number of contemporary sources, including Robert S. Boynton, "How to Make a Guerrilla Documentary," *New York Times Magazine*, July 11, 2004, https://www.nytimes.com/2004/07/11/magazine/how-to-make-a-guerrilla-documentary.html; Dickinson, "How Roger Ailes Built the Fox News Fear Factory"; and Alexandra Kitty, *Outfoxed: Rupert Murdoch's War on Journalism* (New York: Disinformation Company, 2005), based on the film.

76. Jacques Steinberg, "Fox News, Media Elite," *New York Times*, November 8, 2004, citing a study by the Pew Research Center, https://www.nytimes.com/2004/11/08/business/media/fox-news-media-elite.html; the correction appeared in the *Wall Street Journal* on October 26, 2004, A2. The *Journal* would be acquired by News Corp. in 2007.

77. Ken Auletta, "Vox Fox," *New Yorker*, May 26, 2003, https://www.newyorker.com/magazine/2003/05/26/vox-fox.

78. Sherman, *Loudest Voice in the Room*, xv, 342.

79. "Keith Olbermann Suspended Over Political Donations," NBCNews.com, November 5, 2010, quoting Phil Griffin, http://www.nbcnews.com/id/40028929/ns/politics

-decision_2010/t/keith-olbermann-suspended-over-political-donations/; Brian Stelter and Bill Carter, "Olbermann of MSNBC Suspended Over Donations," *New York Times*, November 5, 2010, https://www.nytimes.com/2010/11/06/us/06olbermann.html; Uri Friedman, "Why Did Keith Olbermann Leave MSNBC?," *Atlantic*, January 23, 2011, https://www.theatlantic.com/entertainment/archive/2011/01/why-did-keith-olber mann-leave-msnbc/342545/.

80.   Alessandra Stanley, "How MSNBC Became Fox's Liberal Evil Twin," *New York Times*, August 31, 2012, https://www.nytimes.com/2012/08/31/us/politics/msnbc-as-foxs-liberal -evil-twin.html.

81.   Pew Research Center, "Cable and Internet Loom Large in Fragmented Political News Universe," January 11, 2004, https://www.people-press.org/2004/01/11/cable-and-internet -loom-large-in-fragmented-political-news-universe/.

82.   Jonathan S. Morris, "The Fox News Factor," *International Journal of Press/Politics* 10, no. 3 (2005): 56–79.

83.   "Some News Leaves People Knowing Less," Fairleigh Dickinson University's Public Mind Poll, November 21, 2011, http://publicmind.fdu.edu/2011/knowless/final.pdf; Morris, "Fox News Factor," also finds evidence that Fox viewers are less knowledgable about politics and current events than are viewers of CNN or network news.

84.   Arlie Russell Hochschild, *Strangers in Their Own Land: Anger and Mourning on the American Right* (New York: New Press, 2018), 16, 126–27; see also Peck, *Fox Populism*, on how the network used the populist rhetorical tradition to build its brand.

10. "FAKE BUT ACCURATE"

1.   "The Editors: To Our Readers," *New Republic*, June 1, 1998, 8–9; "To Our Readers," *New Republic*, June 29, 1998, 8–10; Buzz Bissinger, "Shattered Glass," *Vanity Fair*, September 1998, posted online September 5, 2007, https://www.vanityfair.com/magazine/1998 /09/bissinger199809.

2.   Dan Barry, David Barstow, Jonathan D. Glater, Adam Liptak, and Jacques Steinberg, "Correcting the Record: *Times* Reporter Who Resigned Leaves Long Trail of Decep- tion," *New York Times*, May 11, 2003, https://www.nytimes.com/2003/05/11/us/correct ing-the-record-times-reporter-who-resigned-leaves-long-trail-of-deception.html; Jacques Steinberg, "Changes at the *Times*: The Overview; *Times*'s 2 Top Editors Resign After Furor on Writer's Fraud," *New York Times*, June 6, 2003, https://www.nytimes .com/2003/06/06/nyregion/changes-times-overview-times-s-2-top-editors-resign -after-furor-writer-s-fraud.html.

3.   Blake Morrison, "Ex–*USA Today* Reporter Faked Major Stories," *USA Today*, March 19, 2004, 1A; Blake Morrison, Rita Rubin, and Michael Hiestand, "Kelley Issues Apology; More Fabricated Stories Discovered," *USA Today*, April 22, 2004, 10A; Kevin McCoy, "Report: Newsroom Culture Enabled Kelley," *USA Today*, April 22, 2004, 10A.

4.   Jill Rosen, "Who Knows Jack?," *American Journalism Review*, April–May 2004, 31.

5. Maggie Jones Patterson and Steve Urbanski, "What Jayson Blair and Janet Cooke Say About the Press and the Erosion of Public Trust," *Journalism Studies* 7, no. 6 (2006): 828–50; Ivor Shapiro, "Why They Lie: Probing the Explanations for Journalistic Cheating," *Canadian Journal of Communication* 31 (2006): 261–66.

6. Jacques Steinberg, "*Times* Editor to Select Reader Representative," *New York Times*, July 31, 2003, https://www.nytimes.com/2003/07/31/us/times-editor-to-select-reader-representative.html; Daniel Victor, "*New York Times* Will Offer Employee Buyouts and Eliminate Public Editor Role," *New York Times*, May 31, 2017, https://www.nytimes.com/2017/05/31/business/media/new-york-times-buyouts.html.

7. Dennis Ryerson, "The Readers Gave It to Us Straight, Without Any Spin," *Indianapolis Star*, July 13, 2003, E1; *Cleveland Plain Dealer* columnist Connie Schulz quoted in Mark Fitzgerald, "Blair Warning: Readers Everywhere Raise Doubts," *Editor and Publisher*, May 19, 2003, 5. See also Patterson and Urbanski, "What Jayson Blair and Janet Cooke Say"; Matt Carlson, "Gone, but Not Forgotten: Memories of Journalistic Deviance as Metajournalistic Discourse," *Journalism Studies* 15, no. 1 (2014): 33–47.

8. Quoted in Tim Rutten, "Regarding Media: The Blair Affair Fuels a 70-Year-Old Scandal," *Los Angeles Times*, June 4, 2003, E1.

9. Alexander Cockburn, "Beat the Devil: Now, Gods, Stand Up for Fakers!," *Nation*, June 9, 2003, 9; "The Sulzberger Standard," *New York Sun*, May 12, 2003, 6. See also John Berlau, "Duranty's Deception," *Insight on the News*, July 22–August 4, 2003, 18–21.

10. Quoted in Scott R. Maier, "Setting the Record Straight," *Journalism Practice* 1, no. 1 (2007): 34,

11. See Michael Karlsson, Christer Clerwall, and Lars Nord, "Do Not Stand Corrected: Transparency and Users' Attitudes to Inaccurate News and Corrections in Online Journalism," *Journalism & Mass Communication Quarterly* 94, no. 1 (2017): 161, on a small study of Swedish news consumers suggesting that people who didn't trust the media in the first place rarely changed their minds after an outlet published a correction and were less likely to be appeased by the acknowledgment than were people with higher trust in the media. Other recent scholarship focusing on corrections of mistakes in stories about controversial topics has disagreed over the effectiveness of prompt corrections. Brendan Nyhan and Jason Reifler, for instance, argue that correcting mistakes might actually "backfire" by strengthening the misperceptions among readers unwilling to revise their beliefs. But Thomas Wood and Ethan Porter ran experiments that showed "citizens are indeed capable of learning." See Brendan Nyhan and Jason Reifler, "When Corrections Fail: The Persistence of Political Misperceptions," *Political Behavior* 32 (2010): 303–30; Brendan Nyhan, Jason Reifler, and Peter A. Ubel, "The Hazards of Correcting Myths About Health Care Reform," *Medical Care* 51 (2013): 127–32; Thomas Wood and Ethan Porter, "The Elusive Backfire Effect: Mass Attitudes' Steadfast Factual Adherence," *Political Behavior* 41 (2019): 136.

12. Associated Press Managing Editors, *National Credibility Roundtables: 2003 Update: Credibility in Action*, reported and written by Carol Nunnelley (New York: Associated Press, 2003), 1, 13.

13. *Colbert Report*, Comedy Central, October 17, 2005; Adam Sternbergh, "Stephen Colbert Has America by the Ballots," *New York Magazine*, October 2006, https://nymag.com/news/politics/22322/.

14. William Booth, "Reality Is Only an Illusion, Writers Say," *Washington Post*, August 10, 2004, https://www.washingtonpost.com/archive/lifestyle/2004/08/10/reality-is-only-an-illusion-writers-say/1beeafab-a1a2-4956-bbc8-7eee221f88d3/

15. Descriptions of Michael Moore and *Bowling for Columbine* include "manipulating in ways that suit a personal agenda": Stephen Prince, *Firestorm: American Film in the Age of Terrorism* (New York: Columbia University Press, 2009), 154; "shameless exhibitionist," "simplistic," "undeveloped": Ron Briley, "Review: *Bowling for Columbine*," *Journal of American History* 90, no. 3 (December 2003): 1146; "slippery logic, tendentious grandstanding and outright demagoguery": A. O. Scott, "Film Review: Seeking a Smoking Gun in U.S. Violence," *New York Times*, October 11, 2002, https://www.nytimes.com/2002/10/11/movies/film-review-seeking-a-smoking-gun-in-us-violence.html. The documentary's title refers to the false claim that Dylan Klebold and Eric Harris attended their usual early-morning bowling class on the very day they went on to massacre twelve classmates and a teacher.

16. Ken Auletta, "Fortress Bush: Annals of Communications," *New Yorker*, January 19, 2004, https://www.newyorker.com/magazine/2004/01/19/fortress-bush; David Barstow and Robin Stein, "Under Bush, a New Age of Prepackaged TV News," *New York Times*, March 13, 2005, https://www.nytimes.com/2005/03/13/politics/under-bush-a-new-age-of-prepackaged-tv-news.html; David Greenberg, *Republic of Spin: An Inside Story of the American Presidency* (New York: Norton, 2016), 430–32, quoting Joshua Micah Marshall on expert spin.

17. On these points, see, for instance, W. Lance Bennett, Regina G. Lawrence, and Steven Livingston, *When the Press Fails: Political Power and the News Media from Iraq to Katrina* (Chicago: University of Chicago Press, 2007); and Michael Massing, *Now They Tell Us: The American Press and Iraq*, preface by Orville Schell (New York: New York Review of Books, 2004).

18. Michael Isikoff and David Corn, *Hubris: The Inside Story of Spin, Scandal, and the Selling of the Iraq War* (New York: Three Rivers Press, 2007), 35. For a timeline of "what the White House knew and when it knew it," see Frank Rich, *The Greatest Story Ever Sold: The Decline and Fall of Truth from 9/11 to Katrina* (New York: Penguin, 2006), 227–307. For insiders' views on the early determination for war despite the evidence, see, for instance, Ron Suskind, *The Price of Loyalty: George W. Bush, the White House, and the Education of Paul O'Neill* (New York: Simon and Schuster, 2004), 82–86; Bob Woodward, *Plan of Attack* (New York: Simon and Schuster, 2004), 1–8; and the so-called Downing Street Memo, written on July 23, 2002, and first revealed in Michael Smith, "Blair Hit by New Leak of Secret War Plan," *Times* (London), May 1, 2005, 1; and "The Secret Downing Street Memo," *Times* (London), May 1, 2005, 7.

19. Anonymous adviser and Bruce Bartlett quoted in Ron Suskind, "Faith, Certainty, and the Presidency of George W. Bush," *New York Times Magazine*, October 17, 2004,

https://www.nytimes.com/2004/10/17/magazine/faith-certainty-and-the-presidency-of-george-w-bush.html.

20. Massing, *Now They Tell Us*, 61–65; Bennett, Lawrence, and Livingston, *When the Press Fails*, 13–45; Charles Layton, "Miller Brouhaha," *American Journalism Review*, August–September 2003, 30–35.

21. Dana Milbank, "Explanation for Bush's Carrier Landing Altered," *Washington Post*, May 7, 2003, https://www.washingtonpost.com/archive/politics/2003/05/07/explanation-for-bushs-carrier-landing-altered/fc583113-b31f-4dda-91ac-e6b0ac276f43/.

22. Susan Schmidt and Vernon Loeb, "'She Was Fighting to the Death'; Details Emerging of W. Va. Soldier's Capture and Rescue," *Washington Post*, April 3, 2003, https://www.washingtonpost.com/archive/politics/2003/04/03/she-was-fighting-to-the-death/827181d6-bc41-4d13-b20c-ba95fedab997/. The reporters did note that the story was based on battlefield intelligence "whose reliability has yet to be assessed. Pentagon officials said they had heard 'rumors' of Lynch's heroics but had no confirmation."

23. Patrick Rogers, Peter Mikelbank, Rose Ellen O'Connor, Susan Keating, Jane Sims Podesta, and Courtney Rubin, "Saved from Danger: Brave Young Jessica Lynch Survives Captivity—and Torture—to Become a Hero of the Iraqi War," *People*, April 21, 2003, 54.

24. Peter H. Martyn, "Lynch Mob: Pack Journalism and How the Jessica Lynch Story Became Propaganda," *Canadian Journal of Media Studies* 4, no. 1 (November 2008): 124–64; Steve Ritea, "Free Press," *American Journalism Review*, August–September 2003, 10–11.

25. Mitch Potter, "The Real 'Saving Pte. Lynch,'" *Toronto Star*, May 4, 2003, A1; U.S. House of Representatives, Committee on Oversight and Government Reform, *Misleading Information from the Battlefield: The Tillman and Lynch Episodes: First Report* (Washington, DC: U.S. Government Printing Office, 2008), 41–46, 71–75, https://www.govinfo.gov/content/pkg/CRPT-110hrpt858/pdf/CRPT-110hrpt858.pdf. See also John Kampfner, "The Truth About Jessica," *Guardian*, May 15, 2003, https://www.theguardian.com/world/2003/may/15/iraq.usa2; John Kampfner, "War Spin," *Correspondent*, BBC 2, May 18, 2003 (available on DVD); and Pew Research Center, "Jessica Lynch," June 23, 2003, https://www.journalism.org/2003/06/23/jessica-lynch/.

26. Jessica Lynch, "Opening Statement Before House Oversight & Govt. Reform Committee, Delivered 24 April 2007," https://www.americanrhetoric.com/speeches/jessicalynchopeningstatement.htm; "From the Editors: The *Times* and Iraq," *New York Times*, May 26, 2004, https://www.nytimes.com/2004/05/26/world/from-the-editors-the-times-and-iraq.html; Howard Kurtz, "The *Post* on WMDs: An Inside Story; Pre-war Articles Questioning Threat Often Didn't Make Front Page," *Washington Post*, August 12, 2004, https://www.washingtonpost.com/wp-dyn/articles/A58127-2004Aug11.html.

27. "Ignorance, Partisanship Drive False Beliefs about Obama, Iraq," Public Mind Poll, Fairleigh Dickinson University, taken in December 2014 and released January 7, 2015, http://publicmind.fdu.edu/2015/false/. Since, however, the results showed that

41 percent of CNN viewers also believed that WMDs had been found, the correct responses of the MSNBC viewers may represent a happy congruence of reality with their own partisan beliefs.

28. The biggest funder of the Swift Boat group was a wealthy Houston builder who had also donated heavily to Bush and other Texas Republicans; other donors also had links to Bush, his adviser Karl Rove, or other prominent Republicans in the state. The group's claims were quickly debunked by journalists, historians, and some of Kerry's fellow veterans, but they continued to circulate. See Kate Zernike and Jim Rutenberg, "Friendly Fire: The Birth of an Attack on Kerry," *New York Times*, August 20, 2004, https://www.nytimes .com/2004/08/20/us/the-2004-campaign-advertising-friendly-fire-the-birth-of-an -attack-on-kerry.html; "Republican-Funded Group Attacks Kerry's War Record," Annenberg Political Fact Check, Factcheck.org, August 6, 2004, updated August 22, 2004, https://web.archive.org/web/20080703204151/http://www.factcheck.org/article231.html.

29. Dave Moniz and Jim Drinkard, "Guard Commander's Memos Criticize Bush; Documents Cite 'Failure to Perform' to Standards," *USA Today*, September 9, 2004, A4, noting that the White House had not disputed the authenticity of the memos.

30. Dick Thornburgh and Louis D. Boccardi, *Report of the Independent Review Panel on the September 8, 2004, "60 Minutes Wednesday" Segment "For the Record" Concerning President Bush's Texas Air National Guard Service, January 5, 2005*, 153–54, 24, https:// www.cbsnews.com/htdocs/pdf/complete_report/CBS_Report.pdf.

31. CBS's statement quoted in Thornburgh and Boccardi, *Report*, 204.

32. Thornburgh and Boccardi, *Report*, 4, 28, 214–15, 209, 221–22.

33. Thornburgh and Boccardi, *Report*, 2 n. 3; Garance Franke-Ruta, "Blogged Down," *American Prospect*, March 7, 2005, https://prospect.org/article/blogged/.

34. Peggy Noonan, "So Much to Savor," *Wall Street Journal*, November 4, 2004, available at https://peggynoonan.com/282/.

35. Michael Cornfield, Jonathan Carson, Alison Kalis, and Emily Simon, "Buzz, Blogs, and Beyond: The Internet and National Discourse in the Fall of 2004," Pew Research Center, May 16, 2005, 21–22, PIPBlogs051605pdf.

36. Staci D. Kramer, "Prof Pursued by Mob of Bloggers," *Wired*, October 7, 2004, https:// www.wired.com/2004/10/prof-pursued-by-mob-of-bloggers/.

37. Few of the blogs posted in fall 2004 are still available online, but see, for example, Prowler, "Anatomy of a Forgery," *American Spectator*, September 10, 2004, https:// spectator.org/49622_anatomy-forgery/.

38. Corey Pein, "Blog-Gate," *Columbia Journalism Review*, January–February 2005, 30; "Letters," *Columbia Journalism Review*, March–April 2005, 5–6.

39. Cornfield et al., "Buzz, Blogs," 23–24.

40. Douglas Quenqua, "Two DC Firms Ramp Up Efforts Over Latest Presidential Controversies," *PRWeek*, U.S. ed., September 20, 2004, 1; Pein, "Blog-Gate," 32; Peter Wallsten, "GOP Activist Made Allegations on CBS Memos," *Los Angeles Times*, September 18, 2004, A18; Franke-Ruta, "Blogged Down"; Cornfield et al., "Buzz, Blogs," 22–24; Joe Hagan, "Truth or Consequences," *Texas Monthly*, May 2012, https://www.texasmonthly .com/politics/truth-or-consequences/.

41.   See, for example, Charles Johnson, "DC PR Firm Claims Credit for Rathergate," Little
       Green Footballs, September 17, 2004, http://littlegreenfootballs.com/article/12674_DC
       _PR_Firm_Claims_Credit_for_R. For a distancing from the Viguerie connection, see
       Cornfield et al., "Buzz, Blogs," 25.

42.   Mary Mapes, *Truth and Duty: The Press, the President, and the Privilege of Power* (New
       York: St. Martin's, 2005), 316.

43.   Quoted in Marlon Manuel, "Blogger Sheds No Tears for Rather," *Atlanta Journal-
       Constitution*, March 10, 2005, A1, A20.

44.   Some conservatives insisted that the birther rumors had been started by Obama's main
       Democratic rival, Hillary Clinton. But whereas some of her disappointed supporters
       had indeed circulated anonymous rumors about his citizenship during the primary sea-
       son, independent fact-checking organizations found no evidence tying the rumors to
       Clinton herself or to her campaign operation. See, for instance, Robert Farley, "Was
       Hillary Clinton the Original 'Birther'?," *Factcheck*, July 2, 2015, https://www.factcheck
       .org/2015/07/was-hillary-clinton-the-original-birther/; Jon Greenberg, "Did Hillary
       Clinton Start the Obama Birther Movement?," *Politifact*, September 23, 2015, https://
       www.politifact.com/factchecks/2015/sep/23/donald-trump/hillary-clinton-obama
       -birther-fact-check/.

45.   Trudy Lieberman, "The Vince Foster Factory and 'Courage in Journalism,'" *Columbia
       Journalism Review*, March–April 1996, 8–9; Manuel Roig-Franzia, "Inside the Spectac-
       ular Fall of the Granddaddy of Right-Wing Conspiracy Sites," *Washington Post*,
       April 2, 2019, https://www.washingtonpost.com/lifestyle/style/inside-the-spectacular
       -fall-of-the-granddaddy-of-right-wing-conspiracy-sites/2019/04/02/6ac53122-3ba6
       -11e9-a06c-3ec8ed509d15_story.html.

46.   Quoted in Barack Obama, *A Promised Land* (New York: Crown, 2020), 685.

47.   *Where's the Birth Certificate* ranked sixth on the *New York Times's* best-seller list for
       June 5, 2011, and fourteenth a week later. See Adam Berinsky, "The Birthers Are Back,"
       YouGov.com, February 3, 2012, https://today.yougov.com/topics/politics/articles-reports
       /2012/02/03/birthers-are-back. Just before the April 2011 release of the long-form cer-
       tificate, 55 percent of respondents overall believed Obama was a citizen; directly after
       it, 67 percent believed; and in January 2012, 59 percent believed. Among respondents
       identifying as Republican, those numbers were 30 percent, 47 percent, and 27 percent.

48.   Josh Pasek, Tobias H. Stark, Jon A. Krosnick, and Trevor Tompson, "What Motivates
       a Conspiracy Theory? Birther Beliefs, Partisanship, Liberal-Conservative Ideology, and
       Anti-Black Attitudes," *Electoral Studies* 40 (2015): 482–89; Stephanie Kelley-Romano
       and Kathryn L. Carew, "Make America Hate Again: Donald Trump and the Birther
       Conspiracy," *Journal of Hate Studies* 14 (2019): 33–52.

49.   Ashley Parker and Steve Eder, "Inside the Six Weeks Donald Trump Was a Nonstop
       'Birther,'" *New York Times*, July 2, 2016, https://www.nytimes.com/2016/07/03/us
       /politics/donald-trump-birther-obama.html. Trump's Twitter archive, https://www
       .thetrumparchive.com/, includes a number of tweets from 2011 and 2012 about Obama's
       "inconsistent" stories of his religious background, his possibly foreign education, and
       his alleged sympathy for the Muslim Brotherhood.

50. Quoted in Roy Rivenburg, "All the Jokes Fit to Tell," *Los Angeles Times*, May 17, 2003, E1.

51. Quoted in Calvin F. Exoo, *The Pen and the Sword: Press, War, and Terror in the 21st Century* (Los Angeles: Sage, 2010), 178 (misspelling "Corddry" as "Cordrey").

52. Pew Research Center, "Cable and Internet Loom Large in Fragmented Political News Universe," January 11, 2004, https://www.people-press.org/2004/01/11/cable-and -internet-loom-large-in-fragmented-political-news-universe/.

53. Video of Stewart's acceptance speech for the Peabody can be found at http://www .peabodyawards.com/award-profile/the-daily-show-with-jon-stewart-indecision -2000.

54. Jennings quoted in Lauren Feldman, "The News About Comedy: Young Audiences, the *Daily Show*, and Evolving Notions of Journalism," *Journalism* 8, no. 4 (2007): 419; Jon Stewart on "The *Daily Show*'s Jon Stewart," *Now with Bill Moyers*, July 11, 2003, transcript, https://billmoyers.com/content/daily-shows-jon-stewart-transcript/.

CONCLUSION: "A DEGENERATE AND PERVERTED MONSTROSITY"

1. Glen Kessler, "Trump Made 30,573 False or Misleading Claims as President," *Washington Post*, January 23, 2021, https://www.washingtonpost.com/politics/how-fact-checker -tracked-trump-claims/2021/01/23/ad04b69a-5c1d-11eb-a976-bad6431e03e2_story .html. Throughout Trump's administration, the *Post*'s "Fact Checker" column kept a running tab of his false statements.

2. Ralph Pulitzer, *The Profession of Journalism: Accuracy in the News: An Address Before the Pulitzer School of Journalism, Columbia University, New York, Delivered at Earl Hall December 16, 1912* (New York: World, 1912), 16.

3. Brian Stelter, "Sinclair's New Media-Bashing Promos Rankle Local Anchors," CNN-Business.com, March 7, 2018, https://money.cnn.com/2018/03/07/media/sinclair-broad casting-promos-media-bashing/index.html.

4. "About Us," *Ann Arbor Times*, https://annarbortimes.com/about_us; "About Us," *Des Moines Sun*, https://desmoinessun.com/about_us. See also Davey Alba and Jack Nicas, "As Local News Dies, A Pay-for-Play Network Rises in Its Place," *New York Times*, October 18, 2020 (updated October 20, 2020), https://www.nytimes.com/2020/10/18/techno logy/timpone-local-news-metric-media.html; and Priyanjana Bengani, "As Election Looms, a Network of Mysterious 'Pink Slime' Local News Outlets Nearly Triples in Size," *Columbia Journalism Review*, August 4, 2020, https://www.cjr.org/analysis/as -election-looms-a-network-of-mysterious-pink-slime-local-news-outlets-nearly-triples -in-size.php.

5. Sarah Posner, "How Donald Trump's New Campaign Chief Created an Online Haven for White Nationalists," *Mother Jones*, August 22, 2016, quoting Steve Bannon, https:// www.motherjones.com/politics/2016/08/stephen-bannon-donald-trump-alt-right -breitbart-news/; "Who Breitbart Is. . . . Really," Breitbart.com, https://media.breitbart .com/media/2019/11/about-breitbart-news.pdf.

6. Project Veritas, "About," https://www.projectveritas.com/about; Mark Mazzetti and Adam Goldman, "Erik Prince Recruits Ex-spies to Help Infiltrate Liberal Groups," *New York Times*, March 7, 2020, https://www.nytimes.com/2020/03/07/us/politics/erik-prince-project-veritas.html; see also Adam Goldman and Mark Mazzetti, "Ex-spy Was Central to Project Veritas Hiring Effort, Testimony Shows," *New York Times*, October 21, 2020, https://www.nytimes.com/2020/10/21/us/politics/project-veritas-spy.html.

7. "Who Is Alex Jones and What Is the Infowar?" Infowars.com, n.d., page archived in October 2020 at https://archives.infowars.com/about-alex-jones-show/.

8. The slogan about superior accuracy was apparently retired in the spring of 2020; for archived screenshots, see, for instance, https://web.archive.org/web/20190330081454/https://www.thegatewaypundit.com/about/, captured March 30, 2019, and https://web.archive.org/web/20200228175919/https://www.thegatewaypundit.com/, captured February 28, 2020.

9. "About Us," Daily Caller, https://dailycaller.com/about-us. Since the returns from the search for the site's use of the term *correction* and its variants did not appear in chronological order, they were presumably weighted according to popularity. So it's a rough but not irrelevant measure that is also suggestive about its readers' news judgments. (About eighteen of the one hundred items referred to the prison system or the stock market or were otherwise unrelated to errors by journalists.)

10. See, for instance, Glenn Greenwald, "The Rise of Trump Shows the Danger and Sham of Compelled Journalistic 'Neutrality,'" *Intercept*, March 14, 2016, https://theintercept.com/2016/03/14/the-rise-of-trump-shows-the-danger-and-sham-of-compelled-journalistic-neutrality/; Adrienne Russell, "Making Journalism Great Again: Trump and the New Rise of News Activism," in *Trump and the Media*, ed. Pablo J. Boczkowski and Zizi Papacharissi (Cambridge, MA: MIT Press, 2018), 203–212; and Wesley Lowery, "A Reckoning Over Objectivity, Led by Black Journalists," *New York Times*, June 23, 2020, https://www.nytimes.com/2020/06/23/opinion/objectivity-black-journalists-coronavirus.html.

11. Trump Twitter Archive, v2, https://www.thetrumparchive.com/, searching for the term *fake news* used from January 20, 2017, to January 8, 2021; John Bolton, *The Room Where It Happened: A White House Memoir* (New York: Simon and Schuster, 2020), 433.

12. In an appearance on *Meet the Press* on January 22, 2017, White House adviser Kellyanne Conway referred to "alternative facts" regarding the turnout for Trump's inauguration; for an overview, with some caveats, of a number of scholarly and journalistic studies suggesting deep partisan divides in how news consumers responded to coronavirus coverage, see Amelia Thomson-DeVeaux, "Republicans and Democrats See Covid-19 Very Differently. Is That Making People Sick?," FiveThirtyEight.com, July 23, 2020, https://fivethirtyeight.com/features/republicans-and-democrats-see-covid-19-very-differently-is-that-making-people-sick/.

13. Tom Cotton, "Send in the Troops," *New York Times*, June 3, 2020, with the editors' note added on June 5, https://www.nytimes.com/2020/06/03/opinion/tom-cotton-protests-military.html.

14. Matthew Pressman, *On Press: The Liberal Values That Shaped the News* (Cambridge, MA: Harvard University Press, 2018), 184–218; Katherine Fink and Michael Schudson, "The Rise of Contextual Journalism, 1950s–2000s," *Journalism* 15, no. 1 (2014): 3–20.

15.   David Bauder, "Riot? Insurrection? Words Matter in Describing Capitol Siege," AP News, January 14, 2021, https://apnews.com/article/donald-trump-capitol-siege-riots-media-8000ce7db2b176c1be386d945be5fd6a; Alexander Burns, "How the Democrats Planned for Doomsday," *New York Times*, January 24, 2021, https://www.nytimes.com/2021/01/24/us/politics/democrats-trump-election-plan.html. See also, for instance, Rebecca Solnit, "The Violence at the Capitol Was an Attempted Coup. Call It That," *Guardian*, January 6, 2021, https://www.theguardian.com/commentisfree/2021/jan/06/trump-mob-storm-capitol-washington-coup-attempt; and Naunihal Singh, "Was the U.S. Capitol Riot Really a Coup? Here's Why Definitions Matter," *Washington Post*, January 9, 2021, https://www.washingtonpost.com/politics/2021/01/09/was-us-capitol-riot-really-coup-heres-why-definitions-matter/.

16.   Among working journalists who have made this argument are Bill Kovach and Tom Rosenstiel in *The Elements of Journalism: What Newspeople Should Know and the Public Should Expect*, 3rd ed. (New York: Three Rivers, 2014), 101–11; Dean Baquet, interviewed in Jim Waterson, "*New York Times* Editor Says Trump Has Put His Reporters' Lives at Risk," *Guardian*, November 18, 2019, https://www.theguardian.com/media/2019/nov/18/new-york-times-editor-says-trump-has-put-his-reporters-lives-at-risk; and Marty Baron, interviewed in Isaac Chotiner, "Marty Baron Considers His Time at the *Washington Post*," *New Yorker*, February 6, 2021, https://www.newyorker.com/culture/the-new-yorker-interview/marty-baron-considers-his-time-at-the-washington-post. See also Brian McNair, "After Objectivity? Schudson's Sociology of Journalism in the Era of Post-factuality," *Journalism Studies* 18 (2017): 1318–333.

17.   Yochai Benkler, Robert Faris, and Hal Roberts, *Network Propaganda: Manipulation, Disinformation, and Radicalization in American Politics* (New York: Oxford University Press, 2018), 13; Arlie Russell Hochschild, *Strangers in Their Own Land: Anger and Mourning on the American Right* (New York: New Press, 2018), 126–27; Daniel Kreiss, "The Media Are About Identity, Not Information," in *Trump and the Media*, ed. Boczkowski and Papacharissi, 98.

18.   After Ailes resigned in 2016, network executives told a media reporter that the Fox News slogan had "been mocked" and was "too closely associated with Roger," but a spokesperson insisted that "the branding change won't affect programming or editorial decisions." See Gabriel Sherman, "Fox News Is Dropping Its 'Fair & Balanced' Slogan," *New York*, June 14, 2017, https://nymag.com/intelligencer/2017/06/fox-news-is-dropping-its-fair-and-balanced-slogan.html. An ad campaign featuring the slogan "Real News. Real Honest Opinion" debuted in 2018. See Joe Concha, "Fox News Launching New Ad Campaign: 'Real News. Real Honest Opinion,'" *The Hill*, March 12, 2018, https://thehill.com/homenews/media/377926-fox-news-launches-new-ad-campaign-real-news-real-honest-opinion. T-shirts emblazoned with the motto are currently available at the Fox News Shop.

BIBLIOGRAPHY

MANUSCRIPT COLLECTIONS AND ARCHIVES

De Quille, Dan, Papers. BANC MSS P-G 246. Bancroft Library, University of California, Berkeley.

James, E. P. H. "Reminiscences" (1963). Radio Pioneers Project, Oral History Archives. Rare Book & Manuscript Library, Columbia University, New York.

Politisches Archiv des Auswärtigen Amts. Berlin.

World (New York) Records, 1882–1940. Rare Book & Manuscript Library, Columbia University, New York.

DATABASES

Accessible Archives

America's Historical Newspapers (Readex)

Chronicling America (Library of Congress, Washington, DC)

Newspaperarchive.com

Newspapers.com

ProQuest Historical Newspapers

BOOKS, ARTICLES, DISSERTATIONS

1898 Wilmington Race Riot Commission. *1898 Wilmington Race Riot Report*. Raleigh: North Carolina Department of Cultural Resources, 2008, https://digital.ncdcr.gov/digital/collection/p249901coll22/id/5335.

Anderson, Christopher. "Journalism: Expertise, Authority, and Power in Democratic Life." In *The Media and Social Theory*, ed. David Hesmondhalgh and Jason Toynbee, 248–64. London: Routledge, 2008.

Andrews, J. Cutler. *The North Reports the Civil War*. 1955. Reprint. Pittsburgh: University of Pittsburgh Press, 1985.

——. *The South Reports the Civil War*. 1970. Reprint. Pittsburgh: University of Pittsburgh Press, 1985.

Applebaum, Anne. *Red Famine: Stalin's War on Ukraine*. London: Allen Lane, 2017.

Arthur, John. "Reporting, Practical and Theoretical." *Writer* 3 (February 1889): 36–37.

Associated Press Managing Editors. *National Credibility Roundtables: 2003 Update: Credibility in Action*. Reported and written by Carol Nunnelley. New York: Associated Press, 2003.

Atkinson, Rick. *The Day of Battle: The War in Sicily and Italy, 1943–1944*. New York: Holt, 2007.

Auerbach, Jonathan, and Russ Castronovo. "Introduction: Thirteen Propositions About Propaganda." In *The Oxford Handbook of Propaganda Studies*, ed. Jonathan Auerbach and Russ Castronovo, 1–16. Oxford: Oxford University Press, 2013.

Auletta, Ken. "Fortress Bush: Annals of Communications." *New Yorker*, January 19, 2004. https://www.newyorker.com/magazine/2004/01/19/fortress-bush.

——. "Vox Fox." *New Yorker*, May 26, 2003. https://www.newyorker.com/magazine/2003/05/26/vox-fox.

Baldasty, Gerald J. *The Commercialization of News in the Nineteenth Century*. Madison: University of Wisconsin Press, 1992.

Barnhurst, Kevin G., and John Nerone. *The Form of News: A History*. New York: Guilford, 2001.

Barnouw, Erik. *Documentary: A History of the Non-fiction Film*. 2nd ed. New York: Oxford University Press, 1993.

——. *A History of Broadcasting in the United States*. Vol. 1: *A Tower in Babel*. New York: Oxford University Press, 1966.

——. *A History of Broadcasting in the United States*. Vol. 2: *The Golden Web*. New York: Oxford University Press, 1968.

Bayley, Edwin R. *Joe McCarthy and the Press*. Madison: University of Wisconsin Press, 1981.

Benjamin, Louise M. *Freedom of the Air and the Public Interest: First Amendment Rights in Broadcasting to 1935*. Carbondale: Southern Illinois University Press, 2001.

Benkler, Yochai, Robert Faris, and Hal Roberts. *Network Propaganda: Manipulation, Disinformation, and Radicalization in American Politics*. New York: Oxford University Press, 2018.

Bennett, W. Lance, Regina G. Lawrence, and Steven Livingston. *When the Press Fails: Political Power and the News Media from Iraq to Katrina*. Chicago: University of Chicago Press, 2007.

Bent, Silas. *Ballyhoo: The Voice of the Press*. New York: Boni and Liveright, 1927.

Bernays, Edward L. *Crystallizing Public Opinion*. New York: Liveright, 1923.

——. *Propaganda*. New York: Liveright, 1928.

Bernstein, Carl. "The CIA and the Media." *Rolling Stone*, October 20, 1977. http://www.carlbernstein.com/magazine_cia_and_media.php.

Bessie, Simon Michael. *Jazz Journalism: The Story of the Tabloid Newspapers*. 1938. Reprint. New York: Russell and Russell, 1969.

Biel, Michael. "The Making and Use of Recordings in Broadcasting Before 1936." PhD diss., Northwestern University, 1977.

Billington, Ray Allen. "Maria Monk and Her Influence." *Catholic Historical Review* 22, no. 3 (1936): 283–96.

Bird, S. Elizabeth. *For Enquiring Minds: A Cultural Study of Supermarket Tabloids.* Knoxville: University of Tennessee Press, 1992.

Bird, Wendell. *Criminal Dissent: Prosecutions Under the Alien and Sedition Acts of 1798.* Cambridge, MA: Harvard University Press, 2020.

Bissinger, Buzz. "Shattered Glass." *Vanity Fair,* September 1998, posted online September 5, 2007. https://www.vanityfair.com/magazine/1998/09/bissinger199809.

Bitzer, G. W. *Billy Bitzer: His Story.* New York: Farrar, Straus and Giroux, 1973.

Bolton, John. *The Room Where It Happened: A White House Memoir.* New York: Simon and Schuster, 2020.

Botein, Stephen. "'Meer Mechanics' and an Open Press: The Business and Political Strategies of Colonial American Printers." *Perspectives in American History* 9 (1975): 127–225.

——. "Printers and the American Revolution." In *The Press and the American Revolution,* ed. Bernard Bailyn and John B. Hench, 11–57. Boston: Northeastern University Press, 1980.

Bottomore, Stephen. "Filming, Faking, and Propaganda: The Origins of the War Film, 1897–1902." PhD diss., Utrecht University, 2007. https://dspace.library.uu.nl/bitstream/handle/1874/22650/?sequence=6.

——. "The Panicking Audience? Early Cinema and the 'Train Effect.'" *Historical Journal of Film, Radio, and Television* 19, no. 2 (1999): 177–216.

Boylan, James. "Declarations of Independence." *Columbia Journalism Review,* November–December 1986, 30–45.

——. *Pulitzer's School: Columbia University's School of Journalism, 1903–2003.* New York: Columbia University Press, 2003.

Brewer, Susan A. *Why America Fights: Patriotism and War Propaganda from the Philippines to Iraq.* Oxford: Oxford University Press, 2009.

Brill, Steven. "Pressgate." *Brill's Content,* July–August 1998, 122–51.

Brinkley, Alan. *Voices of Protest: Huey Long, Father Coughlin, and the Great Depression.* New York: Vintage, 1982.

Brock, David. *Blinded by the Right: The Conscience of an Ex-conservative.* New York: Crown, 2002.

——. "Confessions of a Right-Wing Hit Man." *Esquire,* July 1997, 52–57.

——. "The Fire This Time." *Esquire,* April 1998, 60–64.

Brokenshire, Norman. *This Is Norman Brokenshire: An Unvarnished Self Portrait.* New York: David McKay, 1954.

Brown, Carolyn S. *The Tall Tale in American Folklore and Literature.* Knoxville: University of Tennessee Press, 1987.

Brown, Charles H. *The Correspondents' War: Journalists in the Spanish-American War.* New York: Scribner's, 1967.

Brown, James A. "Selling Airtime for Controversy: NAB Self-Regulation and Father Coughlin." *Journal of Broadcasting* 24 (1980): 199–224.

Brown, Robert J. *Manipulating the Ether: The Power of Broadcast Radio in Thirties America.* Jefferson, NC: McFarland, 1998.

Browne, Junius Henri. *Four Years in Secessia: Adventures Within and Beyond the Union Lines.* Hartford, CT: O. D. Case, 1865.

Caldwell, Louis G. "Freedom of Speech and Radio Broadcasting." *Annals of the American Academy of Political and Social Science* 177 (1935): 179–207.

Campbell-Copeland, T. *The Ladder of Journalism: How to Climb It.* New York: Forman, 1889.

Carey, James W. "The Press, Public Opinion, and Public Discourse." In *Public Opinion and the Communication of Consent,* ed. Theodore L. Glasser and Charles T. Salmon, 373–402. New York: Guilford, 1995.

Carlson, Matt. "Gone, but Not Forgotten: Memories of Journalistic Deviance as Metajournalistic Discourse." *Journalism Studies* 15, no. 1 (2014): 33–47.

——. *Journalistic Authority: Legitimating News in the Digital Era.* New York: Columbia University Press, 2017.

——. "Metajournalistic Discourse and the Meanings of Journalism: Definitional Control, Boundary Work, and Legitimation." *Communication Theory* 26 (2016): 349–68.

Casey, Steven. *The War Beat, Europe: The American Media at War Against Nazi Germany.* New York: Oxford University Press, 2017.

Cater, Douglass. "The Captive Press." *Reporter* 2 (June 6, 1950): 17–20.

Chernow, Ron. *Alexander Hamilton.* New York: Penguin, 2004.

Chesnut, Mary. *Mary Chesnut's Civil War.* Ed. C. Vann Woodward. New Haven, CT: Yale University Press, 1981.

Chicago Commission on Race Relations. *The Negro in Chicago: A Study of Race Relations and a Race Riot.* Chicago: University of Chicago Press, 1922.

Clark, Charles E. *The Public Prints: The Newspaper in Anglo-American Culture, 1665–1740.* New York: Oxford University Press, 1994.

Cogan, Jacob Katz. "The Reynolds Affair and the Politics of Character." *Journal of the Early Republic* 16 (Autumn 1996): 389–417.

Columbia Journalism Review. "Poll: How Does the Public Think Journalism Happens?" Winter 2019. https://www.cjr.org/special_report/how-does-journalism-happen-poll.php.

Committee on Alleged German Outrages. *Report of the Committee . . . Appointed by His Britannic Majesty's Government and Presided Over by the Right Hon. Viscount Bryce.* London: His Majesty's Stationery Office, 1915.

Conason, Joe, and Gene Lyons. *The Hunting of the President: The Ten-Year Campaign to Destroy Bill and Hillary Clinton.* New York: St. Martin's, 2000.

Conforti, Joseph A. *Lizzie Borden on Trial: Murder, Ethnicity, and Gender.* Lawrence: University Press of Kansas, 2015.

Conniff, Kimberly. "All the Views Fit to Print." *Brill's Content,* March 2001, 105–7, 152–55.

Copeland, David A. *The Idea of a Free Press: The Enlightenment and Its Unruly Legacy.* Evanston, IL: Northwestern University Press, 2006.

Cotts, Cynthia. "Libel Bible." *Village Voice,* February 9, 1999. https://www.villagevoice.com/1999/02/09/libel-bible/.

Creel, George. *How We Advertised America: The First Telling of the Amazing Story of the Committee on Public Information That Carried the Gospel of Americanism to Every Corner of the Globe.* New York: Harper & Brothers, 1920.

Croy, Homer. *How Motion Pictures Are Made.* New York: Harper, 1918.

Crozier, Emmet. *American Reporters on the Western Front 1914–18.* New York: Oxford University Press, 1959.

Czitrom, Daniel J. *Media and the American Mind from Morse to McLuhan.* Chapel Hill: University of North Carolina Press, 1982.

Daniel, Marcus. *Scandal and Civility: Journalism and the Birth of American Democracy.* Oxford: Oxford University Press, 2009.

Daniels, Josephus. *Editor in Politics.* Chapel Hill: University of North Carolina Press, 1941.

Darnton, Robert. *The Forbidden Best-Sellers of Pre-revolutionary France.* London: Fontana, 1997.

Davis, Oscar King. *Released for Publication: Some Inside Political History of Theodore Roosevelt and His Times.* Boston: Houghton Mifflin; Cambridge: Riverside, 1925.

Dewey, Donald. *Buccaneer: James Stuart Blackton and the Birth of American Movies.* Lanham, MD: Rowman and Littlefield, 2016.

Dicken-Garcia, Hazel. *Journalistic Standards in Nineteenth-Century America.* Madison: University of Wisconsin Press, 1989.

Dickinson, Tim. "How Roger Ailes Built the Fox News Fear Factory." *Rolling Stone,* May 25, 2011. https://www.rollingstone.com/politics/politics-news/how-roger-ailes-built-the-fox-news-fear-factory-244652/.

Douglas, Susan J. "Does Textual Analysis Tell Us Anything About Past Audiences?" In *Explorations in Communication and History,* ed. Barbie Zelizer, 66–76. London: Routledge, 2008.

——. *Inventing American Broadcasting 1899–1922.* Baltimore: Johns Hopkins University Press, 1987.

——. *Listening in: Radio and the American Imagination, from Amos 'n' Andy and Edward R. Murrow to Wolfman Jack and Howard Stern.* New York: Random House, 1999.

Downey, Elizabeth A. "A Historical Survey of the International Regulation of Propaganda." *Michigan Yearbook of International Legal Studies* 5, no. 1 (1984): 341–60.

Dreiser, Theodore. *Newspaper Days: An Autobiography.* Ed. T. D. Nostwich. Santa Rosa, CA: Black Sparrow Press, 2000.

Durey, Michael. *"With the Hammer of Truth": James Thomson Callender and America's Early National Heroes.* Charlottesville: University Press of Virginia, 1990.

Eason, David L. "On Journalistic Authority: The Janet Cooke Scandal." *Critical Studies in Mass Communication* 3 (1986): 429–47.

Exoo, Calvin F. *The Pen and the Sword: Press, War, and Terror in the 21st Century.* Los Angeles: Sage, 2010.

Ezra, Elizabeth. *Georges Méliès: The Birth of the Auteur.* Manchester, U.K.: Manchester University Press, 2000.

Fang, Irving E. *Those Radio Commentators!* Ames: Iowa State University Press, 1977.

Feldman, Lauren. "The News About Comedy: Young Audiences, the *Daily Show,* and Evolving Notions of Journalism." *Journalism* 8, no. 4 (2007): 406–27.

Ferrari, Michelle, comp. *Reporting America at War: An Oral History.* With commentary by James Tobin. New York: Hyperion, 2003.

Ferris, John. *The Winds of Barclay Street: The Amusing Life and Sad Demise of the* New York World-Telegram and Sun. Bloomington, IN: Author House, 2013.

Fielding, Raymond. *The American Newsreel: A Complete History, 1911–1967.* 2nd ed. Jefferson, NC: McFarland, 2006.

Fineman, Mia. *Faking It: Manipulated Photography Before Photoshop.* New York: Metropolitan Museum, 2012.

Fink, Katherine, and Michael Schudson. "The Rise of Contextual Journalism, 1950s–2000s." *Journalism* 15, no. 1 (2014): 3–20.

Forde, Kathy Roberts, and Sid Bedingfield, eds. *Journalism and Jim Crow: White Supremacy and the Black Struggle for a New America.* Champaign: University of Illinois Press, 2021.

Forde, Kathy Roberts, and Katherine A. Foss. "'The Facts—the Color!—the Facts': The Idea of a Report in American Print Culture, 1885–1910." *Book History* 15 (2012): 123–51.

Fraser, Antonia. *Love and Louis XIV: The Women in the Life of the Sun King.* New York: Doubleday, 2006.

Frassanito, William A. *Gettysburg: A Journey in Time.* New York: Scribner's, 1975.

Gallagher, Hugh Gregory. *FDR's Splendid Deception.* New York: Dodd, Mead, 1985.

Gamache, Ray. "Breaking Eggs for a Holodomor: Walter Duranty, the *New York Times*, and the Denigration of Gareth Jones." *Journalism History* 39, no. 4 (Winter 2014): 208–18.

Gauger, Michael. "Flickering Images: Live Television Coverage and Viewership of the Army–McCarthy Hearings." *Historian* 67, no. 4 (Winter 2005): 678–93.

Gauvreau, Emile. *Hot News.* New York: Macaulay, 1931.

Giddings, Paula. *Ida, a Sword Among Lions: Ida B. Wells and the Campaign Against Lynching.* New York: Harper Collins, 2008.

Goodman, David. "Before Hate Speech: Charles Coughlin, Free Speech, and Listeners' Rights." *Patterns of Prejudice* 49, no. 3 (2015): 199–224.

Gormley, Ken. *The Death of American Virtue: Clinton vs. Starr.* New York: Crown, 2010.

Greenberg, David. *Republic of Spin: An Inside Story of the American Presidency.* New York: Norton, 2016.

Griffin, Michael. "The Great War Photographs: Constructing Myths of History and Photojournalism." In *Picturing the Past: Media, History, and Photography*, ed. Bonnie Brennen and Hanno Hardt, 122–57. Urbana: University of Illinois Press, 1999.

Grossman, James. "Blowing the Trumpet: The *Chicago Defender* and Black Migration During World War I." *Illinois Historical Journal* 78, no. 2 (1985): 82–96.

Gunning, Tom. "An Aesthetic of Astonishment: Early Film and the (In)Credulous Spectator." In *Film Theory and Criticism: Introductory Readings*, 7th ed., ed. Leo Braudy and Marshall Cohen, 736–50. New York: Oxford University Press, 2009.

Gup, Ted. "Eye of the Storm: Why Jeff Gerth, a Most Accomplished Investigator, Is Also Most Controversial." *Columbia Journalism Review*, May–June 2001, 32–38.

Hackett, Bruce, and Lauren Lutzenhiser. "The Unity of Self and Object." *Western Folklore* 44 (1985): 317–24.

Hagan, Joe. "Truth or Consequences." *Texas Monthly*, May 2012. https://www.texasmonthly.com/politics/truth-or-consequences/.

Hale, William Harlan. "Adventures of a Document: The Strange Sequel to the Kaiser Interview." *Atlantic Monthly*, June 1934, 696–705.

———. "Thus Spoke the Kaiser: The Lost Interview Which Solves an International Mystery." *Atlantic Monthly*, May 1934, 513–23.

Hallin, Daniel C. "The Passing of the 'High Modernism' of American Journalism." *Journal of Communication* 42 (Summer 1992): 14–25.

———. *The "Uncensored War": The Media and Vietnam*. Berkeley: University of California Press, 1989.

Halttunen, Karen. *Confidence Men and Painted Women: A Study of Middle-Class Culture in America, 1830–1870*. New Haven, CT: Yale University Press, 1982.

Hamilton, John Maxwell. *Manipulating the Masses: Woodrow Wilson and the Birth of American Propaganda*. Baton Rouge: Louisiana State University Press, 2020.

Hamilton, Milton W. *The Country Printer: New York State, 1785–1830*. 2nd ed. Port Washington, NY: Ira J. Friedman, 1964.

Hanson, Christopher. "All the News That Fits the Myth." *Columbia Journalism Review*, January–February 2001, 50–53.

Harlow, Alvin F. *Old Wires and New Waves: The History of the Telegraph, Telephone, and Wireless*. New York: Appleton-Century, 1936.

Harris, Neil. *Humbug: The Art of P. T. Barnum*. Chicago: University of Chicago Press, 1973.

———. "Iconography and Intellectual History: The Halftone Effect." In *Cultural Excursions: Marketing Appetites and Cultural Tastes in Modern America*, 304–17. Chicago: University of Chicago Press, 1990.

Hecht, Ben. *A Child of the Century*. 1954. Reprint. New York: Primus, 1985.

Hemment, John C. *Cannon and Camera: Sea and Land Battles of the Spanish-American War in Cuba, Camp Life, and the Return of the Soldiers*. New York: Appleton, 1898.

Henkin, David M. *City Reading: Written Words and Public Spaces in Antebellum New York*. New York: Columbia University Press, 1998.

Henry, Neil. *American Carnival: Journalism Under Siege in an Age of New Media*. Berkeley: University of California Press, 2007.

Hersey, John. "The Legend on the License." *Yale Review* 70 (Autumn 1980): 1–25.

Hickey, Neil. "Is Fox News Fair?" *Columbia Journalism Review*, March–April 1998, 30–35.

Hilgartner, Stephen, and Charles L. Bosk. "The Rise and Fall of Social Problems: A Public Arenas Model." *American Journal of Sociology* 94, no. 1 (July 1988): 53–78.

Hill, A. F. *Secrets of the Sanctum: An Inside View of an Editor's Life*. Philadelphia: Claxton, Remsen, and Haffelfinger, 1875.

Hills, William H. "Advice to Newspaper Correspondents III: Some Hints on Style." *Writer* 1 (June 1887): 49–51.

———. "Advice to Newspaper Correspondents IV: 'Faking.'" *Writer* 1 (November 1887): 154–56.

Hochschild, Arlie Russell. *Strangers in Their Own Land: Anger and Mourning on the American Right*. New York: New Press, 2018.

Hofstadter, Richard. *The Age of Reform from Bryan to F.D.R.* New York: Vintage, 1955.

———. "The Paranoid Style in American Politics." *Harper's*, November 1964, 77–86.

Hughes, Helen MacGill. *News and the Human Interest Story*. 1940. Reprint. New Brunswick, NJ: Transaction, 1981.

Institute for Propaganda Analysis. *The Fine Art of Propaganda: A Study of Father Coughlin's Speeches.* Ed. Alfred McClung Lee and Elizabeth Briant Lee. New York: Harcourt, Brace, 1939.

Irwin, Will. *The Making of a Reporter.* New York: Putnam, 1942.

Isikoff, Michael, and David Corn. *Hubris: The Inside Story of Spin, Scandal, and the Selling of the Iraq War.* New York: Three Rivers Press, 2007.

Jacobs, Lawrence R., and Robert Y. Shapiro. "Presidential Manipulation of Polls and Public Opinion: The Nixon Administration and the Pollsters." *Political Science Quarterly* 110, no. 4 (Winter 1995–1996): 519–38.

Jansen, Sue Curry. "Semantic Tyranny: How Edward L. Bernays Stole Walter Lippmann's Mojo and Got Away with It and Why It Still Matters." *International Journal of Communication* 7 (2013): 1094–111.

——. "'The World's Greatest Adventure in Advertising': Walter Lippmann's Critique of Censorship and Propaganda." In *The Oxford Handbook of Propaganda Studies,* ed. Jonathan Auerbach and Russ Castronovo, 301–25. New York: Oxford University Press, 2013.

Johnson, Haynes. *The Age of Anxiety: McCarthyism to Terrorism.* Orlando, FL: Harcourt, 2005.

Johnson, Robert Underwood. *Remembered Yesterdays.* Boston: Little, Brown, 1923.

Kaplan, Louis. *The Strange Case of William Mumler, Spirit Photographer.* Minneapolis: University of Minnesota Press, 2008.

Karlsson, Michael, Christer Clerwall, and Lars Nord. "Do Not Stand Corrected: Transparency and Users' Attitudes to Inaccurate News and Corrections in Online Journalism." *Journalism & Mass Communication Quarterly* 94, no. 1 (2017): 148–67.

Keller, Ulrich. "Photojournalism Around 1900: The Institutionalization of a Mass Medium." In *Shadow and Substance: Essays on the History of Photography in Honor of Heinz K. Henisch,* ed. Kathleen Collins, 283–303. Bloomfield Hills, MI: Amorphous Institute Press, 1990.

Kelley-Romano, Stephanie, and Kathryn L. Carew. "Make America Hate Again: Donald Trump and the Birther Conspiracy." *Journal of Hate Studies* 14 (2019): 33–52.

Kielbowicz, Richard B. "Newsgathering by Printers' Exchanges Before the Telegraph." *Journalism History* 9, no. 2 (Summer 1982): 42–48.

Kluger, Richard. *The Paper: The Life and Death of the "New York Herald Tribune."* New York: Knopf, 1986.

Knightley, Phillip. *The First Casualty: The War Correspondent as Hero and Myth-Maker from the Crimea to Kosovo.* Rev. ed. Baltimore: Johns Hopkins University Press, 2000.

Knox, Thomas W. *Camp-Fire and Cotton-Field: Southern Adventure in Time of War, Life with the Union Armies, and Residence on a Louisiana Plantation.* New York: Blelock, 1865.

Kovach, Bill, and Tom Rosenstiel. *The Elements of Journalism: What Newspeople Should Know and the Public Should Expect.* 3rd ed. New York: Three Rivers, 2014.

Kracauer, Siegfried. "Cult of Distraction: On Berlin's Picture Palaces." Trans. and ed. Thomas Y. Levin. *New German Critique* 40 (Winter 1987): 91–96.

Kreiss, Daniel. "The Media Are About Identity, Not Information." In *Trump and the Media,* ed. Pablo J. Boczkowski and Zizi Papacharissi, 93–100. Cambridge, MA: MIT Press, 2018.

Kunstler, William M. *The Hall–Mills Murder Case: The Minister and the Choir Singer.* New Brunswick, NJ: Rutgers University Press, 1964.

Layton, Charles. "Miller Brouhaha." *American Journalism Review*, August–September 2003, 30–35.

Lewin, Leonard C. "Is Fact Necessary?" *Columbia Journalism Review*, Winter 1966, 29–34.

Lieberman, Trudy. "Churning Whitewater." *Columbia Journalism Review*, May–June 1994, 26–30.

——. "The Vince Foster Factory and 'Courage in Journalism.'" *Columbia Journalism Review*, March–April 1996, 8–9.

Lippmann, Walter. *Liberty and the News*. New York: Harcourt, Brace and Howe, 1920.

Lippmann, Walter, and Charles Merz. "A Test of the News: An Examination of the News Reports in the *New York Times* on Aspects of the Russian Revolution of Special Importance to Americans, March 1917–March 1920." *New Republic*, supplement, August 4, 1920.

Lipstadt, Deborah E. *Beyond Belief: The American Press and the Coming of the Holocaust 1933–1945*. New York: Free Press, 1986.

Loiperdinger, Martin. "Lumière's 'Arrival of the Train': Cinema's Founding Myth." *Moving Image* 4 (Spring 2004): 89–118.

Loomis, C. Grant. "The Tall Tales of Dan De Quille." *California Folklore Quarterly* 5, no. 1 (January 1946): 26–71.

Lowry, Bates, and Isabel Lowry. "Simultaneous Developments: Documentary Photography and Painless Surgery." In *Young America: The Daguerreotypes of Southworth and Hawes*, ed. Grant B. Romer and Brian Wallis, 75–88. New York: International Center of Photography, 2005.

Lyons, Gene. *Fools for Scandal: How the Media Invented Whitewater*. New York: Franklin Square Press, 1996.

MacLeish, Archibald. *A Time to Act: Selected Addresses*. Boston: Houghton Mifflin, 1943.

Maechler, Stefan. *The Wilkomirski Affair: A Study in Biographical Truth*. Trans. John E. Woods. New York: Schocken Books, 2001.

Maier, Scott R. "Setting the Record Straight." *Journalism Practice* 1, no. 1 (2007): 33–43.

Mallen, Frank. *Sauce for the Gander*. White Plains, NY: Baldwin Books, 1954.

Mapes, Mary. *Truth and Duty: The Press, the President, and the Privilege of Power*. New York: St. Martin's, 2005.

Marlin, Randal. *Propaganda and the Ethics of Persuasion*. Peterborough, Canada: Broadview, 2002.

Martyn, Peter H. "Lynch Mob: Pack Journalism and How the Jessica Lynch Story Became Propaganda." *Canadian Journal of Media Studies* 4, no. 1 (November 2008): 124–64.

Massing, Michael. *Now They Tell Us: The American Press and Iraq*. Preface by Orville Schell. New York: New York Review of Books, 2004.

Matthews, Albert. "The Snake Devices, 1754–1776, and the *Constitutional Courant*, 1765." *Transactions of the Colonial Society of Massachusetts* 11 (1906–1907): 421–46.

Mayer, Jane. *Dark Money: The Hidden History of the Billionaires Behind the Rise of the Radical Right*. New York: Doubleday, 2016.

McClintick, David. "Town Crier for the New Age." *Brill's Content*, November 1998, 112–27.

McNair, Brian. "After Objectivity? Schudson's Sociology of Journalism in the Era of Post-factuality." *Journalism Studies* 18 (2017): 1318–333.

Menning, Ralph R., and Carol Bresnahan Menning. "'Baseless Allegations': Wilhelm II and the Hale Interview of 1908." *Central European History* 16, no. 4 (December 1983): 368–97.

Michaeli, Ethan. *The Defender: How the Legendary Black Newspaper Changed America, from the Age of the Pullman Porters to the Age of Obama.* Boston: Houghton Mifflin Harcourt, 2016.

Miller, Bonnie M. *From Liberation to Conquest: The Visual and Popular Cultures of the Spanish-American War of 1898.* Amherst: University of Massachusetts Press, 2011.

Miller, Merle. *Ike the Soldier: As They Knew Him.* New York: Putnam, 1987.

Mitchell, Greg. *The Campaign of the Century: Upton Sinclair's Race for Governor of California and the Birth of Media Politics.* New York: Random House, 1992.

Molina, Maria D., S. Shyam Sundar, Thai Le, and Dongwon Lee. "Fake News Is Not Simply False Information: A Concept Explication and Taxonomy of Online Content." *American Behavioral Scientist*, October 2019. doi:10.1177/0002764219878224.

Monk, Maria. *Awful Disclosures, by Maria Monk, of the Hotel Dieu Nunnery of Montreal, Revised, with an Appendix . . . Also, a Supplement. . . .* New York: Maria Monk, 1836.

Morris, Errol. *Believing Is Seeing (Observations on the Mysteries of Photography).* New York: Penguin, 2011.

Morris, James McGrath. *Pulitzer: A Life in Politics, Print, and Power.* New York: Harper, 2010.

Morris, Jonathan S. "The Fox News Factor." *International Journal of Press/Politics* 10, no. 3 (2005): 56–79.

Mott, Frank Luther. *American Journalism, a History: 1690–1960.* 3rd ed. New York: Macmillan, 1962.

Musser, Charles. "American Vitagraph: 1897–1901." *Cinema Journal* 22, no. 3 (Spring 1983): 4–46.

——. "The Eden Musee in 1898: The Exhibitor as Creator." *Film & History* 11, no. 4 (December 1981): 73–96.

——. *The Emergence of Cinema: The American Screen to 1907.* New York: Scribner's, 1990.

Nasaw, David. *The Chief: The Life of William Randolph Hearst.* Boston: Houghton Mifflin, 2000.

——. *Going Out: The Rise and Fall of Public Amusements.* New York: Basic, 1993.

National News Council. "Report." *Columbia Journalism Review*, September–October 1981, 76–87.

Neander, Joachim. *The German Corpse Factory: The Master Hoax of British Propaganda in the First World War.* Saarbrücken, Germany: Saarland University Press, 2013.

Nerone, John. "History, Journalism, and the Problem of Truth." In *Assessing Evidence in a Postmodern World*, ed. Bonnie Brennen, 11–29. Milwaukee: Marquette University Press, 2013.

——. *The Media and Public Life: A History.* Cambridge: Polity, 2015.

Newfield, Jack. "Is There a New Journalism?" In *The Reporter as Artist: A Look at the New Journalism Controversy*, ed. Ronald Weber, 299–304. New York: Hastings House, 1974.

Nilsson, Nils Gunnar. "The Origin of the Interview." *Journalism Quarterly* 48 (1971): 707–13.

Nord, David Paul. "Accuracy or Fair Play? Complaining About the Newspaper in Early Twentieth-Century New York." In *New Directions in American Reception Study*, ed. Philip Goldstein and James L. Machor, 233–53. Oxford: Oxford University Press, 2008.

Nyhan, Brendan, and Jason Reifler. "When Corrections Fail: The Persistence of Political Misperceptions." *Political Behavior* 32 (2010): 303–30.

Nyhan, Brendan, Jason Reifler, and Peter A. Ubel. "The Hazards of Correcting Myths About Health Care Reform." *Medical Care* 51 (2013): 127–32.

Obama, Barack. *A Promised Land*. New York: Crown, 2020.

O'Connor, Richard. *Heywood Broun: A Biography*. New York: Putnam, 1975.

Orbison, Charley. "'Fighting Bob' Shuler: Early Radio Crusader." *Journal of Broadcasting* 21, no. 4 (1977): 459–72.

Orvell, Miles. *The Real Thing: Imitation and Authenticity in American Culture, 1880–1940*. Chapel Hill: University of North Carolina Press, 1989.

Orwell, George. *Orwell in "Tribune": "As I Please" and Other Writings 1943-7*. Comp. and ed. Paul Anderson. London: Politico's, 2006.

Oshinsky, David M. *A Conspiracy so Immense: The World of Joe McCarthy*. New York: Free Press, 1983.

Ottley, Roi. *The Lonely Warrior: The Life and Times of Robert S. Abbott*. Washington, DC: Regnery, 1955.

Paltsits, Victor Hugo. "New Light on 'Publick Occurrences': America's First Newspaper." *Proceedings of the American Antiquarian Society* 59 (1949): 75–88.

Pasek, Josh, Tobias H. Stark, Jon A. Krosnick, and Trevor Tompson. "What Motivates a Conspiracy Theory? Birther Beliefs, Partisanship, Liberal-Conservative Ideology, and Anti-Black Attitudes." *Electoral Studies* 40 (2015): 482–89.

Patterson, Maggie Jones, and Steve Urbanski. "What Jayson Blair and Janet Cooke Say About the Press and the Erosion of Public Trust." *Journalism Studies* 7, no. 6 (2006): 828–50.

Peck, Reece. *Fox Populism: Branding Conservatism as Working Class*. Cambridge: Cambridge University Press, 2019.

Pein, Corey. "Blog-Gate." *Columbia Journalism Review*, January–February 2005, 30–35.

Pickard, Victor. "The Strange Life and Death of the Fairness Doctrine: Tracing the Decline of Positive Freedoms in American Policy Discourse." *International Journal of Communication* 12 (2018): 3434–453.

Pizzitola, Louis. *Hearst Over Hollywood: Power, Passion, and Propaganda in the Movies*. New York: Columbia University Press, 2002.

Plimpton, George. "Truman Capote: An Interview" (1966). In *The Reporter as Artist: A Look at the New Journalism Controversy*, ed. Ronald Weber, 188–206. New York: Hastings House, 1974.

Pooley, Jefferson D., and Michael J. Socolow. "Checking Up on *The Invasion from Mars*: Hadley Cantril, Paul F. Lazarsfeld, and the Making of a Misremembered Classic." *International Journal of Communication* 7 (2013): 1919–947.

Pope, Daniel. *The Making of Modern Advertising*. New York: Basic, 1983.

Porter, Edwin H. *The Fall River Tragedy: A History of the Borden Murders*. Fall River, MA: Buffinton, 1893.

Prather, H. Leon, Sr. *We Have Taken a City: Wilmington Racial Massacre and Coup of 1898*. Rutherford, NJ: Fairleigh Dickinson University Press, 1984.

Pressman, Matthew. *On Press: The Liberal Values That Shaped the News*. Cambridge, MA: Harvard University Press, 2018.

Prince, Stephen. *Firestorm: American Film in the Age of Terrorism*. New York: Columbia University Press, 2009.

Pulitzer, Ralph. *The Profession of Journalism: Accuracy in the News: An Address Before the Pulitzer School of Journalism, Columbia University, New York, Delivered at Earl Hall December 16, 1912.* New York: World, 1912.

Putnis, Peter. "SHARE 999: British Government Control of Reuters During World War I." *Media History* 14, no. 2 (2008): 141–65.

Remini, Robert V. *Henry Clay: Statesman for the Union.* New York: Norton, 1991.

Reynolds, David. *The Long Shadow: The Legacies of the Great War in the Twentieth Century.* New York: Norton, 2014.

Rich, Frank. *The Greatest Story Ever Sold: The Decline and Fall of Truth from 9/11 to Katrina.* New York: Penguin, 2006.

Richardson, Albert D. *The Secret Service, the Field, the Dungeon, and the Escape.* Hartford, CT: American, 1865.

Risse, Guenter B. *Plague, Fear, and Politics in San Francisco's Chinatown.* Baltimore: Johns Hopkins University Press, 2012.

Ritea, Steve. "Free Press." *American Journalism Review,* August–September 2003, 10–11.

Roberts, James L., II. "The Roorback Hoax: A Curious Incident in the Election of 1844." *Annotations* 30, no. 3 (September 2002): 16–17.

Roberts, Gene, and Hank Klibanoff. *The Race Beat: The Press, the Civil Rights Struggle, and the Awakening of a Nation.* New York: Knopf, 2006.

Robertson, Michael. *Stephen Crane, Journalism, and the Making of Modern American Literature.* New York: Columbia University Press, 1997.

Roeder, George H., Jr. *The Censored War: American Visual Experience During World War Two.* New Haven, CT: Yale University Press, 1993.

Ross, Stewart Halsey. *Propaganda for War: How the United States Was Conditioned to Fight the Great War of 1914–1918.* Jefferson, NC: McFarland, 1996.

Rothmyer, Karen. "Citizen Scaife." *Columbia Journalism Review,* July–August 1981, 41–50.

——. "Unindicted Co-conspirator?" *Nation,* February 23, 1998, 19–24.

Rowlands, Guy, and Julia Prest. Introduction to *The Third Reign of Louis XIV c. 1682–1715,* ed. Julia Prest and Guy Rowlands, 1–23. London: Routledge, 2017.

Russell, Adrienne. "Making Journalism Great Again: Trump and the New Rise of News Activism." In *Trump and the Media,* ed. Pablo J. Boczkowski and Zizi Papacharissi, 203–12. Cambridge, MA: MIT Press, 2018.

Safire, William. *Before the Fall: An Inside View of the Pre-Watergate White House.* 1975. Reprint. New York: Routledge, 2017.

Sager, Mike. "The Fabulist Who Changed Journalism." *Columbia Journalism Review,* Spring 2016. https://www.cjr.org/the_feature/the_fabulist_who_changed_journalism.php.

Salisbury, Harrison E. *Without Fear or Favor: An Uncompromising Look at the* New York Times. New York: Ballantine, 1980.

Saunders, Frances Stonor. *The Cultural Cold War: The CIA and the World of Arts and Letters.* New York: New Press, 1999.

Schiffrin, Anya. "Fighting Disinformation with Media Literacy—in 1939." *Columbia Journalism Review,* October 10, 2018. https://www.cjr.org/innovations/institute-propaganda-analysis.php.

Schivelbusch, Wolfgang. *The Culture of Defeat: On National Trauma, Mourning, and Recovery.* Trans. Jefferson Chase. New York: Picador, 2004.

Schudson, Michael. *Discovering the News: A Social History of American Newspapers.* New York: Basic, 1978.

——. "Is Journalism a Profession? Objectivity 1.0, Objectivity 2.0, and Beyond." In *Why Journalism Still Matters,* 41–67. Cambridge: Polity, 2018.

——. "Question Authority: A History of the News Interview." In *The Power of News,* 72–93. Cambridge, MA: Harvard University Press, 1995.

Schwartz, A. Brad. *Broadcast Hysteria: Orson Welles's "War of the Worlds" and the Art of Fake News.* New York: Hill and Wang, 2015.

Seelye, John. *War Games: Richard Harding Davis and the New Journalism.* Amherst: University of Massachusetts Press, 2003.

Seitz, Don. C. *Joseph Pulitzer: His Life and Letters.* New York: Simon and Schuster, 1924.

Sevareid, Eric. *Not so Wild a Dream; with a New Introduction by the Author.* 1946. Reprint, New York: Atheneum, 1979.

Shapiro, Ivor. "Why They Lie: Probing the Explanations for Journalistic Cheating." *Canadian Journal of Communication* 31 (2006): 261–66.

Shattuck, H. R. (Harriette Robinson). "Reporters' Ethics." *Writer* 3 (March 1889): 57–58.

Shepard, Alicia C. "How They Blew It." *American Journalism Review,* January–February 2001, 20–27.

Sherman, Gabriel. *The Loudest Voice in the Room: How the Brilliant, Bombastic Roger Ailes Built Fox News—and Divided a Country.* New York: Random House, 2014.

Sherover, Max. *Fakes in American Journalism.* Buffalo, NY: Buffalo Publishing, 1914.

Shi, David E. *Facing Facts: Realism in American Thought and Culture, 1850–1920.* New York: Oxford University Press, 1995.

Shirer, William L. *20th Century Journey: A Memoir of a Life and the Times.* Vol. 2: *The Nightmare Years: 1930–1940.* New York: Little Brown, 1984.

Shuman, Edwin L. *Steps Into Journalism: Helps and Hints for Young Writers.* Evanston, IL: Evanston Press, 1894.

Sloan, William David. "Chaos, Polemics, and America's First Newspaper." *Journalism Quarterly* 70 (1993): 666–81.

Smith, Albert E., with Phil A. Koury. *Two Reels and a Crank.* Garden City, NY: Doubleday, 1952.

Smith, Jeffery A. *War and Press Freedom: The Problem of Prerogative Power.* New York: Oxford University Press, 1999.

Smith, Richard Norton. *The Colonel: The Life and Legend of Robert T. McCormick, 1880–1955.* Boston: Houghton Mifflin, 1997.

Smith, Sally Bedell. *In All His Glory: The Life and Times of William S. Paley, the Legendary Tycoon and His Brilliant Circle.* New York: Touchstone, 1991.

Smith-Pryor, Elizabeth M. *Property Rites: The Rhinelander Trial, Passing, and the Protection of Whiteness.* Chapel Hill: University of North Carolina Press, 2009.

Snyder, Robert L. *Pare Lorentz and the Documentary Film.* Reno: University of Nevada Press, 1994.

Socolow, Michael J. "The Hyped Panic Over 'War of the Worlds.'" *Chronicle of Higher Education*, October 24, 2008, 816–17.

Spencer, David R. *The Yellow Journalism: The Press and America's Emergence as a World Power.* Evanston, IL: Northwestern University Press, 2007.

Starr, Paul. *The Creation of the Media: Political Origins of Modern Communications.* New York: Basic, 2004.

Stead, W. T. *The Americanization of the World; Or, The Trend of the Twentieth Century.* New York: Horace Markley, [1902].

Steffens, Lincoln. *The Autobiography.* New York: Grosset and Dunlap, 1931.

Steinbeck, John. *Once There Was a War.* New York: Viking, 1958.

Stevens, John D. *Sensationalism and the New York Press.* New York: Columbia University Press, 1991.

Stewart, James. *Blood Sport: The President and His Adversaries.* New York: Simon and Schuster, 1996.

Stone, Geoffrey R. *Perilous Times: Free Speech in Wartime from the Sedition Act of 1798 to the War on Terrorism.* New York: Norton, 2004.

Stott, William. *Documentary Expression and Thirties America.* Chicago: University of Chicago Press, 1986.

Streitmatter, Rodger. *Voices of Revolution: The Dissident Press in America.* New York: Columbia University Press, 2001.

Summers, Mark Wahlgren. *The Press Gang: Newspapers and Politics, 1865–1878.* Chapel Hill: University of North Carolina Press, 1994.

Suskind, Ron. *The Price of Loyalty: George W. Bush, the White House, and the Education of Paul O'Neill.* New York: Simon and Schuster, 2004.

Sutherland, James. *The Restoration Newspaper and Its Development.* Cambridge: Cambridge University Press, 1986.

Sweeney, Michael S. *The Military and the Press: An Uneasy Truce.* Evanston, IL: Northwestern University Press, 2006.

Taylor, S. J. *Stalin's Apologist: Walter Duranty, the* New York Times*'s Man in Moscow.* New York: Oxford University Press, 1990.

Thornburgh, Dick, and Louis D. Boccardi. *Report of the Independent Review Panel on the September 8, 2004, "60 Minutes Wednesday" Segment "For the Record" Concerning President Bush's Texas Air National Guard Service, January 5, 2005.* https://www.cbsnews.com/htdocs /pdf/complete_report/CBS_Report.pdf.

Thornton, Brian. "Published Reaction When Murrow Battled McCarthy." *Journalism History* 29, no. 3 (Fall 2003): 133–46.

Tucher, Andie. *Froth and Scum: Truth, Beauty, Goodness, and the Ax-Murder in America's First Mass Medium.* Chapel Hill: University of North Carolina Press, 1994.

——. "'I Believe in Faking': The Dilemma of Photographic Realism at the Dawn of Photojournalism." *Photography and Culture* 10, no. 3 (2017): 195–214.

——. "Reporting for Duty: The Bohemian Brigade, the Civil War, and the Social Construction of the Reporter." *Book History* 9 (2006): 131–57.

——. "The True, the False, and the 'Not Exactly Lying': Making Fakes and Telling Stories in the Age of the Real Thing." In *Literature and Journalism: Inspirations, Intersections, and*

Inventions from Ben Franklin to Stephen Colbert, ed. Mark Canada, 91–118. New York: Palgrave Macmillan, 2013.

——. "Why Journalism History Matters: The Gaffe, the 'Stuff,' and the Historical Imagination." *American Journalism* 31, no. 4 (2014): 432–44.

——. "Why Marmaduke Mizzle and the Good Ship *Wabble* Fooled No One: Fake News and Metajournalistic Discourse in the Era of Journalistic Professionalism." In *Journalists and Knowledge Practices: Histories of Observing the Everyday in the Newspaper Age*, ed. Hansjakob Ziemer. New York: Routledge, forthcoming.

Tye, Larry. *Demagogue: The Life and Long Shadow of Senator Joe McCarthy*. Boston: Houghton Mifflin Harcourt, 2020.

Tyrrell, R. Emmett, Jr. "From Troopergate to Monicagate." *American Spectator*, November 1998, 18–22.

U.S. House of Representatives, Committee on Energy and Commerce. *Election Night Coverage by the Networks, Hearing, 14 February 2001*. Washington, DC: U.S. Government Printing Office, 2001.

U.S. House of Representatives, Committee on Oversight and Government Reform. *Misleading Information from the Battlefield: The Tillman and Lynch Episodes: First Report*. Washington, DC: U.S. Government Printing Office, 2008.

U.S. House of Representatives, Subcommittee on Oversight, Permanent House Select Committee on Intelligence. *The CIA and the Media: Hearings*. 95th Cong., 1st and 2nd sess. Washington, D.C.: U.S. Government Printing Office, 1978.

U.S. Office of Censorship. *Code of Wartime Practices for the American Press*. Washington, DC: U.S. Government Printing Office, June 15, 1942.

U.S. Office of War Information. *Negroes and the War*. Washington, DC: U.S. Government Printing Office, 1942.

U.S. Senate, Committee on Rules and Administration. *Maryland Senatorial Election of 1950: Report*. S. Rep. 647. 82nd Cong., 1st sess. Washington, DC: U.S. Government Printing Office, 1951.

U.S. Senate, Select Committee on Presidential Campaign Activities. *The Senate Watergate Report*. 2 vols. New York: Dell, 1974.

U.S. Senate, Subcommittee of the Committee on Foreign Relations. *State Department Employee Loyalty Investigation. Report . . . Pursuant to S. Res. 231 . . . .* 81st Cong., 2nd sess. Washington, DC: U.S. Government Printing Office, 1950.

Vos, Tim P., and Teri Finneman. "The Early Historical Construction of Journalism's Gatekeeping Role." *Journalism* 18, no. 3 (2017): 265–80.

Vos, Tim P., and Joseph Moore. "Building the Journalistic Paradigm: Beyond Paradigm Repair." *Journalism* 21 (2020): 17–33.

Waisbord, Silvio. *Reinventing Professionalism: Journalism and News in Global Perspective*. Cambridge: Polity Press, 2013.

Walker, Stanley. *City Editor*. Foreword by Alexander Woollcott. 1934. Reprint. Baltimore: Johns Hopkins University Press, 1999.

Weber, Ronald. "Some Sort of Artistic Excitement." In *The Reporter as Artist: A Look at the New Journalism Controversy*, ed. Ronald Weber, 13–26. New York: Hastings House, 1974.

Wertheimer, John. "Mutual Film Reviewed: The Movies, Censorship, and Free Speech in Progressive America." *American Journal of Legal History* 37, no. 2 (April 1993): 158–89.

Whissel, Kristen. "Placing the Spectator on the Scene of History: The Battle Re-enactment at the Turn of the Century, from Buffalo Bill's Wild West to the Early Cinema." *Historical Journal of Film, Radio, and Television* 22, no. 3 (2002): 225–43.

White, Edgar. "The Art of Interviewing." *Writer* 17 (March 1904): 33–35.

White, Graham J. *FDR and the Press.* Chicago: University of Chicago Press, 1979.

White, Richard Grant. "Wedding, Interviewing, et Cetera." *Galaxy*, December 1874, 822–30.

Whitehead, Don. *"Beachhead Don": Reporting the War from the European Theater, 1942–1945.* Ed. John B. Romeiser. New York: Fordham University Press, 2004.

——. *Combat Reporter: Don Whitehead's World War II Diary and Memoirs.* Ed. John B. Romeiser. New York: Fordham University Press, 2006.

Whitney, Joel. *Finks: How the CIA Tricked the World's Best Writers.* New York: OR Books, 2016.

Wilkie, Franc. *Pen and Powder.* Boston: Ticknor, 1888.

Wilson, Trevor. "Lord Bryce's Investigation Into Alleged German Atrocities in Belgium, 1914–15." *Journal of Contemporary History* 14 (1979): 369–83.

Winkler, Allan M. *The Politics of Propaganda: The Office of War Information 1942–1945.* New Haven, CT: Yale University Press, 1978.

Winzen, Peter. *Das Kaiserreich am Abgrund: Die* Daily-Telegraph-*Affäre und das Hale-Interview von 1908: Darstellung und Dokumentation.* Stuttgart, Germany: Franz Steiner, 2002.

Wolfe, Tom. "The New Journalism." In *The New Journalism: An Anthology*, ed. Tom Wolfe and E. W. Johnson, 3–36. New York: Harper and Row, 1973.

Wood, Thomas, and Ethan Porter. "The Elusive Backfire Effect: Mass Attitudes' Steadfast Factual Adherence." *Political Behavior* 41 (2019): 135–63.

Woodward, Bob. *Plan of Attack.* New York: Simon and Schuster, 2004.

Wu, Tim. *The Master Switch: The Rise and Fall of Information Empires.* New York: Vintage, 2011.

York, Byron. "The Life and Death of the *American Spectator*." *Atlantic*, November 2001. https://www.theatlantic.com/magazine/archive/2001/11/the-life-and-death-of-the-american-spectator/302343/.

Zboray, Ronald J., and Mary Saracino Zboray. *Everyday Ideas: Socioliterary Experience Among Antebellum New Englanders.* Knoxville: University of Tennessee Press, 2006.

Zelden, Charles L. *Bush v. Gore: Exposing the Hidden Crisis in American Democracy.* 3rd ed. Lawrence: University Press of Kansas, 2020.

Zucchino, David. *Wilmington's Lie: The Murderous Coup of 1898 and the Rise of White Supremacy.* New York: Atlantic Monthly Press, 2020.

INDEX

New Journalism compared to, 219, 221, 223; objectivity in, 279–80; Stewart and, 274–76; tabloid press and, 146–47
Maintenon, Madame de, 14
Manly, Alexander, 65
Mapes, Mary, 263–64, 265, 268
Marshall, George C., 196
Martian invasion broadcast, 174–79
mass-market advertising, 141–42
Mather, Cotton, 13
Matthews, Herbert, 255
May, Ronald, 203
Mayer, Jane, 245
McCarthy, Joseph R., 199, 208, 217, 280; *Chicago Tribune* and, 200, 203–5, 208–9; critics of, 200, 203; the Establishment and, 200, 205; hearings, 209–10; legacy of, 210–11; objectivity and, 200–201, 204; reporter relationships with, 201–2; television and, 209–10
McCarthyism, 210
McConnell, Mitch, 242
McCormick, Robert, 189, 200, 203–4
McHenry (detective), 69, 70–71
McKinley, William, 80, 108
McPhee, John, 221
media literacy, 182, 284
Meet the Press, 241, 335n12
Méliès, Georges, 103–4, 109
Memogate, 263–69
Memphis Appeal-Avalanche, 66
Mena airport story, 233, 325n44
Merz, Charles, 169
Miller, Dorie, 189
Miller, Judith, 255, 259–60
Miller, Ruth McCormick, 205–6
Mills, Eleanor. *See* Hall-Mills murder
Milton, John, 11
Milwaukee Journal, 200, 201, 203, 218
Missouri Democrat, 52
Mitchel Field, 159
Mitchell, Joseph, 223
Mizzle, Marmaduke M., 168, 314n55

Monk, Maria, 31–34, 294n32
Monthly Recorder, 11
Montreal Gazette, 86
Moody, John, 243, 246–47
moon hoax, 34
Moore, Michael, 257, 330n15
Morgan, J. Pierpont, fake interview with, 79, 83, 301n50
Mormons, 56–57
motion pictures. *See* film
Moyers, Bill, 276
MSNBC, 242, 244, 263, 331n27; Fox News and, 247–49
muckrakers, 130
Mumler, William H., 92, 93; Barnum on, 93–94
Mundt, Karl, 207, 208
Murdoch, Rupert, 232, 241, 242, 246
Murrow, Edward R., 160–61, 200, 205, 209, 210

NAB. *See* National Association of Broadcasters
Nanook of the North, 116–17
Nast, Thomas, 43
Nation, 143, 200, 244; on yellow press, 74
National Association of Broadcasters (NAB), 183
National Board of Review of Motion Pictures, 116
National News Council, 226–27
National Press Club, 237
National Review, 228, 235, 244
Native Americans, fake news about, 22
Nazi Germany, 177, 181; radio in, 180. *See also* Holocaust, reporting on
NBC, 176, 229, 241, 248; ban on prerecorded material, 160–61
Near v. Minnesota, 163–64
Negroes and the War, 187
New Castle News, 303n77
New Deal, 180, 188, 207–8
New England Courant, 19

Printed and bound by CPI Group (UK) Ltd, Croydon, CR0 4YY

23/04/2025

14660940-0004